I0528494

www.ingramcontent.com/pod-product-compliance
Lightning Source LLC
Chambersburg PA
CBHW051317120626
46547CB00015B/2280

* 9 7 8 1 9 5 7 1 0 9 2 9 9 *

במדבר

THE
ISRAEL
BIBLE

NUMBERS

EDITED BY

Rabbi Tuly Weisz

The Israel Bible: Numbers

First Edition, 2021

The Israel Bible was produced by Israel365 in cooperation with Teach for Israel and is used with permission from Teach for Israel. All rights reserved. The English translation was adapted by Israel365 from the JPS Tanakh. Copyright © 1985 by the Jewish Publication Society. All rights reserved.

Cover image used under license from Shutterstock.com

ISBN 978-1-957109-29-9

A CIP catalogue record for this title is available from the British Library

The Israel Bible: Numbers is a holy book that contains the name of God and should be treated with respect.

Table of Contents

Introduction

The Hebrew Bible is commonly known as the *Tanakh* which stands for *Torah* (the Five Books of Moses), *Neviim* (the Prophets) and *Ketuvim* (the Writings). The *Tanakh* consists of 24 books that are considered by Jews to be the word of God. While these books have been referred to as the "Old Testament," many Jews reject this label since it implies the replacement of the Hebrew Bible with something newer and prefer the more authentic Jewish name.

The *Tanakh* is not only the most important book known to man, it is God's word that is perfect and absolute. It is therefore a daunting undertaking to publish an edition of the *Tanakh*, and the responsibilities are awesome. There is no room for error or carelessness in dealing with the eternal word of God. Further, upon embarking on such a serious initiative, we ask ourselves if our efforts are gratuitous. Considering the many editions of the Bible in print, is there truly a need for yet another one?

While there are numerous Bibles in circulation today, its most central aspect – the Land of Israel – has often been overlooked. References to Israel appear on nearly every page, and the city of Jerusalem is specifically referred to hundreds of times throughout the Bible. The essential link between Israel and *Torah* is emphasized repeatedly in verses such as, "For instruction (*Torah*) shall come forth from *Tzion*, the word of *Hashem* from *Yerushalayim*" (Micah 4:2).

The miraculous return of the People of Israel to the Land of Israel in our own generation provides the perfect moment for a new volume to fill this void in biblical literature. *The Israel Bible* includes many special features elucidating God's focus on Israel throughout *Tanakh* and there are many additional, multimedia features available on our website **www.theisraelbible.com**.

Ordering and Presentation – In presenting *The Israel Bible*, our goal is to spread awareness of the biblical significance of the Land of Israel as well as the Jewish people's eternal connection to the land, based on the text of the *Tanakh*, the Hebrew Bible. We aim to honor "the God, the People and the Land of Israel" from an Orthodox Jewish perspective. To that end, *The Israel Bible* follows the traditional Jewish ordering of the books and the customary Hebrew division of chapters. Therefore, for example, we count 24 books of *Tanakh* with *Sefer Divrei Hayamim* (Chronicles) appearing last. It is our hope that our rich content will speak to all Jews and non-Jews who appreciate Israel as the God given land of the Jewish people.

English Translation – Throughout history, Jews have studied the Bible in Hebrew, as any form of translation would miss much of the nuance of the original holy tongue in which *Torah* has been transmitted since the days of Moses. However, as many Jews settled in America in the 19th Century, the need for an English translation became necessary. To be sure, there were already English translations prepared over the centuries by Christians, but in the words of the original editors of the Jewish Publication Society (JPS), "The Jew cannot afford to have his Bible translation prepared for him by others. He cannot have it as a gift, even as he cannot borrow his soul from others."

JPS set out in the late 1800s to publish an authoritative English translation "in the spirit of Jewish tradition." It was compiled over decades by some of the leading Jewish scholars of the time. They formed committees and subcommittees to compare existing English versions, considering medieval and modern Jewish commentators. The monumental JPS translation, originally published in 1917, has been updated in recent years, and *The Israel Bible* is proud to utilize the 1984 New Jewish Publication Society (NJPS) version with its modern, clear language, as well as its wide-ranging acceptance as an accurate and high-quality translation. We applied the NJPS translation verbatim, except for a select list of nouns which we replaced with their traditional Hebrew names. This is true even when we found the NJPS translation to be different than the popular translation of a word or phrase and when the NJPS switched the order of the text for the sake of clarity (see, for example, Ezekiel 24:22–24).

Hebrew Transliteration – To give our readers an authentic *Tanakh* experience, every verse that has commentary is transliterated from Hebrew into English. The Hebrew alphabet chart includes our standards for transliteration and pronunciation of Hebrew verses, enabling readers of *The Israel Bible* to decipher key biblical passages in the holy language. Readers can hear the entire Bible read in Hebrew on our website **www.theisraelbible.com**.

There are various standards when it comes to transliterating Hebrew words into English letters. While we have relied primarily on the classical Hebrew transliteration, we have occasionally deviated for the sake of simplicity, clarity and to reflect common usage.

In addition to whole verses, we have also transliterated many proper nouns in the English translation so that our readers can learn the names of key biblical figures and locations in their Hebrew form. As a rule, we chose to transliterate names of people that were central in the establishment and functioning of the nation of Israel, as well as significant places in the Holy Land. Therefore, regarding Adam's sons, for example, only *Shet* (Seth) is transliterated since it was from him that *Noach* (Noah), and ultimately *Avraham* (Abraham), descended. For this reason, there might be verses or sections of *The Israel Bible* that contains multiple names and only some of them are transliterated.

For the same reason, we have transliterated the names of the books of *Tanakh* when referring to them in our introductions and commentary. When referencing a specific chapter or verse, however, we use the English names of the books in our citations for clarity. We also transliterated ideas and concepts that are central to Judaism such as *Shabbat* (Sabbath), the names of the Jewish holidays and the *Beit Hamikdash* (Temple), as well as biblical measurements. Finally, the name of God is transliterated. Out of respect, Orthodox Jews generally refer to the Lord as *Hashem*, which literally means 'the Name.' Referring to God as *Hashem* reminds us that we feel close to Him but also recognize our distance at the same time. To stress this moniker, we transliterated both the Tetragrammaton as well as the name *Elohim* as *Hashem*.

Study Notes – Our unique commentary was compiled by Orthodox Jewish scholars who live in Israel. It is an anthology in the sense that most of the commentary is not original, but draws from traditional teachings of early Jewish Sages and modern rabbinic commentators. We also include quotations from individuals who have played a significant part in the past century of modern Israeli history including Israeli prime ministers, poets and military leaders.

Our commentary can be broken into four categories, three of which are identified by an icon at the beginning of the study note:

 Israel lessons are indicated with an icon bearing the map of Israel and focus on the Land of Israel and the modern State of Israel.

 Jewish lessons are indicated with a *Torah* scroll and teach a concept in Judaism or a classic idea from rabbinic thought.

 Hebrew lessons are represented by an icon bearing the letter *aleph* and focus on the meaning of a Hebrew word or phrase.

All other comments are considered general comments and are not assigned an icon.

Supplemental Material – In addition to our unique translation and original commentary, *The Israel Bible* offers supplementary material to enrich the learning experience of our readers. Before every book of *Tanakh,* we provide an introduction, as well as information, generally in the form of a map, a chart or a list, which is central to the specific book.

Maps – As the purpose of *The Israel Bible* is to highlight the biblical significance of the Land of Israel, significant time was spent researching and preparing maps to bring the physical contours of the holy land to life with great accuracy. However, since there is a lack of information regarding the precise locations of certain ancient cities, some of the places on our maps are approximate or subject to debate. In these cases, we followed the opinion that we are most comfortable with, but acknowledge that there is room for disagreement. We continue to produce new maps, which are available on our website **www.theisraelbible.com/maps**.

Torah **Readings** – The *Torah* is not just a work that is studied privately, it is also read out loud in synagogue. Every *Shabbat* and holiday a portion of the *Torah* is read, as well as a related section from *Neviim*, the prophets, called the *haftarah.* We included the blessings recited before and after the reading of the *Torah,* a list of the weekly *Torah* portions and their corresponding *haftarot,* and a chart of the *Torah* readings for special days with their corresponding *haftarot.* Readers can always find the current week's *Torah* portion by visiting **www.theisraelbible.com/weekly-torah-portion**. In this volume, we indicate where a new *Torah* portion begins by highlighting the Hebrew verse number with a gray box so readers can follow along with the communal *Torah* readings. Furthermore, we have included prayers for the State of Israel and the soldiers of the Israel Defense Forces (IDF) that are generally recited following the *Torah* reading in synagogue. It is our constant prayer that God watch over the State of Israel and the members of the IDF, who defend Israel every hour of every day.

In 1948, the State of Israel was created providing a modern answer to Isaiah's ancient question, "Is a nation born all at once?" (Isaiah 66:8). *The Israel Bible* was first published in the 70th year of God's miraculous restoration of the People of Israel to the Land of Israel. Jewish wisdom teaches that 70 is a significant number: *Moshe* (Moses) translated the *Torah* into 70 languages for all 70 nations of the world. From our very origins, the Jewish people were meant to be a light unto the 70 nations, spreading God's truth to the masses.

In the seven decades since the modern rebirth of the State of Israel, God's plan has been unfolding with unprecedented speed, dramatic highs and heartbreaking lows. Never has Israel been at the forefront of the world's attention as it is in our generation. Efforts to vilify the Jewish State seem to spread every day across the globe. At the same time, so does the growing movement of millions of non-Jewish biblical Zionists who stand with the nation of Israel as an expression of their commitment to God's word. As we seek to understand the clash of these two conflicting worldviews, the need for *The Israel Bible* has never been so important.

Standing on the great shoulders of those who came before us and emanating from the land that has always served as the birthplace for the Bible, we conclude with a heartfelt prayer: May the Almighty bless our efforts in offering this *Tanakh* to influence the hearts, minds and actions of its readers. In this way, it is our hope to spread God's name so that the publication of *The Israel Bible* brings us one step closer to the final redemption of Israel and the entire world.

Rabbi Tuly Weisz
Editor, *The Israel Bible*

Foreword

The mandate to study God's word daily is interestingly not found in the Five Books of Moses (Pentateuch), but rather in the first book of our prophetic writings: "Let not this Book of the Teaching cease from your lips, but recite it day and night, so that you may observe faithfully all that is written in it. Only then will you prosper in your undertakings and only then will you be successful" (Joshua 1:8). Charged with bringing the Israelites into the land covenantally promised to Abraham, Isaac and Jacob, God ensures Joshua of His protection if the nation observes His ways as dictated in the Divine constitution known as the *Torah*.

In Jewish tradition, Joshua (1:8) is directly linked with Deuteronomy (11:14), "You shall gather in your new grain and wine, and oil."[1] Our Sages deduced from this scriptural combination the importance of merging *Torah* study with a profession. Completely dedicating oneself to the study of *Torah* without having the financial means to sustain this lifestyle can lead one to eventually straying from observance of God's will. Poverty and crime can have an intimate relationship.

We must also be careful that our work does not affect our daily study of Scripture. The addiction of becoming a workaholic and not making *Torah* study a priority can also lead one into temptations that can violate our personal relationship with Him as well as our fellow human beings. The goal is to achieve a healthy balance between our study of God's word and our daily work.

The Deuteronomic verse quoted above is part of the second section of the Shema[2] that discusses the concept of reward and punishment. Sanctifying God by fulfilling His commandments results in the Land of Israel practically benefitting from rains that occur in the right season and reaping the abundance from the fields. However, if the nation follows pagan gods and practices, the consequences are devastating – famine and death. The Land of Israel is intrinsically linked with the keeping of the *Torah*. Covenant Land comes with covenant responsibility.

---

1. Talmud Bavli Berachot 35b
2. Consisting of three sections within the Five Books of Moses (Deut. 6:4–8; 11:13–22 and Numbers 15:37–42), the *Shema* is proclamation of accepting God's Kingdom in our lives, loyalty to His commandments and remembering His redemptive act of liberating us from Egypt. Jews recite the *Shema* twice a day as stated in Deut. 6:7.

Born into slavery, Joshua is now leading His people into the Promised Land. More than 500 years separates him from his ancestral forefather Abraham. The historical narratives that took place between Abraham leaving everything behind to follow God in Genesis 12 and the death of Moses in the last chapter of Deuteronomy are filled with intrigue, suspense, joy, sorrow and hope. What began as a family is now a nation actualizing its mission to be a kingdom of priests to the world. However, for the Israelites to succeed in the Land of Israel, they must see the *Torah* as the only compass to direct their lives.

The biblical episodes after our first entry into the land are well known. Our ancestors' triumphs and sins are all on public record. We learned the harsh reality of Leviticus (18:28) "So let not the land spew you out for defiling it as it spewed out the nation that came before you." Twice, we lost the privilege to be stewards of the Land of Israel and to fulfill our nation state mandate to be a light to the world. However, when the annals of history were ready to archive the Jewish people after the Holocaust, God kept His covenantal promise and gathered us from the four corners of the globe to come home. The year 1948 was a game changer. Biblical prophecies were and are being realized. We are now living in the birth pangs of the messianic era.

In our morning prayers, we recite a series of blessings over the *Torah* that include petitioning God to have a sweet tooth for His word, to study it without any ulterior motive and to have Him to teach it to us. They are some congregations that invoke the following liturgical prayer after the completion of these blessings: *May the Torah be my faith and El Shaddai my help. Blessed be the name of His glorious kingdom forever and all time.*

According to Jewish tradition, the neglect of not blessing the *Torah* before engaging in its study was one of the reasons for the destruction of the Temple.[3] This is deduced from the redundancy of words in Jeremiah (9:12) that talks about Israel not following God: "…Because they forsook the teaching I had set before them. They did not obey Me and they did not follow it [did not make a blessing before studying it]." Our inability to properly cherish God's greatest gift to the world, the *Torah*, led to our eventual exile from our land.

On Israel's Independence Day, Jews around the world recite Psalms 113–118 to express our gratitude to God for His Divine hand in helping establish the State of Israel. We have learned from our past and realize the privilege to see firsthand the land, people and *Torah* operating all together in our generation.

---

3. Babylonian Talmud Nedarim 81a

When Rabbi Tuly Weisz approached me about his intent to publish *The Israel Bible* that would highlight commentary about the special relationship between the land and people, I saw this project as another way to publicly demonstrate our appreciation to God for having the State of Israel. In addition, it is another educational tool to ensure biblical literacy. If we are to truly enjoy the Land of Israel, it is incumbent upon us to continually study the *Torah*. Isaiah once prophesied that the Jewish people would return to Zion with songs, "crowned with everlasting joy" (35:10). *The Israel Bible* provides us the lyrical content to express our joy in living in the land that God calls holy.

Rabbi Shlomo Riskin
Chief Rabbi of Efrat
Founder of the Center for Jewish-Christian
Understanding & Cooperation (CJCUC)

Introduction to Sefer Bamidbar
The Book of Numbers

Introduction and commentary by Shira Schechter

When *Sefer Bamidbar* (literally, 'in the wilderness') begins, the Israelites are in the wilderness, having left Egypt and received the *Torah*, and are preparing to travel to Israel. They are preparing militarily, and hence the English name of this fourth book of the Bible is 'Numbers,' since it begins with a census in which they organize and count their ranks. At the same time, they are also preparing spiritually for their life as a nation, following the laws of the *Torah* in their ancestral homeland.

However, during the course of *Sefer Bamidbar*, the plan becomes derailed. The people complain, turn against *Hashem* and His servant *Moshe*, and arouse the anger of the Almighty. Instead of heading immediately into the land, they are sentenced to wander the desert for forty years. These people lost their chance to enter Israel; only the next generation would be given that opportunity. *Hashem*, Who is merciful and compassionate, suddenly cannot forgive them. What did the people do to deserve such a harsh punishment?

Jewish tradition teaches that the generation of the wilderness committed an inexcusable infraction, in that they rejected *Eretz Yisrael*. In Chapter 14, they cry out, "Why is *Hashem* taking us to that land to fall by the sword?" Instead of eagerly claiming their ancestral heritage and assuming their divine mission, the people second-guess God, cynically call His will into question, and critically reject the greatest of all gifts.

The rest of *Sefer Bamidbar* continues to depict this downward spiral. In Chapter 16, they call into question the legitimacy and qualifications for leadership of *Moshe* and *Aharon*, and rebellion is launched against their leadership. Later, in Chapter 20, the people complain about the lack of water in the wilderness, and in yet another affront to *Hashem*, become involved in idolatry and immoral relations in Chapter 25.

This all started with a rejection of the land. In fact, Jewish tradition teaches that a lack of honor towards the Land of Israel is the source of many calamities throughout history, including the destruction of both Temples in *Yerushalyim*.

The lessons of the Bible are as relevant today as ever before. When studying *Bamidbar*, we must learn the lessons of the incident of the spies, in order to constantly re-evaluate our own relationship with the Land of Israel.

Map of the Journey of the Spies

This map features the places visited by the twelve spies on their mission to scout out the Land of Israel as described in *Sefer Bamidbar* chapter 13.

1. The spies were sent to scout out the Land of Israel from **Kadesh-barnea** in the wilderness of Paran (see Numbers 13:3, 32:8, Deuteronomy 1:19).

2. Moshe commanded the spies to enter Israel from the south, in Hebrew, the **Negev** (Numbers 13:17).

3. After entering from the Negev, the spies came to **Chevron** where they encountered the Anakites, or giants (Numbers 13:22). Wadi Eshcol, where the spies cut a cluster of grapes, pomegranates and figs to bring back to Moshe, was in the area of Chevron (Numbers 13:23–24).

4. The spies walked the length and width of the borders as far north as **Lebo-hamath** (Numbers 13:21).

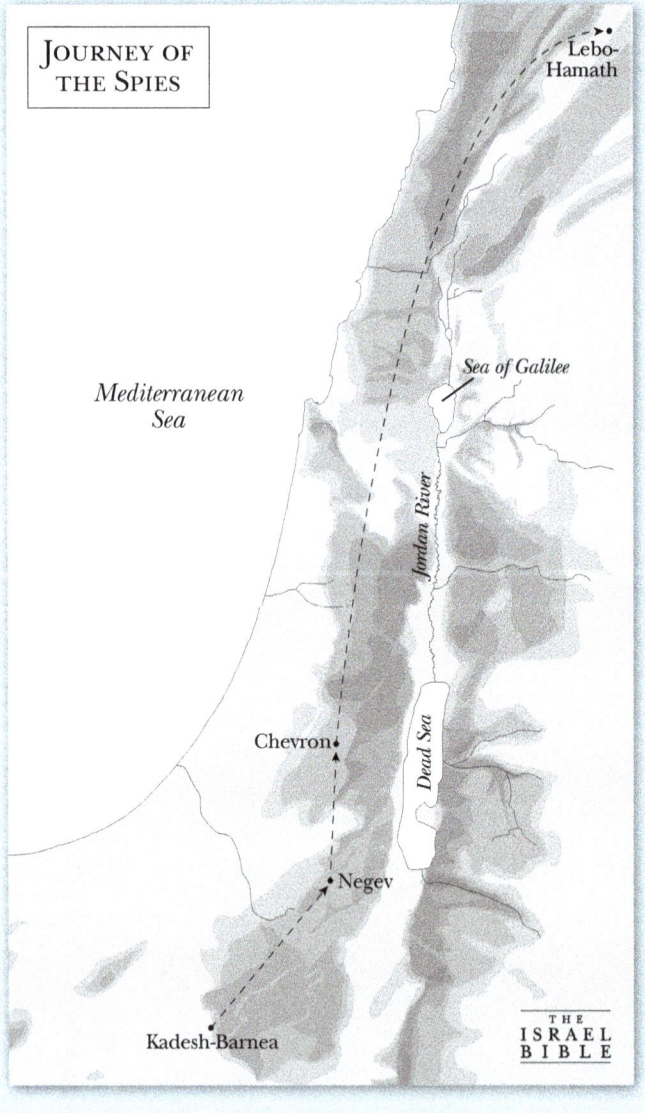

JOURNEY OF THE SPIES

Lebo-Hamath

Mediterranean Sea

Sea of Galilee

Jordan River

Chevron

Dead Sea

Negev

Kadesh-Barnea

THE ISRAEL BIBLE

Numbers

1 ¹ On the first day of the second month, in the second year following the exodus from the land of Egypt, *Hashem* spoke to *Moshe* in the wilderness of Sinai, in the Tent of Meeting, saying:

 וַיְדַבֵּר יְהוָֹה אֶל־מֹשֶׁה בְּמִדְבַּר סִינַי בְּאֹהֶל מוֹעֵד בְּאֶחָד לַחֹדֶשׁ הַשֵּׁנִי בַּשָּׁנָה הַשֵּׁנִית לְצֵאתָם מֵאֶרֶץ מִצְרַיִם לֵאמֹר: א

vai-da-BAYR a-do-NAI el mo-SHEH b'-mid-BAR see-NAI b'-O-hel mo-AYD b'-e-KHAD la-KHO-desh ha-shay-NEE ba-sha-NAH ha-shay-NEET l'-tzay-TAM may-E-retz mitz-RA-yim lay-MOR

² Take a census of the whole Israelite community by the clans of its ancestral houses, listing the names, every male, head by head.

שְׂאוּ אֶת־רֹאשׁ כָּל־עֲדַת בְּנֵי־יִשְׂרָאֵל לְמִשְׁפְּחֹתָם לְבֵית אֲבֹתָם בְּמִסְפַּר שֵׁמוֹת כָּל־זָכָר לְגֻלְגְּלֹתָם: ב

s'-U et ROSH kol a-DAT b'-nay yis-ra-AYL l'-mish-p'-kho-TAM l'-VAYT a-vo-TAM b'-mis-PAR shay-MOT kol za-KHAR l'-gul-g'-lo-TAM

³ You and *Aharon* shall record them by their groups, from the age of twenty years up, all those in *Yisrael* who are able to bear arms.

מִבֶּן עֶשְׂרִים שָׁנָה וָמַעְלָה כָּל־יֹצֵא צָבָא בְּיִשְׂרָאֵל תִּפְקְדוּ אֹתָם לְצִבְאֹתָם אַתָּה וְאַהֲרֹן: ג

⁴ Associated with you shall be a man from each tribe, each one the head of his ancestral house.

וְאִתְּכֶם יִהְיוּ אִישׁ אִישׁ לַמַּטֶּה אִישׁ רֹאשׁ לְבֵית־אֲבֹתָיו הוּא: ד

⁵ These are the names of the men who shall assist you: From *Reuven*, *Elitzur* son of Shedeur.

וְאֵלֶּה שְׁמוֹת הָאֲנָשִׁים אֲשֶׁר יַעַמְדוּ אִתְּכֶם לִרְאוּבֵן אֱלִיצוּר בֶּן־שְׁדֵיאוּר: ה

⁶ From *Shimon*, *Shelumiel* son of Zurishaddai.

לְשִׁמְעוֹן שְׁלֻמִיאֵל בֶּן־צוּרִישַׁדָּי: ו

⁷ From *Yehuda*, *Nachshon* son of *Aminadav*.

לִיהוּדָה נַחְשׁוֹן בֶּן־עַמִּינָדָב: ז

⁸ From *Yissachar*, *Netanel* son of Zuar.

לְיִשָּׂשכָר נְתַנְאֵל בֶּן־צוּעָר: ח

⁹ From *Zevulun*, *Eliav* son of Helon.

לִזְבוּלֻן אֱלִיאָב בֶּן־חֵלֹן: ט

¹⁰ From the sons of *Yosef*: from *Efraim*, *Elishama* son of Ammihud; from *Menashe*, *Gamliel* son of Pedahzur.

לִבְנֵי יוֹסֵף לְאֶפְרַיִם אֱלִישָׁמָע בֶּן־עַמִּיהוּד לִמְנַשֶּׁה גַּמְלִיאֵל בֶּן־פְּדָהצוּר: י

 1:1 In the wilderness of *Sinai*, in the Tent of Meeting After a stay of almost a year in the Sinai Desert where the people received the *Torah*, constructed the *Mishkan* and studied some of their new laws, *Sefer Bamidbar* opens with the preparations to leave the desert and head to the Promised Land. The *Ramban* explains that their entry into *Eretz Yisrael* with the *Torah* in hand was the ultimate goal of the exodus from Egypt. The *Mishkan*, where *Hashem* reveals Himself on a daily basis, will allow the people to carry the experience of revelation at Mount Sinai with them on their journey, and He will ultimately find His permanent resting place on earth in the *Beit Hamikdash* in *Yerushalayim*. In this way, God remains permanently in their midst.

Sunset over the Temple Mount in *Yerushalayim*

1:2 Take a census of the whole Israelite community The foremost commandment given by *Hashem* to *Moshe* and *Aharon* in preparation for travel to the Land of Israel is to count the people. This is one of several censuses described in the Bible, and the first of two in *Sefer Bamidbar*. In fact, the English name of this book, Numbers, derives from these two countings. Since the Israelites are heading toward the Promised Land to conquer and settle it, the census serves to inform the leadership of how many soldiers they have available for their army and among how many people the land would then need to be divided. *Rashi*, however, gives another reason for the count. He explains that *Hashem* counts His people repeatedly, simply because they are precious to Him. Just as someone with a valuable collection will count its contents over and over, so too *Hashem* frequently counts His people, to teach us that every individual is precious to Him.

11 From *Binyamin*, *Avidan* son of Gideoni.

יא לְבִנְיָמִן אֲבִידָן בֶּן־גִּדְעֹנִי:

12 From *Dan*, *Achiezer* son of Ammishaddai.

יב לְדָן אֲחִיעֶזֶר בֶּן־עַמִּישַׁדָּי:

13 From *Asher*, *Pagiel* son of Ochran.

יג לְאָשֵׁר פַּגְעִיאֵל בֶּן־עָכְרָן:

14 From *Gad*, *Elyasaf* son of Deuel.

יד לְגָד אֶלְיָסָף בֶּן־דְּעוּאֵל:

15 From *Naftali*, *Achira* son of Enan.

טו לְנַפְתָּלִי אֲחִירַע בֶּן־עֵינָן:

16 Those are the elected of the assembly, the chieftains of their ancestral tribes: they are the heads of the contingents of *Yisrael*.

טז אֵלֶּה קְרִיאֵי [קְרוּאֵי] הָעֵדָה נְשִׂיאֵי מַטּוֹת אֲבוֹתָם רָאשֵׁי אַלְפֵי יִשְׂרָאֵל הֵם:

17 So *Moshe* and *Aharon* took those men, who were designated by name,

יז וַיִּקַּח מֹשֶׁה וְאַהֲרֹן אֵת הָאֲנָשִׁים הָאֵלֶּה אֲשֶׁר נִקְּבוּ בְּשֵׁמוֹת:

18 and on the first day of the second month they convoked the whole community, who were registered by the clans of their ancestral houses – the names of those aged twenty years and over being listed head by head.

יח וְאֵת כָּל־הָעֵדָה הִקְהִילוּ בְּאֶחָד לַחֹדֶשׁ הַשֵּׁנִי וַיִּתְיַלְדוּ עַל־מִשְׁפְּחֹתָם לְבֵית אֲבֹתָם בְּמִסְפַּר שֵׁמוֹת מִבֶּן עֶשְׂרִים שָׁנָה וָמַעְלָה לְגֻלְגְּלֹתָם:

19 As *Hashem* had commanded *Moshe*, so he recorded them in the wilderness of Sinai.

יט כַּאֲשֶׁר צִוָּה יְהֹוָה אֶת־מֹשֶׁה וַיִּפְקְדֵם בְּמִדְבַּר סִינָי:

20 They totaled as follows: The descendants of *Reuven*, *Yisrael*'s first-born, the registration of the clans of their ancestral house, as listed by name, head by head, all males aged twenty years and over, all who were able to bear arms –

כ וַיִּהְיוּ בְנֵי־רְאוּבֵן בְּכֹר יִשְׂרָאֵל תּוֹלְדֹתָם לְמִשְׁפְּחֹתָם לְבֵית אֲבֹתָם בְּמִסְפַּר שֵׁמוֹת לְגֻלְגְּלֹתָם כָּל־זָכָר מִבֶּן עֶשְׂרִים שָׁנָה וָמַעְלָה כֹּל יֹצֵא צָבָא:

21 those enrolled from the tribe of *Reuven*: 46,500.

כא פְּקֻדֵיהֶם לְמַטֵּה רְאוּבֵן שִׁשָּׁה וְאַרְבָּעִים אֶלֶף וַחֲמֵשׁ מֵאוֹת:

22 Of the descendants of *Shimon*, the registration of the clans of their ancestral house, their enrollment as listed by name, head by head, all males aged twenty years and over, all who were able to bear arms –

כב לִבְנֵי שִׁמְעוֹן תּוֹלְדֹתָם לְמִשְׁפְּחֹתָם לְבֵית אֲבֹתָם פְּקֻדָיו בְּמִסְפַּר שֵׁמוֹת לְגֻלְגְּלֹתָם כָּל־זָכָר מִבֶּן עֶשְׂרִים שָׁנָה וָמַעְלָה כֹּל יֹצֵא צָבָא:

23 those enrolled from the tribe of *Shimon*: 59,300.

כג פְּקֻדֵיהֶם לְמַטֵּה שִׁמְעוֹן תִּשְׁעָה וַחֲמִשִּׁים אֶלֶף וּשְׁלֹשׁ מֵאוֹת:

24 Of the descendants of *Gad*, the registration of the clans of their ancestral house, as listed by name, aged twenty years and over, all who were able to bear arms –

כד לִבְנֵי גָד תּוֹלְדֹתָם לְמִשְׁפְּחֹתָם לְבֵית אֲבֹתָם בְּמִסְפַּר שֵׁמוֹת מִבֶּן עֶשְׂרִים שָׁנָה וָמַעְלָה כֹּל יֹצֵא צָבָא:

25 those enrolled from the tribe of *Gad*: 45,650.

כה פְּקֻדֵיהֶם לְמַטֵּה גָד חֲמִשָּׁה וְאַרְבָּעִים אֶלֶף וְשֵׁשׁ מֵאוֹת וַחֲמִשִּׁים:

26 Of the descendants of *Yehuda*, the registration of the clans of their ancestral house, as listed by name, aged twenty years and over, all who were able to bear arms –

כו לִבְנֵי יְהוּדָה תּוֹלְדֹתָם לְמִשְׁפְּחֹתָם לְבֵית אֲבֹתָם בְּמִסְפַּר שֵׁמֹת מִבֶּן עֶשְׂרִים שָׁנָה וָמַעְלָה כֹּל יֹצֵא צָבָא:

27 those enrolled from the tribe of *Yehuda*: 74,600.

כז פְּקֻדֵיהֶם לְמַטֵּה יְהוּדָה אַרְבָּעָה וְשִׁבְעִים אֶלֶף וְשֵׁשׁ מֵאוֹת:

28 Of the descendants of *Yissachar*, the registration of the clans of their ancestral house, as listed by name, aged twenty years and over, all who were able to bear arms –

כח לִבְנֵי יִשָּׂשכָר תּוֹלְדֹתָם לְמִשְׁפְּחֹתָם לְבֵית אֲבֹתָם בְּמִסְפַּר שֵׁמֹת מִבֶּן עֶשְׂרִים שָׁנָה וָמַעְלָה כֹּל יֹצֵא צָבָא:

29 those enrolled from the tribe of *Yissachar*: 54,400.

כט פְּקֻדֵיהֶם לְמַטֵּה יִשָּׂשכָר אַרְבָּעָה וַחֲמִשִּׁים אֶלֶף וְאַרְבַּע מֵאוֹת:

30 Of the descendants of *Zevulun*, the registration of the clans of their ancestral house, as listed by name, aged twenty years and over, all who were able to bear arms –

ל לִבְנֵי זְבוּלֻן תּוֹלְדֹתָם לְמִשְׁפְּחֹתָם לְבֵית אֲבֹתָם בְּמִסְפַּר שֵׁמֹת מִבֶּן עֶשְׂרִים שָׁנָה וָמַעְלָה כֹּל יֹצֵא צָבָא:

31 those enrolled from the tribe of *Zevulun*: 57,400.

לא פְּקֻדֵיהֶם לְמַטֵּה זְבוּלֻן שִׁבְעָה וַחֲמִשִּׁים אֶלֶף וְאַרְבַּע מֵאוֹת:

32 Of the descendants of *Yosef*: Of the descendants of *Efraim*, the registration of the clans of their ancestral house, as listed by name, aged twenty years and over, all who were able to bear arms –

לב לִבְנֵי יוֹסֵף לִבְנֵי אֶפְרַיִם תּוֹלְדֹתָם לְמִשְׁפְּחֹתָם לְבֵית אֲבֹתָם בְּמִסְפַּר שֵׁמֹת מִבֶּן עֶשְׂרִים שָׁנָה וָמַעְלָה כֹּל יֹצֵא צָבָא:

33 those enrolled from the tribe of *Efraim*: 40,500.

לג פְּקֻדֵיהֶם לְמַטֵּה אֶפְרָיִם אַרְבָּעִים אֶלֶף וַחֲמֵשׁ מֵאוֹת:

34 Of the descendants of *Menashe*, the registration of the clans of their ancestral house, as listed by name, aged twenty years and over, all who were able to bear arms –

לד לִבְנֵי מְנַשֶּׁה תּוֹלְדֹתָם לְמִשְׁפְּחֹתָם לְבֵית אֲבֹתָם בְּמִסְפַּר שֵׁמוֹת מִבֶּן עֶשְׂרִים שָׁנָה וָמַעְלָה כֹּל יֹצֵא צָבָא:

35 those enrolled from the tribe of *Menashe*: 32,200.

לה פְּקֻדֵיהֶם לְמַטֵּה מְנַשֶּׁה שְׁנַיִם וּשְׁלֹשִׁים אֶלֶף וּמָאתָיִם:

36 Of the descendants of *Binyamin*, the registration of the clans of their ancestral house, as listed by name, aged twenty years and over, all who were able to bear arms –

לו לִבְנֵי בִנְיָמִן תּוֹלְדֹתָם לְמִשְׁפְּחֹתָם לְבֵית אֲבֹתָם בְּמִסְפַּר שֵׁמֹת מִבֶּן עֶשְׂרִים שָׁנָה וָמַעְלָה כֹּל יֹצֵא צָבָא:

37 those enrolled from the tribe of *Binyamin*: 35,400.

לז פְּקֻדֵיהֶם לְמַטֵּה בִנְיָמִן חֲמִשָּׁה וּשְׁלֹשִׁים אֶלֶף וְאַרְבַּע מֵאוֹת:

38 Of the descendants of *Dan*, the registration of the clans of their ancestral house, as listed by name, aged twenty years and over, all who were able to bear arms –

לח לִבְנֵי דָן תּוֹלְדֹתָם לְמִשְׁפְּחֹתָם לְבֵית אֲבֹתָם בְּמִסְפַּר שֵׁמֹת מִבֶּן עֶשְׂרִים שָׁנָה וָמַעְלָה כֹּל יֹצֵא צָבָא:

39 those enrolled from the tribe of *Dan*: 62,700.

לט פְּקֻדֵיהֶם לְמַטֵּה דָן שְׁנַיִם וְשִׁשִּׁים אֶלֶף וּשְׁבַע מֵאוֹת:

40 Of the descendants of *Asher*, the registration of the clans of their ancestral house, as listed by name, aged twenty years and over, all who were able to bear arms –

מ לִבְנֵי אָשֵׁר תּוֹלְדֹתָם לְמִשְׁפְּחֹתָם לְבֵית אֲבֹתָם בְּמִסְפַּר שֵׁמֹת מִבֶּן עֶשְׂרִים שָׁנָה וָמַעְלָה כֹּל יֹצֵא צָבָא:

⁴¹ those enrolled from the tribe of *Asher*: 41,500.

מא פְּקֻדֵיהֶם לְמַטֵּה אָשֵׁר אֶחָד וְאַרְבָּעִים אֶלֶף וַחֲמֵשׁ מֵאוֹת:

⁴² [Of] the descendants of *Naftali*, the registration of the clans of their ancestral house as listed by name, aged twenty years and over, all who were able to bear arms –

מב בְּנֵי נַפְתָּלִי תּוֹלְדֹתָם לְמִשְׁפְּחֹתָם לְבֵית אֲבֹתָם בְּמִסְפַּר שֵׁמֹת מִבֶּן עֶשְׂרִים שָׁנָה וָמַעְלָה כֹּל יֹצֵא צָבָא:

⁴³ those enrolled from the tribe of *Naftali*: 53,400.

מג פְּקֻדֵיהֶם לְמַטֵּה נַפְתָּלִי שְׁלֹשָׁה וַחֲמִשִּׁים אֶלֶף וְאַרְבַּע מֵאוֹת:

⁴⁴ Those are the enrollments recorded by *Moshe* and *Aharon* and by the chieftains of *Yisrael*, who were twelve in number, one man to each ancestral house.

מד אֵלֶּה הַפְּקֻדִים אֲשֶׁר פָּקַד מֹשֶׁה וְאַהֲרֹן וּנְשִׂיאֵי יִשְׂרָאֵל שְׁנֵים עָשָׂר אִישׁ אִישׁ־אֶחָד לְבֵית־אֲבֹתָיו הָיוּ:

⁴⁵ All the Israelites, aged twenty years and over, enrolled by ancestral houses, all those in *Yisrael* who were able to bear arms –

מה וַיִּהְיוּ כָּל־פְּקוּדֵי בְנֵי־יִשְׂרָאֵל לְבֵית אֲבֹתָם מִבֶּן עֶשְׂרִים שָׁנָה וָמַעְלָה כָּל־יֹצֵא צָבָא בְּיִשְׂרָאֵל:

⁴⁶ all who were enrolled came to 603,550.

מו וַיִּהְיוּ כָּל־הַפְּקֻדִים שֵׁשׁ־מֵאוֹת אֶלֶף וּשְׁלֹשֶׁת אֲלָפִים וַחֲמֵשׁ מֵאוֹת וַחֲמִשִּׁים:

⁴⁷ The *Leviim*, however, were not recorded among them by their ancestral tribe.

מז וְהַלְוִיִּם לְמַטֵּה אֲבֹתָם לֹא הָתְפָּקְדוּ בְּתוֹכָם:

⁴⁸ For *Hashem* had spoken to *Moshe*, saying:

מח וַיְדַבֵּר יְהֹוָה אֶל־מֹשֶׁה לֵּאמֹר:

⁴⁹ Do not on any account enroll the tribe of *Levi* or take a census of them with the Israelites.

מט אַךְ אֶת־מַטֵּה לֵוִי לֹא תִפְקֹד וְאֶת־רֹאשָׁם לֹא תִשָּׂא בְּתוֹךְ בְּנֵי יִשְׂרָאֵל:

⁵⁰ You shall put the *Leviim* in charge of the *Mishkan* of the Pact, all its furnishings, and everything that pertains to it: they shall carry the *Mishkan* and all its furnishings, and they shall tend it; and they shall camp around the *Mishkan*.

נ וְאַתָּה הַפְקֵד אֶת־הַלְוִיִּם עַל־מִשְׁכַּן הָעֵדֻת וְעַל כָּל־כֵּלָיו וְעַל כָּל־אֲשֶׁר־לוֹ הֵמָּה יִשְׂאוּ אֶת־הַמִּשְׁכָּן וְאֶת־כָּל־כֵּלָיו וְהֵם יְשָׁרְתֻהוּ וְסָבִיב לַמִּשְׁכָּן יַחֲנוּ:

⁵¹ When the *Mishkan* is to set out, the *Leviim* shall take it down, and when the *Mishkan* is to be pitched, the *Leviim* shall set it up; any outsider who encroaches shall be put to death.

נא וּבִנְסֹעַ הַמִּשְׁכָּן יוֹרִידוּ אֹתוֹ הַלְוִיִּם וּבַחֲנֹת הַמִּשְׁכָּן יָקִימוּ אֹתוֹ הַלְוִיִּם וְהַזָּר הַקָּרֵב יוּמָת:

⁵² The Israelites shall encamp troop by troop, each man with his division and each under his standard.

נב וְחָנוּ בְּנֵי יִשְׂרָאֵל אִישׁ עַל־מַחֲנֵהוּ וְאִישׁ עַל־דִּגְלוֹ לְצִבְאֹתָם:

v'-kha-NU b'-NAY yis-ra-AYL EESH al ma-kha-NAY-hu
v'-EESH al dig-LO l'-tziv-o-TAM

1:52 Each under his standard Following the census depicted at the beginning of *Bamidbar*, the Bible describes the layout of the Israelite camp in the desert. At the center of the camp is the *Mishkan*, a reminder that *Hashem* is always at the center of our lives. The *Leviim* surround the *Mishkan*, and the remaining tribes, organized into groups of three, surround the *Leviim*. Each tribe has its own flag featuring an insignia representative of the tribe's unique character; each group of tribes also possessed a distinctive banner. At the First Zionist Congress in 1897, a flag was needed to represent the new movement being formed. David

Flag of Israel

Numbers

53 The *Leviim*, however, shall camp around the *Mishkan* of the Pact, that wrath may not strike the Israelite community; the *Leviim* shall stand guard around the *Mishkan* of the Pact.

נג וְהַלְוִיִּם יַחֲנוּ סָבִיב לְמִשְׁכַּן הָעֵדֻת וְלֹא־יִהְיֶה קֶצֶף עַל־עֲדַת בְּנֵי יִשְׂרָאֵל וְשָׁמְרוּ הַלְוִיִּם אֶת־מִשְׁמֶרֶת מִשְׁכַּן הָעֵדוּת:

54 The Israelites did accordingly; just as *Hashem* had commanded *Moshe*, so they did.

נד וַיַּעֲשׂוּ בְּנֵי יִשְׂרָאֵל כְּכֹל אֲשֶׁר צִוָּה יְהוָה אֶת־מֹשֶׁה כֵּן עָשׂוּ:

2 ¹ *Hashem* spoke to *Moshe* and *Aharon*, saying:

ב א וַיְדַבֵּר יְהוָה אֶל־מֹשֶׁה וְאֶל־אַהֲרֹן לֵאמֹר:

2 The Israelites shall camp each with his standard, under the banners of their ancestral house; they shall camp around the Tent of Meeting at a distance.

ב אִישׁ עַל־דִּגְלוֹ בְאֹתֹת לְבֵית אֲבֹתָם יַחֲנוּ בְּנֵי יִשְׂרָאֵל מִנֶּגֶד סָבִיב לְאֹהֶל־מוֹעֵד יַחֲנוּ:

3 Camped on the front, or east side: the standard of the division of *Yehuda*, troop by troop. Chieftain of the Judites: *Nachshon* son of *Aminadav*.

ג וְהַחֹנִים קֵדְמָה מִזְרָחָה דֶּגֶל מַחֲנֵה יְהוּדָה לְצִבְאֹתָם וְנָשִׂיא לִבְנֵי יְהוּדָה נַחְשׁוֹן בֶּן־עַמִּינָדָב:

v'-ha-kho-NEEM KAY-d'-mah miz-RA-khah DE-gel ma-kha-NAY y'-hu-DAH l'-tziv-o-TAM v'-na-SEE liv-NAY y'-hu-DAH nakh-SHON ben a-mee-na-DAV

4 His troop, as enrolled: 74,600.

ד וּצְבָאוֹ וּפְקֻדֵיהֶם אַרְבָּעָה וְשִׁבְעִים אֶלֶף וְשֵׁשׁ מֵאוֹת:

5 Camping next to it: The tribe of *Yissachar*. Chieftain of the Issacharites: *Netanel* son of Zuar.

ה וְהַחֹנִים עָלָיו מַטֵּה יִשָּׂשכָר וְנָשִׂיא לִבְנֵי יִשָּׂשכָר נְתַנְאֵל בֶּן־צוּעָר:

6 His troop, as enrolled: 54,400.

ו וּצְבָאוֹ וּפְקֻדָיו אַרְבָּעָה וַחֲמִשִּׁים אֶלֶף וְאַרְבַּע מֵאוֹת:

7 The tribe of *Zevulun*. Chieftain of the Zebulunites: *Eliav* son of Helon.

ז מַטֵּה זְבוּלֻן וְנָשִׂיא לִבְנֵי זְבוּלֻן אֱלִיאָב בֶּן־חֵלֹן:

8 His troop, as enrolled: 57,400.

ח וּצְבָאוֹ וּפְקֻדָיו שִׁבְעָה וַחֲמִשִּׁים אֶלֶף וְאַרְבַּע מֵאוֹת:

9 The total enrolled in the division of *Yehuda*: 186,400, for all troops. These shall march first.

ט כָּל־הַפְּקֻדִים לְמַחֲנֵה יְהוּדָה מְאַת אֶלֶף וּשְׁמֹנִים אֶלֶף וְשֵׁשֶׁת־אֲלָפִים וְאַרְבַּע־מֵאוֹת לְצִבְאֹתָם רִאשֹׁנָה יִסָּעוּ:

The emblem of *Yerushalayim* bearing the lion of *Yehuda*

Wolfsohn, a prominent member of the early Zionist movement, described how he came up with the design they ultimately adopted: "What flag would we hang in the Congress Hall? Then an idea struck me. We [already] have a flag – and it is blue and white. The *Tallit* (prayer shawl) with which we wrap ourselves when we pray: that is our symbol. Let us take this *Tallit* from its bag and unroll it before the eyes of Israel and the eyes of all nations. So I ordered a blue and white flag with the Shield of David painted upon it. That is how the national flag, that flew over Congress Hall, came into being."

2:3 The standard of the division of *Yehuda* As the forebear of the Davidic dynasty, *Yehuda* is given a place of honor in the Israelite camp. When the camp is not in motion, the tribe of *Yehuda* camps to the east of the *Mishkan*, which is considered the front, as it is the direction of the rising sun. And when they travel, the tribe of *Yehuda* goes in front, leading the Nation on its journey through the desert. As *Yehuda* led the Nation of Israel to the Promised Land, his descendant, the *Mashiach ben David*, will similarly gather the Children of Israel from all over the world and bring them back to *Eretz Yisrael*.

10 On the south: the standard of the division of *Reuven*, troop by troop. Chieftain of the Reubenites: *Elitzur* son of Shedeur.

י דֶּ֣גֶל מַחֲנֵ֧ה רְאוּבֵ֛ן תֵּימָ֖נָה לְצִבְאֹתָ֑ם וְנָשִׂיא֙ לִבְנֵ֣י רְאוּבֵ֔ן אֱלִיצ֖וּר בֶּן־שְׁדֵיאֽוּר:

11 His troop, as enrolled: 46,500.

יא וּצְבָא֖וֹ וּפְקֻדָ֑יו שִׁשָּׁ֧ה וְאַרְבָּעִ֛ים אֶ֖לֶף וַחֲמֵ֥שׁ מֵאֽוֹת:

12 Camping next to it: The tribe of *Shimon*. Chieftain of the Simeonites: *Shelumiel* son of Zurishaddai.

יב וְהַחוֹנִ֥ם עָלָ֖יו מַטֵּ֣ה שִׁמְע֑וֹן וְנָשִׂיא֙ לִבְנֵ֣י שִׁמְע֔וֹן שְׁלֻמִיאֵ֖ל בֶּן־צוּרִֽי־שַׁדָּֽי:

13 His troop, as enrolled: 59,300.

יג וּצְבָא֖וֹ וּפְקֻדֵיהֶ֑ם תִּשְׁעָ֧ה וַחֲמִשִּׁ֛ים אֶ֖לֶף וּשְׁלֹ֥שׁ מֵאֽוֹת:

14 And the tribe of *Gad*. Chieftain of the Gadites: *Elyasaf* son of Reuel.

יד וְמַטֵּ֖ה גָּ֑ד וְנָשִׂיא֙ לִבְנֵ֣י גָ֔ד אֶלְיָסָ֖ף בֶּן־רְעוּאֵֽל:

15 His troop, as enrolled: 45,650.

טו וּצְבָא֖וֹ וּפְקֻדֵיהֶ֑ם חֲמִשָּׁ֧ה וְאַרְבָּעִ֛ים אֶ֖לֶף וְשֵׁ֥שׁ מֵא֖וֹת וַחֲמִשִּֽׁים:

16 The total enrolled in the division of *Reuven*: 151,450, for all troops. These shall march second.

טז כָּֽל־הַפְּקֻדִ֞ים לְמַחֲנֵ֣ה רְאוּבֵ֗ן מְאַ֪ת אֶ֡לֶף וְאֶחָ֣ד וַחֲמִשִּׁ֥ים אֶ֛לֶף וְאַרְבַּע־מֵא֥וֹת וַחֲמִשִּׁ֖ים לְצִבְאֹתָ֑ם וּשְׁנִיִּ֖ם יִסָּֽעוּ:

17 Then, midway between the divisions, the Tent of Meeting, the division of the *Leviim*, shall move. As they camp, so they shall march, each in position, by their standards.

יז וְנָסַ֧ע אֹֽהֶל־מוֹעֵ֛ד מַחֲנֵ֥ה הַלְוִיִּ֖ם בְּת֣וֹךְ הַֽמַּחֲנֹ֑ת כַּאֲשֶׁ֤ר יַחֲנוּ֙ כֵּ֣ן יִסָּ֔עוּ אִ֥ישׁ עַל־יָד֖וֹ לְדִגְלֵיהֶֽם:

18 On the west: the standard of the division of *Efraim*, troop by troop. Chieftain of the Ephraimites: *Elishama* son of Ammihud.

יח דֶּ֣גֶל מַחֲנֵ֧ה אֶפְרַ֛יִם לְצִבְאֹתָ֖ם יָ֑מָּה וְנָשִׂיא֙ לִבְנֵ֣י אֶפְרַ֔יִם אֱלִישָׁמָ֖ע בֶּן־עַמִּיהֽוּד:

19 His troop, as enrolled: 40,500.

יט וּצְבָא֖וֹ וּפְקֻדֵיהֶ֑ם אַרְבָּעִ֥ים אֶ֖לֶף וַחֲמֵ֥שׁ מֵאֽוֹת:

20 Next to it: The tribe of *Menashe*. Chieftain of the Manassites: *Gamliel* son of Pedahzur.

כ וְעָלָ֖יו מַטֵּ֣ה מְנַשֶּׁ֑ה וְנָשִׂיא֙ לִבְנֵ֣י מְנַשֶּׁ֔ה גַּמְלִיאֵ֖ל בֶּן־פְּדָהצֽוּר:

21 His troop, as enrolled: 32,200.

כא וּצְבָא֖וֹ וּפְקֻדֵיהֶ֑ם שְׁנַ֥יִם וּשְׁלֹשִׁ֛ים אֶ֖לֶף וּמָאתָֽיִם:

22 And the tribe of *Binyamin*. Chieftain of the Benjaminites: *Avidan* son of Gideoni.

כב וּמַטֵּ֖ה בִּנְיָמִ֑ן וְנָשִׂיא֙ לִבְנֵ֣י בִנְיָמִ֔ן אֲבִידָ֖ן בֶּן־גִּדְעֹנִֽי:

23 His troop, as enrolled: 35,400.

כג וּצְבָא֖וֹ וּפְקֻדֵיהֶ֑ם חֲמִשָּׁ֧ה וּשְׁלֹשִׁ֛ים אֶ֖לֶף וְאַרְבַּ֥ע מֵאֽוֹת:

24 The total enrolled in the division of *Efraim*: 108,100 for all troops. These shall march third.

כד כָּֽל־הַפְּקֻדִ֞ים לְמַחֲנֵ֣ה אֶפְרַ֗יִם מְאַ֥ת אֶ֛לֶף וּשְׁמֹנַֽת־אֲלָפִ֖ים וּמֵאָ֑ה לְצִבְאֹתָ֖ם וּשְׁלִשִׁ֥ים יִסָּֽעוּ:

25 On the north: the standard of the division of *Dan*, troop by troop. Chieftain of the Danites: *Achiezer* son of Ammishaddai.

כה דֶּ֣גֶל מַחֲנֵ֥ה דָ֛ן צָפֹ֖נָה לְצִבְאֹתָ֑ם וְנָשִׂיא֙ לִבְנֵ֣י דָ֔ן אֲחִיעֶ֖זֶר בֶּן־עַמִּֽישַׁדָּֽי:

6

26 His troop, as enrolled: 62,700.

כו וּצְבָאוֹ וּפְקֻדֵיהֶם שְׁנַיִם וְשִׁשִּׁים אֶלֶף
וּשְׁבַע מֵאוֹת:

27 Camping next to it: The tribe of *Asher*. Chieftain of the Asherites: *Pagiel* son of Ochran.

כז וְהַחֹנִים עָלָיו מַטֵּה אָשֵׁר וְנָשִׂיא לִבְנֵי
אָשֵׁר פַּגְעִיאֵל בֶּן־עָכְרָן:

28 His troop, as enrolled: 41,500.

כח וּצְבָאוֹ וּפְקֻדֵיהֶם אֶחָד וְאַרְבָּעִים אֶלֶף
וַחֲמֵשׁ מֵאוֹת:

29 And the tribe of *Naftali*. Chieftain of the Naphtalites: *Achira* son of Enan.

כט וּמַטֵּה נַפְתָּלִי וְנָשִׂיא לִבְנֵי נַפְתָּלִי
אֲחִירַע בֶּן־עֵינָן:

30 His troop, as enrolled: 53,400.

ל וּצְבָאוֹ וּפְקֻדֵיהֶם שְׁלֹשָׁה וַחֲמִשִּׁים אֶלֶף
וְאַרְבַּע מֵאוֹת:

31 The total enrolled in the division of *Dan*: 157,600. These shall march last, by their standards.

לא כָּל־הַפְּקֻדִים לְמַחֲנֵה דָן מְאַת אֶלֶף
וְשִׁבְעָה וַחֲמִשִּׁים אֶלֶף וְשֵׁשׁ מֵאוֹת
לָאַחֲרֹנָה יִסְעוּ לְדִגְלֵיהֶם:

32 Those are the enrollments of the Israelites by ancestral houses. The total enrolled in the divisions, for all troops: 603,550.

לב אֵלֶּה פְּקוּדֵי בְנֵי־יִשְׂרָאֵל לְבֵית אֲבֹתָם
כָּל־פְּקוּדֵי הַמַּחֲנֹת לְצִבְאֹתָם שֵׁשׁ־
מֵאוֹת אֶלֶף וּשְׁלֹשֶׁת אֲלָפִים וַחֲמֵשׁ
מֵאוֹת וַחֲמִשִּׁים:

33 The *Leviim*, however, were not recorded among the Israelites, as *Hashem* had commanded *Moshe*.

לג וְהַלְוִיִּם לֹא הָתְפָּקְדוּ בְּתוֹךְ בְּנֵי יִשְׂרָאֵל
כַּאֲשֶׁר צִוָּה יְהֹוָה אֶת־מֹשֶׁה:

34 The Israelites did accordingly; just as *Hashem* had commanded *Moshe*, so they camped by their standards, and so they marched, each with his clan according to his ancestral house.

לד וַיַּעֲשׂוּ בְּנֵי יִשְׂרָאֵל כְּכֹל אֲשֶׁר־צִוָּה יְהֹוָה
אֶת־מֹשֶׁה כֵּן־חָנוּ לְדִגְלֵיהֶם וְכֵן נָסָעוּ
אִישׁ לְמִשְׁפְּחֹתָיו עַל־בֵּית אֲבֹתָיו:

3 ¹ This is the line of *Aharon* and *Moshe* at the time that *Hashem* spoke with *Moshe* on Har Sinai.

ג א וְאֵלֶּה תּוֹלְדֹת אַהֲרֹן וּמֹשֶׁה בְּיוֹם דִּבֶּר
יְהֹוָה אֶת־מֹשֶׁה בְּהַר סִינָי:

*v'-AY-leh to-l'-DOT a-ha-RON u-mo-SHEH b'-YOM
di-BER a-do-NAI et mo-SHEH b'-HAR see-NAI*

² These were the names of *Aharon*'s sons: *Nadav*, the first-born, and *Avihu*, *Elazar* and *Itamar*;

ב וְאֵלֶּה שְׁמוֹת בְּנֵי־אַהֲרֹן הַבְּכֹר נָדָב
וַאֲבִיהוּא אֶלְעָזָר וְאִיתָמָר:

³ those were the names of *Aharon*'s sons, the anointed *Kohanim* who were ordained for priesthood.

ג אֵלֶּה שְׁמוֹת בְּנֵי אַהֲרֹן הַכֹּהֲנִים
הַמְּשֻׁחִים אֲשֶׁר־מִלֵּא יָדָם לְכַהֵן:

3:1 This is the line of *Aharon* and *Moshe* Following these words which introduce the census of the tribe of *Levi*, the Bible goes on to list only the descendants of *Aharon* and not those of *Moshe*, *Levi's* most famous offspring. According to *Rashi*, *Aharon's* descendants were considered to be *Moshe's* as well, since *Moshe* was the one who taught them God's word. Although *Aharon* was their biological father, providing them with physical life, *Moshe* became their spiritual fa-ther, providing for them a life of fulfillment and holiness. Without this spiritual life, their physical lives would have been lacking, devoid of meaning and purpose. How great it is to spread *Hashem's* message to others, for in doing so you are giving them life, just as *Moshe* did.

Rabbi Tuly Weisz teaching the Bible

7

4 But *Nadav* and *Avihu* died by the will of *Hashem*, when they offered alien fire before *Hashem* in the wilderness of Sinai; and they left no sons. So it was *Elazar* and *Itamar* who served as *Kohanim* in the lifetime of their father *Aharon*.

ד וַיָּ֣מָת נָדָ֣ב וַאֲבִיה֣וּא לִפְנֵ֣י יְהֹוָ֡ה בְּהַקְרִבָ֣ם אֵ֣שׁ זָרָה֩ לִפְנֵ֨י יְהֹוָ֜ה בְּמִדְבַּ֣ר סִינַ֗י וּבָנִ֖ים לֹא־הָי֣וּ לָהֶ֑ם וַיְכַהֵ֤ן אֶלְעָזָר֙ וְאִ֣יתָמָ֔ר עַל־פְּנֵ֖י אַהֲרֹ֥ן אֲבִיהֶֽם׃

5 *Hashem* spoke to *Moshe*, saying:

ה וַיְדַבֵּ֥ר יְהֹוָ֖ה אֶל־מֹשֶׁ֥ה לֵּאמֹֽר׃

6 Advance the tribe of *Levi* and place them in attendance upon *Aharon* the *Kohen* to serve him.

ו הַקְרֵב֙ אֶת־מַטֵּ֣ה לֵוִ֔י וְהַֽעֲמַדְתָּ֣ אֹת֔וֹ לִפְנֵ֖י אַהֲרֹ֣ן הַכֹּהֵ֑ן וְשֵׁרְת֖וּ אֹתֽוֹ׃

7 They shall perform duties for him and for the whole community before the Tent of Meeting, doing the work of the *Mishkan*.

ז וְשָׁמְר֣וּ אֶת־מִשְׁמַרְתּ֗וֹ וְאֶת־מִשְׁמֶ֙רֶת֙ כָּל־הָ֣עֵדָ֔ה לִפְנֵ֖י אֹ֣הֶל מוֹעֵ֑ד לַעֲבֹ֖ד אֶת־עֲבֹדַ֥ת הַמִּשְׁכָּֽן׃

8 They shall take charge of all the furnishings of the Tent of Meeting – a duty on behalf of the Israelites – doing the work of the *Mishkan*.

ח וְשָׁמְר֗וּ אֶֽת־כָּל־כְּלֵי֙ אֹ֣הֶל מוֹעֵ֔ד וְאֶת־מִשְׁמֶ֖רֶת בְּנֵ֣י יִשְׂרָאֵ֑ל לַעֲבֹ֖ד אֶת־עֲבֹדַ֥ת הַמִּשְׁכָּֽן׃

9 You shall assign the *Leviim* to *Aharon* and to his sons: they are formally assigned to him from among the Israelites.

ט וְנָתַתָּה֙ אֶת־הַלְוִיִּ֔ם לְאַהֲרֹ֖ן וּלְבָנָ֑יו נְתוּנִ֨ם נְתוּנִ֥ם הֵ֙מָּה֙ ל֔וֹ מֵאֵ֖ת בְּנֵ֥י יִשְׂרָאֵֽל׃

10 You shall make *Aharon* and his sons responsible for observing their priestly duties; and any outsider who encroaches shall be put to death.

י וְאֶת־אַהֲרֹ֤ן וְאֶת־בָּנָיו֙ תִּפְקֹ֔ד וְשָׁמְר֖וּ אֶת־כְּהֻנָּתָ֑ם וְהַזָּ֥ר הַקָּרֵ֖ב יוּמָֽת׃

11 *Hashem* spoke to *Moshe*, saying:

יא וַיְדַבֵּ֥ר יְהֹוָ֖ה אֶל־מֹשֶׁ֥ה לֵּאמֹֽר׃

12 I hereby take the *Leviim* from among the Israelites in place of all the first-born, the first issue of the womb among the Israelites: the *Leviim* shall be Mine.

יב וַאֲנִ֞י הִנֵּ֧ה לָקַ֣חְתִּי אֶת־הַלְוִיִּ֗ם מִתּוֹךְ֙ בְּנֵ֣י יִשְׂרָאֵ֔ל תַּ֛חַת כָּל־בְּכ֥וֹר פֶּ֣טֶר רֶ֖חֶם מִבְּנֵ֣י יִשְׂרָאֵ֑ל וְהָ֥יוּ לִ֖י הַלְוִיִּֽם׃

13 For every first-born is Mine: at the time that I smote every first-born in the land of Egypt, I consecrated every first-born in *Yisrael*, man and beast, to Myself, to be Mine, *Hashem*'s.

יג כִּ֣י לִי֮ כָּל־בְּכוֹר֒ בְּיוֹם֩ הַכֹּתִ֨י כָל־בְּכ֜וֹר בְּאֶ֣רֶץ מִצְרַ֗יִם הִקְדַּ֣שְׁתִּי לִ֤י כָל־בְּכוֹר֙ בְּיִשְׂרָאֵ֔ל מֵאָדָ֖ם עַד־בְּהֵמָ֑ה לִ֥י יִהְי֖וּ אֲנִ֥י יְהֹוָֽה׃

14 *Hashem* spoke to *Moshe* in the wilderness of Sinai, saying:

יד וַיְדַבֵּ֤ר יְהֹוָה֙ אֶל־מֹשֶׁ֔ה בְּמִדְבַּ֥ר סִינַ֖י לֵאמֹֽר׃

15 Record the *Leviim* by ancestral house and by clan; record every male among them from the age of one month up.

טו פְּקֹד֙ אֶת־בְּנֵ֣י לֵוִ֔י לְבֵ֥ית אֲבֹתָ֖ם לְמִשְׁפְּחֹתָ֑ם כָּל־זָכָ֛ר מִבֶּן־חֹ֥דֶשׁ וָמַ֖עְלָה תִּפְקְדֵֽם׃

16 So *Moshe* recorded them at the command of *Hashem*, as he was bidden.

טז וַיִּפְקֹ֥ד אֹתָ֛ם מֹשֶׁ֖ה עַל־פִּ֣י יְהֹוָ֑ה כַּאֲשֶׁ֖ר צֻוָּֽה׃

17 These were the sons of *Levi* by name: *Gershon*, *Kehat*, and *Merari*.

יז וַיִּֽהְיוּ־אֵ֥לֶּה בְנֵֽי־לֵוִ֖י בִּשְׁמֹתָ֑ם גֵּרְשׁ֕וֹן וּקְהָ֖ת וּמְרָרִֽי׃

18 These were the names of the sons of *Gershon* by clan: Libni and *Shim'i*.

יח וְאֵ֛לֶּה שְׁמ֥וֹת בְּנֵֽי־גֵרְשׁ֖וֹן לְמִשְׁפְּחֹתָ֑ם לִבְנִ֖י וְשִׁמְעִֽי׃

19 The sons of *Kehat* by clan: *Amram* and Izhar, *Chevron* and Uzziel.

יט וּבְנֵי קְהָת לְמִשְׁפְּחֹתָם עַמְרָם וְיִצְהָר חֶבְרוֹן וְעֻזִּיאֵל:

20 The sons of *Merari* by clan: Mahli and Mushi. These were the clans of the *Leviim* within their ancestral houses:

כ וּבְנֵי מְרָרִי לְמִשְׁפְּחֹתָם מַחְלִי וּמוּשִׁי אֵלֶּה הֵם מִשְׁפְּחֹת הַלֵּוִי לְבֵית אֲבֹתָם:

21 To *Gershon* belonged the clan of the Libnites and the clan of the Shim'ites; those were the clans of the Gershonites.

כא לְגֵרְשׁוֹן מִשְׁפַּחַת הַלִּבְנִי וּמִשְׁפַּחַת הַשִּׁמְעִי אֵלֶּה הֵם מִשְׁפְּחֹת הַגֵּרְשֻׁנִּי:

22 The recorded entries of all their males from the age of one month up, as recorded, came to 7,500.

כב פְּקֻדֵיהֶם בְּמִסְפַּר כָּל־זָכָר מִבֶּן־חֹדֶשׁ וָמָעְלָה פְּקֻדֵיהֶם שִׁבְעַת אֲלָפִים וַחֲמֵשׁ מֵאוֹת:

23 The clans of the Gershonites were to camp behind the *Mishkan*, to the west.

כג מִשְׁפְּחֹת הַגֵּרְשֻׁנִּי אַחֲרֵי הַמִּשְׁכָּן יַחֲנוּ יָמָּה:

24 The chieftain of the ancestral house of the Gershonites was *Elyasaf* son of Lael.

כד וּנְשִׂיא בֵית־אָב לַגֵּרְשֻׁנִּי אֶלְיָסָף בֶּן־לָאֵל:

25 The duties of the Gershonites in the Tent of Meeting comprised: the *Mishkan*, the tent, its covering, and the screen for the entrance of the Tent of Meeting;

כה וּמִשְׁמֶרֶת בְּנֵי־גֵרְשׁוֹן בְּאֹהֶל מוֹעֵד הַמִּשְׁכָּן וְהָאֹהֶל מִכְסֵהוּ וּמָסַךְ פֶּתַח אֹהֶל מוֹעֵד:

26 the hangings of the enclosure, the screen for the entrance of the enclosure which surrounds the *Mishkan*, the cords thereof, and the *Mizbayach* – all the service connected with these.

כו וְקַלְעֵי הֶחָצֵר וְאֶת־מָסַךְ פֶּתַח הֶחָצֵר אֲשֶׁר עַל־הַמִּשְׁכָּן וְעַל־הַמִּזְבֵּחַ סָבִיב וְאֵת מֵיתָרָיו לְכֹל עֲבֹדָתוֹ:

27 To *Kehat* belonged the clan of the Amramites, the clan of the Izharites, the clan of the Chevronites, and the clan of the Uzzielites; those were the clans of the Kohathites.

כז וְלִקְהָת מִשְׁפַּחַת הָעַמְרָמִי וּמִשְׁפַּחַת הַיִּצְהָרִי וּמִשְׁפַּחַת הַחֶבְרֹנִי וּמִשְׁפַּחַת הָעָזִּיאֵלִי אֵלֶּה הֵם מִשְׁפְּחֹת הַקְּהָתִי:

28 All the listed males from the age of one month up came to 8,600, attending to the duties of the sanctuary.

כח בְּמִסְפַּר כָּל־זָכָר מִבֶּן־חֹדֶשׁ וָמָעְלָה שְׁמֹנַת אֲלָפִים וְשֵׁשׁ מֵאוֹת שֹׁמְרֵי מִשְׁמֶרֶת הַקֹּדֶשׁ:

29 The clans of the Kohathites were to camp along the south side of the *Mishkan*.

כט מִשְׁפְּחֹת בְּנֵי־קְהָת יַחֲנוּ עַל יֶרֶךְ הַמִּשְׁכָּן תֵּימָנָה:

30 The chieftain of the ancestral house of the Kohathite clans was *Elitzafan* son of Uzziel.

ל וּנְשִׂיא בֵית־אָב לְמִשְׁפְּחֹת הַקְּהָתִי אֱלִיצָפָן בֶּן־עֻזִּיאֵל:

31 Their duties comprised: the ark, the table, the *menorah*, the *mizbachot*, and the sacred utensils that were used with them, and the screen – all the service connected with these.

לא וּמִשְׁמַרְתָּם הָאָרֹן וְהַשֻּׁלְחָן וְהַמְּנֹרָה וְהַמִּזְבְּחֹת וּכְלֵי הַקֹּדֶשׁ אֲשֶׁר יְשָׁרְתוּ בָּהֶם וְהַמָּסָךְ וְכֹל עֲבֹדָתוֹ:

32 The head chieftain of the *Leviim* was *Elazar* son of *Aharon* the *Kohen*, in charge of those attending to the duties of the sanctuary.

לב וּנְשִׂיא נְשִׂיאֵי הַלֵּוִי אֶלְעָזָר בֶּן־אַהֲרֹן הַכֹּהֵן פְּקֻדַּת שֹׁמְרֵי מִשְׁמֶרֶת הַקֹּדֶשׁ:

Numbers

33 To *Merari* belonged the clan of the Mahlites and the clan of the Mushites; those were the clans of *Merari*.

לג לִמְרָרִי מִשְׁפַּחַת הַמַּחְלִי וּמִשְׁפַּחַת הַמּוּשִׁי אֵלֶּה הֵם מִשְׁפְּחֹת מְרָרִי:

34 The recorded entries of all their males from the age of one month up came to 6,200.

לד וּפְקֻדֵיהֶם בְּמִסְפַּר כָּל־זָכָר מִבֶּן־חֹדֶשׁ וָמָעְלָה שֵׁשֶׁת אֲלָפִים וּמָאתָיִם:

35 The chieftain of the ancestral house of the clans of *Merari* was *Tzuriel* son of *Avichayil*. They were to camp along the north side of the *Mishkan*.

לה וּנְשִׂיא בֵית־אָב לְמִשְׁפְּחֹת מְרָרִי צוּרִיאֵל בֶּן־אֲבִיחָיִל עַל יֶרֶךְ הַמִּשְׁכָּן יַחֲנוּ צָפֹנָה:

36 The assigned duties of the Merarites comprised: the planks of the *Mishkan*, its bars, posts, and sockets, and all its furnishings – all the service connected with these;

לו וּפְקֻדַּת מִשְׁמֶרֶת בְּנֵי מְרָרִי קַרְשֵׁי הַמִּשְׁכָּן וּבְרִיחָיו וְעַמֻּדָיו וַאֲדָנָיו וְכָל־כֵּלָיו וְכֹל עֲבֹדָתוֹ:

37 also the posts around the enclosure and their sockets, pegs, and cords.

לז וְעַמֻּדֵי הֶחָצֵר סָבִיב וְאַדְנֵיהֶם וִיתֵדֹתָם וּמֵיתְרֵיהֶם:

38 Those who were to camp before the *Mishkan*, in front – before the Tent of Meeting, on the east – were *Moshe* and *Aharon* and his sons, attending to the duties of the sanctuary, as a duty on behalf of the Israelites; and any outsider who encroached was to be put to death.

לח וְהַחֹנִים לִפְנֵי הַמִּשְׁכָּן קֵדְמָה לִפְנֵי אֹהֶל־מוֹעֵד מִזְרָחָה מֹשֶׁה וְאַהֲרֹן וּבָנָיו שֹׁמְרִים מִשְׁמֶרֶת הַמִּקְדָּשׁ לְמִשְׁמֶרֶת בְּנֵי יִשְׂרָאֵל וְהַזָּר הַקָּרֵב יוּמָת:

39 All the *Leviim* who were recorded, whom at *Hashem*'s command *Moshe* and *Aharon* recorded by their clans, all the males from the age of one month up, came to 22,000.

לט כָּל־פְּקוּדֵי הַלְוִיִּם אֲשֶׁר פָּקַד מֹשֶׁה וְאַהֲרֹן עַל־פִּי יְהֹוָה לְמִשְׁפְּחֹתָם כָּל־זָכָר מִבֶּן־חֹדֶשׁ וָמַעְלָה שְׁנַיִם וְעֶשְׂרִים אָלֶף:

40 *Hashem* said to *Moshe*: Record every first-born male of *B'nei Yisrael* from the age of one month up, and make a list of their names;

מ וַיֹּאמֶר יְהֹוָה אֶל־מֹשֶׁה פְּקֹד כָּל־בְּכֹר זָכָר לִבְנֵי יִשְׂרָאֵל מִבֶּן־חֹדֶשׁ וָמָעְלָה וְשָׂא אֵת מִסְפַּר שְׁמֹתָם:

41 and take the *Leviim* for Me, *Hashem*, in place of every first-born among *B'nei Yisrael*, and the cattle of the *Leviim* in place of every first-born among the cattle of the Israelites.

מא וְלָקַחְתָּ אֶת־הַלְוִיִּם לִי אֲנִי יְהֹוָה תַּחַת כָּל־בְּכֹר בִּבְנֵי יִשְׂרָאֵל וְאֵת בֶּהֱמַת הַלְוִיִּם תַּחַת כָּל־בְּכוֹר בְּבֶהֱמַת בְּנֵי יִשְׂרָאֵל:

42 So *Moshe* recorded all the first-born among the Israelites, as *Hashem* had commanded him.

מב וַיִּפְקֹד מֹשֶׁה כַּאֲשֶׁר צִוָּה יְהֹוָה אֹתוֹ אֶת־כָּל־בְּכֹר בִּבְנֵי יִשְׂרָאֵל:

43 All the first-born males as listed by name, recorded from the age of one month up, came to 22,273.

מג וַיְהִי כָל־בְּכוֹר זָכָר בְּמִסְפַּר שֵׁמוֹת מִבֶּן־חֹדֶשׁ וָמַעְלָה לִפְקֻדֵיהֶם שְׁנַיִם וְעֶשְׂרִים אֶלֶף שְׁלֹשָׁה וְשִׁבְעִים וּמָאתָיִם:

44 *Hashem* spoke to *Moshe*, saying:

מד וַיְדַבֵּר יְהֹוָה אֶל־מֹשֶׁה לֵּאמֹר:

45 Take the *Leviim* in place of all the first-born among *B'nei Yisrael*, and the cattle of the *Leviim* in place of their cattle; and the *Leviim* shall be Mine, *Hashem*'s.

מה קַח אֶת־הַלְוִיִּם תַּחַת כָּל־בְּכוֹר בִּבְנֵי יִשְׂרָאֵל וְאֶת־בֶּהֱמַת הַלְוִיִּם תַּחַת בְּהֶמְתָּם וְהָיוּ־לִי הַלְוִיִּם אֲנִי יְהֹוָה:

46 And as the redemption price of the 273 Israelite first-born over and above the number of the *Leviim*,

מו וְאֵת פְּדוּיֵי הַשְּׁלֹשָׁה וְהַשִּׁבְעִים וְהַמָּאתָיִם הָעֹדְפִים עַל־הַלְוִיִּם מִבְּכוֹר בְּנֵי יִשְׂרָאֵל:

Numbers

⁴⁷ take five *shekalim* per head – take this by the sanctuary weight, twenty *geira* to the *shekel* –

מז וְלָקַחְתָּ חֲמֵ֤שֶׁת חֲמֵ֨שֶׁת שְׁקָלִ֖ים לַגֻּלְגֹּ֑לֶת בְּשֶׁ֣קֶל הַקֹּ֔דֶשׁ תִּקָּ֖ח עֶשְׂרִ֥ים גֵּרָ֖ה הַשָּֽׁקֶל׃

⁴⁸ and give the money to *Aharon* and his sons as the redemption price for those who are in excess.

מח וְנָתַתָּ֣ה הַכֶּ֗סֶף לְאַהֲרֹ֖ן וּלְבָנָ֑יו פְּדוּיֵ֖י הָעֹדְפִ֥ים בָּהֶֽם׃

⁴⁹ So *Moshe* took the redemption money from those over and above the ones redeemed by the *Leviim*;

מט וַיִּקַּ֣ח מֹשֶׁ֔ה אֵ֖ת כֶּ֣סֶף הַפִּדְי֑וֹם מֵאֵת֙ הָעֹ֣דְפִ֔ים עַ֖ל פְּדוּיֵ֥י הַלְוִיִּֽם׃

⁵⁰ he took the money from the first-born of the Israelites, 1,365 sanctuary *shekalim*.

נ מֵאֵ֗ת בְּכ֛וֹר בְּנֵ֥י יִשְׂרָאֵ֖ל לָקַ֣ח אֶת־הַכָּ֑סֶף חֲמִשָּׁ֤ה וְשִׁשִּׁים֙ וּשְׁלֹ֣שׁ מֵא֔וֹת וָאֶ֖לֶף בְּשֶׁ֥קֶל הַקֹּֽדֶשׁ׃

⁵¹ And *Moshe* gave the redemption money to *Aharon* and his sons at *Hashem*'s bidding, as *Hashem* had commanded *Moshe*.

נא וַיִּתֵּ֨ן מֹשֶׁ֜ה אֶת־כֶּ֧סֶף הַפְּדֻיִ֛ם לְאַהֲרֹ֖ן וּלְבָנָ֑יו עַל־פִּ֥י יְהֹוָ֖ה כַּאֲשֶׁ֛ר צִוָּ֥ה יְהֹוָ֖ה אֶת־מֹשֶֽׁה׃

4 ¹ *Hashem* spoke to *Moshe* and *Aharon*, saying:

ד א וַיְדַבֵּ֣ר יְהֹוָ֔ה אֶל־מֹשֶׁ֥ה וְאֶֽל־אַהֲרֹ֖ן לֵאמֹֽר׃

² Take a [separate] census of the Kohathites among the *Leviim*, by the clans of their ancestral house,

ב נָשֹׂ֗א אֶת־רֹאשׁ֙ בְּנֵ֣י קְהָ֔ת מִתּ֖וֹךְ בְּנֵ֣י לֵוִ֑י לְמִשְׁפְּחֹתָ֖ם לְבֵ֥ית אֲבֹתָֽם׃

³ from the age of thirty years up to the age of fifty, all who are subject to service, to perform tasks for the Tent of Meeting.

ג מִבֶּ֨ן שְׁלֹשִׁ֤ים שָׁנָה֙ וָמַ֔עְלָה וְעַ֖ד בֶּן־חֲמִשִּׁ֣ים שָׁנָ֑ה כָּל־בָּא֙ לַצָּבָ֔א לַעֲשׂ֥וֹת מְלָאכָ֖ה בְּאֹ֥הֶל מוֹעֵֽד׃

⁴ This is the responsibility of the Kohathites in the Tent of Meeting: the most sacred objects.

ד זֹ֛את עֲבֹדַ֥ת בְּנֵי־קְהָ֖ת בְּאֹ֣הֶל מוֹעֵ֑ד קֹ֖דֶשׁ הַקֳּדָשִֽׁים׃

⁵ At the breaking of camp, *Aharon* and his sons shall go in and take down the screening curtain and cover the *Aron HaBrit* with it.

ה וּבָ֨א אַהֲרֹ֤ן וּבָנָיו֙ בִּנְסֹ֣עַ הַֽמַּחֲנֶ֔ה וְהוֹרִ֕דוּ אֵ֖ת פָּרֹ֣כֶת הַמָּסָ֑ךְ וְכִסּוּ־בָ֕הּ אֵ֖ת אֲרֹ֥ן הָעֵדֻֽת׃

⁶ They shall lay a covering of dolphin skin over it and spread a cloth of pure blue on top; and they shall put its poles in place.

ו וְנָתְנ֣וּ עָלָ֗יו כְּס֚וּי ע֣וֹר תַּ֔חַשׁ וּפָרְשׂ֧וּ בֶֽגֶד־כְּלִ֥יל תְּכֵ֖לֶת מִלְמָ֑עְלָה וְשָׂמ֖וּ בַּדָּֽיו׃

⁷ Over the table of display they shall spread a blue cloth; they shall place upon it the bowls, the ladles, the jars, and the libation jugs; and the regular bread shall rest upon it.

ז וְעַ֣ל ׀ שֻׁלְחַ֣ן הַפָּנִ֗ים יִפְרְשׂוּ֮ בֶּ֣גֶד תְּכֵ֒לֶת֒ וְנָתְנ֣וּ עָ֠לָ֠יו אֶת־הַקְּעָרֹ֤ת וְאֶת־הַכַּפֹּת֙ וְאֶת־הַמְּנַקִּיֹּ֔ת וְאֵ֖ת קְשׂ֣וֹת הַנָּ֑סֶךְ וְלֶ֥חֶם הַתָּמִ֖יד עָלָ֥יו יִהְיֶֽה׃

⁸ They shall spread over these a crimson cloth which they shall cover with a covering of dolphin skin; and they shall put the poles in place.

ח וּפָרְשׂ֣וּ עֲלֵיהֶ֗ם בֶּ֚גֶד תּוֹלַ֣עַת שָׁנִ֔י וְכִסּ֣וּ אֹת֔וֹ בְּמִכְסֵ֖ה ע֣וֹר תָּ֑חַשׁ וְשָׂמ֖וּ אֶת־בַּדָּֽיו׃

⁹ Then they shall take a blue cloth and cover the *menorah* for lighting, with its lamps, its tongs, and its fire pans, as well as all the oil vessels that are used in its service.

ט וְלָקְח֣וּ בֶּ֣גֶד תְּכֵ֗לֶת וְכִסּ֞וּ אֶת־מְנֹרַ֤ת הַמָּאוֹר֙ וְאֶת־נֵ֣רֹתֶ֔יהָ וְאֶת־מַלְקָחֶ֖יהָ וְאֶת־מַחְתֹּתֶ֑יהָ וְאֵת֙ כָּל־כְּלֵ֣י שַׁמְנָ֔הּ אֲשֶׁ֥ר יְשָׁרְתוּ־לָ֖הּ בָּהֶֽם׃

¹⁰ They shall put it and all its furnishings into a covering of dolphin skin, which they shall then place on a carrying frame.

י וְנָתְנ֤וּ אֹתָהּ֙ וְאֶת־כָּל־כֵּלֶ֔יהָ אֶל־מִכְסֵ֖ה ע֣וֹר תָּ֑חַשׁ וְנָתְנ֖וּ עַל־הַמּֽוֹט׃

11

11 Next they shall spread a blue cloth over the *Mizbayach* of gold and cover it with a covering of dolphin skin; and they shall put its poles in place.

יא וְעַל מִזְבַּח הַזָּהָב יִפְרְשׂוּ בֶּגֶד תְּכֵלֶת וְכִסּוּ אֹתוֹ בְּמִכְסֵה עוֹר תָּחַשׁ וְשָׂמוּ אֶת־בַּדָּיו:

12 They shall take all the service vessels with which the service in the sanctuary is performed, put them into a blue cloth and cover them with a covering of dolphin skin, which they shall then place on a carrying frame.

יב וְלָקְחוּ אֶת־כָּל־כְּלֵי הַשָּׁרֵת אֲשֶׁר יְשָׁרְתוּ־בָם בַּקֹּדֶשׁ וְנָתְנוּ אֶל־בֶּגֶד תְּכֵלֶת וְכִסּוּ אוֹתָם בְּמִכְסֵה עוֹר תָּחַשׁ וְנָתְנוּ עַל־הַמּוֹט:

13 They shall remove the ashes from the [copper] *Mizbayach* and spread a purple cloth over it.

יג וְדִשְּׁנוּ אֶת־הַמִּזְבֵּחַ וּפָרְשׂוּ עָלָיו בֶּגֶד אַרְגָּמָן:

14 Upon it they shall place all the vessels that are used in its service: the fire pans, the flesh hooks, the scrapers, and the basins – all the vessels of the *Mizbayach* – and over it they shall spread a covering of dolphin skin; and they shall put its poles in place.

יד וְנָתְנוּ עָלָיו אֶת־כָּל־כֵּלָיו אֲשֶׁר יְשָׁרְתוּ עָלָיו בָּהֶם אֶת־הַמַּחְתֹּת אֶת־הַמִּזְלָגֹת וְאֶת־הַיָּעִים וְאֶת־הַמִּזְרָקֹת כֹּל כְּלֵי הַמִּזְבֵּחַ וּפָרְשׂוּ עָלָיו כְּסוּי עוֹר תָּחַשׁ וְשָׂמוּ בַדָּיו:

15 When *Aharon* and his sons have finished covering the sacred objects and all the furnishings of the sacred objects at the breaking of camp, only then shall the Kohathites come and lift them, so that they do not come in contact with the sacred objects and die. These things in the Tent of Meeting shall be the porterage of the Kohathites.

טו וְכִלָּה אַהֲרֹן־וּבָנָיו לְכַסֹּת אֶת־הַקֹּדֶשׁ וְאֶת־כָּל־כְּלֵי הַקֹּדֶשׁ בִּנְסֹעַ הַמַּחֲנֶה וְאַחֲרֵי־כֵן יָבֹאוּ בְנֵי־קְהָת לָשֵׂאת וְלֹא־יִגְּעוּ אֶל־הַקֹּדֶשׁ וָמֵתוּ אֵלֶּה מַשָּׂא בְנֵי־קְהָת בְּאֹהֶל מוֹעֵד:

16 Responsibility shall rest with *Elazar* son of *Aharon* the *Kohen* for the lighting oil, the aromatic incense, the regular meal offering, and the anointing oil – responsibility for the whole *Mishkan* and for everything consecrated that is in it or in its vessels.

טז וּפְקֻדַּת אֶלְעָזָר בֶּן־אַהֲרֹן הַכֹּהֵן שֶׁמֶן הַמָּאוֹר וּקְטֹרֶת הַסַּמִּים וּמִנְחַת הַתָּמִיד וְשֶׁמֶן הַמִּשְׁחָה פְּקֻדַּת כָּל־הַמִּשְׁכָּן וְכָל־אֲשֶׁר־בּוֹ בְּקֹדֶשׁ וּבְכֵלָיו:

17 *Hashem* spoke to *Moshe* and *Aharon*, saying:

יז וַיְדַבֵּר יְהוָה אֶל־מֹשֶׁה וְאֶל־אַהֲרֹן לֵאמֹר:

18 Do not let the group of Kohathite clans be cut off from the *Leviim*.

יח אַל־תַּכְרִיתוּ אֶת־שֵׁבֶט מִשְׁפְּחֹת הַקְּהָתִי מִתּוֹךְ הַלְוִיִּם:

al takh-REE-tu et SHAY-vet mish-p'-KHOT ha-k'-ha-TEE mi-TOKH hal-vi-YIM

4:18 Do not let the group of Kohathites clans be cut off from the *Leviim* The children of *Kehat*, one of the three sons of *Levi*, are responsible for the most sacred parts of the *Mishkan*, including the Holy of Holies and the *Aron*. When the people break camp and begin a new journey, the Kohathites must dismantle the Holy of Holies and cover the *Aron*. However, due to its elevated holiness they are required to do so without viewing the inside of the Holy of Holies, since merely looking at it carries the strictest of penalties. Interestingly, *Moshe* and *Aharon* are the ones who are commanded, "Do not let the group of Kohathite clans be cut off..." They are the ones responsible for making sure that the Kohathites do not mistakenly look into the Holy of Holies and incur the death penalty. Not only does *Hashem* care about the life of every individual, He holds us all responsible for looking out for, and caring about, each other.

Israeli children at the beach

19 Do this with them, that they may live and not die when they approach the most sacred objects: let *Aharon* and his sons go in and assign each of them to his duties and to his porterage.

יט וְזֹאת עֲשׂוּ לָהֶם וְחָיוּ וְלֹא יָמֻתוּ בְּגִשְׁתָּם אֶת־קֹדֶשׁ הַקֳּדָשִׁים אַהֲרֹן וּבָנָיו יָבֹאוּ וְשָׂמוּ אוֹתָם אִישׁ אִישׁ עַל־עֲבֹדָתוֹ וְאֶל־מַשָּׂאוֹ:

20 But let not [the Kohathites] go inside and witness the dismantling of the sanctuary, lest they die.

כ וְלֹא־יָבֹאוּ לִרְאוֹת כְּבַלַּע אֶת־הַקֹּדֶשׁ וָמֵתוּ:

21 *Hashem* spoke to *Moshe*:

כא וַיְדַבֵּר יְהֹוָה אֶל־מֹשֶׁה לֵּאמֹר:

22 Take a census of the Gershonites also, by their ancestral house and by their clans.

כב נָשֹׂא אֶת־רֹאשׁ בְּנֵי גֵרְשׁוֹן גַּם־הֵם לְבֵית אֲבֹתָם לְמִשְׁפְּחֹתָם:

23 Record them from the age of thirty years up to the age of fifty, all who are subject to service in the performance of tasks for the Tent of Meeting.

כג מִבֶּן שְׁלֹשִׁים שָׁנָה וָמַעְלָה עַד בֶּן־חֲמִשִּׁים שָׁנָה תִּפְקֹד אוֹתָם כָּל־הַבָּא לִצְבֹא צָבָא לַעֲבֹד עֲבֹדָה בְּאֹהֶל מוֹעֵד:

24 These are the duties of the Gershonite clans as to labor and porterage:

כד זֹאת עֲבֹדַת מִשְׁפְּחֹת הַגֵּרְשֻׁנִּי לַעֲבֹד וּלְמַשָּׂא:

25 they shall carry the cloths of the *Mishkan*, the Tent of Meeting with its covering, the covering of dolphin skin that is on top of it, and the screen for the entrance of the Tent of Meeting;

כה וְנָשְׂאוּ אֶת־יְרִיעֹת הַמִּשְׁכָּן וְאֶת־אֹהֶל מוֹעֵד מִכְסֵהוּ וּמִכְסֵה הַתַּחַשׁ אֲשֶׁר־עָלָיו מִלְמָעְלָה וְאֶת־מָסַךְ פֶּתַח אֹהֶל מוֹעֵד:

26 the hangings of the enclosure, the screen at the entrance of the gate of the enclosure that surrounds the *Mishkan*, the cords thereof, and the *Mizbayach*, and all their service equipment and all their accessories; and they shall perform the service.

כו וְאֵת קַלְעֵי הֶחָצֵר וְאֶת־מָסַךְ פֶּתַח שַׁעַר הֶחָצֵר אֲשֶׁר עַל־הַמִּשְׁכָּן וְעַל־הַמִּזְבֵּחַ סָבִיב וְאֵת מֵיתְרֵיהֶם וְאֶת־כָּל־כְּלֵי עֲבֹדָתָם וְאֵת כָּל־אֲשֶׁר יֵעָשֶׂה לָהֶם וְעָבָדוּ:

27 All the duties of the Gershonites, all their porterage and all their service, shall be performed on orders from *Aharon* and his sons; you shall make them responsible for attending to all their porterage.

כז עַל־פִּי אַהֲרֹן וּבָנָיו תִּהְיֶה כָּל־עֲבֹדַת בְּנֵי הַגֵּרְשֻׁנִּי לְכָל־מַשָּׂאָם וּלְכֹל עֲבֹדָתָם וּפְקַדְתֶּם עֲלֵהֶם בְּמִשְׁמֶרֶת אֵת כָּל־מַשָּׂאָם:

28 Those are the duties of the Gershonite clans for the Tent of Meeting; they shall attend to them under the direction of *Itamar* son of *Aharon* the *Kohen*.

כח זֹאת עֲבֹדַת מִשְׁפְּחֹת בְּנֵי הַגֵּרְשֻׁנִּי בְּאֹהֶל מוֹעֵד וּמִשְׁמַרְתָּם בְּיַד אִיתָמָר בֶּן־אַהֲרֹן הַכֹּהֵן:

29 As for the Merarites, you shall record them by the clans of their ancestral house;

כט בְּנֵי מְרָרִי לְמִשְׁפְּחֹתָם לְבֵית־אֲבֹתָם תִּפְקֹד אֹתָם:

30 you shall record them from the age of thirty years up to the age of fifty, all who are subject to service in the performance of the duties for the Tent of Meeting.

ל מִבֶּן שְׁלֹשִׁים שָׁנָה וָמַעְלָה וְעַד בֶּן־חֲמִשִּׁים שָׁנָה תִּפְקְדֵם כָּל־הַבָּא לַצָּבָא לַעֲבֹד אֶת־עֲבֹדַת אֹהֶל מוֹעֵד:

31 These are their porterage tasks in connection with their various duties for the Tent of Meeting: the planks, the bars, the posts, and the sockets of the *Mishkan*;

לא וְזֹאת מִשְׁמֶרֶת מַשָּׂאָם לְכָל־עֲבֹדָתָם בְּאֹהֶל מוֹעֵד קַרְשֵׁי הַמִּשְׁכָּן וּבְרִיחָיו וְעַמּוּדָיו וַאֲדָנָיו:

³² the posts around the enclosure and their sockets, pegs, and cords – all these furnishings and their service: you shall list by name the objects that are their porterage tasks.

לב וְעַמּוּדֵי הֶחָצֵר סָבִיב וְאַדְנֵיהֶם וִיתֵדֹתָם וּמֵיתְרֵיהֶם לְכָל־כְּלֵיהֶם וּלְכֹל עֲבֹדָתָם וּבְשֵׁמֹת תִּפְקְדוּ אֶת־כְּלֵי מִשְׁמֶרֶת מַשָּׂאָם:

³³ Those are the duties of the Merarite clans, pertaining to their various duties in the Tent of Meeting under the direction of *Itamar* son of *Aharon* the *Kohen*.

לג זֹאת עֲבֹדַת מִשְׁפְּחֹת בְּנֵי מְרָרִי לְכָל־ עֲבֹדָתָם בְּאֹהֶל מוֹעֵד בְּיַד אִיתָמָר בֶּן־ אַהֲרֹן הַכֹּהֵן:

³⁴ So *Moshe, Aharon,* and the chieftains of the community recorded the Kohathites by the clans of their ancestral house,

לד וַיִּפְקֹד מֹשֶׁה וְאַהֲרֹן וּנְשִׂיאֵי הָעֵדָה אֶת־בְּנֵי הַקְּהָתִי לְמִשְׁפְּחֹתָם וּלְבֵית אֲבֹתָם:

³⁵ from the age of thirty years up to the age of fifty, all who were subject to service for work relating to the Tent of Meeting.

לה מִבֶּן שְׁלֹשִׁים שָׁנָה וָמַעְלָה וְעַד בֶּן־ חֲמִשִּׁים שָׁנָה כָּל־הַבָּא לַצָּבָא לַעֲבֹדָה בְּאֹהֶל מוֹעֵד:

³⁶ Those recorded by their clans came to 2,750.

לו וַיִּהְיוּ פְקֻדֵיהֶם לְמִשְׁפְּחֹתָם אַלְפַּיִם שְׁבַע מֵאוֹת וַחֲמִשִּׁים:

³⁷ That was the enrollment of the Kohathite clans, all those who performed duties relating to the Tent of Meeting, whom *Moshe* and *Aharon* recorded at the command of *Hashem* through *Moshe*.

לז אֵלֶּה פְקוּדֵי מִשְׁפְּחֹת הַקְּהָתִי כָּל־ הָעֹבֵד בְּאֹהֶל מוֹעֵד אֲשֶׁר פָּקַד מֹשֶׁה וְאַהֲרֹן עַל־פִּי יְהֹוָה בְּיַד־מֹשֶׁה:

³⁸ The Gershonites who were recorded by the clans of their ancestral house,

לח וּפְקוּדֵי בְּנֵי גֵרְשׁוֹן לְמִשְׁפְּחוֹתָם וּלְבֵית אֲבֹתָם:

³⁹ from the age of thirty years up to the age of fifty, all who were subject to service for work relating to the Tent of Meeting –

לט מִבֶּן שְׁלֹשִׁים שָׁנָה וָמַעְלָה וְעַד בֶּן־ חֲמִשִּׁים שָׁנָה כָּל־הַבָּא לַצָּבָא לַעֲבֹדָה בְּאֹהֶל מוֹעֵד:

⁴⁰ those recorded by the clans of their ancestral house came to 2,630.

מ וַיִּהְיוּ פְּקֻדֵיהֶם לְמִשְׁפְּחֹתָם לְבֵית אֲבֹתָם אַלְפַּיִם וְשֵׁשׁ מֵאוֹת וּשְׁלֹשִׁים:

⁴¹ That was the enrollment of the Gershonite clans, all those performing duties relating to the Tent of Meeting whom *Moshe* and *Aharon* recorded at the command of *Hashem*.

מא אֵלֶּה פְקוּדֵי מִשְׁפְּחֹת בְּנֵי גֵרְשׁוֹן כָּל־ הָעֹבֵד בְּאֹהֶל מוֹעֵד אֲשֶׁר פָּקַד מֹשֶׁה וְאַהֲרֹן עַל־פִּי יְהֹוָה:

⁴² The enrollment of the Merarite clans by the clans of their ancestral house,

מב וּפְקוּדֵי מִשְׁפְּחֹת בְּנֵי מְרָרִי לְמִשְׁפְּחֹתָם לְבֵית אֲבֹתָם:

⁴³ from the age of thirty years up to the age of fifty, all who were subject to service for work relating to the Tent of Meeting –

מג מִבֶּן שְׁלֹשִׁים שָׁנָה וָמַעְלָה וְעַד בֶּן־ חֲמִשִּׁים שָׁנָה כָּל־הַבָּא לַצָּבָא לַעֲבֹדָה בְּאֹהֶל מוֹעֵד:

⁴⁴ those recorded by their clans came to 3,200.

מד וַיִּהְיוּ פְקֻדֵיהֶם לְמִשְׁפְּחֹתָם שְׁלֹשֶׁת אֲלָפִים וּמָאתָיִם:

⁴⁵ That was the enrollment of the Merarite clans which *Moshe* and *Aharon* recorded at the command of *Hashem* through *Moshe*.

מה אֵלֶּה פְקוּדֵי מִשְׁפְּחֹת בְּנֵי מְרָרִי אֲשֶׁר פָּקַד מֹשֶׁה וְאַהֲרֹן עַל־פִּי יְהֹוָה בְּיַד־ מֹשֶׁה:

Numbers

46 All the *Leviim* whom *Moshe, Aharon,* and the chieftains of *Yisrael* recorded by the clans of their ancestral houses,

מו כָּל־הַפְּקֻדִים אֲשֶׁר פָּקַד מֹשֶׁה וְאַהֲרֹן וּנְשִׂיאֵי יִשְׂרָאֵל אֶת־הַלְוִיִּם לְמִשְׁפְּחֹתָם וּלְבֵית אֲבֹתָם:

47 from the age of thirty years up to the age of fifty, all who were subject to duties of service and porterage relating to the Tent of Meeting –

מז מִבֶּן שְׁלֹשִׁים שָׁנָה וָמַעְלָה וְעַד בֶּן־חֲמִשִּׁים שָׁנָה כָּל־הַבָּא לַעֲבֹד עֲבֹדַת עֲבֹדָה וַעֲבֹדַת מַשָּׂא בְּאֹהֶל מוֹעֵד:

48 those recorded came to 8,580.

מח וַיִּהְיוּ פְּקֻדֵיהֶם שְׁמֹנַת אֲלָפִים וַחֲמֵשׁ מֵאוֹת וּשְׁמֹנִים:

49 Each one was given responsibility for his service and porterage at the command of *Hashem* through *Moshe,* and each was recorded as *Hashem* had commanded *Moshe.*

מט עַל־פִּי יְהֹוָה פָּקַד אוֹתָם בְּיַד־מֹשֶׁה אִישׁ אִישׁ עַל־עֲבֹדָתוֹ וְעַל־מַשָּׂאוֹ וּפְקֻדָיו אֲשֶׁר־צִוָּה יְהֹוָה אֶת־מֹשֶׁה:

5 1 *Hashem* spoke to *Moshe,* saying:

ה א וַיְדַבֵּר יְהֹוָה אֶל־מֹשֶׁה לֵּאמֹר:

2 Instruct the Israelites to remove from camp anyone with an eruption or a discharge and anyone defiled by a corpse.

ב צַו אֶת־בְּנֵי יִשְׂרָאֵל וִישַׁלְּחוּ מִן־הַמַּחֲנֶה כָּל־צָרוּעַ וְכָל־זָב וְכֹל טָמֵא לָנָפֶשׁ:

3 Remove male and female alike; put them outside the camp so that they do not defile the camp of those in whose midst I dwell.

ג מִזָּכָר עַד־נְקֵבָה תְּשַׁלֵּחוּ אֶל־מִחוּץ לַמַּחֲנֶה תְּשַׁלְּחוּם וְלֹא יְטַמְּאוּ אֶת־מַחֲנֵיהֶם אֲשֶׁר אֲנִי שֹׁכֵן בְּתוֹכָם:

4 The Israelites did so, putting them outside the camp; as *Hashem* had spoken to *Moshe,* so the Israelites did.

ד וַיַּעֲשׂוּ־כֵן בְּנֵי יִשְׂרָאֵל וַיְשַׁלְּחוּ אוֹתָם אֶל־מִחוּץ לַמַּחֲנֶה כַּאֲשֶׁר דִּבֶּר יְהֹוָה אֶל־מֹשֶׁה כֵּן עָשׂוּ בְּנֵי יִשְׂרָאֵל:

5 *Hashem* spoke to *Moshe,* saying:

ה וַיְדַבֵּר יְהֹוָה אֶל־מֹשֶׁה לֵּאמֹר:

6 Speak to the Israelites: When a man or woman commits any wrong toward a fellow man, thus breaking faith with *Hashem,* and that person realizes his guilt,

ו דַּבֵּר אֶל־בְּנֵי יִשְׂרָאֵל אִישׁ אוֹ־אִשָּׁה כִּי יַעֲשׂוּ מִכָּל־חַטֹּאת הָאָדָם לִמְעֹל מַעַל בַּיהֹוָה וְאָשְׁמָה הַנֶּפֶשׁ הַהִוא:

da-BAYR el b'-NAY yis-ra-AYL EESH o i-SHAH KEE ya-a-SU mi-kol kha-TOT ha-a-DAM lim-OL MA-al ba-a-do-NAI v'-a-sh'-MAH ha-NE-fesh ha-HEE

5:6 When a man or woman commits any wrong toward a fellow man After describing the camp of Israel in the desert with the *Mishkan* at its center, the *Torah* continues by detailing a series of laws that are seemingly unrelated to the camp, or to each other: Laws concerning theft, the wayward wife, and the nazirite. The connection between these different topics may be that all of these laws have to do with the high level of holiness and morality that the Children of Israel are expected to maintain, not only in their relationship with *Hashem,* but also in their human interactions. These laws represent three different types of relationships that require this type of sensitivity: Relations between a person and his fellow (theft), between a person and his family (the wayward wife), and between a person and himself (nazirite). Those who desire to ensure that *Hashem*'s presence will continue to rest among them must ensure that all their interpersonal interactions are characterized by respect and sensitivity.

Two Israeli girls cleaning garbage from a park

7 he shall confess the wrong that he has done. He shall make restitution in the principal amount and add one-fifth to it, giving it to him whom he has wronged.

ז וְהִתְוַדּוּ אֶת־חַטָּאתָם אֲשֶׁר עָשׂוּ וְהֵשִׁיב אֶת־אֲשָׁמוֹ בְּרֹאשׁוֹ וַחֲמִישִׁתוֹ יֹסֵף עָלָיו וְנָתַן לַאֲשֶׁר אָשַׁם לֽוֹ׃

8 If the man has no kinsman to whom restitution can be made, the amount repaid shall go to *Hashem* for the *Kohen* – in addition to the ram of expiation with which expiation is made on his behalf.

ח וְאִם־אֵין לָאִישׁ גֹּאֵל לְהָשִׁיב הָאָשָׁם אֵלָיו הָאָשָׁם הַמּוּשָׁב לַיהֹוָה לַכֹּהֵן מִלְּבַד אֵיל הַכִּפֻּרִים אֲשֶׁר יְכַפֶּר־בּוֹ עָלָֽיו׃

9 So, too, any gift among the sacred donations that the Israelites offer shall be the *Kohen's*.

ט וְכָל־תְּרוּמָה לְכָל־קָדְשֵׁי בְנֵי־יִשְׂרָאֵל אֲשֶׁר־יַקְרִיבוּ לַכֹּהֵן לוֹ יִהְיֶֽה׃

10 And each shall retain his sacred donations: each *Kohen* shall keep what is given to him.

י וְאִישׁ אֶת־קֳדָשָׁיו לוֹ יִהְיוּ אִישׁ אֲשֶׁר־יִתֵּן לַכֹּהֵן לוֹ יִהְיֶֽה׃

11 *Hashem* spoke to *Moshe*, saying:

יא וַיְדַבֵּר יְהֹוָה אֶל־מֹשֶׁה לֵּאמֹֽר׃

12 Speak to *B'nei Yisrael* and say to them: If any man's wife has gone astray and broken faith with him

יב דַּבֵּר אֶל־בְּנֵי יִשְׂרָאֵל וְאָמַרְתָּ אֲלֵהֶם אִישׁ אִישׁ כִּי־תִשְׂטֶה אִשְׁתּוֹ וּמָעֲלָה בוֹ מָֽעַל׃

13 in that a man has had carnal relations with her unbeknown to her husband, and she keeps secret the fact that she has defiled herself without being forced, and there is no witness against her –

יג וְשָׁכַב אִישׁ אֹתָהּ שִׁכְבַת־זֶרַע וְנֶעְלַם מֵעֵינֵי אִישָׁהּ וְנִסְתְּרָה וְהִיא נִטְמָאָה וְעֵד אֵין בָּהּ וְהִוא לֹא נִתְפָּֽשָׂה׃

14 but a fit of jealousy comes over him and he is wrought up about the wife who has defiled herself; or if a fit of jealousy comes over one and he is wrought up about his wife although she has not defiled herself –

יד וְעָבַר עָלָיו רֽוּחַ־קִנְאָה וְקִנֵּא אֶת־אִשְׁתּוֹ וְהִוא נִטְמָאָה אוֹ־עָבַר עָלָיו רֽוּחַ־קִנְאָה וְקִנֵּא אֶת־אִשְׁתּוֹ וְהִיא לֹא נִטְמָֽאָה׃

15 the man shall bring his wife to the *Kohen*. And he shall bring as an offering for her one-tenth of an *efah* of barley flour. No oil shall be poured upon it and no frankincense shall be laid on it, for it is a meal offering of jealousy, a meal offering of remembrance which recalls wrongdoing.

טו וְהֵבִיא הָאִישׁ אֶת־אִשְׁתּוֹ אֶל־הַכֹּהֵן וְהֵבִיא אֶת־קָרְבָּנָהּ עָלֶיהָ עֲשִׂירִת הָאֵיפָה קֶמַח שְׂעֹרִים לֹא־יִצֹק עָלָיו שֶׁמֶן וְלֹא־יִתֵּן עָלָיו לְבֹנָה כִּי־מִנְחַת קְנָאֹת הוּא מִנְחַת זִכָּרוֹן מַזְכֶּרֶת עָוֺֽן׃

16 The *Kohen* shall bring her forward and have her stand before *Hashem*.

טז וְהִקְרִיב אֹתָהּ הַכֹּהֵן וְהֶעֱמִדָהּ לִפְנֵי יְהֹוָֽה׃

17 The *Kohen* shall take sacral water in an earthen vessel and, taking some of the earth that is on the floor of the *Mishkan*, the *Kohen* shall put it into the water.

יז וְלָקַח הַכֹּהֵן מַיִם קְדֹשִׁים בִּכְלִי־חָרֶשׂ וּמִן־הֶעָפָר אֲשֶׁר יִהְיֶה בְּקַרְקַע הַמִּשְׁכָּן יִקַּח הַכֹּהֵן וְנָתַן אֶל־הַמָּֽיִם׃

18 After he has made the woman stand before *Hashem*, the *Kohen* shall bare the woman's head and place upon her hands the meal offering of remembrance, which is a meal offering of jealousy. And in the *Kohen's* hands shall be the water of bitterness that induces the spell.

יח וְהֶעֱמִיד הַכֹּהֵן אֶת־הָאִשָּׁה לִפְנֵי יְהֹוָה וּפָרַע אֶת־רֹאשׁ הָֽאִשָּׁה וְנָתַן עַל־כַּפֶּיהָ אֵת מִנְחַת הַזִּכָּרוֹן מִנְחַת קְנָאֹת הִוא וּבְיַד הַכֹּהֵן יִהְיוּ מֵי הַמָּרִים הַמְאָֽרֲרִֽים׃

Numbers

19 The *Kohen* shall adjure the woman, saying to her, "If no man has lain with you, if you have not gone astray in defilement while married to your husband, be immune to harm from this water of bitterness that induces the spell.

יט וְהִשְׁבִּיעַ אֹתָהּ הַכֹּהֵן וְאָמַר אֶל־הָאִשָּׁה אִם־לֹא שָׁכַב אִישׁ אֹתָךְ וְאִם־לֹא שָׂטִית טֻמְאָה תַּחַת אִישֵׁךְ הִנָּקִי מִמֵּי הַמָּרִים הַמְאָרֲרִים הָאֵלֶּה:

20 But if you have gone astray while married to your husband and have defiled yourself, if a man other than your husband has had carnal relations with you" –

כ וְאַתְּ כִּי שָׂטִית תַּחַת אִישֵׁךְ וְכִי נִטְמֵאת וַיִּתֵּן אִישׁ בָּךְ אֶת־שְׁכָבְתּוֹ מִבַּלְעֲדֵי אִישֵׁךְ:

21 here the *Kohen* shall administer the curse of adjuration to the woman, as the *Kohen* goes on to say to the woman – "may *Hashem* make you a curse and an imprecation among your people, as *Hashem* causes your thigh to sag and your belly to distend;

כא וְהִשְׁבִּיעַ הַכֹּהֵן אֶת־הָאִשָּׁה בִּשְׁבֻעַת הָאָלָה וְאָמַר הַכֹּהֵן לָאִשָּׁה יִתֵּן יְהֹוָה אוֹתָךְ לְאָלָה וְלִשְׁבֻעָה בְּתוֹךְ עַמֵּךְ בְּתֵת יְהֹוָה אֶת־יְרֵכֵךְ נֹפֶלֶת וְאֶת־בִּטְנֵךְ צָבָה:

22 may this water that induces the spell enter your body, causing the belly to distend and the thigh to sag." And the woman shall say, "*Amen, Amen!*"

כב וּבָאוּ הַמַּיִם הַמְאָרֲרִים הָאֵלֶּה בְּמֵעַיִךְ לַצְבּוֹת בֶּטֶן וְלַנְפִּל יָרֵךְ וְאָמְרָה הָאִשָּׁה אָמֵן אָמֵן:

23 The *Kohen* shall put these curses down in writing and rub it off into the water of bitterness.

כג וְכָתַב אֶת־הָאָלֹת הָאֵלֶּה הַכֹּהֵן בַּסֵּפֶר וּמָחָה אֶל־מֵי הַמָּרִים:

24 He is to make the woman drink the water of bitterness that induces the spell, so that the spell-inducing water may enter into her to bring on bitterness.

כד וְהִשְׁקָה אֶת־הָאִשָּׁה אֶת־מֵי הַמָּרִים הַמְאָרֲרִים וּבָאוּ בָהּ הַמַּיִם הַמְאָרֲרִים לְמָרִים:

25 Then the *Kohen* shall take from the woman's hand the meal offering of jealousy, elevate the meal offering before *Hashem*, and present it on the *Mizbayach*.

כה וְלָקַח הַכֹּהֵן מִיַּד הָאִשָּׁה אֵת מִנְחַת הַקְּנָאֹת וְהֵנִיף אֶת־הַמִּנְחָה לִפְנֵי יְהֹוָה וְהִקְרִיב אֹתָהּ אֶל־הַמִּזְבֵּחַ:

26 The *Kohen* shall scoop out of the meal offering a token part of it and turn it into smoke on the *Mizbayach*. Last, he shall make the woman drink the water.

כו וְקָמַץ הַכֹּהֵן מִן־הַמִּנְחָה אֶת־אַזְכָּרָתָהּ וְהִקְטִיר הַמִּזְבֵּחָה וְאַחַר יַשְׁקֶה אֶת־הָאִשָּׁה אֶת־הַמָּיִם:

27 Once he has made her drink the water – if she has defiled herself by breaking faith with her husband, the spell-inducing water shall enter into her to bring on bitterness, so that her belly shall distend and her thigh shall sag; and the woman shall become a curse among her people.

כז וְהִשְׁקָהּ אֶת־הַמַּיִם וְהָיְתָה אִם־נִטְמְאָה וַתִּמְעֹל מַעַל בְּאִישָׁהּ וּבָאוּ בָהּ הַמַּיִם הַמְאָרֲרִים לְמָרִים וְצָבְתָה בִטְנָהּ וְנָפְלָה יְרֵכָהּ וְהָיְתָה הָאִשָּׁה לְאָלָה בְּקֶרֶב עַמָּהּ:

28 But if the woman has not defiled herself and is pure, she shall be unharmed and able to retain seed.

כח וְאִם־לֹא נִטְמְאָה הָאִשָּׁה וּטְהֹרָה הִוא וְנִקְּתָה וְנִזְרְעָה זָרַע:

29 This is the ritual in cases of jealousy, when a woman goes astray while married to her husband and defiles herself,

כט זֹאת תּוֹרַת הַקְּנָאֹת אֲשֶׁר תִּשְׂטֶה אִשָּׁה תַּחַת אִישָׁהּ וְנִטְמָאָה:

30 or when a fit of jealousy comes over a man and he is wrought up over his wife: the woman shall be made to stand before *Hashem* and the *Kohen* shall carry out all this ritual with her.

31 The man shall be clear of guilt; but that woman shall suffer for her guilt.

6 1 *Hashem* spoke to *Moshe*, saying:

2 Speak to the Israelites and say to them: If anyone, man or woman, explicitly utters a nazirite's vow, to set himself apart for *Hashem*,

3 he shall abstain from wine and any other intoxicant; he shall not drink vinegar of wine or of any other intoxicant, neither shall he drink anything in which grapes have been steeped, nor eat grapes fresh or dried.

4 Throughout his term as nazirite, he may not eat anything that is obtained from the grapevine, even seeds or skin.

5 Throughout the term of his vow as nazirite, no razor shall touch his head; it shall remain consecrated until the completion of his term as nazirite of *Hashem*, the hair of his head being left to grow untrimmed.

6 Throughout the term that he has set apart for *Hashem*, he shall not go in where there is a dead person.

7 Even if his father or mother, or his brother or sister should die, he must not defile himself for them, since hair set apart for his God is upon his head:

8 throughout his term as nazirite he is consecrated to *Hashem*.

9 If a person dies suddenly near him, defiling his consecrated hair, he shall shave his head on the day he becomes clean; he shall shave it on the seventh day.

10 On the eighth day he shall bring two turtledoves or two pigeons to the *Kohen*, at the entrance of the Tent of Meeting.

11 The *Kohen* shall offer one as a sin offering and the other as a burnt offering, and make expiation on his behalf for the guilt that he incurred through the corpse. That same day he shall reconsecrate his head

ל אוֹ־אִישׁ אֲשֶׁר תַּעֲבֹר עָלָיו רוּחַ קִנְאָה וְקִנֵּא אֶת־אִשְׁתּוֹ וְהֶעֱמִיד אֶת־הָאִשָּׁה לִפְנֵי יְהוָֹה וְעָשָׂה לָהּ הַכֹּהֵן אֵת כָּל־הַתּוֹרָה הַזֹּאת:

לא וְנִקָּה הָאִישׁ מֵעָוֹן וְהָאִשָּׁה הַהִוא תִּשָּׂא אֶת־עֲוֹנָהּ:

ו א וַיְדַבֵּר יְהוָֹה אֶל־מֹשֶׁה לֵּאמֹר:

ב דַּבֵּר אֶל־בְּנֵי יִשְׂרָאֵל וְאָמַרְתָּ אֲלֵהֶם אִישׁ אוֹ־אִשָּׁה כִּי יַפְלִא לִנְדֹּר נֶדֶר נָזִיר לְהַזִּיר לַיהוָֹה:

ג מִיַּיִן וְשֵׁכָר יַזִּיר חֹמֶץ יַיִן וְחֹמֶץ שֵׁכָר לֹא יִשְׁתֶּה וְכָל־מִשְׁרַת עֲנָבִים לֹא יִשְׁתֶּה וַעֲנָבִים לַחִים וִיבֵשִׁים לֹא יֹאכֵל:

ד כֹּל יְמֵי נִזְרוֹ מִכֹּל אֲשֶׁר יֵעָשֶׂה מִגֶּפֶן הַיַּיִן מֵחַרְצַנִּים וְעַד־זָג לֹא יֹאכֵל:

ה כָּל־יְמֵי נֶדֶר נִזְרוֹ תַּעַר לֹא־יַעֲבֹר עַל־רֹאשׁוֹ עַד־מְלֹאת הַיָּמִם אֲשֶׁר־יַזִּיר לַיהוָֹה קָדֹשׁ יִהְיֶה גַּדֵּל פֶּרַע שְׂעַר רֹאשׁוֹ:

ו כָּל־יְמֵי הַזִּירוֹ לַיהוָֹה עַל־נֶפֶשׁ מֵת לֹא יָבֹא:

ז לְאָבִיו וּלְאִמּוֹ לְאָחִיו וּלְאַחֹתוֹ לֹא־יִטַּמָּא לָהֶם בְּמֹתָם כִּי נֵזֶר אֱלֹהָיו עַל־רֹאשׁוֹ:

ח כֹּל יְמֵי נִזְרוֹ קָדֹשׁ הוּא לַיהוָֹה:

ט וְכִי־יָמוּת מֵת עָלָיו בְּפֶתַע פִּתְאֹם וְטִמֵּא רֹאשׁ נִזְרוֹ וְגִלַּח רֹאשׁוֹ בְּיוֹם טָהֳרָתוֹ בַּיּוֹם הַשְּׁבִיעִי יְגַלְּחֶנּוּ:

י וּבַיּוֹם הַשְּׁמִינִי יָבִא שְׁתֵּי תֹרִים אוֹ שְׁנֵי בְּנֵי יוֹנָה אֶל־הַכֹּהֵן אֶל־פֶּתַח אֹהֶל מוֹעֵד:

יא וְעָשָׂה הַכֹּהֵן אֶחָד לְחַטָּאת וְאֶחָד לְעֹלָה וְכִפֶּר עָלָיו מֵאֲשֶׁר חָטָא עַל־הַנָּפֶשׁ וְקִדַּשׁ אֶת־רֹאשׁוֹ בַּיּוֹם הַהוּא:

Numbers

¹² and rededicate to *Hashem* his term as nazirite; and he shall bring a lamb in its first year as a penalty offering. The previous period shall be void, since his consecrated hair was defiled.

יב וְהִזִּיר לַיהוָֹה אֶת־יְמֵי נִזְרוֹ וְהֵבִיא כֶּבֶשׂ בֶּן־שְׁנָתוֹ לְאָשָׁם וְהַיָּמִים הָרִאשֹׁנִים יִפְּלוּ כִּי טָמֵא נִזְרוֹ:

¹³ This is the ritual for the nazirite: On the day that his term as nazirite is completed, he shall be brought to the entrance of the Tent of Meeting.

יג וְזֹאת תּוֹרַת הַנָּזִיר בְּיוֹם מְלֹאת יְמֵי נִזְרוֹ יָבִיא אֹתוֹ אֶל־פֶּתַח אֹהֶל מוֹעֵד:

¹⁴ As his offering to *Hashem* he shall present: one male lamb in its first year, without blemish, for a burnt offering; one ewe lamb in its first year, without blemish, for a sin offering; one ram without blemish for an offering of well-being;

יד וְהִקְרִיב אֶת־קָרְבָּנוֹ לַיהוָֹה כֶּבֶשׂ בֶּן־שְׁנָתוֹ תָמִים אֶחָד לְעֹלָה וְכַבְשָׂה אַחַת בַּת־שְׁנָתָהּ תְּמִימָה לְחַטָּאת וְאַיִל־אֶחָד תָּמִים לִשְׁלָמִים:

v'-hik-REEV et kor-ba-NO la-a-do-NAI KE-ves ben sh'-na-TO ta-MEEM e-KHAD l'-o-LAH v'-khav-SAH a-KHAT bat sh'-na-TAH t'-mee-MAH l'-kha-TAT v'-a-yil e-KHAD ta-MEEM lish-la-MEEM

¹⁵ a basket of unleavened cakes of choice flour with oil mixed in, and unleavened wafers spread with oil; and the proper meal offerings and libations.

טו וְסַל מַצּוֹת סֹלֶת חַלֹּת בְּלוּלֹת בַּשֶּׁמֶן וּרְקִיקֵי מַצּוֹת מְשֻׁחִים בַּשָּׁמֶן וּמִנְחָתָם וְנִסְכֵּיהֶם:

¹⁶ The *Kohen* shall present them before *Hashem* and offer the sin offering and the burnt offering.

טז וְהִקְרִיב הַכֹּהֵן לִפְנֵי יְהוָֹה וְעָשָׂה אֶת־חַטָּאתוֹ וְאֶת־עֹלָתוֹ:

¹⁷ He shall offer the ram as a sacrifice of well-being to *Hashem*, together with the basket of unleavened cakes; the *Kohen* shall also offer the meal offerings and the libations.

יז וְאֶת־הָאַיִל יַעֲשֶׂה זֶבַח שְׁלָמִים לַיהוָֹה עַל סַל הַמַּצּוֹת וְעָשָׂה הַכֹּהֵן אֶת־מִנְחָתוֹ וְאֶת־נִסְכּוֹ:

¹⁸ The nazirite shall then shave his consecrated hair, at the entrance of the Tent of Meeting, and take the locks of his consecrated hair and put them on the fire that is under the sacrifice of well-being.

יח וְגִלַּח הַנָּזִיר פֶּתַח אֹהֶל מוֹעֵד אֶת־רֹאשׁ נִזְרוֹ וְלָקַח אֶת־שְׂעַר רֹאשׁ נִזְרוֹ וְנָתַן עַל־הָאֵשׁ אֲשֶׁר־תַּחַת זֶבַח הַשְּׁלָמִים:

¹⁹ The *Kohen* shall take the shoulder of the ram when it has been boiled, one unleavened cake from the basket, and one unleavened wafer, and place them on the hands of the nazirite after he has shaved his consecrated hair.

יט וְלָקַח הַכֹּהֵן אֶת־הַזְּרֹעַ בְּשֵׁלָה מִן־הָאַיִל וְחַלַּת מַצָּה אַחַת מִן־הַסַּל וּרְקִיק מַצָּה אֶחָד וְנָתַן עַל־כַּפֵּי הַנָּזִיר אַחַר הִתְגַּלְּחוֹ אֶת־נִזְרוֹ:

📜 **6:14 For a sin offering** The nazirite is someone who takes it upon himself to abstain from wine, from cutting his hair and from contracting spiritual impurity from a dead body. He accepts these voluntary restrictions for the purpose of coming closer to *Hashem* and elevating himself spiritually. In essence, a nazirite removes himself from the ills of society so that he can remain pure and holy. At first glance, this seems admirable, something to be lauded and emulated. Indeed, the verse refers to the nazirite as "consecrated to *Hashem*" (verse 8). However, at the completion of his period of abstinence, the nazirite is required to bring a sin-offering.

What is his sin? The Talmud (*Taanit* 11a) explains that while it is important to set aside time to work on oneself and one's personal growth, the ideal is not to remove oneself from society completely. Rather, we must try to elevate ourselves within society and bring the rest of the world up with us.

Grapes in a vineyard in *Gush Etzion*

20 The *Kohen* shall elevate them as an elevation offering before *Hashem*; and this shall be a sacred donation for the *Kohen*, in addition to the breast of the elevation offering and the thigh of gift offering. After that the nazirite may drink wine.

כ וְהֵנִיף אוֹתָם הַכֹּהֵן תְּנוּפָה לִפְנֵי יְהוָה קֹדֶשׁ הוּא לַכֹּהֵן עַל חֲזֵה הַתְּנוּפָה וְעַל שׁוֹק הַתְּרוּמָה וְאַחַר יִשְׁתֶּה הַנָּזִיר יָיִן:

21 Such is the obligation of a nazirite; except that he who vows an offering to God of what he can afford, beyond his nazirite requirements, must do exactly according to the vow that he has made beyond his obligation as a nazirite.

כא זֹאת תּוֹרַת הַנָּזִיר אֲשֶׁר יִדֹּר קָרְבָּנוֹ לַיהוָה עַל נִזְרוֹ מִלְּבַד אֲשֶׁר־תַּשִּׂיג יָדוֹ כְּפִי נִדְרוֹ אֲשֶׁר יִדֹּר כֵּן יַעֲשֶׂה עַל תּוֹרַת נִזְרוֹ:

22 *Hashem* spoke to *Moshe*:

כב וַיְדַבֵּר יְהוָה אֶל־מֹשֶׁה לֵּאמֹר:

23 Speak to *Aharon* and his sons: Thus shall you bless the people of *Yisrael*. Say to them:

כג דַּבֵּר אֶל־אַהֲרֹן וְאֶל־בָּנָיו לֵאמֹר כֹּה תְבָרֲכוּ אֶת־בְּנֵי יִשְׂרָאֵל אָמוֹר לָהֶם:

da-BAYR el ah-ha-RON v'-el ba-NAV lay-MOR KOH
t'-va-r'-KHU et b'-NAY yis-ra-AYL a-MOR la-HEM

24 *Hashem* bless you and protect you!

כד יְבָרֶכְךָ יְהוָה וְיִשְׁמְרֶךָ:

y'-va-re-kh'-KHA a-do-NAI v'-yish-m'-RE-kha

25 *Hashem* deal kindly and graciously with you!

כה יָאֵר יְהוָה פָּנָיו אֵלֶיךָ וִיחֻנֶּךָּ:

ya-AYR a-do-NAI pa-NAV ay-LE-kha vee-khu-NE-ka

26 *Hashem* bestow His favor upon you and grant you peace!

כו יִשָּׂא יְהוָה פָּנָיו אֵלֶיךָ וְיָשֵׂם לְךָ שָׁלוֹם:

yi-SA a-do-NAI pa-NAV ay-LE-kha v'-ya-SAYM l'-KHA sha-LOM

27 Thus they shall link My name with the people of *Yisrael*, and I will bless them.

כז וְשָׂמוּ אֶת־שְׁמִי עַל־בְּנֵי יִשְׂרָאֵל וַאֲנִי אֲבָרֲכֵם:

7 1 On the day that *Moshe* finished setting up the *Mishkan*, he anointed and consecrated it and all its furnishings, as well as the *Mizbayach* and its utensils. When he had anointed and consecrated them,

ז א וַיְהִי בְּיוֹם כַּלּוֹת מֹשֶׁה לְהָקִים אֶת־הַמִּשְׁכָּן וַיִּמְשַׁח אֹתוֹ וַיְקַדֵּשׁ אֹתוֹ וְאֶת־כָּל־כֵּלָיו וְאֶת־הַמִּזְבֵּחַ וְאֶת־כָּל־כֵּלָיו וַיִּמְשָׁחֵם וַיְקַדֵּשׁ אֹתָם:

2 the chieftains of *Yisrael*, the heads of ancestral houses, namely, the chieftains of the tribes, those who were in charge of enrollment, drew near

ב וַיַּקְרִיבוּ נְשִׂיאֵי יִשְׂרָאֵל רָאשֵׁי בֵּית אֲבֹתָם הֵם נְשִׂיאֵי הַמַּטֹּת הֵם הָעֹמְדִים עַל־הַפְּקֻדִים:

6:26 Bestow His favor upon you and grant you peace The Priestly Blessing uttered by the *Kohanim* contains three parts. It begins with a blessing for prosperity and safety, continues with a blessing for *Hashem*'s grace, and climaxes with a blessing of peace. Indeed, the Sages of the *Mishna* (*Oktzin* 3:12) taught that "God found no vessel to contain His blessings, other than peace." In Israel, the Priestly Blessing is recited publicly each day by individuals possessing a family tradition that they are among the descendants of *Aharon*, a group whose lineage has been verified in recent years by DNA testing. We pray every day for the total fulfillment of the Priestly Blessing, when the Jewish people will live peacefully in *Eretz Yisrael*.

The Priestly Blessing at the Western Wall

Numbers

3 and brought their offering before *Hashem*: six draught carts and twelve oxen, a cart for every two chieftains and an ox for each one. When they had brought them before the *Mishkan*,

4 *Hashem* said to *Moshe*:

5 Accept these from them for use in the service of the Tent of Meeting, and give them to the *Leviim* according to their respective services.

6 *Moshe* took the carts and the oxen and gave them to the *Leviim*.

7 Two carts and four oxen he gave to the Gershonites, as required for their service,

8 and four carts and eight oxen he gave to the Merarites, as required for their service – under the direction of *Itamar* son of *Aharon* the *Kohen*.

9 But to the Kohathites he did not give any; since theirs was the service of the [most] sacred objects, their porterage was by shoulder.

10 The chieftains also brought the dedication offering for the *Mizbayach* upon its being anointed. As the chieftains were presenting their offerings before the *Mizbayach*,

va-yak-REE-vu han-si-EEM AYT kha-nu-KAT ha-miz-BAY-akh
b'-YOM hi-ma-SHAKH o-TO va-yak-REE-vu ha-n'-see-IM
et kor-ba-NAM lif-NAY ha-miz-BAY-akh

11 *Hashem* said to *Moshe*: Let them present their offerings for the dedication of the *Mizbayach*, one chieftain each day.

12 The one who presented his offering on the first day was *Nachshon* son of *Aminadav* of the tribe of *Yehuda*.

13 His offering: one silver bowl weighing 130 *shekalim* and one silver basin of 70 *shekalim* by the sanctuary weight, both filled with choice flour with oil mixed in, for a meal offering;

ג וַיָּבִיאוּ אֶת־קׇרְבָּנָם לִפְנֵי יְהֹוָה שֵׁשׁ־עֶגְלֹת צָב וּשְׁנֵי עָשָׂר בָּקָר עֲגָלָה עַל־שְׁנֵי הַנְּשִׂאִים וְשׁוֹר לְאֶחָד וַיַּקְרִיבוּ אוֹתָם לִפְנֵי הַמִּשְׁכָּן:

ד וַיֹּאמֶר יְהֹוָה אֶל־מֹשֶׁה לֵּאמֹר:

ה קַח מֵאִתָּם וְהָיוּ לַעֲבֹד אֶת־עֲבֹדַת אֹהֶל מוֹעֵד וְנָתַתָּה אוֹתָם אֶל־הַלְוִיִּם אִישׁ כְּפִי עֲבֹדָתוֹ:

ו וַיִּקַּח מֹשֶׁה אֶת־הָעֲגָלֹת וְאֶת־הַבָּקָר וַיִּתֵּן אוֹתָם אֶל־הַלְוִיִּם:

ז אֵת שְׁתֵּי הָעֲגָלֹת וְאֵת אַרְבַּעַת הַבָּקָר נָתַן לִבְנֵי גֵרְשׁוֹן כְּפִי עֲבֹדָתָם:

ח וְאֵת אַרְבַּע הָעֲגָלֹת וְאֵת שְׁמֹנַת הַבָּקָר נָתַן לִבְנֵי מְרָרִי כְּפִי עֲבֹדָתָם בְּיַד אִיתָמָר בֶּן־אַהֲרֹן הַכֹּהֵן:

ט וְלִבְנֵי קְהָת לֹא נָתָן כִּי־עֲבֹדַת הַקֹּדֶשׁ עֲלֵהֶם בַּכָּתֵף יִשָּׂאוּ:

י וַיַּקְרִיבוּ הַנְּשִׂאִים אֵת חֲנֻכַּת הַמִּזְבֵּחַ בְּיוֹם הִמָּשַׁח אֹתוֹ וַיַּקְרִיבוּ הַנְּשִׂיאִם אֶת־קׇרְבָּנָם לִפְנֵי הַמִּזְבֵּחַ:

יא וַיֹּאמֶר יְהֹוָה אֶל־מֹשֶׁה נָשִׂיא אֶחָד לַיּוֹם נָשִׂיא אֶחָד לַיּוֹם יַקְרִיבוּ אֶת־קׇרְבָּנָם לַחֲנֻכַּת הַמִּזְבֵּחַ:

יב וַיְהִי הַמַּקְרִיב בַּיּוֹם הָרִאשׁוֹן אֶת־קׇרְבָּנוֹ נַחְשׁוֹן בֶּן־עַמִּינָדָב לְמַטֵּה יְהוּדָה:

יג וְקׇרְבָּנוֹ קַעֲרַת־כֶּסֶף אַחַת שְׁלֹשִׁים וּמֵאָה מִשְׁקָלָהּ מִזְרָק אֶחָד כֶּסֶף שִׁבְעִים שֶׁקֶל בְּשֶׁקֶל הַקֹּדֶשׁ שְׁנֵיהֶם מְלֵאִים סֹלֶת בְּלוּלָה בַשֶּׁמֶן לְמִנְחָה:

Model of the second Beit Hamikdash in Yerushalayim

7:10 The chieftains also brought the dedication offering for the *Mizbayach* Chapter 7 describes the donations given by the tribal leaders in celebration of the sanctification of the *Mishkan*. After the donations of the chieftains are ac-cepted, they are inspired to bring offerings in celebration of the dedication of the altar. Following this example, the inaugurations of the First and Second Temples were also celebrated with an abundance of offerings (I Kings 8:62–63, Ezra 6:17). We await the day on which we will celebrate the inauguration of the third *Beit Hamikdash* in this same manner.

14 one gold ladle of 10 *shekalim*, filled with incense;

יד כַּף אַחַת עֲשָׂרָה זָהָב מְלֵאָה קְטֹרֶת:

15 one bull of the herd, one ram, and one lamb in its first year, for a burnt offering;

טו פַּר אֶחָד בֶּן־בָּקָר אַיִל אֶחָד כֶּבֶשׂ־אֶחָד בֶּן־שְׁנָתוֹ לְעֹלָה:

16 one goat for a sin offering;

טז שְׂעִיר־עִזִּים אֶחָד לְחַטָּאת:

17 and for his sacrifice of well-being: two oxen, five rams, five he-goats, and five yearling lambs. That was the offering of *Nachshon* son of *Aminadav*.

יז וּלְזֶבַח הַשְּׁלָמִים בָּקָר שְׁנַיִם אֵילִם חֲמִשָּׁה עַתּוּדִים חֲמִשָּׁה כְּבָשִׂים בְּנֵי־שָׁנָה חֲמִשָּׁה זֶה קָרְבַּן נַחְשׁוֹן בֶּן־עַמִּינָדָב:

18 On the second day, *Netanel* son of Zuar, chieftain of *Yissachar*, made his offering.

יח בַּיּוֹם הַשֵּׁנִי הִקְרִיב נְתַנְאֵל בֶּן־צוּעָר נְשִׂיא יִשָּׂשכָר:

19 He presented as his offering: one silver bowl weighing 130 *shekalim* and one silver basin of 70 *shekalim* by the sanctuary weight, both filled with choice flour with oil mixed in, for a meal offering;

יט הִקְרִב אֶת־קָרְבָּנוֹ קַעֲרַת־כֶּסֶף אַחַת שְׁלֹשִׁים וּמֵאָה מִשְׁקָלָהּ מִזְרָק אֶחָד כֶּסֶף שִׁבְעִים שֶׁקֶל בְּשֶׁקֶל הַקֹּדֶשׁ שְׁנֵיהֶם מְלֵאִים סֹלֶת בְּלוּלָה בַשֶּׁמֶן לְמִנְחָה:

20 one gold ladle of 10 *shekalim*, filled with incense;

כ כַּף אַחַת עֲשָׂרָה זָהָב מְלֵאָה קְטֹרֶת:

21 one bull of the herd, one ram, and one lamb in its first year, for a burnt offering;

כא פַּר אֶחָד בֶּן־בָּקָר אַיִל אֶחָד כֶּבֶשׂ־אֶחָד בֶּן־שְׁנָתוֹ לְעֹלָה:

22 one goat for a sin offering;

כב שְׂעִיר־עִזִּים אֶחָד לְחַטָּאת:

23 and for his sacrifice of well-being: two oxen, five rams, five he-goats, and five yearling lambs. That was the offering of *Netanel* son of Zuar.

כג וּלְזֶבַח הַשְּׁלָמִים בָּקָר שְׁנַיִם אֵילִם חֲמִשָּׁה עַתּוּדִים חֲמִשָּׁה כְּבָשִׂים בְּנֵי־שָׁנָה חֲמִשָּׁה זֶה קָרְבַּן נְתַנְאֵל בֶּן־צוּעָר:

24 On the third day, it was the chieftain of the Zebulunites, *Eliav* son of Helon.

כד בַּיּוֹם הַשְּׁלִישִׁי נָשִׂיא לִבְנֵי זְבוּלֻן אֱלִיאָב בֶּן־חֵלֹן:

25 His offering: one silver bowl weighing 130 *shekalim* and one silver basin of 70 *shekalim* by the sanctuary weight, both filled with choice flour with oil mixed in, for a meal offering;

כה קָרְבָּנוֹ קַעֲרַת־כֶּסֶף אַחַת שְׁלֹשִׁים וּמֵאָה מִשְׁקָלָהּ מִזְרָק אֶחָד כֶּסֶף שִׁבְעִים שֶׁקֶל בְּשֶׁקֶל הַקֹּדֶשׁ שְׁנֵיהֶם מְלֵאִים סֹלֶת בְּלוּלָה בַשֶּׁמֶן לְמִנְחָה:

26 one gold ladle of 10 *shekalim*, filled with incense;

כו כַּף אַחַת עֲשָׂרָה זָהָב מְלֵאָה קְטֹרֶת:

27 one bull of the herd, one ram, and one lamb in its first year, for a burnt offering;

כז פַּר אֶחָד בֶּן־בָּקָר אַיִל אֶחָד כֶּבֶשׂ־אֶחָד בֶּן־שְׁנָתוֹ לְעֹלָה:

28 one goat for a sin offering;

כח שְׂעִיר־עִזִּים אֶחָד לְחַטָּאת:

29 and for his sacrifice of well-being: two oxen, five rams, five he-goats, and five yearling lambs. That was the offering of *Eliav* son of Helon.

כט וּלְזֶבַח הַשְּׁלָמִים בָּקָר שְׁנַיִם אֵילִם חֲמִשָּׁה עַתֻּדִים חֲמִשָּׁה כְּבָשִׂים בְּנֵי־שָׁנָה חֲמִשָּׁה זֶה קָרְבַּן אֱלִיאָב בֶּן־חֵלֹן:

30 On the fourth day, it was the chieftain of the Reubenites, *Elitzur* son of Shedeur.

ל בַּיּוֹם הָרְבִיעִי נָשִׂיא לִבְנֵי רְאוּבֵן אֱלִיצוּר בֶּן־שְׁדֵיאוּר:

Numbers

³¹ His offering: one silver bowl weighing 130 *shekalim* and one silver basin of 70 *shekalim* by the sanctuary weight, both filled with choice flour with oil mixed in, for a meal offering;

לא קׇרְבָּנ֞וֹ קַֽעֲרַת־כֶּ֣סֶף אַחַ֗ת שְׁלֹשִׁ֣ים וּמֵאָה֮ מִשְׁקָלָהּ֒ מִזְרָ֤ק אֶחָד֙ כֶּ֔סֶף שִׁבְעִ֥ים שֶׁ֖קֶל בְּשֶׁ֣קֶל הַקֹּ֑דֶשׁ שְׁנֵיהֶ֣ם ׀ מְלֵאִ֗ים סֹ֛לֶת בְּלוּלָ֥ה בַשֶּׁ֖מֶן לְמִנְחָֽה:

³² one gold ladle of 10 *shekalim*, filled with incense;

לב כַּ֥ף אַחַ֛ת עֲשָׂרָ֥ה זָהָ֖ב מְלֵאָ֥ה קְטֹֽרֶת:

³³ one bull of the herd, one ram, and one lamb in its first year, for a burnt offering;

לג פַּ֣ר אֶחָ֞ד בֶּן־בָּקָ֗ר אַ֧יִל אֶחָ֛ד כֶּֽבֶשׂ־אֶחָ֥ד בֶּן־שְׁנָת֖וֹ לְעֹלָֽה:

³⁴ one goat for a sin offering;

לד שְׂעִיר־עִזִּ֥ים אֶחָ֖ד לְחַטָּֽאת:

³⁵ and for his sacrifice of well-being: two oxen, five rams, five he-goats, and five yearling lambs. That was the offering of *Elitzur* son of Shedeur.

לה וּלְזֶ֣בַח הַשְּׁלָמִים֮ בָּקָ֣ר שְׁנַ֒יִם֒ אֵילִ֤ם חֲמִשָּׁה֙ עַתֻּדִ֣ים חֲמִשָּׁ֔ה כְּבָשִׂ֥ים בְּנֵי־שָׁנָ֖ה חֲמִשָּׁ֑ה זֶ֛ה קׇרְבַּ֥ן אֱלִיצ֖וּר בֶּן־שְׁדֵיאֽוּר:

³⁶ On the fifth day, it was the chieftain of the Simeonites, *Shelumiel* son of Zurishaddai.

לו בַּיּוֹם֙ הַֽחֲמִישִׁ֔י נָשִׂ֖יא לִבְנֵ֣י שִׁמְע֑וֹן שְׁלֻֽמִיאֵ֖ל בֶּן־צֽוּרִישַׁדָּֽי:

³⁷ His offering: one silver bowl weighing 130 *shekalim* and one silver basin of 70 *shekalim* by the sanctuary weight, both filled with choice flour with oil mixed in, for a meal offering;

לז קׇרְבָּנ֞וֹ קַֽעֲרַת־כֶּ֣סֶף אַחַ֗ת שְׁלֹשִׁ֣ים וּמֵאָה֮ מִשְׁקָלָהּ֒ מִזְרָ֤ק אֶחָד֙ כֶּ֔סֶף שִׁבְעִ֥ים שֶׁ֖קֶל בְּשֶׁ֣קֶל הַקֹּ֑דֶשׁ שְׁנֵיהֶ֣ם ׀ מְלֵאִ֗ים סֹ֛לֶת בְּלוּלָ֥ה בַשֶּׁ֖מֶן לְמִנְחָֽה:

³⁸ one gold ladle of 10 *shekalim*, filled with incense;

לח כַּ֥ף אַחַ֛ת עֲשָׂרָ֥ה זָהָ֖ב מְלֵאָ֥ה קְטֹֽרֶת:

³⁹ one bull of the herd, one ram, and one lamb in its first year, for a burnt offering;

לט פַּ֣ר אֶחָ֞ד בֶּן־בָּקָ֗ר אַ֧יִל אֶחָ֛ד כֶּֽבֶשׂ־אֶחָ֥ד בֶּן־שְׁנָת֖וֹ לְעֹלָֽה:

⁴⁰ one goat for a sin offering;

מ שְׂעִיר־עִזִּ֥ים אֶחָ֖ד לְחַטָּֽאת

⁴¹ and for his sacrifice of well-being: two oxen, five rams, five he-goats, and five yearling lambs. That was the offering of *Shelumiel* son of Zurishaddai.

מא וּלְזֶ֣בַח הַשְּׁלָמִים֮ בָּקָ֣ר שְׁנַ֒יִם֒ אֵילִ֤ם חֲמִשָּׁה֙ עַתֻּדִ֣ים חֲמִשָּׁ֔ה כְּבָשִׂ֥ים בְּנֵי־שָׁנָ֖ה חֲמִשָּׁ֑ה זֶ֛ה קׇרְבַּ֥ן שְׁלֻֽמִיאֵ֖ל בֶּן־צֽוּרִישַׁדָּֽי:

⁴² On the sixth day, it was the chieftain of the Gadites, *Elyasaf* son of Deuel.

מב בַּיּוֹם֙ הַשִּׁשִּׁ֔י נָשִׂ֖יא לִבְנֵ֣י גָ֑ד אֶלְיָסָ֖ף בֶּן־דְּעוּאֵֽל:

⁴³ His offering: one silver bowl weighing 130 *shekalim* and one silver basin of 70 *shekalim* by the sanctuary weight, both filled with choice flour with oil mixed in, for a meal offering;

מג קׇרְבָּנ֞וֹ קַֽעֲרַת־כֶּ֣סֶף אַחַ֗ת שְׁלֹשִׁ֣ים וּמֵאָה֮ מִשְׁקָלָהּ֒ מִזְרָ֤ק אֶחָד֙ כֶּ֔סֶף שִׁבְעִ֥ים שֶׁ֖קֶל בְּשֶׁ֣קֶל הַקֹּ֑דֶשׁ שְׁנֵיהֶ֣ם ׀ מְלֵאִ֗ים סֹ֛לֶת בְּלוּלָ֥ה בַשֶּׁ֖מֶן לְמִנְחָֽה:

⁴⁴ one gold ladle of 10 *shekalim*, filled with incense;

מד כַּ֥ף אַחַ֛ת עֲשָׂרָ֥ה זָהָ֖ב מְלֵאָ֥ה קְטֹֽרֶת:

⁴⁵ one bull of the herd, one ram, and one lamb in its first year, for a burnt offering;

מה פַּ֣ר אֶחָ֞ד בֶּן־בָּקָ֗ר אַ֧יִל אֶחָ֛ד כֶּֽבֶשׂ־אֶחָ֥ד בֶּן־שְׁנָת֖וֹ לְעֹלָֽה:

⁴⁶ one goat for a sin offering;

מו שְׂעִיר־עִזִּ֥ים אֶחָ֖ד לְחַטָּֽאת:

⁴⁷ and for his sacrifice of well-being: two oxen, five rams, five he-goats, and five yearling lambs. That was the offering of *Elyasaf* son of Deuel.

מז וּלְזֶ֣בַח הַשְּׁלָמִים֮ בָּקָ֣ר שְׁנַ֒יִם֒ אֵילִ֤ם חֲמִשָּׁה֙ עַתֻּדִ֣ים חֲמִשָּׁ֔ה כְּבָשִׂ֥ים בְּנֵי־שָׁנָ֖ה חֲמִשָּׁ֑ה זֶ֛ה קׇרְבַּ֥ן אֶלְיָסָ֖ף בֶּן־דְּעוּאֵֽל:

48   On the seventh day, it was the chieftain of the Ephraimites, *Elishama* son of Ammihud.

מח בַּיּוֹם֙ הַשְּׁבִיעִ֔י נָשִׂ֖יא לִבְנֵ֣י אֶפְרָ֑יִם אֱלִישָׁמָ֖ע בֶּן־עַמִּיהֽוּד:

49   His offering: one silver bowl weighing 130 *shekalim* and one silver basin of 70 *shekalim* by the sanctuary weight, both filled with choice flour with oil mixed in, for a meal offering;

מט קָרְבָּנ֞וֹ קַֽעֲרַת־כֶּ֣סֶף אַחַ֗ת שְׁלֹשִׁ֣ים וּמֵאָה֮ מִשְׁקָלָהּ֒ מִזְרָ֤ק אֶחָד֙ כֶּ֔סֶף שִׁבְעִ֥ים שֶׁ֖קֶל בְּשֶׁ֣קֶל הַקֹּ֑דֶשׁ שְׁנֵיהֶ֣ם מְלֵאִ֗ים סֹ֛לֶת בְּלוּלָ֥ה בַשֶּׁ֖מֶן לְמִנְחָֽה:

50   one gold ladle of 10 *shekalim*, filled with incense;

נ כַּ֥ף אַחַ֛ת עֲשָׂרָ֥ה זָהָ֖ב מְלֵאָ֥ה קְטֹֽרֶת:

51   one bull of the herd, one ram, and one lamb in its first year, for a burnt offering;

נא פַּ֣ר אֶחָ֞ד בֶּן־בָּקָ֗ר אַ֧יִל אֶחָ֛ד כֶּֽבֶשׂ־אֶחָ֥ד בֶּן־שְׁנָת֖וֹ לְעֹלָֽה:

52   one goat for a sin offering;

נב שְׂעִיר־עִזִּ֥ים אֶחָ֖ד לְחַטָּֽאת:

53   and for his sacrifice of well-being: two oxen, five rams, five he-goats, and five yearling lambs. That was the offering of *Elishama* son of Ammihud.

נג וּלְזֶ֣בַח הַשְּׁלָמִים֮ בָּקָ֣ר שְׁנַ֒יִם֒ אֵילִ֤ם חֲמִשָּׁה֙ עַתֻּדִ֣ים חֲמִשָּׁ֔ה כְּבָשִׂ֥ים בְּנֵֽי־שָׁנָ֖ה חֲמִשָּׁ֑ה זֶ֛ה קָרְבַּ֥ן אֱלִֽישָׁמָ֖ע בֶּן־עַמִּיהֽוּד:

54   On the eighth day, it was the chieftain of the Manassites, *Gamliel* son of Pedahzur.

נד בַּיּוֹם֙ הַשְּׁמִינִ֔י נָשִׂ֖יא לִבְנֵ֣י מְנַשֶּׁ֑ה גַּמְלִיאֵ֖ל בֶּן־פְּדָהצֽוּר:

55   His offering: one silver bowl weighing 130 *shekalim* and one silver basin of 70 *shekalim* by the sanctuary weight, both filled with choice flour with oil mixed in, for a meal offering;

נה קָרְבָּנ֞וֹ קַֽעֲרַת־כֶּ֣סֶף אַחַ֗ת שְׁלֹשִׁ֣ים וּמֵאָה֮ מִשְׁקָלָהּ֒ מִזְרָ֤ק אֶחָד֙ כֶּ֔סֶף שִׁבְעִ֥ים שֶׁ֖קֶל בְּשֶׁ֣קֶל הַקֹּ֑דֶשׁ שְׁנֵיהֶ֣ם מְלֵאִ֗ים סֹ֛לֶת בְּלוּלָ֥ה בַשֶּׁ֖מֶן לְמִנְחָֽה:

56   one gold ladle of 10 *shekalim*, filled with incense;

נו כַּ֥ף אַחַ֛ת עֲשָׂרָ֥ה זָהָ֖ב מְלֵאָ֥ה קְטֹֽרֶת:

57   one bull of the herd, one ram, and one lamb in its first year, for a burnt offering;

נז פַּ֣ר אֶחָ֞ד בֶּן־בָּקָ֗ר אַ֧יִל אֶחָ֛ד כֶּֽבֶשׂ־אֶחָ֥ד בֶּן־שְׁנָת֖וֹ לְעֹלָֽה:

58   one goat for a sin offering;

נח שְׂעִיר־עִזִּ֥ים אֶחָ֖ד לְחַטָּֽאת:

59   and for his sacrifice of well-being: two oxen, five rams, five he-goats, and five yearling lambs. That was the offering of *Gamliel* son of Pedahzur.

נט וּלְזֶ֣בַח הַשְּׁלָמִים֮ בָּקָ֣ר שְׁנַ֒יִם֒ אֵילִ֤ם חֲמִשָּׁה֙ עַתֻּדִ֣ים חֲמִשָּׁ֔ה כְּבָשִׂ֥ים בְּנֵֽי־שָׁנָ֖ה חֲמִשָּׁ֑ה זֶ֛ה קָרְבַּ֥ן גַּמְלִיאֵ֖ל בֶּן־פְּדָה צֽוּר:

60   On the ninth day, it was the chieftain of the Benjaminites, *Avidan* son of Gideoni.

ס בַּיּוֹם֙ הַתְּשִׁיעִ֔י נָשִׂ֖יא לִבְנֵ֣י בִנְיָמִ֑ן אֲבִידָ֖ן בֶּן־גִּדְעֹנִֽי:

61   His offering: one silver bowl weighing 130 *shekalim* and one silver basin of 70 *shekalim* by the sanctuary weight, both filled with choice flour with oil mixed in, for a meal offering;

סא קָרְבָּנ֞וֹ קַֽעֲרַת־כֶּ֣סֶף אַחַ֗ת שְׁלֹשִׁ֣ים וּמֵאָה֮ מִשְׁקָלָהּ֒ מִזְרָ֤ק אֶחָד֙ כֶּ֔סֶף שִׁבְעִ֥ים שֶׁ֖קֶל בְּשֶׁ֣קֶל הַקֹּ֑דֶשׁ שְׁנֵיהֶ֣ם מְלֵאִ֗ים סֹ֛לֶת בְּלוּלָ֥ה בַשֶּׁ֖מֶן לְמִנְחָֽה:

62   one gold ladle of 10 *shekalim*, filled with incense;

סב כַּ֥ף אַחַ֛ת עֲשָׂרָ֥ה זָהָ֖ב מְלֵאָ֥ה קְטֹֽרֶת:

63   one bull of the herd, one ram, and one lamb in its first year, for a burnt offering;

סג פַּ֣ר אֶחָ֞ד בֶּן־בָּקָ֗ר אַ֧יִל אֶחָ֛ד כֶּֽבֶשׂ־אֶחָ֥ד בֶּן־שְׁנָת֖וֹ לְעֹלָֽה:

64   one goat for a sin offering;

סד שְׂעִיר־עִזִּ֥ים אֶחָ֖ד לְחַטָּֽאת:

Numbers

65 and for his sacrifice of well-being: two oxen, five rams, five he-goats, and five yearling lambs. That was the offering of *Avidan* son of Gideoni.

סה וּלְזֶבַח הַשְּׁלָמִים בָּקָר שְׁנַיִם אֵילִם חֲמִשָּׁה עַתֻּדִים חֲמִשָּׁה כְּבָשִׂים בְּנֵי־שָׁנָה חֲמִשָּׁה זֶה קָרְבַּן אֲבִידָן בֶּן־גִּדְעֹנִי:

66 On the tenth day, it was the chieftain of the Danites, *Achiezer* son of Ammishaddai.

סו בַּיּוֹם הָעֲשִׂירִי נָשִׂיא לִבְנֵי דָן אֲחִיעֶזֶר בֶּן־עַמִּישַׁדָּי:

67 His offering: one silver bowl weighing 130 *shekalim* and one silver basin of 70 *shekalim* by the sanctuary weight, both filled with choice flour with oil mixed in, for a meal offering;

סז קָרְבָּנוֹ קַעֲרַת־כֶּסֶף אַחַת שְׁלֹשִׁים וּמֵאָה מִשְׁקָלָהּ מִזְרָק אֶחָד כֶּסֶף שִׁבְעִים שֶׁקֶל בְּשֶׁקֶל הַקֹּדֶשׁ שְׁנֵיהֶם מְלֵאִים סֹלֶת בְּלוּלָה בַשֶּׁמֶן לְמִנְחָה:

68 one gold ladle of 10 *shekalim*, filled with incense;

סח כַּף אַחַת עֲשָׂרָה זָהָב מְלֵאָה קְטֹרֶת:

69 one bull of the herd, one ram, and one lamb in its first year, for a burnt offering;

סט פַּר אֶחָד בֶּן־בָּקָר אַיִל אֶחָד כֶּבֶשׂ־אֶחָד בֶּן־שְׁנָתוֹ לְעֹלָה:

70 one goat for a sin offering;

ע שְׂעִיר־עִזִּים אֶחָד לְחַטָּאת:

71 and for his sacrifice of well-being: two oxen, five rams, five he-goats, and five yearling lambs. That was the offering of *Achiezer* son of Ammishaddai.

עא וּלְזֶבַח הַשְּׁלָמִים בָּקָר שְׁנַיִם אֵילִם חֲמִשָּׁה עַתֻּדִים חֲמִשָּׁה כְּבָשִׂים בְּנֵי־שָׁנָה חֲמִשָּׁה זֶה קָרְבַּן אֲחִיעֶזֶר בֶּן־עַמִּישַׁדָּי:

72 On the eleventh day, it was the chieftain of the Asherites, *Pagiel* son of Ochran.

עב בְּיוֹם עַשְׁתֵּי עָשָׂר יוֹם נָשִׂיא לִבְנֵי אָשֵׁר פַּגְעִיאֵל בֶּן־עָכְרָן:

73 His offering: one silver bowl weighing 130 *shekalim* and one silver basin of 70 *shekalim* by the sanctuary weight, both filled with choice flour with oil mixed in, for a meal offering;

עג קָרְבָּנוֹ קַעֲרַת־כֶּסֶף אַחַת שְׁלֹשִׁים וּמֵאָה מִשְׁקָלָהּ מִזְרָק אֶחָד כֶּסֶף שִׁבְעִים שֶׁקֶל בְּשֶׁקֶל הַקֹּדֶשׁ שְׁנֵיהֶם מְלֵאִים סֹלֶת בְּלוּלָה בַשֶּׁמֶן לְמִנְחָה:

74 one gold ladle of 10 *shekalim*, filled with incense;

עד כַּף אַחַת עֲשָׂרָה זָהָב מְלֵאָה קְטֹרֶת:

75 one bull of the herd, one ram, and one lamb in its first year, for a burnt offering;

עה פַּר אֶחָד בֶּן־בָּקָר אַיִל אֶחָד כֶּבֶשׂ־אֶחָד בֶּן־שְׁנָתוֹ לְעֹלָה:

76 one goat for a sin offering;

עו שְׂעִיר־עִזִּים אֶחָד לְחַטָּאת:

77 and for his sacrifice of well-being: two oxen, five rams, five he-goats, and five yearling lambs. That was the offering of *Pagiel* son of Ochran.

עז וּלְזֶבַח הַשְּׁלָמִים בָּקָר שְׁנַיִם אֵילִם חֲמִשָּׁה עַתֻּדִים חֲמִשָּׁה כְּבָשִׂים בְּנֵי־שָׁנָה חֲמִשָּׁה זֶה קָרְבַּן פַּגְעִיאֵל בֶּן־עָכְרָן:

78 On the twelfth day, it was the chieftain of the Naphtalites, *Achira* son of Enan.

עח בְּיוֹם שְׁנֵים עָשָׂר יוֹם נָשִׂיא לִבְנֵי נַפְתָּלִי אֲחִירַע בֶּן־עֵינָן:

79 His offering: one silver bowl weighing 130 *shekalim* and one silver basin of 70 *shekalim* by the sanctuary weight, both filled with choice flour with oil mixed in, for a meal offering;

עט קָרְבָּנוֹ קַעֲרַת־כֶּסֶף אַחַת שְׁלֹשִׁים וּמֵאָה מִשְׁקָלָהּ מִזְרָק אֶחָד כֶּסֶף שִׁבְעִים שֶׁקֶל בְּשֶׁקֶל הַקֹּדֶשׁ שְׁנֵיהֶם מְלֵאִים סֹלֶת בְּלוּלָה בַשֶּׁמֶן לְמִנְחָה:

80 one gold ladle of 10 *shekalim*, filled with incense;

פ כַּף אַחַת עֲשָׂרָה זָהָב מְלֵאָה קְטֹרֶת:

81 one bull of the herd, one ram, and one lamb in its first year, for a burnt offering;

פא פַּר אֶחָד בֶּן־בָּקָר אַיִל אֶחָד כֶּבֶשׂ־אֶחָד בֶּן־שְׁנָתוֹ לְעֹלָה:

82   one goat for a sin offering;

פב   שְׂעִיר־עִזִּים אֶחָד לְחַטָּאת:

83   and for his sacrifice of well-being: two oxen, five rams, five he-goats, and five yearling lambs. That was the offering of *Achira* son of Enan.

פג   וּלְזֶבַח הַשְּׁלָמִים בָּקָר שְׁנַיִם אֵילִם חֲמִשָּׁה עַתֻּדִים חֲמִשָּׁה כְּבָשִׂים בְּנֵי־שָׁנָה חֲמִשָּׁה זֶה קָרְבַּן אֲחִירַע בֶּן־עֵינָן:

84   This was the dedication offering for the *Mizbayach* from the chieftains of *Yisrael* upon its being anointed: silver bowls, 12; silver basins, 12; gold ladles, 12.

פד   זֹאת חֲנֻכַּת הַמִּזְבֵּחַ בְּיוֹם הִמָּשַׁח אֹתוֹ מֵאֵת נְשִׂיאֵי יִשְׂרָאֵל קַעֲרֹת כֶּסֶף שְׁתֵּים עֶשְׂרֵה מִזְרְקֵי־כֶסֶף שְׁנֵים עָשָׂר כַּפּוֹת זָהָב שְׁתֵּים עֶשְׂרֵה:

85   Silver per bowl, 130; per basin, 70. Total silver of vessels, 2,400 sanctuary *shekalim*.

פה   שְׁלֹשִׁים וּמֵאָה הַקְּעָרָה הָאַחַת כֶּסֶף וְשִׁבְעִים הַמִּזְרָק הָאֶחָד כֹּל כֶּסֶף הַכֵּלִים אַלְפַּיִם וְאַרְבַּע־מֵאוֹת בְּשֶׁקֶל הַקֹּדֶשׁ:

86   The 12 gold ladles filled with incense – 10 sanctuary *shekalim* per ladle – total gold of the ladles, 120.

פו   כַּפּוֹת זָהָב שְׁתֵּים־עֶשְׂרֵה מְלֵאֹת קְטֹרֶת עֲשָׂרָה עֲשָׂרָה הַכַּף בְּשֶׁקֶל הַקֹּדֶשׁ כָּל־זְהַב הַכַּפּוֹת עֶשְׂרִים וּמֵאָה:

87   Total of herd animals for burnt offerings, 12 bulls; of rams, 12; of yearling lambs, 12 – with their proper meal offerings; of goats for sin offerings, 12.

פז   כָּל־הַבָּקָר לָעֹלָה שְׁנֵים עָשָׂר פָּרִים אֵילִם שְׁנֵים־עָשָׂר כְּבָשִׂים בְּנֵי־שָׁנָה שְׁנֵים עָשָׂר וּמִנְחָתָם וּשְׂעִירֵי עִזִּים שְׁנֵים עָשָׂר לְחַטָּאת:

88   Total of herd animals for sacrifices of well-being, 24 bulls; of rams, 60; of he-goats, 60; of yearling lambs, 60. That was the dedication offering for the *Mizbayach* after its anointing.

פח   וְכֹל בְּקַר זֶבַח הַשְּׁלָמִים עֶשְׂרִים וְאַרְבָּעָה פָּרִים אֵילִם שִׁשִּׁים עַתֻּדִים שִׁשִּׁים כְּבָשִׂים בְּנֵי־שָׁנָה שִׁשִּׁים זֹאת חֲנֻכַּת הַמִּזְבֵּחַ אַחֲרֵי הִמָּשַׁח אֹתוֹ:

89   When *Moshe* went into the Tent of Meeting to speak with Him, he would hear the Voice addressing him from above the cover that was on top of the *Aron HaBrit* between the two cherubim; thus He spoke to him.

פט   וּבְבֹא מֹשֶׁה אֶל־אֹהֶל מוֹעֵד לְדַבֵּר אִתּוֹ וַיִּשְׁמַע אֶת־הַקּוֹל מִדַּבֵּר אֵלָיו מֵעַל הַכַּפֹּרֶת אֲשֶׁר עַל־אֲרֹן הָעֵדֻת מִבֵּין שְׁנֵי הַכְּרֻבִים וַיְדַבֵּר אֵלָיו:

8 ¹   *Hashem* spoke to *Moshe*, saying:

ח א   וַיְדַבֵּר יְהֹוָה אֶל־מֹשֶׁה לֵּאמֹר:

2   Speak to *Aharon* and say to him, "When you mount the lamps, let the seven lamps give light at the front of the *menorah*."

ב   דַּבֵּר אֶל־אַהֲרֹן וְאָמַרְתָּ אֵלָיו בְּהַעֲלֹתְךָ אֶת־הַנֵּרֹת אֶל־מוּל פְּנֵי הַמְּנוֹרָה יָאִירוּ שִׁבְעַת הַנֵּרוֹת:

da-BAYR el a-ha-RON v'-a-mar-TA ay-LAV b'-ha-a-lo-t'-KHA et ha-nay-ROT
el MUL p'-NAY ha-m'-no-RAH ya-EE-ru shiv-AT ha-nay-ROT

8:2 When you mount the lamps *Aharon* is charged with the daily task of lighting the lamps of the *menorah* in the *Mishkan*. The *Ramban* adds that many centuries later, a small group of priests who descended from the family of *Aharon* boldly led a revolt against the mighty Syrian-Greek army. After miraculously defeating the enemy, the Maccabees re- claimed the *Beit Hamikdash* and sought pure olive oil to kindle the *menorah* which had been extin- guished. Due to the scarcity of pure oil to be found in the *Beit Hamikdash*, *Hashem* performed a second miracle, causing one day's supply of oil to

PM Netanyahu lighting a *menorah* at the Western Wall

3 *Aharon* did so; he mounted the lamps at the front of the *menorah*, as *Hashem* had commanded *Moshe*. –

ג וַיַּעַשׂ כֵּן אַהֲרֹן אֶל־מוּל פְּנֵי הַמְּנוֹרָה הֶעֱלָה נֵרֹתֶיהָ כַּאֲשֶׁר צִוָּה יְהֹוָה אֶת־מֹשֶׁה:

4 Now this is how the *menorah* was made: it was hammered work of gold, hammered from base to petal. According to the pattern that *Hashem* had shown *Moshe*, so was the *menorah* made.

ד וְזֶה מַעֲשֵׂה הַמְּנֹרָה מִקְשָׁה זָהָב עַד־יְרֵכָהּ עַד־פִּרְחָהּ מִקְשָׁה הִוא כַּמַּרְאֶה אֲשֶׁר הֶרְאָה יְהֹוָה אֶת־מֹשֶׁה כֵּן עָשָׂה אֶת־הַמְּנֹרָה:

5 *Hashem* spoke to *Moshe*, saying:

ה וַיְדַבֵּר יְהֹוָה אֶל־מֹשֶׁה לֵּאמֹר:

6 Take the *Leviim* from among the Israelites and cleanse them.

ו קַח אֶת־הַלְוִיִּם מִתּוֹךְ בְּנֵי יִשְׂרָאֵל וְטִהַרְתָּ אֹתָם:

7 This is what you shall do to them to cleanse them: sprinkle on them water of purification, and let them go over their whole body with a razor, and wash their clothes; thus they shall be cleansed.

ז וְכֹה־תַעֲשֶׂה לָהֶם לְטַהֲרָם הַזֵּה עֲלֵיהֶם מֵי חַטָּאת וְהֶעֱבִירוּ תַעַר עַל־כָּל־בְּשָׂרָם וְכִבְּסוּ בִגְדֵיהֶם וְהִטֶּהָרוּ:

8 Let them take a bull of the herd, and with it a meal offering of choice flour with oil mixed in, and you take a second bull of the herd for a sin offering.

ח וְלָקְחוּ פַּר בֶּן־בָּקָר וּמִנְחָתוֹ סֹלֶת בְּלוּלָה בַשָּׁמֶן וּפַר־שֵׁנִי בֶן־בָּקָר תִּקַּח לְחַטָּאת:

9 You shall bring the *Leviim* forward before the Tent of Meeting. Assemble the whole Israelite community,

ט וְהִקְרַבְתָּ אֶת־הַלְוִיִּם לִפְנֵי אֹהֶל מוֹעֵד וְהִקְהַלְתָּ אֶת־כָּל־עֲדַת בְּנֵי יִשְׂרָאֵל:

10 and bring the *Leviim* forward before *Hashem*. Let the Israelites lay their hands upon the *Leviim*,

י וְהִקְרַבְתָּ אֶת־הַלְוִיִּם לִפְנֵי יְהֹוָה וְסָמְכוּ בְנֵי־יִשְׂרָאֵל אֶת־יְדֵיהֶם עַל־הַלְוִיִּם:

11 and let *Aharon* designate the *Leviim* before *Hashem* as an elevation offering from the Israelites, that they may perform the service of *Hashem*.

יא וְהֵנִיף אַהֲרֹן אֶת־הַלְוִיִּם תְּנוּפָה לִפְנֵי יְהֹוָה מֵאֵת בְּנֵי יִשְׂרָאֵל וְהָיוּ לַעֲבֹד אֶת־עֲבֹדַת יְהֹוָה:

12 The *Leviim* shall now lay their hands upon the heads of the bulls; one shall be offered to *Hashem* as a sin offering and the other as a burnt offering, to make expiation for the *Leviim*.

יב וְהַלְוִיִּם יִסְמְכוּ אֶת־יְדֵיהֶם עַל רֹאשׁ הַפָּרִים וַעֲשֵׂה אֶת־הָאֶחָד חַטָּאת וְאֶת־הָאֶחָד עֹלָה לַיהֹוָה לְכַפֵּר עַל־הַלְוִיִּם:

13 You shall place the *Leviim* in attendance upon *Aharon* and his sons, and designate them as an elevation offering to *Hashem*.

יג וְהַעֲמַדְתָּ אֶת־הַלְוִיִּם לִפְנֵי אַהֲרֹן וְלִפְנֵי בָנָיו וְהֵנַפְתָּ אֹתָם תְּנוּפָה לַיהֹוָה:

14 Thus you shall set the *Leviim* apart from the Israelites, and the *Leviim* shall be Mine.

יד וְהִבְדַּלְתָּ אֶת־הַלְוִיִּם מִתּוֹךְ בְּנֵי יִשְׂרָאֵל וְהָיוּ לִי הַלְוִיִּם:

15 Thereafter the *Leviim* shall be qualified for the service of the Tent of Meeting, once you have cleansed them and designated them as an elevation offering.

טו וְאַחֲרֵי־כֵן יָבֹאוּ הַלְוִיִּם לַעֲבֹד אֶת־אֹהֶל מוֹעֵד וְטִהַרְתָּ אֹתָם וְהֵנַפְתָּ אֹתָם תְּנוּפָה:

burn for a full eight days, until new oil was produced. In perpetual commemoration of these miracles, the Jewish people light their own *menorah* lamps for eight nights every year, when they celebrate *Chanukah*.

16 For they are formally assigned to Me from among the Israelites: I have taken them for Myself in place of all the first issue of the womb, of all the first-born of the Israelites.

טז כִּי נְתֻנִים נְתֻנִים הֵמָּה לִי מִתּוֹךְ בְּנֵי יִשְׂרָאֵל תַּחַת פִּטְרַת כָּל־רֶחֶם בְּכוֹר כֹּל מִבְּנֵי יִשְׂרָאֵל לָקַחְתִּי אֹתָם לִי:

17 For every first-born among the Israelites, man as well as beast, is Mine; I consecrated them to Myself at the time that I smote every first-born in the land of Egypt.

יז כִּי לִי כָל־בְּכוֹר בִּבְנֵי יִשְׂרָאֵל בָּאָדָם וּבַבְּהֵמָה בְּיוֹם הַכֹּתִי כָל־בְּכוֹר בְּאֶרֶץ מִצְרַיִם הִקְדַּשְׁתִּי אֹתָם לִי:

18 Now I take the *Leviim* instead of every first-born of the Israelites;

יח וָאֶקַּח אֶת־הַלְוִיִּם תַּחַת כָּל־בְּכוֹר בִּבְנֵי יִשְׂרָאֵל:

19 and from among the Israelites I formally assign the *Leviim* to *Aharon* and his sons, to perform the service for the Israelites in the Tent of Meeting and to make expiation for the Israelites, so that no plague may afflict the Israelites for coming too near the sanctuary.

יט וָאֶתְּנָה אֶת־הַלְוִיִּם נְתֻנִים לְאַהֲרֹן וּלְבָנָיו מִתּוֹךְ בְּנֵי יִשְׂרָאֵל לַעֲבֹד אֶת־עֲבֹדַת בְּנֵי־יִשְׂרָאֵל בְּאֹהֶל מוֹעֵד וּלְכַפֵּר עַל־בְּנֵי יִשְׂרָאֵל וְלֹא יִהְיֶה בִּבְנֵי יִשְׂרָאֵל נֶגֶף בְּגֶשֶׁת בְּנֵי־יִשְׂרָאֵל אֶל־הַקֹּדֶשׁ:

20 *Moshe*, *Aharon*, and the whole Israelite community did with the *Leviim* accordingly; just as *Hashem* had commanded *Moshe* in regard to the *Leviim*, so the Israelites did with them.

כ וַיַּעַשׂ מֹשֶׁה וְאַהֲרֹן וְכָל־עֲדַת בְּנֵי־יִשְׂרָאֵל לַלְוִיִּם כְּכֹל אֲשֶׁר־צִוָּה יְהֹוָה אֶת־מֹשֶׁה לַלְוִיִּם כֵּן־עָשׂוּ לָהֶם בְּנֵי יִשְׂרָאֵל:

21 The *Leviim* purified themselves and washed their clothes; and *Aharon* designated them as an elevation offering before *Hashem*, and *Aharon* made expiation for them to cleanse them.

כא וַיִּתְחַטְּאוּ הַלְוִיִּם וַיְכַבְּסוּ בִּגְדֵיהֶם וַיָּנֶף אַהֲרֹן אֹתָם תְּנוּפָה לִפְנֵי יְהֹוָה וַיְכַפֵּר עֲלֵיהֶם אַהֲרֹן לְטַהֲרָם:

22 Thereafter the *Leviim* were qualified to perform their service in the Tent of Meeting, under *Aharon* and his sons. As *Hashem* had commanded *Moshe* in regard to the *Leviim*, so they did to them.

כב וְאַחֲרֵי־כֵן בָּאוּ הַלְוִיִּם לַעֲבֹד אֶת־עֲבֹדָתָם בְּאֹהֶל מוֹעֵד לִפְנֵי אַהֲרֹן וְלִפְנֵי בָנָיו כַּאֲשֶׁר צִוָּה יְהֹוָה אֶת־מֹשֶׁה עַל־הַלְוִיִּם כֵּן עָשׂוּ לָהֶם:

23 *Hashem* spoke to *Moshe*, saying:

כג וַיְדַבֵּר יְהֹוָה אֶל־מֹשֶׁה לֵּאמֹר:

24 This is the rule for the *Leviim*. From twenty-five years of age up they shall participate in the work force in the service of the Tent of Meeting;

כד זֹאת אֲשֶׁר לַלְוִיִּם מִבֶּן חָמֵשׁ וְעֶשְׂרִים שָׁנָה וָמַעְלָה יָבוֹא לִצְבֹא צָבָא בַּעֲבֹדַת אֹהֶל מוֹעֵד:

25 but at the age of fifty they shall retire from the work force and shall serve no more.

כה וּמִבֶּן חֲמִשִּׁים שָׁנָה יָשׁוּב מִצְּבָא הָעֲבֹדָה וְלֹא יַעֲבֹד עוֹד:

26 They may assist their brother *Leviim* at the Tent of Meeting by standing guard, but they shall perform no labor. Thus you shall deal with the *Leviim* in regard to their duties.

כו וְשֵׁרֵת אֶת־אֶחָיו בְּאֹהֶל מוֹעֵד לִשְׁמֹר מִשְׁמֶרֶת וַעֲבֹדָה לֹא יַעֲבֹד כָּכָה תַּעֲשֶׂה לַלְוִיִּם בְּמִשְׁמְרֹתָם:

9 ¹ *Hashem* spoke to *Moshe* in the wilderness of Sinai, on the first new moon of the second year following the exodus from the land of Egypt, saying:

ט א וַיְדַבֵּר יְהֹוָה אֶל־מֹשֶׁה בְמִדְבַּר־סִינַי בַּשָּׁנָה הַשֵּׁנִית לְצֵאתָם מֵאֶרֶץ מִצְרַיִם בַּחֹדֶשׁ הָרִאשׁוֹן לֵאמֹר:

2 Let *B'nei Yisrael* offer the *Pesach* sacrifice at its set time:

ב וְיַעֲשׂוּ בְנֵי־יִשְׂרָאֵל אֶת־הַפָּסַח בְּמוֹעֲדוֹ:

Numbers

3 you shall offer it on the fourteenth day of this month, at twilight, at its set time; you shall offer it in accordance with all its rules and rites.

ג בְּאַרְבָּעָה עָשָׂר־יוֹם בַּחֹדֶשׁ הַזֶּה בֵּין הָעַרְבַּיִם תַּעֲשׂוּ אֹתוֹ בְּמוֹעֲדוֹ כְּכָל־חֻקֹּתָיו וּכְכָל־מִשְׁפָּטָיו תַּעֲשׂוּ אֹתוֹ:

4 *Moshe* instructed the Israelites to offer the *Pesach* sacrifice;

ד וַיְדַבֵּר מֹשֶׁה אֶל־בְּנֵי יִשְׂרָאֵל לַעֲשֹׂת הַפָּסַח:

5 and they offered the *Pesach* sacrifice in the first month, on the fourteenth day of the month, at twilight, in the wilderness of Sinai. Just as *Hashem* had commanded *Moshe*, so the Israelites did.

ה וַיַּעֲשׂוּ אֶת־הַפֶּסַח בָּרִאשׁוֹן בְּאַרְבָּעָה עָשָׂר יוֹם לַחֹדֶשׁ בֵּין הָעַרְבַּיִם בְּמִדְבַּר סִינָי כְּכֹל אֲשֶׁר צִוָּה יְהוָה אֶת־מֹשֶׁה כֵּן עָשׂוּ בְּנֵי יִשְׂרָאֵל:

va-ya-a-SU et ha-PE-sakh ba-ri-SHON b'-ar-ba-AH a-SAR YOM la-KHO-desh BAYN ha-ar-BA-yim b'-mid-BAR see-NAI k'-KHOL a-SHER tzi-VAH a-do-NAI et mo-SHEH KAYN a-SU b'-NAY yis-ra-AYL

6 But there were some men who were unclean by reason of a corpse and could not offer the *Pesach* sacrifice on that day. Appearing that same day before *Moshe* and *Aharon*,

ו וַיְהִי אֲנָשִׁים אֲשֶׁר הָיוּ טְמֵאִים לְנֶפֶשׁ אָדָם וְלֹא־יָכְלוּ לַעֲשֹׂת־הַפֶּסַח בַּיּוֹם הַהוּא וַיִּקְרְבוּ לִפְנֵי מֹשֶׁה וְלִפְנֵי אַהֲרֹן בַּיּוֹם הַהוּא:

7 those men said to them, "Unclean though we are by reason of a corpse, why must we be debarred from presenting *Hashem*'s offering at its set time with the rest of the Israelites?"

ז וַיֹּאמְרוּ הָאֲנָשִׁים הָהֵמָּה אֵלָיו אֲנַחְנוּ טְמֵאִים לְנֶפֶשׁ אָדָם לָמָּה נִגָּרַע לְבִלְתִּי הַקְרִב אֶת־קָרְבַּן יְהוָה בְּמֹעֲדוֹ בְּתוֹךְ בְּנֵי יִשְׂרָאֵל:

8 *Moshe* said to them, "Stand by, and let me hear what instructions *Hashem* gives about you."

ח וַיֹּאמֶר אֲלֵהֶם מֹשֶׁה עִמְדוּ וְאֶשְׁמְעָה מַה־יְצַוֶּה יְהוָה לָכֶם:

9 And *Hashem* spoke to *Moshe*, saying:

ט וַיְדַבֵּר יְהוָה אֶל־מֹשֶׁה לֵּאמֹר:

10 Speak to *B'nei Yisrael*, saying: When any of you or of your posterity who are defiled by a corpse or are on a long journey would offer a *Pesach* sacrifice to *Hashem*,

י דַּבֵּר אֶל־בְּנֵי יִשְׂרָאֵל לֵאמֹר אִישׁ אִישׁ כִּי־יִהְיֶה־טָמֵא לָנֶפֶשׁ אוֹ בְדֶרֶךְ רְחֹקָה לָכֶם אוֹ לְדֹרֹתֵיכֶם וְעָשָׂה פֶסַח לַיהוָה:

11 they shall offer it in the second month, on the fourteenth day of the month, at twilight. They shall eat it with unleavened bread and bitter herbs,

יא בַּחֹדֶשׁ הַשֵּׁנִי בְּאַרְבָּעָה עָשָׂר יוֹם בֵּין הָעַרְבַּיִם יַעֲשׂוּ אֹתוֹ עַל־מַצּוֹת וּמְרֹרִים יֹאכְלֻהוּ:

12 and they shall not leave any of it over until morning. They shall not break a bone of it. They shall offer it in strict accord with the law of the *Pesach* sacrifice.

יב לֹא־יַשְׁאִירוּ מִמֶּנּוּ עַד־בֹּקֶר וְעֶצֶם לֹא יִשְׁבְּרוּ־בוֹ כְּכָל־חֻקַּת הַפֶּסַח יַעֲשׂוּ אֹתוֹ:

A table set for the *Pesach* seder

9:5 And they offered the *Pesach* sacrifice in the first month Before embarking on their journey through the desert, the Children of Israel observed the holiday of *Pesach*, commemorating the day they had left Egypt one year previously. Although the Israelites were already able to celebrate their release from bondage, their ultimate freedom was still to come; it would be realized only once they were settled in their own land. A nation is truly free only when it inhabits its own land under its own leadership. For this reason, the *Pesach seder* meal ends with the declaration, "Next year in *Yerushalayim*." The Jewish people can only be truly free when they are all living in *Eretz Yisrael*.

13 But if a man who is clean and not on a journey refrains from offering the *Pesach* sacrifice, that person shall be cut off from his kin, for he did not present *Hashem*'s offering at its set time; that man shall bear his guilt.

יג וְהָאִישׁ אֲשֶׁר־הוּא טָהוֹר וּבְדֶרֶךְ לֹא־הָיָה וְחָדַל לַעֲשׂוֹת הַפֶּסַח וְנִכְרְתָה הַנֶּפֶשׁ הַהִוא מֵעַמֶּיהָ כִּי קָרְבַּן יְהֹוָה לֹא הִקְרִיב בְּמֹעֲדוֹ חֶטְאוֹ יִשָּׂא הָאִישׁ הַהוּא:

14 And when a stranger who resides with you would offer a *Pesach* sacrifice to *Hashem*, he must offer it in accordance with the rules and rites of the *Pesach* sacrifice. There shall be one law for you, whether stranger or citizen of the country.

יד וְכִי־יָגוּר אִתְּכֶם גֵּר וְעָשָׂה פֶסַח לַיהֹוָה כְּחֻקַּת הַפֶּסַח וּכְמִשְׁפָּטוֹ כֵּן יַעֲשֶׂה חֻקָּה אַחַת יִהְיֶה לָכֶם וְלַגֵּר וּלְאֶזְרַח הָאָרֶץ:

15 On the day that the *Mishkan* was set up, the cloud covered the *Mishkan*, the Tent of the Pact; and in the evening it rested over the *Mishkan* in the likeness of fire until morning.

טו וּבְיוֹם הָקִים אֶת־הַמִּשְׁכָּן כִּסָּה הֶעָנָן אֶת־הַמִּשְׁכָּן לְאֹהֶל הָעֵדֻת וּבָעֶרֶב יִהְיֶה עַל־הַמִּשְׁכָּן כְּמַרְאֵה־אֵשׁ עַד־בֹּקֶר:

16 It was always so: the cloud covered it, appearing as fire by night.

טז כֵּן יִהְיֶה תָמִיד הֶעָנָן יְכַסֶּנּוּ וּמַרְאֵה־אֵשׁ לָיְלָה:

17 And whenever the cloud lifted from the Tent, the Israelites would set out accordingly; and at the spot where the cloud settled, there the Israelites would make camp.

יז וּלְפִי הֵעָלֹת הֶעָנָן מֵעַל הָאֹהֶל וְאַחֲרֵי כֵן יִסְעוּ בְּנֵי יִשְׂרָאֵל וּבִמְקוֹם אֲשֶׁר יִשְׁכָּן־שָׁם הֶעָנָן שָׁם יַחֲנוּ בְּנֵי יִשְׂרָאֵל:

18 At a command of *Hashem* the Israelites broke camp, and at a command of *Hashem* they made camp: they remained encamped as long as the cloud stayed over the *Mishkan*.

יח עַל־פִּי יְהֹוָה יִסְעוּ בְּנֵי יִשְׂרָאֵל וְעַל־פִּי יְהֹוָה יַחֲנוּ כָּל־יְמֵי אֲשֶׁר יִשְׁכֹּן הֶעָנָן עַל־הַמִּשְׁכָּן יַחֲנוּ:

al PEE a-do-NAI yis-U b'-NAY yis-ra-AYL v'-al PEE a-do-NAI ya-kha-NU
kol y'-MAY a-SHER yish-KON he-a-NAN al ha-mish-KAN ya-kha-NU

19 When the cloud lingered over the *Mishkan* many days, the Israelites observed *Hashem*'s mandate and did not journey on.

יט וּבְהַאֲרִיךְ הֶעָנָן עַל־הַמִּשְׁכָּן יָמִים רַבִּים וְשָׁמְרוּ בְנֵי־יִשְׂרָאֵל אֶת־מִשְׁמֶרֶת יְהֹוָה וְלֹא יִסָּעוּ:

20 At such times as the cloud rested over the *Mishkan* for but a few days, they remained encamped at a command of *Hashem*, and broke camp at a command of *Hashem*.

כ וְיֵשׁ אֲשֶׁר יִהְיֶה הֶעָנָן יָמִים מִסְפָּר עַל־הַמִּשְׁכָּן עַל־פִּי יְהֹוָה יַחֲנוּ וְעַל־פִּי יְהֹוָה יִסָּעוּ:

21 And at such times as the cloud stayed from evening until morning, they broke camp as soon as the cloud lifted in the morning. Day or night, whenever the cloud lifted, they would break camp.

כא וְיֵשׁ אֲשֶׁר־יִהְיֶה הֶעָנָן מֵעֶרֶב עַד־בֹּקֶר וְנַעֲלָה הֶעָנָן בַּבֹּקֶר וְנָסָעוּ אוֹ יוֹמָם וָלַיְלָה וְנַעֲלָה הֶעָנָן וְנָסָעוּ:

22 Whether it was two days or a month or a year – however long the cloud lingered over the *Mishkan* – the Israelites remained encamped and did not set out; only when it lifted did they break camp.

כב אוֹ־יֹמַיִם אוֹ־חֹדֶשׁ אוֹ־יָמִים בְּהַאֲרִיךְ הֶעָנָן עַל־הַמִּשְׁכָּן לִשְׁכֹּן עָלָיו יַחֲנוּ בְנֵי־יִשְׂרָאֵל וְלֹא יִסָּעוּ וּבְהֵעָלֹתוֹ יִסָּעוּ:

23 On a sign from *Hashem* they made camp and on a sign from *Hashem* they broke camp; they observed *Hashem*'s mandate at *Hashem*'s bidding through *Moshe*.

כג עַל־פִּ֣י יְהֹוָ֗ה יַחֲנוּ֙ וְעַל־פִּ֣י יְהֹוָ֖ה יִסָּ֑עוּ אֶת־מִשְׁמֶ֤רֶת יְהֹוָה֙ שָׁמָ֔רוּ עַל־פִּ֥י יְהֹוָ֖ה בְּיַד־מֹשֶֽׁה׃

10 1 *Hashem* spoke to *Moshe*, saying:

י א וַיְדַבֵּ֥ר יְהֹוָ֖ה אֶל־מֹשֶׁ֥ה לֵּאמֹֽר׃

2 Have two silver trumpets made; make them of hammered work. They shall serve you to summon the community and to set the divisions in motion.

ב עֲשֵׂ֣ה לְךָ֗ שְׁתֵּי֙ חֲצֽוֹצְרֹ֣ת כֶּ֔סֶף מִקְשָׁ֖ה תַּעֲשֶׂ֣ה אֹתָ֑ם וְהָי֤וּ לְךָ֙ לְמִקְרָ֣א הָֽעֵדָ֔ה וּלְמַסַּ֖ע אֶת־הַֽמַּחֲנֽוֹת׃

3 When both are blown in long blasts, the whole community shall assemble before you at the entrance of the Tent of Meeting;

ג וְתָקְע֖וּ בָּהֵ֑ן וְנֽוֹעֲד֤וּ אֵלֶ֙יךָ֙ כׇּל־הָ֣עֵדָ֔ה אֶל־פֶּ֖תַח אֹ֥הֶל מוֹעֵֽד׃

4 and if only one is blown, the chieftains, heads of *Yisrael*'s contingents, shall assemble before you.

ד וְאִם־בְּאַחַ֖ת יִתְקָ֑עוּ וְנֽוֹעֲד֤וּ אֵלֶ֙יךָ֙ הַנְּשִׂיאִ֔ים רָאשֵׁ֖י אַלְפֵ֥י יִשְׂרָאֵֽל׃

5 But when you sound short blasts, the divisions encamped on the east shall move forward;

ה וּתְקַעְתֶּ֖ם תְּרוּעָ֑ה וְנָֽסְעוּ֙ הַֽמַּחֲנ֔וֹת הַחֹנִ֖ים קֵֽדְמָה׃

6 and when you sound short blasts a second time, those encamped on the south shall move forward. Thus short blasts shall be blown for setting them in motion,

ו וּתְקַעְתֶּ֤ם תְּרוּעָה֙ שֵׁנִ֔ית וְנָֽסְעוּ֙ הַֽמַּחֲנ֔וֹת הַחֹנִ֖ים תֵּימָ֑נָה תְּרוּעָ֥ה יִתְקְע֖וּ לְמַסְעֵיהֶֽם׃

7 while to convoke the congregation you shall blow long blasts, not short ones.

ז וּבְהַקְהִ֖יל אֶת־הַקָּהָ֑ל תִּתְקְע֖וּ וְלֹ֥א תָרִֽיעוּ׃

8 The trumpets shall be blown by *Aharon*'s sons, the *Kohanim*; they shall be for you an institution for all time throughout the ages.

ח וּבְנֵ֤י אַהֲרֹן֙ הַכֹּ֣הֲנִ֔ים יִתְקְע֖וּ בַּֽחֲצֹֽצְר֑וֹת וְהָי֥וּ לָכֶ֛ם לְחֻקַּ֥ת עוֹלָ֖ם לְדֹרֹֽתֵיכֶֽם׃

9 When you are at war in your land against an aggressor who attacks you, you shall sound short blasts on the trumpets, that you may be remembered before *Hashem* your God and be delivered from your enemies.

ט וְכִֽי־תָבֹ֨אוּ מִלְחָמָ֜ה בְּאַרְצְכֶ֗ם עַל־הַצַּר֙ הַצֹּרֵ֣ר אֶתְכֶ֔ם וַהֲרֵֽעֹתֶ֖ם בַּֽחֲצֹֽצְר֑וֹת וְנִזְכַּרְתֶּ֗ם לִפְנֵי֙ יְהֹוָ֣ה אֱלֹֽהֵיכֶ֔ם וְנֽוֹשַׁעְתֶּ֖ם מֵאֹֽיְבֵיכֶֽם׃

10 And on your joyous occasions – your fixed festivals and new moon days – you shall sound the trumpets over your burnt offerings and your sacrifices of well-being. They shall be a reminder of you before your God: I, *Hashem*, am your God.

י וּבְי֨וֹם שִׂמְחַתְכֶ֜ם וּֽבְמֽוֹעֲדֵיכֶ֗ם וּבְרָאשֵׁ֣י חׇדְשֵׁיכֶ֔ם וּתְקַעְתֶּ֣ם בַּחֲצֹ֣צְרֹ֔ת עַ֚ל עֹלֹ֣תֵיכֶ֔ם וְעַ֖ל זִבְחֵ֣י שַׁלְמֵיכֶ֑ם וְהָי֨וּ לָכֶ֤ם לְזִכָּרוֹן֙ לִפְנֵ֣י אֱלֹֽהֵיכֶ֔ם אֲנִ֖י יְהֹוָ֥ה אֱלֹֽהֵיכֶֽם׃

11 In the second year, on the twentieth day of the second month, the cloud lifted from the *Mishkan* of the Pact

יא וַיְהִ֞י בַּשָּׁנָ֧ה הַשֵּׁנִ֛ית בַּחֹ֥דֶשׁ הַשֵּׁנִ֖י בְּעֶשְׂרִ֣ים בַּחֹ֑דֶשׁ נַעֲלָה֙ הֶֽעָנָ֔ן מֵעַ֖ל מִשְׁכַּ֥ן הָעֵדֻֽת׃

12 and the Israelites set out on their journeys from the wilderness of Sinai. The cloud came to rest in the wilderness of Paran.

יב וַיִּסְע֧וּ בְנֵֽי־יִשְׂרָאֵ֛ל לְמַסְעֵיהֶ֖ם מִמִּדְבַּ֣ר סִינָ֑י וַיִּשְׁכֹּ֥ן הֶעָנָ֖ן בְּמִדְבַּ֥ר פָּארָֽן׃

13 When the march was to begin, at *Hashem*'s command through *Moshe*,

יג וַיִּסְע֖וּ בָּרִֽאשֹׁנָ֑ה עַל־פִּ֥י יְהֹוָ֖ה בְּיַד־מֹשֶֽׁה׃

14 the first standard to set out, troop by troop, was the division of *Yehuda*. In command of its troops was *Nachshon* son of *Aminadav*;

יד וַיִּסַּ֞ע דֶּ֣גֶל מַחֲנֵ֧ה בְנֵֽי־יְהוּדָ֛ה בָּרִאשֹׁנָ֖ה לְצִבְאֹתָ֑ם וְעַ֨ל־צְבָא֔וֹ נַחְשׁ֖וֹן בֶּן־עַמִּינָדָֽב:

15 in command of the tribal troop of *Yissachar*, *Netanel* son of Zuar;

טו וְעַ֨ל־צְבָ֔א מַטֵּ֖ה בְּנֵ֣י יִשָּׂשכָ֑ר נְתַנְאֵ֖ל בֶּן־צוּעָֽר:

16 and in command of the tribal troop of *Zevulun*, *Eliav* son of Helon.

טז וְעַ֨ל־צְבָ֔א מַטֵּ֖ה בְּנֵ֣י זְבוּלֻ֑ן אֱלִיאָ֖ב בֶּן־חֵלֹֽן:

17 Then the *Mishkan* would be taken apart; and the Gershonites and the Merarites, who carried the *Mishkan*, would set out.

יז וְהוּרַ֖ד הַמִּשְׁכָּ֑ן וְנָסְע֤וּ בְנֵֽי־גֵרְשׁוֹן֙ וּבְנֵ֣י מְרָרִ֔י נֹשְׂאֵ֖י הַמִּשְׁכָּֽן:

18 The next standard to set out, troop by troop, was the division of *Reuven*. In command of its troop was *Elitzur* son of Shedeur;

יח וְנָסַ֗ע דֶּ֚גֶל מַחֲנֵ֣ה רְאוּבֵ֔ן לְצִבְאֹתָ֑ם וְעַ֨ל־צְבָא֔וֹ אֱלִיצ֖וּר בֶּן־שְׁדֵיאֽוּר:

19 in command of the tribal troop of *Shimon*, *Shelumiel* son of Zurishaddai;

יט וְעַ֨ל־צְבָ֔א מַטֵּ֖ה בְּנֵ֣י שִׁמְע֑וֹן שְׁלֻֽמִיאֵ֖ל בֶּן־צוּרִֽי שַׁדָּֽי:

20 and in command of the tribal troop of *Gad*, *Elyasaf* son of Deuel.

כ וְעַ֨ל־צְבָ֔א מַטֵּ֖ה בְנֵי־גָ֑ד אֶלְיָסָ֖ף בֶּן־דְּעוּאֵֽל:

21 Then the Kohathites, who carried the sacred objects, would set out; and by the time they arrived, the *Mishkan* would be set up again.

כא וְנָסְעוּ֙ הַקְּהָתִ֔ים נֹשְׂאֵ֖י הַמִּקְדָּ֑שׁ וְהֵקִ֥ימוּ אֶת־הַמִּשְׁכָּ֖ן עַד־בֹּאָֽם:

22 The next standard to set out, troop by troop, was the division of *Efraim*. In command of its troop was *Elishama* son of Ammihud;

כב וְנָסַ֗ע דֶּ֛גֶל מַחֲנֵ֥ה בְנֵֽי־אֶפְרַ֖יִם לְצִבְאֹתָ֑ם וְעַ֨ל־צְבָא֔וֹ אֱלִישָׁמָ֖ע בֶּן־עַמִּיהֽוּד:

23 in command of the tribal troop of *Menashe*, *Gamliel* son of Pedahzur;

כג וְעַ֨ל־צְבָ֔א מַטֵּ֖ה בְּנֵ֣י מְנַשֶּׁ֑ה גַּמְלִיאֵ֖ל בֶּן־פְּדָה צֽוּר:

24 and in command of the tribal troop of *Binyamin*, *Avidan* son of Gideoni.

כד וְעַ֨ל־צְבָ֔א מַטֵּ֖ה בְּנֵ֣י בִנְיָמִ֑ן אֲבִידָ֖ן בֶּן־גִּדְעוֹנִֽי:

25 Then, as the rear guard of all the divisions, the standard of the division of *Dan* would set out, troop by troop. In command of its troop was *Achiezer* son of Ammishaddai;

כה וְנָסַ֗ע דֶּ֚גֶל מַחֲנֵ֣ה בְנֵי־דָ֔ן מְאַסֵּ֖ף לְכָל־הַמַּחֲנֹ֑ת לְצִבְאֹתָ֑ם וְעַ֨ל־צְבָא֔וֹ אֲחִיעֶ֖זֶר בֶּן־עַמִּֽי שַׁדָּֽי:

26 in command of the tribal troop of *Asher*, *Pagiel* son of Ochran;

כו וְעַ֨ל־צְבָ֔א מַטֵּ֖ה בְּנֵ֣י אָשֵׁ֑ר פַּגְעִיאֵ֖ל בֶּן־עָכְרָֽן:

27 and in command of the tribal troop of *Naftali*, *Achira* son of Enan.

כז וְעַ֨ל־צְבָ֔א מַטֵּ֖ה בְּנֵ֣י נַפְתָּלִ֑י אֲחִירַ֖ע בֶּן־עֵינָֽן:

28 Such was the order of march of the Israelites, as they marched troop by troop.

כח אֵ֜לֶּה מַסְעֵ֧י בְנֵֽי־יִשְׂרָאֵ֛ל לְצִבְאֹתָ֖ם וַיִּסָּֽעוּ:

29 *Moshe* said to Hobab son of Reuel the Midianite, *Moshe's* father-in-law, "We are setting out for the place of which *Hashem* has said, 'I will give it to you.' Come with us and we will be generous with you; for *Hashem* has promised to be generous to *Yisrael*."

כט וַיֹּאמֶר מֹשֶׁה לְחֹבָב בֶּן־רְעוּאֵל הַמִּדְיָנִי חֹתֵן מֹשֶׁה נֹסְעִים אֲנַחְנוּ אֶל־הַמָּקוֹם אֲשֶׁר אָמַר יְהֹוָה אֹתוֹ אֶתֵּן לָכֶם לְכָה אִתָּנוּ וְהֵטַבְנוּ לָךְ כִּי־יְהֹוָה דִּבֶּר־טוֹב עַל־יִשְׂרָאֵל:

va-YO-mer mo-SHEH l'-kho-VAV ben r'-u-AYL ha-mid-ya-NEE kho-TAYN mo-SHEH no-s'-EEM a-NAKH-nu el ha-ma-KOM a-SHER a-MAR a-do-NAI o-TO e-TAYN la-KHEM l'-KHAH i-TA-nu v'-hay-TAV-nu LAKH kee a-do-NAI di-ber TOV al yis-ra-AYL

30 "I will not go," he replied to him, "but will return to my native land."

ל וַיֹּאמֶר אֵלָיו לֹא אֵלֵךְ כִּי אִם־אֶל־אַרְצִי וְאֶל־מוֹלַדְתִּי אֵלֵךְ:

31 He said, "Please do not leave us, inasmuch as you know where we should camp in the wilderness and can be our guide.

לא וַיֹּאמֶר אַל־נָא תַּעֲזֹב אֹתָנוּ כִּי עַל־כֵּן יָדַעְתָּ חֲנֹתֵנוּ בַּמִּדְבָּר וְהָיִיתָ לָּנוּ לְעֵינָיִם:

32 So if you come with us, we will extend to you the same bounty that *Hashem* grants us."

לב וְהָיָה כִּי־תֵלֵךְ עִמָּנוּ וְהָיָה הַטּוֹב הַהוּא אֲשֶׁר יֵיטִיב יְהֹוָה עִמָּנוּ וְהֵטַבְנוּ לָךְ:

33 They marched from the mountain of *Hashem* a distance of three days. The *Aron* Brit *Hashem* traveled in front of them on that three days' journey to seek out a resting place for them;

לג וַיִּסְעוּ מֵהַר יְהֹוָה דֶּרֶךְ שְׁלֹשֶׁת יָמִים וַאֲרוֹן בְּרִית־יְהֹוָה נֹסֵעַ לִפְנֵיהֶם דֶּרֶךְ שְׁלֹשֶׁת יָמִים לָתוּר לָהֶם מְנוּחָה:

34 and *Hashem's* cloud kept above them by day, as they moved on from camp.

לד וַעֲנַן יְהֹוָה עֲלֵיהֶם יוֹמָם בְּנָסְעָם מִן־הַמַּחֲנֶה:

35 When the *Aron* was to set out, *Moshe* would say: Advance, *Hashem*! May Your enemies be scattered, And may Your foes flee before You!

לה וַיְהִי בִּנְסֹעַ הָאָרֹן וַיֹּאמֶר מֹשֶׁה קוּמָה יְהֹוָה וְיָפֻצוּ אֹיְבֶיךָ וְיָנֻסוּ מְשַׂנְאֶיךָ מִפָּנֶיךָ:

vai-HEE bin-SO-a ha-a-RON va-YO-mer mo-SHEH ku-MAH a-do-NAI v'-ya-FU-tzu o-y'-VE-kka v'-ya-NU-su m'-san-E-khah mi-pa-NE-khah

36 And when it halted, he would say: Return, *Hashem*, You who are *Yisrael's* myriads of thousands!

לו וּבְנֻחֹה יֹאמַר שׁוּבָה יְהֹוָה רִבְבוֹת אַלְפֵי יִשְׂרָאֵל:

uv-nu-KHOH yo-MAR shu-VAH a-do-NAI ri-v'-VOT al-FAY yis-ra-AYL

11 1 The people took to complaining bitterly before *Hashem*. *Hashem* heard and was incensed: a fire of *Hashem* broke out against them, ravaging the outskirts of the camp.

א וַיְהִי הָעָם כְּמִתְאֹנְנִים רַע בְּאָזְנֵי יְהֹוָה וַיִּשְׁמַע יְהֹוָה וַיִּחַר אַפּוֹ וַתִּבְעַר־בָּם אֵשׁ יְהֹוָה וַתֹּאכַל בִּקְצֵה הַמַּחֲנֶה:

The Israel Bible

10:35–36 When the *Aron* was to set out The Holy Ark travels with the Jewish people throughout their journey to the Promised Land, reminding them of God's presence within their camp. The Ark of the Covenant contained the Tablets of the Law – concretizing and symbolizing the entire *Torah* given to *Moshe* by *Hashem*. Just as the *Aron* was the focal point of the Israelites' existence in the desert, so too the Bible must always be the central focus of our own lives.

² The people cried out to *Moshe*. *Moshe* prayed to *Hashem*, and the fire died down.

ב וַיִּצְעַק הָעָם אֶל־מֹשֶׁה וַיִּתְפַּלֵּל מֹשֶׁה אֶל־יְהֹוָה וַתִּשְׁקַע הָאֵשׁ:

³ That place was named Taberah, because a fire of *Hashem* had broken out against them.

ג וַיִּקְרָא שֵׁם־הַמָּקוֹם הַהוּא תַּבְעֵרָה כִּי־בָעֲרָה בָם אֵשׁ יְהֹוָה:

⁴ The riffraff in their midst felt a gluttonous craving; and then the Israelites wept and said, "If only we had meat to eat!

ד וְהָאסַפְסֻף אֲשֶׁר בְּקִרְבּוֹ הִתְאַוּוּ תַּאֲוָה וַיָּשֻׁבוּ וַיִּבְכּוּ גַּם בְּנֵי יִשְׂרָאֵל וַיֹּאמְרוּ מִי יַאֲכִלֵנוּ בָּשָׂר:

⁵ We remember the fish that we used to eat free in Egypt, the cucumbers, the melons, the leeks, the onions, and the garlic.

ה זָכַרְנוּ אֶת־הַדָּגָה אֲשֶׁר־נֹאכַל בְּמִצְרַיִם חִנָּם אֵת הַקִּשֻּׁאִים וְאֵת הָאֲבַטִּחִים וְאֶת־הֶחָצִיר וְאֶת־הַבְּצָלִים וְאֶת־הַשּׁוּמִים:

⁶ Now our gullets are shriveled. There is nothing at all! Nothing but this manna to look to!"

ו וְעַתָּה נַפְשֵׁנוּ יְבֵשָׁה אֵין כֹּל בִּלְתִּי אֶל־הַמָּן עֵינֵינוּ:

⁷ Now the manna was like coriander seed, and in color it was like bdellium.

ז וְהַמָּן כִּזְרַע־גַּד הוּא וְעֵינוֹ כְּעֵין הַבְּדֹלַח:

⁸ The people would go about and gather it, grind it between millstones or pound it in a mortar, boil it in a pot, and make it into cakes. It tasted like rich cream.

ח שָׁטוּ הָעָם וְלָקְטוּ וְטָחֲנוּ בָרֵחַיִם אוֹ דָכוּ בַּמְּדֹכָה וּבִשְּׁלוּ בַּפָּרוּר וְעָשׂוּ אֹתוֹ עֻגוֹת וְהָיָה טַעְמוֹ כְּטַעַם לְשַׁד הַשָּׁמֶן:

⁹ When the dew fell on the camp at night, the manna would fall upon it.

ט וּבְרֶדֶת הַטַּל עַל־הַמַּחֲנֶה לָיְלָה יֵרֵד הַמָּן עָלָיו:

¹⁰ *Moshe* heard the people weeping, every clan apart, each person at the entrance of his tent. *Hashem* was very angry, and *Moshe* was distressed.

י וַיִּשְׁמַע מֹשֶׁה אֶת־הָעָם בֹּכֶה לְמִשְׁפְּחֹתָיו אִישׁ לְפֶתַח אָהֳלוֹ וַיִּחַר־אַף יְהֹוָה מְאֹד וּבְעֵינֵי מֹשֶׁה רָע:

¹¹ And *Moshe* said to *Hashem*, "Why have You dealt ill with Your servant, and why have I not enjoyed Your favor, that You have laid the burden of all this people upon me?

יא וַיֹּאמֶר מֹשֶׁה אֶל־יְהֹוָה לָמָה הֲרֵעֹתָ לְעַבְדֶּךָ וְלָמָּה לֹא־מָצָתִי חֵן בְּעֵינֶיךָ לָשׂוּם אֶת־מַשָּׂא כָּל־הָעָם הַזֶּה עָלָי:

¹² Did I conceive all this people, did I bear them, that You should say to me, 'Carry them in your bosom as a nurse carries an infant,' to the land that You have promised on oath to their fathers?

יב הֶאָנֹכִי הָרִיתִי אֵת כָּל־הָעָם הַזֶּה אִם־אָנֹכִי יְלִדְתִּיהוּ כִּי־תֹאמַר אֵלַי שָׂאֵהוּ בְחֵיקֶךָ כַּאֲשֶׁר יִשָּׂא הָאֹמֵן אֶת־הַיֹּנֵק עַל הָאֲדָמָה אֲשֶׁר נִשְׁבַּעְתָּ לַאֲבֹתָיו:

¹³ Where am I to get meat to give to all this people, when they whine before me and say, 'Give us meat to eat!'

יג מֵאַיִן לִי בָּשָׂר לָתֵת לְכָל־הָעָם הַזֶּה כִּי־יִבְכּוּ עָלַי לֵאמֹר תְּנָה־לָּנוּ בָשָׂר וְנֹאכֵלָה:

¹⁴ I cannot carry all this people by myself, for it is too much for me.

יד לֹא־אוּכַל אָנֹכִי לְבַדִּי לָשֵׂאת אֶת־כָּל־הָעָם הַזֶּה כִּי כָבֵד מִמֶּנִּי:

¹⁵ If You would deal thus with me, kill me rather, I beg You, and let me see no more of my wretchedness!"

טו וְאִם־כָּכָה אַתְּ־עֹשֶׂה לִּי הָרְגֵנִי נָא הָרֹג אִם־מָצָאתִי חֵן בְּעֵינֶיךָ וְאַל־אֶרְאֶה בְּרָעָתִי:

Numbers

¹⁶ Then *Hashem* said to *Moshe*, "Gather for Me seventy of *Yisrael*'s elders of whom you have experience as elders and officers of the people, and bring them to the Tent of Meeting and let them take their place there with you.

טז וַיֹּאמֶר יְהוָֹה אֶל־מֹשֶׁה אֶסְפָה־לִּי שִׁבְעִים אִישׁ מִזִּקְנֵי יִשְׂרָאֵל אֲשֶׁר יָדַעְתָּ כִּי־הֵם זִקְנֵי הָעָם וְשֹׁטְרָיו וְלָקַחְתָּ אֹתָם אֶל־אֹהֶל מוֹעֵד וְהִתְיַצְּבוּ שָׁם עִמָּךְ:

¹⁷ I will come down and speak with you there, and I will draw upon the spirit that is on you and put it upon them; they shall share the burden of the people with you, and you shall not bear it alone.

יז וְיָרַדְתִּי וְדִבַּרְתִּי עִמְּךָ שָׁם וְאָצַלְתִּי מִן־הָרוּחַ אֲשֶׁר עָלֶיךָ וְשַׂמְתִּי עֲלֵיהֶם וְנָשְׂאוּ אִתְּךָ בְּמַשָּׂא הָעָם וְלֹא־תִשָּׂא אַתָּה לְבַדֶּךָ:

v'-ya-rad-TEE v'-di-bar-TEE i-m'-KHA SHAM v'-a-tzal-TEE min ha-RU-akh a-SHER a-LE-kha v'-sam-TEE a-lay-HEM v'-na-s'-U i-t'-KHA b'-ma-SA ha-AM v'-lo ti-SA a-TAH l'-va-DE-kha

¹⁸ And say to the people: Purify yourselves for tomorrow and you shall eat meat, for you have kept whining before *Hashem* and saying, 'If only we had meat to eat! Indeed, we were better off in Egypt!' *Hashem* will give you meat and you shall eat.

יח וְאֶל־הָעָם תֹּאמַר הִתְקַדְּשׁוּ לְמָחָר וַאֲכַלְתֶּם בָּשָׂר כִּי בְּכִיתֶם בְּאָזְנֵי יְהוָֹה לֵאמֹר מִי יַאֲכִלֵנוּ בָּשָׂר כִּי־טוֹב לָנוּ בְּמִצְרָיִם וְנָתַן יְהוָֹה לָכֶם בָּשָׂר וַאֲכַלְתֶּם:

¹⁹ You shall eat not one day, not two, not even five days or ten or twenty,

יט לֹא יוֹם אֶחָד תֹּאכְלוּן וְלֹא יוֹמָיִם וְלֹא חֲמִשָּׁה יָמִים וְלֹא עֲשָׂרָה יָמִים וְלֹא עֶשְׂרִים יוֹם:

²⁰ but a whole month, until it comes out of your nostrils and becomes loathsome to you. For you have rejected *Hashem* who is among you, by whining before Him and saying, 'Oh, why did we ever leave Egypt!'"

כ עַד חֹדֶשׁ יָמִים עַד אֲשֶׁר־יֵצֵא מֵאַפְּכֶם וְהָיָה לָכֶם לְזָרָא יַעַן כִּי־מְאַסְתֶּם אֶת־ יְהוָֹה אֲשֶׁר בְּקִרְבְּכֶם וַתִּבְכּוּ לְפָנָיו לֵאמֹר לָמָּה זֶּה יָצָאנוּ מִמִּצְרָיִם:

²¹ But *Moshe* said, "The people who are with me number six hundred thousand men; yet You say, 'I will give them enough meat to eat for a whole month.'

כא וַיֹּאמֶר מֹשֶׁה שֵׁשׁ־מֵאוֹת אֶלֶף רַגְלִי הָעָם אֲשֶׁר אָנֹכִי בְּקִרְבּוֹ וְאַתָּה אָמַרְתָּ בָּשָׂר אֶתֵּן לָהֶם וְאָכְלוּ חֹדֶשׁ יָמִים:

Replica of the Temple *menorah*

11:17 And I will draw upon the spirit that is on you and put it upon them In his commentary to this verse, *Rashi*, compares *Moshe* to a candle. Just as one candle can light many others without diminishing its own flame, *Moshe*'s spirit will inspire the seventy elders he is about to gather, but his own spirit will not become lacking as a result. Candles are often thought of as a symbol of spirituality. The *Shabbat* is brought in with the lighting of candles, and its completion is marked with the *havdala* ceremony, which also features a lit candle. Just as the flame of a candle can illuminate a dark room, the holiness of *Shabbat* is meant to radiate and illuminate the rest of the week. Similarly, candles were lit daily on the *menorah*, 'lamp,' in the *Beit Hamikdash*. According to the Sages of the *Midrash*, the *menorah* was not designed to provide light in the sanctuary, but rather to spread light and holiness to the rest of the world. For this reason, the windows of the *Beit Hamikdash* were constructed with a unique design, narrow on the inside and wide on the outside (see I Kings 6:4). The *Beit Hamikdash* in *Yerushalayim* is the source of holiness in the world; it is the duty of the Children of Israel to spread that holiness and serve as a "light unto the nations" (Isaiah 42:6, 49:6).

22 Could enough flocks and herds be slaughtered to suffice them? Or could all the fish of the sea be gathered for them to suffice them?"

23 And *Hashem* answered *Moshe*, "Is there a limit to *Hashem*'s power? You shall soon see whether what I have said happens to you or not!"

24 *Moshe* went out and reported the words of *Hashem* to the people. He gathered seventy of the people's elders and stationed them around the Tent.

25 Then *Hashem* came down in a cloud and spoke to him; He drew upon the spirit that was on him and put it upon the seventy elders. And when the spirit rested upon them, they spoke in ecstasy, but did not continue.

26 Two men, one named Eldad and the other Medad, had remained in camp; yet the spirit rested upon them – they were among those recorded, but they had not gone out to the Tent – and they spoke in ecstasy in the camp.

27 A youth ran out and told *Moshe*, saying, "Eldad and Medad are acting the *navi* in the camp!"

28 And *Yehoshua* son of Nun, *Moshe*'s attendant from his youth, spoke up and said, "My lord *Moshe*, restrain them!"

29 But *Moshe* said to him, "Are you wrought up on my account? Would that all *Hashem*'s people were *Neviim*, that *Hashem* put His spirit upon them!"

30 *Moshe* then reentered the camp together with the elders of *Yisrael*.

31 A wind from *Hashem* started up, swept quail from the sea and strewed them over the camp, about a day's journey on this side and about a day's journey on that side, all around the camp, and some two *amot* deep on the ground.

32 The people set to gathering quail all that day and night and all the next day – even he who gathered least had ten *chomarim* – and they spread them out all around the camp.

33 The meat was still between their teeth, nor yet chewed, when the anger of *Hashem* blazed forth against the people and *Hashem* struck the people with a very severe plague.

כב הֲצֹאן וּבָקָר יִשָּׁחֵט לָהֶם וּמָצָא לָהֶם אִם אֶת־כָּל־דְּגֵי הַיָּם יֵאָסֵף לָהֶם וּמָצָא לָהֶם:

כג וַיֹּאמֶר יְהֹוָה אֶל־מֹשֶׁה הֲיַד יְהֹוָה תִּקְצָר עַתָּה תִרְאֶה הֲיִקְרְךָ דְבָרִי אִם־לֹא:

כד וַיֵּצֵא מֹשֶׁה וַיְדַבֵּר אֶל־הָעָם אֵת דִּבְרֵי יְהֹוָה וַיֶּאֱסֹף שִׁבְעִים אִישׁ מִזִּקְנֵי הָעָם וַיַּעֲמֵד אֹתָם סְבִיבֹת הָאֹהֶל:

כה וַיֵּרֶד יְהֹוָה בֶּעָנָן וַיְדַבֵּר אֵלָיו וַיָּאצֶל מִן־הָרוּחַ אֲשֶׁר עָלָיו וַיִּתֵּן עַל־שִׁבְעִים אִישׁ הַזְּקֵנִים וַיְהִי כְּנוֹחַ עֲלֵיהֶם הָרוּחַ וַיִּתְנַבְּאוּ וְלֹא יָסָפוּ:

כו וַיִּשָּׁאֲרוּ שְׁנֵי־אֲנָשִׁים בַּמַּחֲנֶה שֵׁם הָאֶחָד אֶלְדָּד וְשֵׁם הַשֵּׁנִי מֵידָד וַתָּנַח עֲלֵיהֶם הָרוּחַ וְהֵמָּה בַּכְּתֻבִים וְלֹא יָצְאוּ הָאֹהֱלָה וַיִּתְנַבְּאוּ בַּמַּחֲנֶה:

כז וַיָּרָץ הַנַּעַר וַיַּגֵּד לְמֹשֶׁה וַיֹּאמַר אֶלְדָּד וּמֵידָד מִתְנַבְּאִים בַּמַּחֲנֶה:

כח וַיַּעַן יְהוֹשֻׁעַ בִּן־נוּן מְשָׁרֵת מֹשֶׁה מִבְּחֻרָיו וַיֹּאמַר אֲדֹנִי מֹשֶׁה כְּלָאֵם:

כט וַיֹּאמֶר לוֹ מֹשֶׁה הַמְקַנֵּא אַתָּה לִי וּמִי יִתֵּן כָּל־עַם יְהֹוָה נְבִיאִים כִּי־יִתֵּן יְהֹוָה אֶת־רוּחוֹ עֲלֵיהֶם:

ל וַיֵּאָסֵף מֹשֶׁה אֶל־הַמַּחֲנֶה הוּא וְזִקְנֵי יִשְׂרָאֵל:

לא וְרוּחַ נָסַע מֵאֵת יְהֹוָה וַיָּגָז שַׂלְוִים מִן־הַיָּם וַיִּטֹּשׁ עַל־הַמַּחֲנֶה כְּדֶרֶךְ יוֹם כֹּה וּכְדֶרֶךְ יוֹם כֹּה סְבִיבוֹת הַמַּחֲנֶה וּכְאַמָּתַיִם עַל־פְּנֵי הָאָרֶץ:

לב וַיָּקָם הָעָם כָּל־הַיּוֹם הַהוּא וְכָל־הַלַּיְלָה וְכֹל יוֹם הַמָּחֳרָת וַיַּאַסְפוּ אֶת־הַשְּׂלָו הַמַּמְעִיט אָסַף עֲשָׂרָה חֳמָרִים וַיִּשְׁטְחוּ לָהֶם שָׁטוֹחַ סְבִיבוֹת הַמַּחֲנֶה:

לג הַבָּשָׂר עוֹדֶנּוּ בֵּין שִׁנֵּיהֶם טֶרֶם יִכָּרֵת וְאַף יְהֹוָה חָרָה בָעָם וַיַּךְ יְהֹוָה בָּעָם מַכָּה רַבָּה מְאֹד:

³⁴ That place was named Kibroth-hattaavah, because the people who had the craving were buried there.

לד וַיִּקְרָ֛א אֶת־שֵֽׁם־הַמָּק֥וֹם הַה֖וּא קִבְר֣וֹת הַֽתַּאֲוָ֑ה כִּי־שָׁם֙ קָֽבְר֔וּ אֶת־הָעָ֖ם הַמִּתְאַוִּֽים׃

³⁵ Then the people set out from Kibroth-hattaavah for Hazeroth. When they were in Hazeroth,

לה מִקִּבְר֧וֹת הַֽתַּאֲוָ֛ה נָֽסְע֥וּ הָעָ֖ם חֲצֵר֑וֹת וַיִּֽהְי֖וּ בַּחֲצֵרֽוֹת׃

12 ¹ *Miriam* and *Aharon* spoke against *Moshe* because of the Cushite woman he had married: "He married a Cushite woman!"

יב א וַתְּדַבֵּ֨ר מִרְיָ֤ם וְאַֽהֲרֹן֙ בְּמֹשֶׁ֔ה עַל־אֹד֛וֹת הָאִשָּׁ֥ה הַכֻּשִׁ֖ית אֲשֶׁ֣ר לָקָ֑ח כִּֽי־אִשָּׁ֥ה כֻשִׁ֖ית לָקָֽח׃

² They said, "Has *Hashem* spoken only through *Moshe*? Has He not spoken through us as well?" *Hashem* heard it.

ב וַיֹּֽאמְר֗וּ הֲרַ֤ק אַךְ־בְּמֹשֶׁה֙ דִּבֶּ֣ר יְהֹוָ֔ה הֲלֹ֖א גַּם־בָּ֣נוּ דִבֵּ֑ר וַיִּשְׁמַ֖ע יְהֹוָֽה׃

³ Now *Moshe* was a very humble man, more so than any other man on earth.

ג וְהָאִ֥ישׁ מֹשֶׁ֖ה עָנָ֣ו [עָנָ֣יו] מְאֹ֑ד מִכֹּל֙ הָֽאָדָ֔ם אֲשֶׁ֖ר עַל־פְּנֵ֥י הָֽאֲדָמָֽה׃

⁴ Suddenly *Hashem* called to *Moshe*, *Aharon*, and *Miriam*, "Come out, you three, to the Tent of Meeting." So the three of them went out.

ד וַיֹּ֨אמֶר יְהֹוָ֜ה פִּתְאֹ֗ם אֶל־מֹשֶׁ֤ה וְאֶֽל־אַֽהֲרֹן֙ וְאֶל־מִרְיָ֔ם צְא֥וּ שְׁלָשְׁתְּכֶ֖ם אֶל־אֹ֣הֶל מוֹעֵ֑ד וַיֵּֽצְא֖וּ שְׁלָשְׁתָּֽם׃

⁵ *Hashem* came down in a pillar of cloud, stopped at the entrance of the Tent, and called out, "*Aharon* and *Miriam*!" The two of them came forward;

ה וַיֵּ֤רֶד יְהֹוָה֙ בְּעַמּ֣וּד עָנָ֔ן וַיַּֽעֲמֹ֖ד פֶּ֣תַח הָאֹ֑הֶל וַיִּקְרָא֙ אַֽהֲרֹ֣ן וּמִרְיָ֔ם וַיֵּֽצְא֖וּ שְׁנֵיהֶֽם׃

⁶ and He said, "Hear these My words: When a *navi* of *Hashem* arises among you, I make Myself known to him in a vision, I speak with him in a dream.

ו וַיֹּ֖אמֶר שִׁמְעוּ־נָ֣א דְבָרָ֑י אִם־יִֽהְיֶה֙ נְבִ֣יאֲכֶ֔ם יְהֹוָ֗ה בַּמַּרְאָה֙ אֵלָ֣יו אֶתְוַדָּ֔ע בַּֽחֲל֖וֹם אֲדַבֶּר־בּֽוֹ׃

⁷ Not so with My servant *Moshe*; he is trusted throughout My household.

ז לֹא־כֵ֖ן עַבְדִּ֣י מֹשֶׁ֑ה בְּכָל־בֵּיתִ֖י נֶֽאֱמָ֥ן הֽוּא׃

⁸ With him I speak mouth to mouth, plainly and not in riddles, and he beholds the likeness of *Hashem*. How then did you not shrink from speaking against My servant *Moshe*!"

ח פֶּ֣ה אֶל־פֶּ֞ה אֲדַבֶּר־בּ֗וֹ וּמַרְאֶה֙ וְלֹ֣א בְחִידֹ֔ת וּתְמֻנַ֥ת יְהֹוָ֖ה יַבִּ֑יט וּמַדּ֙וּעַ֙ לֹ֣א יְרֵאתֶ֔ם לְדַבֵּ֖ר בְּעַבְדִּ֥י בְמֹשֶֽׁה׃

*PEH el PEH a-da-bayr BO u-mar-EH v'-LO v'-khee-DOT ut-mu-NAT a-do-NAI
ya-BEET u-ma-DU-a LO y'-ray-TEM l'-da-BAYR b'-av-DEE v'-mo-SHEH*

⁹ Still incensed with them, *Hashem* departed.

ט וַיִּֽחַר־אַ֧ף יְהֹוָ֛ה בָּ֖ם וַיֵּלַֽךְ׃

A spring morning in Samaria

12:8 With him I speak mouth to mouth The prophecy of *Moshe* was qualitatively different than that of any other prophet to have ever lived. According to Jewish teachings, prophets generally received their prophecy in a dream or trance, and were given a message that they needed to decode before they could deliver it to the people. They expressed and wrote these messages in their own words, though the messages themselves were divine. *Moshe's* prophecy, though, was different. As the verse indicates, he spoke to God, as it were, "face to face." When receiving his prophecy, *Moshe* was fully conscious, and he heard *Hashem's* messages word for word. It is through this level of prophecy that the Five Books of *Moshe* were written; not only are the messages of the books divine, but the words themselves were given directly by *Hashem*.

10 As the cloud withdrew from the Tent, there was *Miriam* stricken with snow-white scales! When *Aharon* turned toward *Miriam*, he saw that she was stricken with scales.

י וְהֶעָנָן סָר מֵעַל הָאֹהֶל וְהִנֵּה מִרְיָם מְצֹרַעַת כַּשָּׁלֶג וַיִּפֶן אַהֲרֹן אֶל־מִרְיָם וְהִנֵּה מְצֹרָעַת:

11 And *Aharon* said to *Moshe*, "O my lord, account not to us the sin which we committed in our folly.

יא וַיֹּאמֶר אַהֲרֹן אֶל־מֹשֶׁה בִּי אֲדֹנִי אַל־נָא תָשֵׁת עָלֵינוּ חַטָּאת אֲשֶׁר נוֹאַלְנוּ וַאֲשֶׁר חָטָאנוּ:

12 Let her not be as one dead, who emerges from his mother's womb with half his flesh eaten away."

יב אַל־נָא תְהִי כַּמֵּת אֲשֶׁר בְּצֵאתוֹ מֵרֶחֶם אִמּוֹ וַיֵּאָכֵל חֲצִי בְשָׂרוֹ:

13 So *Moshe* cried out to *Hashem*, saying, "O *Hashem*, pray heal her!"

יג וַיִּצְעַק מֹשֶׁה אֶל־יְהֹוָה לֵאמֹר אֵל נָא רְפָא נָא לָהּ:

14 But *Hashem* said to *Moshe*, "If her father spat in her face, would she not bear her shame for seven days? Let her be shut out of camp for seven days, and then let her be readmitted."

יד וַיֹּאמֶר יְהֹוָה אֶל־מֹשֶׁה וְאָבִיהָ יָרֹק יָרַק בְּפָנֶיהָ הֲלֹא תִכָּלֵם שִׁבְעַת יָמִים תִּסָּגֵר שִׁבְעַת יָמִים מִחוּץ לַמַּחֲנֶה וְאַחַר תֵּאָסֵף:

15 So *Miriam* was shut out of camp seven days; and the people did not march on until *Miriam* was readmitted.

טו וַתִּסָּגֵר מִרְיָם מִחוּץ לַמַּחֲנֶה שִׁבְעַת יָמִים וְהָעָם לֹא נָסַע עַד־הֵאָסֵף מִרְיָם:

16 After that the people set out from Hazeroth and encamped in the wilderness of Paran.

טז וְאַחַר נָסְעוּ הָעָם מֵחֲצֵרוֹת וַיַּחֲנוּ בְּמִדְבַּר פָּארָן:

3 1 *Hashem* spoke to *Moshe*, saying,

יג א וַיְדַבֵּר יְהֹוָה אֶל־מֹשֶׁה לֵּאמֹר:

2 "Send men to scout the land of Canaan, which I am giving to *B'nei Yisrael*; send one man from each of their ancestral tribes, each one a chieftain among them."

ב שְׁלַח־לְךָ אֲנָשִׁים וְיָתֻרוּ אֶת־אֶרֶץ כְּנַעַן אֲשֶׁר־אֲנִי נֹתֵן לִבְנֵי יִשְׂרָאֵל אִישׁ אֶחָד אִישׁ אֶחָד לְמַטֵּה אֲבֹתָיו תִּשְׁלָחוּ כֹּל נָשִׂיא בָהֶם:

3 So *Moshe*, by *Hashem*'s command, sent them out from the wilderness of Paran, all the men being leaders of the Israelites.

ג וַיִּשְׁלַח אֹתָם מֹשֶׁה מִמִּדְבַּר פָּארָן עַל־פִּי יְהֹוָה כֻּלָּם אֲנָשִׁים רָאשֵׁי בְנֵי־יִשְׂרָאֵל הֵמָּה:

4 And these were their names: From the tribe of *Reuven*, Shamua son of Zaccur.

ד וְאֵלֶּה שְׁמוֹתָם לְמַטֵּה רְאוּבֵן שַׁמּוּעַ בֶּן־זַכּוּר:

5 From the tribe of *Shimon*, Shafat son of Hori.

ה לְמַטֵּה שִׁמְעוֹן שָׁפָט בֶּן־חוֹרִי:

6 From the tribe of *Yehuda*, Kalev son of Jephunneh.

ו לְמַטֵּה יְהוּדָה כָּלֵב בֶּן־יְפֻנֶּה:

7 From the tribe of *Yissachar*, Yigal son of *Yosef*.

ז לְמַטֵּה יִשָּׂשכָר יִגְאָל בֶּן־יוֹסֵף:

8 From the tribe of *Efraim*, Hoshea son of Nun.

ח לְמַטֵּה אֶפְרָיִם הוֹשֵׁעַ בִּן־נוּן:

9 From the tribe of *Binyamin*, Palti son of Rafu.

ט לְמַטֵּה בִנְיָמִן פַּלְטִי בֶּן־רָפוּא:

10 From the tribe of *Zevulun*, Gadiel son of Sodi.

י לְמַטֵּה זְבוּלֻן גַּדִּיאֵל בֶּן־סוֹדִי:

11 From the tribe of *Yosef*, namely, the tribe of *Menashe*, Gadi son of Susi.

יא לְמַטֵּה יוֹסֵף לְמַטֵּה מְנַשֶּׁה גַּדִּי בֶּן־סוּסִי:

12 From the tribe of *Dan, Amiel* son of Gemalli.

יב לְמַטֵּה דָן עַמִּיאֵל בֶּן־גְּמַלִּי:

13 From the tribe of *Asher, Setur* son of Michael.

יג לְמַטֵּה אָשֵׁר סְתוּר בֶּן־מִיכָאֵל:

14 From the tribe of *Naftali, Nachbi* son of Vophsi.

יד לְמַטֵּה נַפְתָּלִי נַחְבִּי בֶּן־וָפְסִי:

15 From the tribe of *Gad, Geuel* son of Machi.

טו לְמַטֵּה גָד גְּאוּאֵל בֶּן־מָכִי:

16 Those were the names of the men whom *Moshe* sent to scout the land; but *Moshe* changed the name of *Hoshea* son of *Nun* to *Yehoshua.*

טז אֵלֶּה שְׁמוֹת הָאֲנָשִׁים אֲשֶׁר־שָׁלַח מֹשֶׁה לָתוּר אֶת־הָאָרֶץ וַיִּקְרָא מֹשֶׁה לְהוֹשֵׁעַ בִּן־נוּן יְהוֹשֻׁעַ:

17 When *Moshe* sent them to scout the land of Canaan, he said to them, "Go up there into the *Negev* and on into the hill country,

יז וַיִּשְׁלַח אֹתָם מֹשֶׁה לָתוּר אֶת־אֶרֶץ כְּנָעַן וַיֹּאמֶר אֲלֵהֶם עֲלוּ זֶה בַּנֶּגֶב וַעֲלִיתֶם אֶת־הָהָר:

18 and see what kind of country it is. Are the people who dwell in it strong or weak, few or many?

יח וּרְאִיתֶם אֶת־הָאָרֶץ מַה־הִוא וְאֶת־הָעָם הַיֹּשֵׁב עָלֶיהָ הֶחָזָק הוּא הֲרָפֶה הַמְעַט הוּא אִם־רָב:

19 Is the country in which they dwell good or bad? Are the towns they live in open or fortified?

יט וּמָה הָאָרֶץ אֲשֶׁר־הוּא יֹשֵׁב בָּהּ הֲטוֹבָה הִוא אִם־רָעָה וּמָה הֶעָרִים אֲשֶׁר־הוּא יוֹשֵׁב בָּהֵנָּה הַבְּמַחֲנִים אִם בְּמִבְצָרִים:

20 Is the soil rich or poor? Is it wooded or not? And take pains to bring back some of the fruit of the land." – Now it happened to be the season of the first ripe grapes.

כ וּמָה הָאָרֶץ הַשְּׁמֵנָה הִוא אִם־רָזָה הֲיֵשׁ־בָּהּ עֵץ אִם־אַיִן וְהִתְחַזַּקְתֶּם וּלְקַחְתֶּם מִפְּרִי הָאָרֶץ וְהַיָּמִים יְמֵי בִּכּוּרֵי עֲנָבִים:

21 They went up and scouted the land, from the wilderness of Zin to Rehob, at Lebo-hamath.

כא וַיַּעֲלוּ וַיָּתֻרוּ אֶת־הָאָרֶץ מִמִּדְבַּר־צִן עַד־רְחֹב לְבֹא חֲמָת:

22 They went up into the *Negev* and came to *Chevron,* where lived Ahiman, Sheshai, and Talmai, the Anakites. – Now *Chevron* was founded seven years before Zoan of Egypt. –

כב וַיַּעֲלוּ בַנֶּגֶב וַיָּבֹא עַד־חֶבְרוֹן וְשָׁם אֲחִימַן שֵׁשַׁי וְתַלְמַי יְלִידֵי הָעֲנָק וְחֶבְרוֹן שֶׁבַע שָׁנִים נִבְנְתָה לִפְנֵי צֹעַן מִצְרָיִם:

va-ya-a-LU va-NE-gev va-ya-VO ad khev-RON v'-SHAM a-khi-MAN
shay-SHAI v'-tal-MAI y'-lee-DAY ha-a-NAK v'-khev-RON SHE-va
sha-NEEM niv-ni-TAH lif-NAY TZO-an mitz-RA-yim

23 They reached the wadi Eshcol, and there they cut down a branch with a single cluster of grapes – it had to be borne on a carrying frame by two of them – and some pomegranates and figs.

כג וַיָּבֹאוּ עַד־נַחַל אֶשְׁכֹּל וַיִּכְרְתוּ מִשָּׁם זְמוֹרָה וְאֶשְׁכּוֹל עֲנָבִים אֶחָד וַיִּשָּׂאֻהוּ בַמּוֹט בִּשְׁנָיִם וּמִן־הָרִמֹּנִים וּמִן־הַתְּאֵנִים:

24 That place was named the wadi Eshcol because of the cluster that the Israelites cut down there.

כד לַמָּקוֹם הַהוּא קָרָא נַחַל אֶשְׁכּוֹל עַל אֹדוֹת הָאֶשְׁכּוֹל אֲשֶׁר־כָּרְתוּ מִשָּׁם בְּנֵי יִשְׂרָאֵל:

25 At the end of forty days they returned from scouting the land.

כה וַיָּשֻׁבוּ מִתּוּר הָאָרֶץ מִקֵּץ אַרְבָּעִים יוֹם:

²⁶ They went straight to *Moshe* and *Aharon* and the whole Israelite community at Kadesh in the wilderness of Paran, and they made their report to them and to the whole community, as they showed them the fruit of the land.

כו וַיֵּלְכוּ וַיָּבֹאוּ אֶל־מֹשֶׁה וְאֶל־אַהֲרֹן וְאֶל־
כָּל־עֲדַת בְּנֵי־יִשְׂרָאֵל אֶל־מִדְבַּר פָּארָן
קָדֵשָׁה וַיָּשִׁיבוּ אוֹתָם דָּבָר וְאֶת־כָּל־
הָעֵדָה וַיַּרְאוּם אֶת־פְּרִי הָאָרֶץ:

²⁷ This is what they told him: "We came to the land you sent us to; it does indeed flow with milk and honey, and this is its fruit.

כז וַיְסַפְּרוּ־לוֹ וַיֹּאמְרוּ בָּאנוּ אֶל־הָאָרֶץ
אֲשֶׁר שְׁלַחְתָּנוּ וְגַם זָבַת חָלָב וּדְבַשׁ
הִוא וְזֶה־פִּרְיָהּ:

vai-sa-p'-ru LO va-YO-m'-RU BA-nu el ha-A-retz a-SHER sh'-lakh-
TA-nu v'-GAM za-VAT kha-LAV u-d'-VASH HEE v'-zeh pir-YAH

²⁸ However, the people who inhabit the country are powerful, and the cities are fortified and very large; moreover, we saw the Anakites there.

כח אֶפֶס כִּי־עַז הָעָם הַיֹּשֵׁב בָּאָרֶץ וְהֶעָרִים
בְּצֻרוֹת גְּדֹלֹת מְאֹד וְגַם־יְלִדֵי הָעֲנָק
רָאִינוּ שָׁם:

²⁹ Amalekites dwell in the *Negev* region; Hittites, Jebusites, and Amorites inhabit the hill country; and Canaanites dwell by the Sea and along the *Yarden*."

כט עֲמָלֵק יוֹשֵׁב בְּאֶרֶץ הַנֶּגֶב וְהַחִתִּי
וְהַיְבוּסִי וְהָאֱמֹרִי יוֹשֵׁב בָּהָר וְהַכְּנַעֲנִי
יֹשֵׁב עַל־הַיָּם וְעַל יַד הַיַּרְדֵּן:

³⁰ *Kalev* hushed the people before *Moshe* and said, "Let us by all means go up, and we shall gain possession of it, for we shall surely overcome it."

ל וַיַּהַס כָּלֵב אֶת־הָעָם אֶל־מֹשֶׁה וַיֹּאמֶר
עָלֹה נַעֲלֶה וְיָרַשְׁנוּ אֹתָהּ כִּי־יָכוֹל נוּכַל
לָהּ:

va-ya-HAS ka-LAYV et ha-AM el mo-SHEH va-YO-mer a-LOH
na-a-LEH v'-ya-RASH-nu o-TAH kee ya-KHOL nu-KHAL LAH

³¹ But the men who had gone up with him said, "We cannot attack that people, for it is stronger than we."

לא וְהָאֲנָשִׁים אֲשֶׁר־עָלוּ עִמּוֹ אָמְרוּ לֹא
נוּכַל לַעֲלוֹת אֶל־הָעָם כִּי־חָזָק הוּא
מִמֶּנּוּ:

³² Thus they spread calumnies among the Israelites about the land they had scouted, saying, "The country that we traversed and scouted is one that devours its settlers. All the people that we saw in it are men of great size;

לב וַיֹּצִיאוּ דִּבַּת הָאָרֶץ אֲשֶׁר תָּרוּ אֹתָהּ
אֶל־בְּנֵי יִשְׂרָאֵל לֵאמֹר הָאָרֶץ אֲשֶׁר
עָבַרְנוּ בָהּ לָתוּר אֹתָהּ אֶרֶץ אֹכֶלֶת
יוֹשְׁבֶיהָ הִוא וְכָל־הָעָם אֲשֶׁר־רָאִינוּ
בְתוֹכָהּ אַנְשֵׁי מִדּוֹת:

13:27 This is what they told him The spies' slanderous report against *Eretz Yisrael* is one of the worst, if not the single gravest, sin described in the Bible. *Moshe* sends one representative from each tribe to scout out the land, and ten of the twelve return with a negative report. Only *Kalev* and *Yehoshua* have faith in *Hashem* and speak positively about the Land of Israel. Whereas *Hashem* forgives many sins throughout the Bible, slandering *Eretz Yisrael* is unacceptable, and the entire generation is punished for accepting the report. They are condemned to wander in the desert for forty years until the entire generation of the spies dies, as they no longer deserve to enter the Promised Land. Like *Kalev* and *Yehoshua*, we must not fall into the trap of criticizing the greatest of all God's gifts. Rather, we must speak positively about Israel at every opportunity.

A field of wildflowers in the Negev

40

Numbers

33 we saw the Nephilim there – the Anakites are part of the Nephilim – and we looked like grasshoppers to ourselves, and so we must have looked to them."

לג וְשָׁ֣ם רָאִ֗ינוּ אֶת־הַנְּפִילִ֛ים בְּנֵ֥י עֲנָ֖ק מִן־הַנְּפִלִ֑ים וַנְּהִ֤י בְעֵינֵ֙ינוּ֙ כַּֽחֲגָבִ֔ים וְכֵ֥ן הָיִ֖ינוּ בְּעֵינֵיהֶֽם׃

v'-SHAM ra-EE-nu et ha-n'-fee-LEEM b'-NAY a-NAK min ha-n'-fee-LEEM
va-n'-HEE v'-ay-NAY-nu ka-kha-ga-VEEM v'-KHAYN ha-YEE-nu b'-ay-nay-HEM

14 ¹ The whole community broke into loud cries, and the people wept that night.

יד א וַתִּשָּׂא֙ כָּל־הָ֣עֵדָ֔ה וַֽיִּתְּנ֖וּ אֶת־קוֹלָ֑ם וַיִּבְכּ֥וּ הָעָ֖ם בַּלַּ֥יְלָה הַהֽוּא׃

va-ti-SA kol HA-ay-DAH va-yi-t'-NU et ko-LAM
va-yiv-KU ha-AM ba-LAI-lah ha-HU

² All the Israelites railed against *Moshe* and *Aharon*. "If only we had died in the land of Egypt," the whole community shouted at them, "or if only we might die in this wilderness!

ב וַיִּלֹּ֙נוּ֙ עַל־מֹשֶׁ֣ה וְעַֽל־אַהֲרֹ֔ן כֹּ֖ל בְּנֵ֣י יִשְׂרָאֵ֑ל וַיֹּאמְר֨וּ אֲלֵהֶ֜ם כָּל־הָעֵדָ֗ה לוּ־מַ֙תְנוּ֙ בְּאֶ֣רֶץ מִצְרַ֔יִם א֛וֹ בַּמִּדְבָּ֥ר הַזֶּ֖ה לוּ־מָֽתְנוּ׃

³ Why is *Hashem* taking us to that land to fall by the sword? Our wives and children will be carried off! It would be better for us to go back to Egypt!"

ג וְלָמָ֣ה יְ֠הֹוָה מֵבִ֨יא אֹתָ֜נוּ אֶל־הָאָ֤רֶץ הַזֹּאת֙ לִנְפֹּ֣ל בַּחֶ֔רֶב נָשֵׁ֥ינוּ וְטַפֵּ֖נוּ יִהְי֣וּ לָבַ֑ז הֲל֣וֹא ט֥וֹב לָ֖נוּ שׁ֥וּב מִצְרָֽיְמָה׃

⁴ And they said to one another, "Let us head back for Egypt."

ד וַיֹּאמְר֖וּ אִ֣ישׁ אֶל־אָחִ֑יו נִתְּנָ֥ה רֹ֖אשׁ וְנָשׁ֥וּבָה מִצְרָֽיְמָה׃

⁵ Then *Moshe* and *Aharon* fell on their faces before all the assembled congregation of the Israelites.

ה וַיִּפֹּ֥ל מֹשֶׁ֛ה וְאַהֲרֹ֖ן עַל־פְּנֵיהֶ֑ם לִפְנֵ֕י כָּל־קְהַ֥ל עֲדַ֖ת בְּנֵ֥י יִשְׂרָאֵֽל׃

⁶ And *Yehoshua* son of *Nun* and *Kalev* son of Jephunneh, of those who had scouted the land, rent their clothes

ו וִֽיהוֹשֻׁ֣עַ בִּן־נ֗וּן וְכָלֵב֙ בֶּן־יְפֻנֶּ֔ה מִן־הַתָּרִ֖ים אֶת־הָאָ֑רֶץ קָרְע֖וּ בִּגְדֵיהֶֽם׃

13:33 And so we must have looked to them. In comparison to the giants living in Canaan, the spies report that "we looked like grasshoppers to ourselves, and so we must have looked to them." Rabbi Menachem Mendel of Kotzk, a Hasidic leader in the nineteenth century, suggests that the sin of the spies was that they worried about what others thought of them. As emissaries of *Hashem*, they should have been concerned only with fulfilling their mission, despite how they might be perceived by the people around them. We all have a special mission, to spread God's messages to the world. Since we know we are fulfilling *Hashem's* work, we should not worry about what others will think about us.

14:1 And the people wept that night The Sages explain that *Hashem* intentionally selected the ninth day of the month of *Av* as the day upon which both the first and second Temples would be destroyed. According to Jewish tradition, This is because it was on this day that the twelve spies returned from their mission to scout out *Eretz Yisrael*. As reported in the coming verses, following their pessimistic and libelous report,

the people cried out to God in fear: "If only we had died in the land of Egypt… or if only we might die in this wilderness! Why is *Hashem* taking us to that land to fall by the sword? Our wives and children will be carried off! It would be better for us to go back to Egypt!" (Numbers 14:2–3). The Talmud (*Taanit* 29a) records that *Hashem* reprimanded the people for their lack of faith and said: "As you cried on the ninth of *Av* for no reason, this day will become a day of crying for all future generations." The events surrounding the destruc-

Mourning on the 9th of Av

tion of the *Beit Hamikdash* are linked back to the biblical account of the twelve spies, to illustrate that all of Jewish history is inexorably interwoven, and is the unfolding of *Hashem's* plan. We must never forget that one of the keys to the rebuilding of the *Beit Hamikdash* and the heralding in of the Messianic Era is our unquestioning trust in God, and appreciation of *Eretz Yisrael*.

41

7 and exhorted the whole Israelite community: "The land that we traversed and scouted is an exceedingly good land.

וַיֹּאמְרוּ אֶל־כָּל־עֲדַת בְּנֵי־יִשְׂרָאֵל לֵאמֹר הָאָרֶץ אֲשֶׁר עָבַרְנוּ בָהּ לָתוּר אֹתָהּ טוֹבָה הָאָרֶץ מְאֹד מְאֹד: ז

va-YO-m'-RU el kol a-DAT b'-nay yis-ra-AYL lay-MOR ha-A-retz a-SHER a-VAR-nu VAH la-TUR o-TAH to-VAH ha-A-retz m'-OD m'-OD

8 If *Hashem* is pleased with us, He will bring us into that land, a land that flows with milk and honey, and give it to us;

אִם־חָפֵץ בָּנוּ יְהֹוָה וְהֵבִיא אֹתָנוּ אֶל־הָאָרֶץ הַזֹּאת וּנְתָנָהּ לָנוּ אֶרֶץ אֲשֶׁר־הִוא זָבַת חָלָב וּדְבָשׁ: ח

im kha-FAYTZ BA-nu a-do-NAI v'-hay-VEE o-TA-nu el ha-A-retz ha-ZOT u-n'-ta-NAH LA-nu E-retz a-sher HEE za-VAT kha-LAV u-d'-VASH

9 only you must not rebel against *Hashem*. Have no fear then of the people of the country, for they are our prey: their protection has departed from them, but *Hashem* is with us. Have no fear of them!"

אַךְ בַּיהֹוָה אַל־תִּמְרֹדוּ וְאַתֶּם אַל־תִּירְאוּ אֶת־עַם הָאָרֶץ כִּי לַחְמֵנוּ הֵם סָר צִלָּם מֵעֲלֵיהֶם וַיהֹוָה אִתָּנוּ אַל־תִּירָאֻם: ט

10 As the whole community threatened to pelt them with stones, the Presence of *Hashem* appeared in the Tent of Meeting to all the Israelites.

וַיֹּאמְרוּ כָּל־הָעֵדָה לִרְגּוֹם אֹתָם בָּאֲבָנִים וּכְבוֹד יְהֹוָה נִרְאָה בְּאֹהֶל מוֹעֵד אֶל־כָּל־בְּנֵי יִשְׂרָאֵל: י

11 And *Hashem* said to *Moshe*, "How long will this people spurn Me, and how long will they have no faith in Me despite all the signs that I have performed in their midst?

וַיֹּאמֶר יְהֹוָה אֶל־מֹשֶׁה עַד־אָנָה יְנַאֲצֻנִי הָעָם הַזֶּה וְעַד־אָנָה לֹא־יַאֲמִינוּ בִי בְּכֹל הָאֹתוֹת אֲשֶׁר עָשִׂיתִי בְּקִרְבּוֹ: יא

12 I will strike them with pestilence and disown them, and I will make of you a nation far more numerous than they!"

אַכֶּנּוּ בַדֶּבֶר וְאוֹרִשֶׁנּוּ וְאֶעֱשֶׂה אֹתְךָ לְגוֹי־גָּדוֹל וְעָצוּם מִמֶּנּוּ: יב

13 But *Moshe* said to *Hashem*, "When the Egyptians, from whose midst You brought up this people in Your might, hear the news,

וַיֹּאמֶר מֹשֶׁה אֶל־יְהֹוָה וְשָׁמְעוּ מִצְרַיִם כִּי־הֶעֱלִיתָ בְכֹחֲךָ אֶת־הָעָם הַזֶּה מִקִּרְבּוֹ: יג

14 they will tell it to the inhabitants of that land. Now they have heard that You, *Hashem*, are in the midst of this people; that You, *Hashem*, appear in plain sight when Your cloud rests over them and when You go before them in a pillar of cloud by day and in a pillar of fire by night.

וְאָמְרוּ אֶל־יוֹשֵׁב הָאָרֶץ הַזֹּאת שָׁמְעוּ כִּי־אַתָּה יְהֹוָה בְּקֶרֶב הָעָם הַזֶּה אֲשֶׁר־עַיִן בְּעַיִן נִרְאָה אַתָּה יְהֹוָה וַעֲנָנְךָ עֹמֵד עֲלֵהֶם וּבְעַמֻּד עָנָן אַתָּה הֹלֵךְ לִפְנֵיהֶם יוֹמָם וּבְעַמּוּד אֵשׁ לָיְלָה: יד

14:7–8 If *Hashem* is pleased with us After the negative report of ten of the twelve spies, *Kalev* responds by saying that if *Hashem* desires that the People of Israel live in *Eretz Yisrael*, He will make sure that they will inherit it, despite the many obstacles. *Hashem* desired to give the land to His chosen nation then, and He desires for them to have it now. There are certainly deterrents from living in, and loving, the land of Israel. For example, it is surrounded by hostile neighbors and there are constant security threats. Nevertheless, God has returned the land to the Children of Israel. Let us not repeat the mistake of the ten spies by minimizing God's great gift to our generation.

Iron Dome rocket interceptions over Ashdod

15 If then You slay this people to a man, the nations who have heard Your fame will say,

טו וְהֵמַתָּה אֶת־הָעָם הַזֶּה כְּאִישׁ אֶחָד וְאָמְרוּ הַגּוֹיִם אֲשֶׁר־שָׁמְעוּ אֶת־שִׁמְעֲךָ לֵאמֹר:

16 'It must be because *Hashem* was powerless to bring that people into the land He had promised them on oath that He slaughtered them in the wilderness.'

טז מִבִּלְתִּי יְכֹלֶת יְהֹוָה לְהָבִיא אֶת־הָעָם הַזֶּה אֶל־הָאָרֶץ אֲשֶׁר־נִשְׁבַּע לָהֶם וַיִּשְׁחָטֵם בַּמִּדְבָּר:

17 Therefore, I pray, let my Lord's forbearance be great, as You have declared, saying,

יז וְעַתָּה יִגְדַּל־נָא כֹּחַ אֲדֹנָי כַּאֲשֶׁר דִּבַּרְתָּ לֵאמֹר:

18 '*Hashem*! slow to anger and abounding in kindness; forgiving iniquity and transgression; yet not remitting all punishment, but visiting the iniquity of fathers upon children, upon the third and fourth generations.'

יח יְהֹוָה אֶרֶךְ אַפַּיִם וְרַב־חֶסֶד נֹשֵׂא עָוֹן וָפָשַׁע וְנַקֵּה לֹא יְנַקֶּה פֹּקֵד עֲוֹן אָבוֹת עַל־בָּנִים עַל־שִׁלֵּשִׁים וְעַל־רִבֵּעִים:

19 Pardon, I pray, the iniquity of this people according to Your great kindness, as You have forgiven this people ever since Egypt."

יט סְלַח־נָא לַעֲוֹן הָעָם הַזֶּה כְּגֹדֶל חַסְדֶּךָ וְכַאֲשֶׁר נָשָׂאתָה לָעָם הַזֶּה מִמִּצְרַיִם וְעַד־הֵנָּה:

20 And *Hashem* said, "I pardon, as you have asked.

כ וַיֹּאמֶר יְהֹוָה סָלַחְתִּי כִּדְבָרֶךָ:

21 Nevertheless, as I live and as *Hashem*'s Presence fills the whole world,

כא וְאוּלָם חַי־אָנִי וְיִמָּלֵא כְבוֹד־יְהֹוָה אֶת־כָּל־הָאָרֶץ:

22 none of the men who have seen My Presence and the signs that I have performed in Egypt and in the wilderness, and who have tried Me these many times and have disobeyed Me,

כב כִּי כָל־הָאֲנָשִׁים הָרֹאִים אֶת־כְּבֹדִי וְאֶת־אֹתֹתַי אֲשֶׁר־עָשִׂיתִי בְמִצְרַיִם וּבַמִּדְבָּר וַיְנַסּוּ אֹתִי זֶה עֶשֶׂר פְּעָמִים וְלֹא שָׁמְעוּ בְּקוֹלִי:

23 shall see the land that I promised on oath to their fathers; none of those who spurn Me shall see it.

כג אִם־יִרְאוּ אֶת־הָאָרֶץ אֲשֶׁר נִשְׁבַּעְתִּי לַאֲבֹתָם וְכָל־מְנַאֲצַי לֹא יִרְאוּהָ:

24 But My servant *Kalev*, because he was imbued with a different spirit and remained loyal to Me – him will I bring into the land that he entered, and his offspring shall hold it as a possession.

כד וְעַבְדִּי כָלֵב עֵקֶב הָיְתָה רוּחַ אַחֶרֶת עִמּוֹ וַיְמַלֵּא אַחֲרָי וַהֲבִיאֹתִיו אֶל־הָאָרֶץ אֲשֶׁר־בָּא שָׁמָּה וְזַרְעוֹ יוֹרִשֶׁנָּה:

25 Now the Amalekites and the Canaanites occupy the valleys. Start out, then, tomorrow and march into the wilderness by way of the Sea of Reeds."

כה וְהָעֲמָלֵקִי וְהַכְּנַעֲנִי יוֹשֵׁב בָּעֵמֶק מָחָר פְּנוּ וּסְעוּ לָכֶם הַמִּדְבָּר דֶּרֶךְ יַם־סוּף:

26 *Hashem* spoke further to *Moshe* and *Aharon*,

כו וַיְדַבֵּר יְהֹוָה אֶל־מֹשֶׁה וְאֶל־אַהֲרֹן לֵאמֹר:

27 "How much longer shall that wicked community keep muttering against Me? Very well, I have heeded the incessant muttering of the Israelites against Me.

כז עַד־מָתַי לָעֵדָה הָרָעָה הַזֹּאת אֲשֶׁר הֵמָּה מַלִּינִים עָלָי אֶת־תְּלֻנּוֹת בְּנֵי יִשְׂרָאֵל אֲשֶׁר הֵמָּה מַלִּינִים עָלַי שָׁמָעְתִּי:

28 Say to them: 'As I live,' says *Hashem*, 'I will do to you just as you have urged Me.

כח אֱמֹר אֲלֵהֶם חַי־אָנִי נְאֻם־יְהֹוָה אִם־לֹא כַּאֲשֶׁר דִּבַּרְתֶּם בְּאָזְנָי כֵּן אֶעֱשֶׂה לָכֶם:

29 In this very wilderness shall your carcasses drop.
Of all of you who were recorded in your various
lists from the age of twenty years up, you who have
muttered against Me,

כט בַּמִּדְבָּ֣ר הַזֶּה֩ יִפְּל֨וּ פִגְרֵיכֶ֜ם וְכָל־
פְּקֻדֵיכֶם֙ לְכָל־מִסְפַּרְכֶ֔ם מִבֶּ֛ן עֶשְׂרִ֥ים
שָׁנָ֖ה וָמָ֑עְלָה אֲשֶׁ֥ר הֲלִינֹתֶ֖ם עָלָֽי:

30 not one shall enter the land in which I swore to
settle you – save *Kalev* son of Jephunneh and
Yehoshua son of *Nun*.

ל אִם־אַתֶּם֙ תָּבֹ֣אוּ אֶל־הָאָ֔רֶץ אֲשֶׁ֤ר
נָשָׂ֙אתִי֙ אֶת־יָדִ֔י לְשַׁכֵּ֥ן אֶתְכֶ֖ם בָּ֑הּ כִּ֚י
אִם־כָּלֵ֣ב בֶּן־יְפֻנֶּ֔ה וִיהוֹשֻׁ֖עַ בִּן־נֽוּן:

31 Your children who, you said, would be carried off –
these will I allow to enter; they shall know the land
that you have rejected.

לא וְטַ֨פְּכֶ֔ם אֲשֶׁ֥ר אֲמַרְתֶּ֖ם לָבַ֣ז יִֽהְיֶ֑ה
וְהֵבֵיאתִ֣י אֹתָ֔ם וְיָֽדְעוּ֙ אֶת־הָאָ֔רֶץ אֲשֶׁ֥ר
מְאַסְתֶּ֖ם בָּֽהּ:

32 But your carcasses shall drop in this wilderness,

לב וּפִגְרֵיכֶ֖ם אַתֶּ֑ם יִפְּל֖וּ בַּמִּדְבָּ֥ר הַזֶּֽה:

33 while your children roam the wilderness for forty
years, suffering for your faithlessness, until the last
of your carcasses is down in the wilderness.

לג וּ֠בְנֵיכֶ֠ם יִֽהְי֨וּ רֹעִ֤ים בַּמִּדְבָּר֙ אַרְבָּעִ֣ים
שָׁנָ֔ה וְנָֽשְׂא֖וּ אֶת־זְנֽוּתֵיכֶ֑ם עַד־תֹּ֥ם
פִּגְרֵיכֶ֖ם בַּמִּדְבָּֽר:

34 You shall bear your punishment for forty years,
corresponding to the number of days – forty days –
that you scouted the land: a year for each day. Thus
you shall know what it means to thwart Me.

לד בְּמִסְפַּ֣ר הַיָּמִ֡ים אֲשֶׁר־תַּרְתֶּם֩ אֶת־
הָאָ֜רֶץ אַרְבָּעִ֣ים יוֹם֙ י֤וֹם לַשָּׁנָה֙ י֣וֹם
לַשָּׁנָ֔ה תִּשְׂאוּ֙ אֶת־עֲוֹנֹֽתֵיכֶ֔ם אַרְבָּעִ֖ים
שָׁנָ֑ה וִֽידַעְתֶּ֖ם אֶת־תְּנֽוּאָתִֽי:

35 I *Hashem* have spoken: Thus will I do to all that
wicked band that has banded together against Me:
in this very wilderness they shall die to the last
man.'"

לה אֲנִ֣י יְהֹוָה֮ דִּבַּ֒רְתִּי֒ אִם־לֹ֣א ׀ זֹ֣את אֶֽעֱשֶׂ֗ה
לְכָל־הָֽעֵדָ֤ה הָֽרָעָה֙ הַזֹּ֔את הַנּֽוֹעָדִ֖ים עָלָ֑י
בַּמִּדְבָּ֥ר הַזֶּ֛ה יִתַּ֖מּוּ וְשָׁ֥ם יָמֻֽתוּ:

36 As for the men whom *Moshe* sent to scout the
land, those who came back and caused the whole
community to mutter against him by spreading
calumnies about the land –

לו וְהָ֣אֲנָשִׁ֔ים אֲשֶׁר־שָׁלַ֥ח מֹשֶׁ֖ה לָת֣וּר אֶת־
הָאָ֑רֶץ וַיָּשֻׁ֗בוּ וילונו [וַיַּלִּ֤ינוּ] עָלָיו֙ אֶת־
כָּל־הָ֣עֵדָ֔ה לְהוֹצִ֥יא דִבָּ֖ה עַל־הָאָֽרֶץ:

37 those who spread such calumnies about the land
died of plague, by the will of *Hashem*.

לז וַיָּמֻ֙תוּ֙ הָֽאֲנָשִׁ֔ים מֽוֹצִאֵ֥י דִבַּת־הָאָ֖רֶץ
רָעָ֑ה בַּמַּגֵּפָ֖ה לִפְנֵ֥י יְהֹוָֽה:

38 Of those men who had gone to scout the land, only
Yehoshua son of *Nun* and *Kalev* son of Jephunneh
survived.

לח וִֽיהוֹשֻׁ֣עַ בִּן־נ֔וּן וְכָלֵ֖ב בֶּן־יְפֻנֶּ֑ה חָי֗וּ
מִן־הָֽאֲנָשִׁ֣ים הָהֵ֔ם הַהֹֽלְכִ֖ים לָת֥וּר אֶת־
הָאָֽרֶץ:

39 When *Moshe* repeated these words to all the
Israelites, the people were overcome by grief.

לט וַיְדַבֵּ֤ר מֹשֶׁה֙ אֶת־הַדְּבָרִ֣ים הָאֵ֔לֶּה אֶל־
כָּל־בְּנֵ֖י יִשְׂרָאֵ֑ל וַיִּֽתְאַבְּל֥וּ הָעָ֖ם מְאֹֽד:

40 Early next morning they set out toward the crest of
the hill country, saying, "We are prepared to go up
to the place that *Hashem* has spoken of, for we were
wrong."

מ וַיַּשְׁכִּ֣מוּ בַבֹּ֔קֶר וַיַּֽעֲל֥וּ אֶל־רֹאשׁ־הָהָ֖ר
לֵאמֹ֑ר הִנֶּ֗נּוּ וְעָלִ֛ינוּ אֶל־הַמָּק֛וֹם אֲשֶׁר־
אָמַ֥ר יְהֹוָ֖ה כִּ֥י חָטָֽאנוּ:

41 But *Moshe* said, "Why do you transgress *Hashem*'s
command? This will not succeed.

מא וַיֹּ֣אמֶר מֹשֶׁ֔ה לָ֥מָּה זֶּ֛ה אַתֶּ֥ם עֹֽבְרִ֖ים
אֶת־פִּ֣י יְהֹוָ֑ה וְהִ֖וא לֹ֥א תִצְלָֽח:

42 Do not go up, lest you be routed by your enemies,
for *Hashem* is not in your midst.

מב אַֽל־תַּֽעֲל֔וּ כִּ֛י אֵ֥ין יְהֹוָ֖ה בְּקִרְבְּכֶ֑ם וְלֹא֙
תִּנָּ֣גְפ֔וּ לִפְנֵ֖י אֹֽיְבֵיכֶֽם:

43 For the Amalekites and the Canaanites will be there to face you, and you will fall by the sword, inasmuch as you have turned from following *Hashem* and *Hashem* will not be with you."

מג כִּי הָעֲמָלֵקִי וְהַכְּנַעֲנִי שָׁם לִפְנֵיכֶם וּנְפַלְתֶּם בֶּחָרֶב כִּי־עַל־כֵּן שַׁבְתֶּם מֵאַחֲרֵי יְהֹוָה וְלֹא־יִהְיֶה יְהֹוָה עִמָּכֶם:

44 Yet defiantly they marched toward the crest of the hill country, though neither *Hashem*'s *Aron HaBrit* nor *Moshe* stirred from the camp.

מד וַיַּעְפִּלוּ לַעֲלוֹת אֶל־רֹאשׁ הָהָר וַאֲרוֹן בְּרִית־יְהֹוָה וּמֹשֶׁה לֹא־מָשׁוּ מִקֶּרֶב הַמַּחֲנֶה:

45 And the Amalekites and the Canaanites who dwelt in that hill country came down and dealt them a shattering blow at Hormah.

מה וַיֵּרֶד הָעֲמָלֵקִי וְהַכְּנַעֲנִי הַיֹּשֵׁב בָּהָר הַהוּא וַיַּכּוּם וַיַּכְּתוּם עַד־הַחָרְמָה:

15 1 *Hashem* spoke to *Moshe*, saying:

טו א וַיְדַבֵּר יְהֹוָה אֶל־מֹשֶׁה לֵּאמֹר:

2 Speak to *B'nei Yisrael* and say to them: When you enter the land that I am giving you to settle in,

ב דַּבֵּר אֶל־בְּנֵי יִשְׂרָאֵל וְאָמַרְתָּ אֲלֵהֶם כִּי תָבֹאוּ אֶל־אֶרֶץ מוֹשְׁבֹתֵיכֶם אֲשֶׁר אֲנִי נֹתֵן לָכֶם:

3 and would present an offering by fire to *Hashem* from the herd or from the flock, be it burnt offering or sacrifice, in fulfillment of a vow explicitly uttered, or as a freewill offering, or at your fixed occasions, producing an odor pleasing to *Hashem*:

ג וַעֲשִׂיתֶם אִשֶּׁה לַיהֹוָה עֹלָה אוֹ־זֶבַח לְפַלֵּא־נֶדֶר אוֹ בִנְדָבָה אוֹ בְּמֹעֲדֵיכֶם לַעֲשׂוֹת רֵיחַ נִיחֹחַ לַיהֹוָה מִן־הַבָּקָר אוֹ מִן־הַצֹּאן:

4 The person who presents the offering to *Hashem* shall bring as a meal offering: a tenth of a measure of choice flour with a quarter of a *hin* of oil mixed in.

ד וְהִקְרִיב הַמַּקְרִיב קָרְבָּנוֹ לַיהֹוָה מִנְחָה סֹלֶת עִשָּׂרוֹן בָּלוּל בִּרְבִעִית הַהִין שָׁמֶן:

5 You shall also offer, with the burnt offering or the sacrifice, a quarter of a *hin* of wine as a libation for each sheep.

ה וְיַיִן לַנֶּסֶךְ רְבִיעִית הַהִין תַּעֲשֶׂה עַל־הָעֹלָה אוֹ לַזָּבַח לַכֶּבֶשׂ הָאֶחָד:

6 In the case of a ram, you shall present as a meal offering: two-tenths of a measure of choice flour with a third of a *hin* of oil mixed in;

ו אוֹ לָאַיִל תַּעֲשֶׂה מִנְחָה סֹלֶת שְׁנֵי עֶשְׂרֹנִים בְּלוּלָה בַשֶּׁמֶן שְׁלִשִׁית הַהִין:

7 and a third of a *hin* of wine as a libation – as an offering of pleasing odor to *Hashem*.

ז וְיַיִן לַנֶּסֶךְ שְׁלִשִׁית הַהִין תַּקְרִיב רֵיחַ־נִיחֹחַ לַיהֹוָה:

8 And if it is an animal from the herd that you offer to *Hashem* as a burnt offering or as a sacrifice, in fulfillment of a vow explicitly uttered or as an offering of well-being,

ח וְכִי־תַעֲשֶׂה בֶן־בָּקָר עֹלָה אוֹ־זֶבַח לְפַלֵּא־נֶדֶר אוֹ־שְׁלָמִים לַיהֹוָה:

9 there shall be offered a meal offering along with the animal: three-tenths of a measure of choice flour with half a *hin* of oil mixed in;

ט וְהִקְרִיב עַל־בֶּן־הַבָּקָר מִנְחָה סֹלֶת שְׁלֹשָׁה עֶשְׂרֹנִים בָּלוּל בַּשֶּׁמֶן חֲצִי הַהִין:

10 and as libation you shall offer half a *hin* of wine – these being offerings by fire of pleasing odor to *Hashem*.

י וְיַיִן תַּקְרִיב לַנֶּסֶךְ חֲצִי הַהִין אִשֵּׁה רֵיחַ־נִיחֹחַ לַיהֹוָה:

11 Thus shall be done with each ox, with each ram, and with any sheep or goat,

12 as many as you offer; you shall do thus with each one, as many as there are.

13 Every citizen, when presenting an offering by fire of pleasing odor to *Hashem*, shall do so with them.

14 And when, throughout the ages, a stranger who has taken up residence with you, or one who lives among you, would present an offering by fire of pleasing odor to *Hashem* – as you do, so shall it be done by

15 the rest of the congregation. There shall be one law for you and for the resident stranger; it shall be a law for all time throughout the ages. You and the stranger shall be alike before *Hashem*;

16 the same ritual and the same rule shall apply to you and to the stranger who resides among you.

17 *Hashem* spoke to *Moshe*, saying:

18 Speak to *B'nei Yisrael* and say to them: When you enter the land to which I am taking you

19 and you eat of the bread of the land, you shall set some aside as a gift to *Hashem*:

20 as the first yield of your baking, you shall set aside a loaf as a gift; you shall set it aside as a gift like the gift from the threshing floor.

21 You shall make a gift to *Hashem* from the first yield of your baking, throughout the ages.

may-ray-SHEET a-ri-so-tay-KHEM ti-t'-NU la-do-NAI t'-ru-MAH l'-do-RO-tay-KHEM

22 If you unwittingly fail to observe any one of the commandments that *Hashem* has declared to *Moshe* –

יא כָּכָה יֵעָשֶׂה לַשּׁוֹר הָאֶחָד אוֹ לָאַיִל הָאֶחָד אוֹ־לַשֶּׂה בַכְּבָשִׂים אוֹ בָעִזִּים:

יב כַּמִּסְפָּר אֲשֶׁר תַּעֲשׂוּ כָּכָה תַּעֲשׂוּ לָאֶחָד כְּמִסְפָּרָם:

יג כָּל־הָאֶזְרָח יַעֲשֶׂה־כָּכָה אֶת־אֵלֶּה לְהַקְרִיב אִשֵּׁה רֵיחַ־נִיחֹחַ לַיהוָה:

יד וְכִי־יָגוּר אִתְּכֶם גֵּר אוֹ אֲשֶׁר־בְּתוֹכְכֶם לְדֹרֹתֵיכֶם וְעָשָׂה אִשֵּׁה רֵיחַ־נִיחֹחַ לַיהוָה כַּאֲשֶׁר תַּעֲשׂוּ כֵּן יַעֲשֶׂה:

טו הַקָּהָל חֻקָּה אַחַת לָכֶם וְלַגֵּר הַגָּר חֻקַּת עוֹלָם לְדֹרֹתֵיכֶם כָּכֶם כַּגֵּר יִהְיֶה לִפְנֵי יְהוָה:

טז תּוֹרָה אַחַת וּמִשְׁפָּט אֶחָד יִהְיֶה לָכֶם וְלַגֵּר הַגָּר אִתְּכֶם:

יז וַיְדַבֵּר יְהוָה אֶל־מֹשֶׁה לֵּאמֹר:

יח דַּבֵּר אֶל־בְּנֵי יִשְׂרָאֵל וְאָמַרְתָּ אֲלֵהֶם בְּבֹאֲכֶם אֶל־הָאָרֶץ אֲשֶׁר אֲנִי מֵבִיא אֶתְכֶם שָׁמָּה:

יט וְהָיָה בַּאֲכָלְכֶם מִלֶּחֶם הָאָרֶץ תָּרִימוּ תְרוּמָה לַיהוָה:

כ רֵאשִׁית עֲרִסֹתֵכֶם חַלָּה תָּרִימוּ תְרוּמָה כִּתְרוּמַת גֹּרֶן כֵּן תָּרִימוּ אֹתָהּ:

כא מֵרֵאשִׁית עֲרִסֹתֵיכֶם תִּתְּנוּ לַיהוָה תְּרוּמָה לְדֹרֹתֵיכֶם:

כב וְכִי תִשְׁגּוּ וְלֹא תַעֲשׂוּ אֵת כָּל־הַמִּצְוֹת הָאֵלֶּה אֲשֶׁר־דִּבֶּר יְהוָה אֶל־מֹשֶׁה:

Separating the challah from the dough

15:21 You shall make a gift to *Hashem* from the first yield of your baking The commandment to separate a portion of dough for the *Kohanim*, known as *challah* (חלה), went into effect only once the people entered the Land of Israel. This dough is given to the *Kohanim*, since they did not receive their own portion of land through which they could sustain themselves. The job of the *Kohanim* is to educate the people and work in the *Beit Hamikdash*, thereby providing the Nation with spiritual sustenance. In turn, they are provided with physical sustenance from the portions of the other tribes. Such is one's existence in *Eretz Yisrael* – the physical and spiritual are continuously intertwined.

23 anything that *Hashem* has enjoined upon you through *Moshe* – from the day that *Hashem* gave the commandment and on through the ages:

כג אֵת כָּל־אֲשֶׁר צִוָּה יְהֹוָה אֲלֵיכֶם בְּיַד־מֹשֶׁה מִן־הַיּוֹם אֲשֶׁר צִוָּה יְהֹוָה וָהָלְאָה לְדֹרֹתֵיכֶם:

24 If this was done unwittingly, through the inadvertence of the community, the whole community shall present one bull of the herd as a burnt offering of pleasing odor to *Hashem*, with its proper meal offering and libation, and one he-goat as a sin offering.

כד וְהָיָה אִם מֵעֵינֵי הָעֵדָה נֶעֶשְׂתָה לִשְׁגָגָה וְעָשׂוּ כָל־הָעֵדָה פַּר בֶּן־בָּקָר אֶחָד לְעֹלָה לְרֵיחַ נִיחֹחַ לַיהֹוָה וּמִנְחָתוֹ וְנִסְכּוֹ כַּמִּשְׁפָּט וּשְׂעִיר־עִזִּים אֶחָד לְחַטָּת:

25 The *Kohen* shall make expiation for the whole Israelite community and they shall be forgiven; for it was an error, and for their error they have brought their offering, an offering by fire to *Hashem* and their sin offering before *Hashem*.

כה וְכִפֶּר הַכֹּהֵן עַל־כָּל־עֲדַת בְּנֵי יִשְׂרָאֵל וְנִסְלַח לָהֶם כִּי־שְׁגָגָה הִוא וְהֵם הֵבִיאוּ אֶת־קָרְבָּנָם אִשֶּׁה לַיהֹוָה וְחַטָּאתָם לִפְנֵי יְהֹוָה עַל־שִׁגְגָתָם:

26 The whole Israelite community and the stranger residing among them shall be forgiven, for it happened to the entire people through error.

כו וְנִסְלַח לְכָל־עֲדַת בְּנֵי יִשְׂרָאֵל וְלַגֵּר הַגָּר בְּתוֹכָם כִּי לְכָל־הָעָם בִּשְׁגָגָה:

27 In case it is an individual who has sinned unwittingly, he shall offer a she-goat in its first year as a sin offering.

כז וְאִם־נֶפֶשׁ אַחַת תֶּחֱטָא בִשְׁגָגָה וְהִקְרִיבָה עֵז בַּת־שְׁנָתָהּ לְחַטָּאת:

28 The *Kohen* shall make expiation before *Hashem* on behalf of the person who erred, for he sinned unwittingly, making such expiation for him that he may be forgiven.

כח וְכִפֶּר הַכֹּהֵן עַל־הַנֶּפֶשׁ הַשֹּׁגֶגֶת בְּחֶטְאָה בִשְׁגָגָה לִפְנֵי יְהֹוָה לְכַפֵּר עָלָיו וְנִסְלַח לוֹ:

29 For the citizen among the Israelites and for the stranger who resides among them – you shall have one ritual for anyone who acts in error.

כט הָאֶזְרָח בִּבְנֵי יִשְׂרָאֵל וְלַגֵּר הַגָּר בְּתוֹכָם תּוֹרָה אַחַת יִהְיֶה לָכֶם לָעֹשֶׂה בִּשְׁגָגָה:

30 But the person, be he citizen or stranger, who acts defiantly reviles *Hashem*; that person shall be cut off from among his people.

ל וְהַנֶּפֶשׁ אֲשֶׁר־תַּעֲשֶׂה בְּיָד רָמָה מִן־הָאֶזְרָח וּמִן־הַגֵּר אֶת־יְהֹוָה הוּא מְגַדֵּף וְנִכְרְתָה הַנֶּפֶשׁ הַהִוא מִקֶּרֶב עַמָּהּ:

31 Because he has spurned the word of *Hashem* and violated His commandment, that person shall be cut off – he bears his guilt.

לא כִּי דְבַר־יְהֹוָה בָּזָה וְאֶת־מִצְוָתוֹ הֵפַר הִכָּרֵת תִּכָּרֵת הַנֶּפֶשׁ הַהִוא עֲוֹנָה בָהּ:

32 Once, when the Israelites were in the wilderness, they came upon a man gathering wood on the *Shabbat* day.

לב וַיִּהְיוּ בְנֵי־יִשְׂרָאֵל בַּמִּדְבָּר וַיִּמְצְאוּ אִישׁ מְקֹשֵׁשׁ עֵצִים בְּיוֹם הַשַּׁבָּת:

33 Those who found him as he was gathering wood brought him before *Moshe*, *Aharon*, and the whole community.

לג וַיַּקְרִיבוּ אֹתוֹ הַמֹּצְאִים אֹתוֹ מְקֹשֵׁשׁ עֵצִים אֶל־מֹשֶׁה וְאֶל־אַהֲרֹן וְאֶל כָּל־הָעֵדָה:

34 He was placed in custody, for it had not been specified what should be done to him.

לד וַיַּנִּיחוּ אֹתוֹ בַּמִּשְׁמָר כִּי לֹא פֹרַשׁ מַה־יֵּעָשֶׂה לוֹ:

35 Then *Hashem* said to *Moshe*, "The man shall be put to death: the whole community shall pelt him with stones outside the camp."

לה וַיֹּאמֶר יְהוָה אֶל־מֹשֶׁה מוֹת יוּמַת הָאִישׁ רָגוֹם אֹתוֹ בָאֲבָנִים כָּל־הָעֵדָה מִחוּץ לַמַּחֲנֶה:

36 So the whole community took him outside the camp and stoned him to death – as *Hashem* had commanded *Moshe*.

לו וַיֹּצִיאוּ אֹתוֹ כָּל־הָעֵדָה אֶל־מִחוּץ לַמַּחֲנֶה וַיִּרְגְּמוּ אֹתוֹ בָּאֲבָנִים וַיָּמֹת כַּאֲשֶׁר צִוָּה יְהוָה אֶת־מֹשֶׁה:

37 *Hashem* said to *Moshe* as follows:

לז וַיֹּאמֶר יְהוָה אֶל־מֹשֶׁה לֵּאמֹר:

38 Speak to *B'nei Yisrael* and instruct them to make for themselves fringes on the corners of their garments throughout the ages; let them attach a cord of blue to the fringe at each corner.

לח דַּבֵּר אֶל־בְּנֵי יִשְׂרָאֵל וְאָמַרְתָּ אֲלֵהֶם וְעָשׂוּ לָהֶם צִיצִת עַל־כַּנְפֵי בִגְדֵיהֶם לְדֹרֹתָם וְנָתְנוּ עַל־צִיצִת הַכָּנָף פְּתִיל תְּכֵלֶת:

*da-BAYR el b'-NAY yis-ra-AYL v'-a-mar-TA a-lay-HEM v'-a-SU
la-HEM tzee-TZIT al kan-FAY vig-day-HEM l'-do-ro-TAM
v'-na-t'-NU al tzee-TZIT ha-ka-NAF p'-TEEL t'-KHAY-let*

39 That shall be your fringe; look at it and recall all the commandments of *Hashem* and observe them, so that you do not follow your heart and eyes in your lustful urge.

לט וְהָיָה לָכֶם לְצִיצִת וּרְאִיתֶם אֹתוֹ וּזְכַרְתֶּם אֶת־כָּל־מִצְוֺת יְהוָה וַעֲשִׂיתֶם אֹתָם וְלֹא־תָתוּרוּ אַחֲרֵי לְבַבְכֶם וְאַחֲרֵי עֵינֵיכֶם אֲשֶׁר־אַתֶּם זֹנִים אַחֲרֵיהֶם:

40 Thus you shall be reminded to observe all My commandments and to be holy to your God.

מ לְמַעַן תִּזְכְּרוּ וַעֲשִׂיתֶם אֶת־כָּל־מִצְוֺתָי וִהְיִיתֶם קְדֹשִׁים לֵאלֹהֵיכֶם:

41 I *Hashem* am your God, who brought you out of the land of Egypt to be your God: I, *Hashem* your God.

מא אֲנִי יְהוָה אֱלֹהֵיכֶם אֲשֶׁר הוֹצֵאתִי אֶתְכֶם מֵאֶרֶץ מִצְרַיִם לִהְיוֹת לָכֶם לֵאלֹהִים אֲנִי יְהוָה אֱלֹהֵיכֶם:

16 1 Now *Korach*, son of Izhar son of *Kehat* son of *Levi*, betook himself, along with *Datan* and *Aviram* sons of *Eliav*, and On son of Peleth – descendants of *Reuven* –

טז א וַיִּקַּח קֹרַח בֶּן־יִצְהָר בֶּן־קְהָת בֶּן־לֵוִי וְדָתָן וַאֲבִירָם בְּנֵי אֱלִיאָב וְאוֹן בֶּן־פֶּלֶת בְּנֵי רְאוּבֵן:

2 to rise up against *Moshe*, together with two hundred and fifty Israelites, chieftains of the community, chosen in the assembly, men of repute.

ב וַיָּקֻמוּ לִפְנֵי מֹשֶׁה וַאֲנָשִׁים מִבְּנֵי־ יִשְׂרָאֵל חֲמִשִּׁים וּמָאתָיִם נְשִׂיאֵי עֵדָה קְרִאֵי מוֹעֵד אַנְשֵׁי־שֵׁם:

15:38 A cord of blue The biblical blue color *techelet* (תכלת) is mentioned numerous times in the Bible. *Rashi* explains that this color, worn on the fringes known as *tzitzit* (ציצית) placed on the corners of four-cornered garments, is meant to remind us of the sky, and, by extension, of *Hashem* and His constant presence in our lives. For close to fifteen hundred years, the source of this special blue dye had been lost to the world. In an exciting discovery in recent years, marine biologists together with Talmudic researchers have identified the source of *techelet* as a small snail found off the coast of northern Israel, near Haifa. Today, for the first time in centuries, people are once again wearing *techelet* on their *tzitzit*. From even the smallest sea creature, we continue to see the wonders of the Bible come to life in *Eretz Yisrael*.

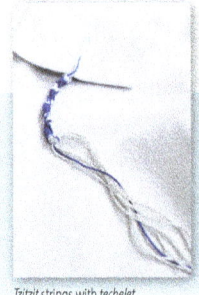

Tzitzit strings with *techelet*

³ They combined against *Moshe* and *Aharon* and said to them, "You have gone too far! For all the community are holy, all of them, and *Hashem* is in their midst. Why then do you raise yourselves above *Hashem*'s congregation?"

ג וַיִּקָּהֲלוּ עַל־מֹשֶׁה וְעַל־אַהֲרֹן וַיֹּאמְרוּ אֲלֵהֶם רַב־לָכֶם כִּי כָל־הָעֵדָה כֻּלָּם קְדֹשִׁים וּבְתוֹכָם יְהוָה וּמַדּוּעַ תִּתְנַשְּׂאוּ עַל־קְהַל יְהוָה:

> va-yi-ka-ha-LU al mo-SHEH v'-al a-ha-RON va-yo-m'-RU a-lay-HEM
> rav la-KHEM KEE khol ha-ay-DAH ku-LAM k'do-SHEEM uv-to-KHAM
> a-do-NAI u-ma-DU-a tit-na-s'-U al k'-HAL a-do-NAI

⁴ When *Moshe* heard this, he fell on his face.

ד וַיִּשְׁמַע מֹשֶׁה וַיִּפֹּל עַל־פָּנָיו:

⁵ Then he spoke to *Korach* and all his company, saying, "Come morning, *Hashem* will make known who is His and who is holy, and will grant him access to Himself; He will grant access to the one He has chosen.

ה וַיְדַבֵּר אֶל־קֹרַח וְאֶל־כָּל־עֲדָתוֹ לֵאמֹר בֹּקֶר וְיֹדַע יְהוָה אֶת־אֲשֶׁר־לוֹ וְאֶת־הַקָּדוֹשׁ וְהִקְרִיב אֵלָיו וְאֵת אֲשֶׁר יִבְחַר־בּוֹ יַקְרִיב אֵלָיו:

⁶ Do this: You, *Korach* and all your band, take fire pans,

ו זֹאת עֲשׂוּ קְחוּ־לָכֶם מַחְתּוֹת קֹרַח וְכָל־עֲדָתוֹ:

⁷ and tomorrow put fire in them and lay incense on them before *Hashem*. Then the man whom *Hashem* chooses, he shall be the holy one. You have gone too far, sons of *Levi*!"

ז וּתְנוּ בָהֵן אֵשׁ וְשִׂימוּ עֲלֵיהֶן קְטֹרֶת לִפְנֵי יְהוָה מָחָר וְהָיָה הָאִישׁ אֲשֶׁר־יִבְחַר יְהוָה הוּא הַקָּדוֹשׁ רַב־לָכֶם בְּנֵי לֵוִי:

⁸ *Moshe* said further to *Korach*, "Hear me, sons of *Levi*.

ח וַיֹּאמֶר מֹשֶׁה אֶל־קֹרַח שִׁמְעוּ־נָא בְּנֵי לֵוִי:

⁹ Is it not enough for you that the God of *Yisrael* has set you apart from the community of *Yisrael* and given you access to Him, to perform the duties of *Hashem*'s *Mishkan* and to minister to the community and serve them?

ט הַמְעַט מִכֶּם כִּי־הִבְדִּיל אֱלֹהֵי יִשְׂרָאֵל אֶתְכֶם מֵעֲדַת יִשְׂרָאֵל לְהַקְרִיב אֶתְכֶם אֵלָיו לַעֲבֹד אֶת־עֲבֹדַת מִשְׁכַּן יְהוָה וְלַעֲמֹד לִפְנֵי הָעֵדָה לְשָׁרְתָם:

¹⁰ Now that He has advanced you and all your fellow *Leviim* with you, do you seek the priesthood too?

י וַיַּקְרֵב אֹתְךָ וְאֶת־כָּל־אַחֶיךָ בְנֵי־לֵוִי אִתָּךְ וּבִקַּשְׁתֶּם גַּם־כְּהֻנָּה:

¹¹ Truly, it is against *Hashem* that you and all your company have banded together. For who is *Aharon* that you should rail against him?"

יא לָכֵן אַתָּה וְכָל־עֲדָתְךָ הַנֹּעָדִים עַל־יְהוָה וְאַהֲרֹן מַה־הוּא כִּי תלונו [תַלִּינוּ] עָלָיו:

Blowing the *shofar* (ram's horn) against a cloudy sky

16:3 Why then do you raise yourselves above *Hashem's* congregation? *Korach* rebels against his cousins *Moshe* and *Aharon*, accusing them of taking positions of power for themselves. He declares that the entire Nation of Israel is holy, and therefore questions why *Moshe* and *Aharon* have raised themselves above the rest of the congregation. In making this claim, *Korach* not only implies that *Moshe* and *Aharon* inappropriately chose the leadership positions for themselves, thereby denying *Hashem's* role in their appointment. He also makes the erroneous claim that every individual in the nation is on the same level of holiness. While it is true that everyone is endowed with an element of Godliness, it is up to each person to elevate himself or herself to even greater levels of holiness. The exact degree of a person's holiness, therefore, depends on their individual achievements.

12 *Moshe* sent for *Datan* and *Aviram*, sons of *Eliav*; but they said, "We will not come!

יב וַיִּשְׁלַ֣ח מֹשֶׁ֔ה לִקְרֹ֛א לְדָתָ֥ן וְלַאֲבִירָ֖ם בְּנֵ֣י אֱלִיאָ֑ב וַיֹּאמְר֖וּ לֹ֥א נַעֲלֶֽה׃

13 Is it not enough that you brought us from a land flowing with milk and honey to have us die in the wilderness, that you would also lord it over us?

יג הַמְעַ֗ט כִּ֤י הֶעֱלִיתָ֙נוּ֙ מֵאֶ֜רֶץ זָבַ֤ת חָלָב֙ וּדְבַ֔שׁ לַהֲמִיתֵ֖נוּ בַּמִּדְבָּ֑ר כִּֽי־תִשְׂתָּרֵ֥ר עָלֵ֖ינוּ גַּם־הִשְׂתָּרֵֽר׃

14 Even if you had brought us to a land flowing with milk and honey, and given us possession of fields and vineyards, should you gouge out those men's eyes? We will not come!"

יד אַ֡ף לֹ֣א אֶל־אֶ֩רֶץ֩ זָבַ֨ת חָלָ֜ב וּדְבַ֗שׁ הֲבִ֣יאֹתָ֔נוּ וַתִּ֨תֶּן־לָ֔נוּ נַחֲלַ֖ת שָׂדֶ֣ה וָכָ֑רֶם הַעֵינֵ֞י הָאֲנָשִׁ֥ים הָהֵ֛ם תְּנַקֵּ֖ר לֹ֥א נַעֲלֶֽה׃

15 *Moshe* was much aggrieved and he said to *Hashem*, "Pay no regard to their oblation. I have not taken the ass of any one of them, nor have I wronged any one of them."

טו וַיִּ֤חַר לְמֹשֶׁה֙ מְאֹ֔ד וַיֹּ֙אמֶר֙ אֶל־יְהֹוָ֔ה אַל־תֵּ֖פֶן אֶל־מִנְחָתָ֑ם לֹ֣א חֲמ֤וֹר אֶחָד֙ מֵהֶ֣ם נָשָׂ֔אתִי וְלֹ֥א הֲרֵעֹ֖תִי אֶת־אַחַ֥ד מֵהֶֽם׃

16 And *Moshe* said to *Korach*, "Tomorrow, you and all your company appear before *Hashem*, you and they and *Aharon*.

טז וַיֹּ֤אמֶר מֹשֶׁה֙ אֶל־קֹ֔רַח אַתָּה֙ וְכׇל־עֲדָ֣תְךָ֔ הֱי֖וּ לִפְנֵ֣י יְהֹוָ֑ה אַתָּ֥ה וָהֵ֛ם וְאַהֲרֹ֖ן מָחָֽר׃

17 Each of you take his fire pan and lay incense on it, and each of you bring his fire pan before *Hashem*, two hundred and fifty fire pans; you and *Aharon* also [bring] your fire pans."

יז וּקְח֣וּ ׀ אִ֣ישׁ מַחְתָּת֗וֹ וּנְתַתֶּ֤ם עֲלֵיהֶם֙ קְטֹ֔רֶת וְהִקְרַבְתֶּ֞ם לִפְנֵ֤י יְהֹוָה֙ אִ֣ישׁ מַחְתָּת֔וֹ חֲמִשִּׁ֥ים וּמָאתַ֖יִם מַחְתֹּ֑ת וְאַתָּ֥ה וְאַהֲרֹ֖ן אִ֥ישׁ מַחְתָּתֽוֹ׃

18 Each of them took his fire pan, put fire in it, laid incense on it, and took his place at the entrance of the Tent of Meeting, as did *Moshe* and *Aharon*.

יח וַיִּקְח֞וּ אִ֣ישׁ מַחְתָּת֗וֹ וַיִּתְּנ֤וּ עֲלֵיהֶם֙ אֵ֔שׁ וַיָּשִׂ֥ימוּ עֲלֵיהֶ֖ם קְטֹ֑רֶת וַֽיַּעַמְד֗וּ פֶּ֛תַח אֹ֥הֶל מוֹעֵ֖ד וּמֹשֶׁ֥ה וְאַהֲרֹֽן׃

19 *Korach* gathered the whole community against them at the entrance of the Tent of Meeting. Then the Presence of *Hashem* appeared to the whole community,

יט וַיַּקְהֵ֨ל עֲלֵיהֶ֥ם קֹ֙רַח֙ אֶת־כׇּל־הָ֣עֵדָ֔ה אֶל־פֶּ֖תַח אֹ֣הֶל מוֹעֵ֑ד וַיֵּרָ֥א כְבוֹד־יְהֹוָ֖ה אֶל־כׇּל־הָעֵדָֽה׃

20 and *Hashem* spoke to *Moshe* and *Aharon*, saying,

כ וַיְדַבֵּ֣ר יְהֹוָ֔ה אֶל־מֹשֶׁ֥ה וְאֶֽל־אַהֲרֹ֖ן לֵאמֹֽר׃

21 "Stand back from this community that I may annihilate them in an instant!"

כא הִבָּ֣דְל֔וּ מִתּ֖וֹךְ הָעֵדָ֣ה הַזֹּ֑את וַאֲכַלֶּ֥ה אֹתָ֖ם כְּרָֽגַע׃

22 But they fell on their faces and said, "O *Hashem*, Source of the breath of all flesh! When one man sins, will You be wrathful with the whole community?"

כב וַיִּפְּל֤וּ עַל־פְּנֵיהֶם֙ וַיֹּ֣אמְר֔וּ אֵ֕ל אֱלֹהֵ֥י הָרוּחֹ֖ת לְכׇל־בָּשָׂ֑ר הָאִ֤ישׁ אֶחָד֙ יֶחֱטָ֔א וְעַ֥ל כׇּל־הָעֵדָ֖ה תִּקְצֹֽף׃

23 *Hashem* spoke to *Moshe*, saying,

כג וַיְדַבֵּ֥ר יְהֹוָ֖ה אֶל־מֹשֶׁ֥ה לֵּאמֹֽר׃

24 "Speak to the community and say: Withdraw from about the abodes of *Korach, Datan*, and *Aviram*."

כד דַּבֵּ֥ר אֶל־הָעֵדָ֖ה לֵאמֹ֑ר הֵֽעָלוּ֙ מִסָּבִ֔יב לְמִשְׁכַּן־קֹ֖רַח דָּתָ֥ן וַאֲבִירָֽם׃

25 *Moshe* rose and went to *Datan* and *Aviram*, the elders of *Yisrael* following him.

כה וַיָּ֣קׇם מֹשֶׁ֔ה וַיֵּ֖לֶךְ אֶל־דָּתָ֣ן וַאֲבִירָ֑ם וַיֵּלְכ֥וּ אַחֲרָ֖יו זִקְנֵ֥י יִשְׂרָאֵֽל׃

26 He addressed the community, saying, "Move away from the tents of these wicked men and touch nothing that belongs to them, lest you be wiped out for all their sins."

כו וַיְדַבֵּר אֶל־הָעֵדָה לֵאמֹר סוּרוּ נָא מֵעַל אָהֳלֵי הָאֲנָשִׁים הָרְשָׁעִים הָאֵלֶּה וְאַל־תִּגְּעוּ בְּכָל־אֲשֶׁר לָהֶם פֶּן־תִּסָּפוּ בְּכָל־חַטֹּאתָם:

27 So they withdrew from about the abodes of *Korach*, *Datan*, and *Aviram*. Now *Datan* and *Aviram* had come out and they stood at the entrance of their tents, with their wives, their children, and their little ones.

כז וַיֵּעָלוּ מֵעַל מִשְׁכַּן־קֹרַח דָּתָן וַאֲבִירָם מִסָּבִיב וְדָתָן וַאֲבִירָם יָצְאוּ נִצָּבִים פֶּתַח אָהֳלֵיהֶם וּנְשֵׁיהֶם וּבְנֵיהֶם וְטַפָּם:

28 And *Moshe* said, "By this you shall know that it was *Hashem* who sent me to do all these things; that they are not of my own devising:

כח וַיֹּאמֶר מֹשֶׁה בְּזֹאת תֵּדְעוּן כִּי־יְהוָה שְׁלָחַנִי לַעֲשׂוֹת אֵת כָּל־הַמַּעֲשִׂים הָאֵלֶּה כִּי־לֹא מִלִּבִּי:

29 if these men die as all men do, if their lot be the common fate of all mankind, it was not *Hashem* who sent me.

כט אִם־כְּמוֹת כָּל־הָאָדָם יְמֻתוּן אֵלֶּה וּפְקֻדַּת כָּל־הָאָדָם יִפָּקֵד עֲלֵיהֶם לֹא יְהוָה שְׁלָחָנִי:

30 But if *Hashem* brings about something unheard-of, so that the ground opens its mouth and swallows them up with all that belongs to them, and they go down alive into Sheol, you shall know that these men have spurned *Hashem*."

ל וְאִם־בְּרִיאָה יִבְרָא יְהוָה וּפָצְתָה הָאֲדָמָה אֶת־פִּיהָ וּבָלְעָה אֹתָם וְאֶת־כָּל־אֲשֶׁר לָהֶם וְיָרְדוּ חַיִּים שְׁאֹלָה וִידַעְתֶּם כִּי נִאֲצוּ הָאֲנָשִׁים הָאֵלֶּה אֶת־יְהוָה:

31 Scarcely had he finished speaking all these words when the ground under them burst asunder,

לא וַיְהִי כְּכַלֹּתוֹ לְדַבֵּר אֵת כָּל־הַדְּבָרִים הָאֵלֶּה וַתִּבָּקַע הָאֲדָמָה אֲשֶׁר תַּחְתֵּיהֶם:

32 and the earth opened its mouth and swallowed them up with their households, all *Korach*'s people and all their possessions.

לב וַתִּפְתַּח הָאָרֶץ אֶת־פִּיהָ וַתִּבְלַע אֹתָם וְאֶת־בָּתֵּיהֶם וְאֵת כָּל־הָאָדָם אֲשֶׁר לְקֹרַח וְאֵת כָּל־הָרְכוּשׁ:

33 They went down alive into Sheol, with all that belonged to them; the earth closed over them and they vanished from the midst of the congregation.

לג וַיֵּרְדוּ הֵם וְכָל־אֲשֶׁר לָהֶם חַיִּים שְׁאֹלָה וַתְּכַס עֲלֵיהֶם הָאָרֶץ וַיֹּאבְדוּ מִתּוֹךְ הַקָּהָל:

34 All *Yisrael* around them fled at their shrieks, for they said, "The earth might swallow us!"

לד וְכָל־יִשְׂרָאֵל אֲשֶׁר סְבִיבֹתֵיהֶם נָסוּ לְקֹלָם כִּי אָמְרוּ פֶּן־תִּבְלָעֵנוּ הָאָרֶץ:

35 And a fire went forth from *Hashem* and consumed the two hundred and fifty men offering the incense.

לה וְאֵשׁ יָצְאָה מֵאֵת יְהוָה וַתֹּאכַל אֵת הַחֲמִשִּׁים וּמָאתַיִם אִישׁ מַקְרִיבֵי הַקְּטֹרֶת:

17 1 *Hashem* spoke to *Moshe*, saying:

יז א וַיְדַבֵּר יְהוָה אֶל־מֹשֶׁה לֵּאמֹר:

2 Order *Elazar* son of *Aharon* the *Kohen* to remove the fire pans – for they have become sacred – from among the charred remains; and scatter the coals abroad.

ב אֱמֹר אֶל־אֶלְעָזָר בֶּן־אַהֲרֹן הַכֹּהֵן וְיָרֵם אֶת־הַמַּחְתֹּת מִבֵּין הַשְּׂרֵפָה וְאֶת־הָאֵשׁ זְרֵה־הָלְאָה כִּי קָדֵשׁוּ:

3 [Remove] the fire pans of those who have sinned at the cost of their lives, and let them be made into hammered sheets as plating for the *Mizbayach* – for once they have been used for offering to *Hashem*, they have become sacred – and let them serve as a warning to the people of *Yisrael*.

ג אֶת־מַחְתּוֹת הַחַטָּאִים הָאֵלֶּה בְּנַפְשֹׁתָם וְעָשׂוּ אֹתָם רִקֻּעֵי פַחִים צִפּוּי לַמִּזְבֵּחַ כִּי־הִקְרִיבֻם לִפְנֵי־יְהוָה וַיִּקְדָּשׁוּ וְיִהְיוּ לְאוֹת לִבְנֵי יִשְׂרָאֵל:

4 *Elazar* the *Kohen* took the copper fire pans which had been used for offering by those who died in the fire; and they were hammered into plating for the *Mizbayach*,

ד וַיִּקַּח אֶלְעָזָר הַכֹּהֵן אֵת מַחְתּוֹת הַנְּחֹשֶׁת אֲשֶׁר הִקְרִיבוּ הַשְּׂרֻפִים וַיְרַקְּעוּם צִפּוּי לַמִּזְבֵּחַ:

5 as *Hashem* had ordered him through *Moshe*. It was to be a reminder to the Israelites, so that no outsider – one not of *Aharon*'s offspring – should presume to offer incense before *Hashem* and suffer the fate of *Korach* and his band.

ה זִכָּרוֹן לִבְנֵי יִשְׂרָאֵל לְמַעַן אֲשֶׁר לֹא־יִקְרַב אִישׁ זָר אֲשֶׁר לֹא מִזֶּרַע אַהֲרֹן הוּא לְהַקְטִיר קְטֹרֶת לִפְנֵי יְהוָה וְלֹא־יִהְיֶה כְקֹרַח וְכַעֲדָתוֹ כַּאֲשֶׁר דִּבֶּר יְהוָה בְּיַד־מֹשֶׁה לוֹ:

6 Next day the whole Israelite community railed against *Moshe* and *Aharon*, saying, "You two have brought death upon *Hashem*'s people!"

ו וַיִּלֹּנוּ כָּל־עֲדַת בְּנֵי־יִשְׂרָאֵל מִמָּחֳרָת עַל־מֹשֶׁה וְעַל־אַהֲרֹן לֵאמֹר אַתֶּם הֲמִתֶּם אֶת־עַם יְהוָה:

7 But as the community gathered against them, *Moshe* and *Aharon* turned toward the Tent of Meeting; the cloud had covered it and the Presence of *Hashem* appeared.

ז וַיְהִי בְּהִקָּהֵל הָעֵדָה עַל־מֹשֶׁה וְעַל־אַהֲרֹן וַיִּפְנוּ אֶל־אֹהֶל מוֹעֵד וְהִנֵּה כִסָּהוּ הֶעָנָן וַיֵּרָא כְּבוֹד יְהוָה:

8 When *Moshe* and *Aharon* reached the Tent of Meeting,

ח וַיָּבֹא מֹשֶׁה וְאַהֲרֹן אֶל־פְּנֵי אֹהֶל מוֹעֵד:

9 *Hashem* spoke to *Moshe*, saying,

ט וַיְדַבֵּר יְהוָה אֶל־מֹשֶׁה לֵּאמֹר:

10 "Remove yourselves from this community, that I may annihilate them in an instant." They fell on their faces.

י הֵרֹמּוּ מִתּוֹךְ הָעֵדָה הַזֹּאת וַאֲכַלֶּה אֹתָם כְּרָגַע וַיִּפְּלוּ עַל־פְּנֵיהֶם:

11 Then *Moshe* said to *Aharon*, "Take the fire pan, and put on it fire from the *Mizbayach*. Add incense and take it quickly to the community and make expiation for them. For wrath has gone forth from *Hashem*: the plague has begun!"

יא וַיֹּאמֶר מֹשֶׁה אֶל־אַהֲרֹן קַח אֶת־הַמַּחְתָּה וְתֶן־עָלֶיהָ אֵשׁ מֵעַל הַמִּזְבֵּחַ וְשִׂים קְטֹרֶת וְהוֹלֵךְ מְהֵרָה אֶל־הָעֵדָה וְכַפֵּר עֲלֵיהֶם כִּי־יָצָא הַקֶּצֶף מִלִּפְנֵי יְהוָה הֵחֵל הַנָּגֶף:

12 *Aharon* took it, as *Moshe* had ordered, and ran to the midst of the congregation, where the plague had begun among the people. He put on the incense and made expiation for the people;

יב וַיִּקַּח אַהֲרֹן כַּאֲשֶׁר דִּבֶּר מֹשֶׁה וַיָּרָץ אֶל־תּוֹךְ הַקָּהָל וְהִנֵּה הֵחֵל הַנֶּגֶף בָּעָם וַיִּתֵּן אֶת־הַקְּטֹרֶת וַיְכַפֵּר עַל־הָעָם:

13 he stood between the dead and the living until the plague was checked.

יג וַיַּעֲמֹד בֵּין־הַמֵּתִים וּבֵין הַחַיִּים וַתֵּעָצַר הַמַּגֵּפָה:

14 Those who died of the plague came to fourteen thousand and seven hundred, aside from those who died on account of *Korach*.

יד וַיִּהְיוּ הַמֵּתִים בַּמַּגֵּפָה אַרְבָּעָה עָשָׂר אֶלֶף וּשְׁבַע מֵאוֹת מִלְּבַד הַמֵּתִים עַל־דְּבַר־קֹרַח:

¹⁵ *Aharon* then returned to *Moshe* at the entrance of the Tent of Meeting, since the plague was checked.

טו וַיָּשָׁב אַהֲרֹן אֶל־מֹשֶׁה אֶל־פֶּתַח אֹהֶל מוֹעֵד וְהַמַּגֵּפָה נֶעֱצָרָה:

¹⁶ *Hashem* spoke to *Moshe*, saying:

טז וַיְדַבֵּר יְהוָֹה אֶל־מֹשֶׁה לֵּאמֹר:

¹⁷ Speak to *B'nei Yisrael* and take from them – from the chieftains of their ancestral houses – one staff for each chieftain of an ancestral house: twelve staffs in all. Inscribe each man's name on his staff,

יז דַּבֵּר ׀ אֶל־בְּנֵי יִשְׂרָאֵל וְקַח מֵאִתָּם מַטֶּה מַטֶּה לְבֵית אָב מֵאֵת כָּל־נְשִׂיאֵהֶם לְבֵית אֲבֹתָם שְׁנֵים עָשָׂר מַטּוֹת אִישׁ אֶת־שְׁמוֹ תִּכְתֹּב עַל־מַטֵּהוּ:

¹⁸ there being one staff for each head of an ancestral house; also inscribe *Aharon*'s name on the staff of *Levi*.

יח וְאֵת שֵׁם אַהֲרֹן תִּכְתֹּב עַל־מַטֵּה לֵוִי כִּי מַטֶּה אֶחָד לְרֹאשׁ בֵּית אֲבוֹתָם:

¹⁹ Deposit them in the Tent of Meeting before the Pact, where I meet with you.

יט וְהִנַּחְתָּם בְּאֹהֶל מוֹעֵד לִפְנֵי הָעֵדוּת אֲשֶׁר אִוָּעֵד לָכֶם שָׁמָּה:

²⁰ The staff of the man whom I choose shall sprout, and I will rid Myself of the incessant mutterings of the Israelites against you.

כ וְהָיָה הָאִישׁ אֲשֶׁר אֶבְחַר־בּוֹ מַטֵּהוּ יִפְרָח וַהֲשִׁכֹּתִי מֵעָלַי אֶת־תְּלֻנּוֹת בְּנֵי יִשְׂרָאֵל אֲשֶׁר הֵם מַלִּינִם עֲלֵיכֶם:

²¹ *Moshe* spoke thus to the Israelites. Their chieftains gave him a staff for each chieftain of an ancestral house, twelve staffs in all; among these staffs was that of *Aharon*.

כא וַיְדַבֵּר מֹשֶׁה אֶל־בְּנֵי יִשְׂרָאֵל וַיִּתְּנוּ אֵלָיו ׀ כָּל־נְשִׂיאֵיהֶם מַטֶּה לְנָשִׂיא אֶחָד מַטֶּה לְנָשִׂיא אֶחָד לְבֵית אֲבֹתָם שְׁנֵים עָשָׂר מַטּוֹת וּמַטֵּה אַהֲרֹן בְּתוֹךְ מַטּוֹתָם:

²² *Moshe* deposited the staffs before *Hashem*, in the Tent of the Pact.

כב וַיַּנַּח מֹשֶׁה אֶת־הַמַּטֹּת לִפְנֵי יְהוָֹה בְּאֹהֶל הָעֵדֻת:

²³ The next day *Moshe* entered the Tent of the Pact, and there the staff of *Aharon* of the house of *Levi* had sprouted: it had brought forth sprouts, produced blossoms, and borne almonds.

כג וַיְהִי מִמָּחֳרָת וַיָּבֹא מֹשֶׁה אֶל־אֹהֶל הָעֵדוּת וְהִנֵּה פָּרַח מַטֵּה־אַהֲרֹן לְבֵית לֵוִי וַיֹּצֵא פֶרַח וַיָּצֵץ צִיץ וַיִּגְמֹל שְׁקֵדִים:

vai-HEE mi-ma-kha-RAT va-ya-VO mo-SHEH el O-hel ha-ay-DUT
v'-hi-NAY pa-RAKH ma-tay a-ha-RON l'-VAYT lay-VEE va-YO-tzay
FE-rakh va-YA-tzaytz TZEETZ va-yig-MOL sh'-kay-DEEM

17:23 The staff of *Aharon* of the house of *Levi* had sprouted Legendary Israeli storyteller Rabbi S.Z. Kahana tells a story about three clergymen who were on a visit to Mount Zion in 1965. When they asked the Jewish curator of Mt. Zion why the Jews insist on claiming Jerusalem as the capital of the Israel instead of letting it remain an international city, he replied with an example from this chapter. When *Moshe* appointed *Aharon* as the *Kohen Gadol*, 'High Priest,' the people objected and murmured. Neither the earthquake that swallowed *Korach* and his followers nor the plague that followed were enough to convince the people that *Aharon* had been appointed

Mount Zion

by God. It was only once his staff blossomed, showing the vitality of life, that they accepted *Aharon* as the *Kohen*. The curator invited the visiting clergymen to climb up with him to the mountain's observation tower. "From here, you can see both the old and new Jerusalem. In the old Arab-controlled section of the city, as you can observe, there is desolation: ruins, desert, and rocks. On our side is the new Jerusalem, where over 150,000 Jews have settled. You can see our new homes and schools, the new hospital and the new university. Everywhere you look, you see life, growth, and vitality. You ask: To whom does Jerusalem belong? It belongs to those who make it bud and blossom, to those who make it live and grow." Half a century later, Jewish Jerusalem continues to show even more incredible signs of life and vitality. *Yerushalayim* in Jewish hands is indeed ordained by *Hashem*, just as the budding of *Aharon*'s staff demonstrated his divine selection.

24 *Moshe* then brought out all the staffs from before *Hashem* to all the Israelites; each identified and recovered his staff.

כד וַיֹּצֵא מֹשֶׁה אֶת־כָּל־הַמַּטֹּת מִלִּפְנֵי יְהֹוָה אֶל־כָּל־בְּנֵי יִשְׂרָאֵל וַיִּרְאוּ וַיִּקְחוּ אִישׁ מַטֵּהוּ:

25 *Hashem* said to *Moshe*, "Put *Aharon*'s staff back before the Pact, to be kept as a lesson to rebels, so that their mutterings against Me may cease, lest they die."

כה וַיֹּאמֶר יְהֹוָה אֶל־מֹשֶׁה הָשֵׁב אֶת־מַטֵּה אַהֲרֹן לִפְנֵי הָעֵדוּת לְמִשְׁמֶרֶת לְאוֹת לִבְנֵי־מֶרִי וּתְכַל תְּלוּנֹּתָם מֵעָלַי וְלֹא יָמֻתוּ:

26 This *Moshe* did; just as *Hashem* had commanded him, so he did.

כו וַיַּעַשׂ מֹשֶׁה כַּאֲשֶׁר צִוָּה יְהֹוָה אֹתוֹ כֵּן עָשָׂה:

27 But the Israelites said to *Moshe*, "Lo, we perish! We are lost, all of us lost!

כז וַיֹּאמְרוּ בְּנֵי יִשְׂרָאֵל אֶל־מֹשֶׁה לֵאמֹר הֵן גָּוַעְנוּ אָבַדְנוּ כֻּלָּנוּ אָבַדְנוּ:

28 Everyone who so much as ventures near *Hashem*'s *Mishkan* must die. Alas, we are doomed to perish!"

כח כֹּל הַקָּרֵב הַקָּרֵב אֶל־מִשְׁכַּן יְהֹוָה יָמוּת הַאִם תַּמְנוּ לִגְוֹעַ:

18 1 *Hashem* said to *Aharon*: You and your sons and the ancestral house under your charge shall bear any guilt connected with the sanctuary; you and your sons alone shall bear any guilt connected with your priesthood.

יח א וַיֹּאמֶר יְהֹוָה אֶל־אַהֲרֹן אַתָּה וּבָנֶיךָ וּבֵית־אָבִיךָ אִתָּךְ תִּשְׂאוּ אֶת־עֲוֹן הַמִּקְדָּשׁ וְאַתָּה וּבָנֶיךָ אִתָּךְ תִּשְׂאוּ אֶת־עֲוֹן כְּהֻנַּתְכֶם:

2 You shall also associate with yourself your kinsmen the tribe of *Levi*, your ancestral tribe, to be attached to you and to minister to you, while you and your sons under your charge are before the Tent of the Pact.

ב וְגַם אֶת־אַחֶיךָ מַטֵּה לֵוִי שֵׁבֶט אָבִיךָ הַקְרֵב אִתָּךְ וְיִלָּווּ עָלֶיךָ וִישָׁרְתוּךָ וְאַתָּה וּבָנֶיךָ אִתָּךְ לִפְנֵי אֹהֶל הָעֵדֻת:

3 They shall discharge their duties to you and to the Tent as a whole, but they must not have any contact with the furnishings of the Shrine or with the *Mizbayach*, lest both they and you die.

ג וְשָׁמְרוּ מִשְׁמַרְתְּךָ וּמִשְׁמֶרֶת כָּל־הָאֹהֶל אַךְ אֶל־כְּלֵי הַקֹּדֶשׁ וְאֶל־הַמִּזְבֵּחַ לֹא יִקְרָבוּ וְלֹא־יָמֻתוּ גַם־הֵם גַּם־אַתֶּם:

4 They shall be attached to you and discharge the duties of the Tent of Meeting, all the service of the Tent; but no outsider shall intrude upon you

ד וְנִלְווּ עָלֶיךָ וְשָׁמְרוּ אֶת־מִשְׁמֶרֶת אֹהֶל מוֹעֵד לְכֹל עֲבֹדַת הָאֹהֶל וְזָר לֹא־יִקְרַב אֲלֵיכֶם:

5 as you discharge the duties connected with the Shrine and the *Mizbayach*, that wrath may not again strike the Israelites.

ה וּשְׁמַרְתֶּם אֵת מִשְׁמֶרֶת הַקֹּדֶשׁ וְאֵת מִשְׁמֶרֶת הַמִּזְבֵּחַ וְלֹא־יִהְיֶה עוֹד קֶצֶף עַל־בְּנֵי יִשְׂרָאֵל:

6 I hereby take your fellow *Leviim* from among the Israelites; they are assigned to you in dedication to *Hashem*, to do the work of the Tent of Meeting;

ו וַאֲנִי הִנֵּה לָקַחְתִּי אֶת־אֲחֵיכֶם הַלְוִיִּם מִתּוֹךְ בְּנֵי יִשְׂרָאֵל לָכֶם מַתָּנָה נְתֻנִים לַיהֹוָה לַעֲבֹד אֶת־עֲבֹדַת אֹהֶל מוֹעֵד:

7 while you and your sons shall be careful to perform your priestly duties in everything pertaining to the *Mizbayach* and to what is behind the curtain. I make your priesthood a service of dedication; any outsider who encroaches shall be put to death.

ז וְאַתָּה וּבָנֶיךָ אִתְּךָ תִּשְׁמְרוּ אֶת־כְּהֻנַּתְכֶם לְכָל־דְּבַר הַמִּזְבֵּחַ וּלְמִבֵּית לַפָּרֹכֶת וַעֲבַדְתֶּם עֲבֹדַת מַתָּנָה אֶתֵּן אֶת־כְּהֻנַּתְכֶם וְהַזָּר הַקָּרֵב יוּמָת:

8 *Hashem* spoke further to *Aharon*: I hereby give you charge of My gifts, all the sacred donations of the Israelites; I grant them to you and to your sons as a perquisite, a due for all time.

ח וַיְדַבֵּר יְהוָה אֶל־אַהֲרֹן וַאֲנִי הִנֵּה נָתַתִּי לְךָ אֶת־מִשְׁמֶרֶת תְּרוּמֹתָי לְכָל־קָדְשֵׁי בְנֵי־יִשְׂרָאֵל לְךָ נְתַתִּים לְמָשְׁחָה וּלְבָנֶיךָ לְחָק־עוֹלָם:

> vai-da-BAYR a-do-NAI el a-ha-RON v-a-NEE hi-NAY na-TA-tee
> l'-KHA et mish-ME-ret t'-ru-mo-TAI l'-khol kod-SHAY v'-nay yis-ra-AYL
> l'-KHA n'-ta-TEEM l'-mosh-KHAH ul-va-NE-kha l'-khok o-LAM

9 This shall be yours from the most holy sacrifices, the offerings by fire: every such offering that they render to Me as most holy sacrifices, namely, every meal offering, sin offering, and guilt offering of theirs, shall belong to you and your sons.

ט זֶה־יִהְיֶה לְךָ מִקֹּדֶשׁ הַקֳּדָשִׁים מִן־הָאֵשׁ כָּל־קָרְבָּנָם לְכָל־מִנְחָתָם וּלְכָל־חַטָּאתָם וּלְכָל־אֲשָׁמָם אֲשֶׁר יָשִׁיבוּ לִי קֹדֶשׁ קָדָשִׁים לְךָ הוּא וּלְבָנֶיךָ:

10 You shall partake of them as most sacred donations: only males may eat them; you shall treat them as consecrated.

י בְּקֹדֶשׁ הַקֳּדָשִׁים תֹּאכְלֶנּוּ כָּל־זָכָר יֹאכַל אֹתוֹ קֹדֶשׁ יִהְיֶה־לָּךְ:

11 This, too, shall be yours: the gift offerings of their contributions, all the elevation offerings of the Israelites, I give to you, to your sons, and to the daughters that are with you, as a due for all time; everyone of your household who is clean may eat it.

יא וְזֶה־לְּךָ תְּרוּמַת מַתָּנָם לְכָל־תְּנוּפֹת בְּנֵי יִשְׂרָאֵל לְךָ נְתַתִּים וּלְבָנֶיךָ וְלִבְנֹתֶיךָ אִתְּךָ לְחָק־עוֹלָם כָּל־טָהוֹר בְּבֵיתְךָ יֹאכַל אֹתוֹ:

12 All the best of the new oil, wine, and grain – the choice parts that they present to *Hashem* – I give to you.

יב כֹּל חֵלֶב יִצְהָר וְכָל־חֵלֶב תִּירוֹשׁ וְדָגָן רֵאשִׁיתָם אֲשֶׁר־יִתְּנוּ לַיהוָה לְךָ נְתַתִּים:

13 The first fruits of everything in their land, that they bring to *Hashem*, shall be yours; everyone of your household who is clean may eat them.

יג בִּכּוּרֵי כָּל־אֲשֶׁר בְּאַרְצָם אֲשֶׁר־יָבִיאוּ לַיהוָה לְךָ יִהְיֶה כָּל־טָהוֹר בְּבֵיתְךָ יֹאכְלֶנּוּ:

14 Everything that has been proscribed in *Yisrael* shall be yours.

יד כָּל־חֵרֶם בְּיִשְׂרָאֵל לְךָ יִהְיֶה:

15 The first issue of the womb of every being, man or beast, that is offered to *Hashem*, shall be yours; but you shall have the first-born of man redeemed, and you shall also have the firstling of unclean animals redeemed.

טו כָּל־פֶּטֶר רֶחֶם לְכָל־בָּשָׂר אֲשֶׁר־יַקְרִיבוּ לַיהוָה בָּאָדָם וּבַבְּהֵמָה יִהְיֶה־לָּךְ אַךְ פָּדֹה תִפְדֶּה אֵת בְּכוֹר הָאָדָם וְאֵת בְּכוֹר־הַבְּהֵמָה הַטְּמֵאָה תִּפְדֶּה:

16 Take as their redemption price, from the age of one month up, the money equivalent of five *shekalim* by the sanctuary weight, which is twenty *geira*.

טז וּפְדוּיָו מִבֶּן־חֹדֶשׁ תִּפְדֶּה בְּעֶרְכְּךָ כֶּסֶף חֲמֵשֶׁת שְׁקָלִים בְּשֶׁקֶל הַקֹּדֶשׁ עֶשְׂרִים גֵּרָה הוּא:

A basket of fruit grown in Israel

18:8 I grant them to you and to your sons as a perquisite The gifts and tithes presented to the *Kohanim* and *Leviim* are additional examples of commandments that apply only in the Land of Israel. Like the portion of *challah* (Numbers 15:17–21), these are gifts given to the spiritual leaders of Israel to provide for their physical sustenance in exchange for the spiritual sustenance they offered to the people. Since they have no portion of land of their own, the *Kohanim* and *Leviim* are dependent on the rest of the nation for their physical nourishment, while the spiritual work that they do elevates everyone else's existence in the land.

17 But the firstlings of cattle, sheep, or goats may not be redeemed; they are consecrated. You shall dash their blood against the *Mizbayach*, and turn their fat into smoke as an offering by fire for a pleasing odor to *Hashem*.

יז אַךְ בְּכוֹר־שׁוֹר אוֹ־בְכוֹר כֶּשֶׂב אוֹ־בְכוֹר עֵז לֹא תִפְדֶּה קֹדֶשׁ הֵם אֶת־דָּמָם תִּזְרֹק עַל־הַמִּזְבֵּחַ וְאֶת־חֶלְבָּם תַּקְטִיר אִשֶּׁה לְרֵיחַ נִיחֹחַ לַיהֹוָה׃

18 But their meat shall be yours: it shall be yours like the breast of elevation offering and like the right thigh.

יח וּבְשָׂרָם יִהְיֶה־לָּךְ כַּחֲזֵה הַתְּנוּפָה וּכְשׁוֹק הַיָּמִין לְךָ יִהְיֶה׃

19 All the sacred gifts that the Israelites set aside for *Hashem* I give to you, to your sons, and to the daughters that are with you, as a due for all time. It shall be an everlasting covenant of salt before *Hashem* for you and for your offspring as well.

יט כֹּל תְּרוּמֹת הַקֳּדָשִׁים אֲשֶׁר יָרִימוּ בְנֵי־יִשְׂרָאֵל לַיהֹוָה נָתַתִּי לְךָ וּלְבָנֶיךָ וְלִבְנֹתֶיךָ אִתְּךָ לְחָק־עוֹלָם בְּרִית מֶלַח עוֹלָם הִוא לִפְנֵי יְהֹוָה לְךָ וּלְזַרְעֲךָ אִתָּךְ׃

20 And *Hashem* said to *Aharon*: You shall, however, have no territorial share among them or own any portion in their midst; I am your portion and your share among the Israelites.

כ וַיֹּאמֶר יְהֹוָה אֶל־אַהֲרֹן בְּאַרְצָם לֹא תִנְחָל וְחֵלֶק לֹא־יִהְיֶה לְךָ בְּתוֹכָם אֲנִי חֶלְקְךָ וְנַחֲלָתְךָ בְּתוֹךְ בְּנֵי יִשְׂרָאֵל׃

21 And to the *Leviim* I hereby give all the tithes in *Yisrael* as their share in return for the services that they perform, the services of the Tent of Meeting.

כא וְלִבְנֵי לֵוִי הִנֵּה נָתַתִּי כָּל־מַעֲשֵׂר בְּיִשְׂרָאֵל לְנַחֲלָה חֵלֶף עֲבֹדָתָם אֲשֶׁר־הֵם עֹבְדִים אֶת־עֲבֹדַת אֹהֶל מוֹעֵד׃

22 Henceforth, Israelites shall not trespass on the Tent of Meeting, and thus incur guilt and die:

כב וְלֹא־יִקְרְבוּ עוֹד בְּנֵי יִשְׂרָאֵל אֶל־אֹהֶל מוֹעֵד לָשֵׂאת חֵטְא לָמוּת׃

23 only *Leviim* shall perform the services of the Tent of Meeting; others would incur guilt. It is the law for all time throughout the ages. But they shall have no territorial share among the Israelites;

כג וְעָבַד הַלֵּוִי הוּא אֶת־עֲבֹדַת אֹהֶל מוֹעֵד וְהֵם יִשְׂאוּ עֲוֺנָם חֻקַּת עוֹלָם לְדֹרֹתֵיכֶם וּבְתוֹךְ בְּנֵי יִשְׂרָאֵל לֹא יִנְחֲלוּ נַחֲלָה׃

24 for it is the tithes set aside by the Israelites as a gift to *Hashem* that I give to the *Leviim* as their share. Therefore I have said concerning them: They shall have no territorial share among the Israelites.

כד כִּי אֶת־מַעְשַׂר בְּנֵי־יִשְׂרָאֵל אֲשֶׁר יָרִימוּ לַיהֹוָה תְּרוּמָה נָתַתִּי לַלְוִיִּם לְנַחֲלָה עַל־כֵּן אָמַרְתִּי לָהֶם בְּתוֹךְ בְּנֵי יִשְׂרָאֵל לֹא יִנְחֲלוּ נַחֲלָה׃

25 *Hashem* spoke to *Moshe*, saying:

כה וַיְדַבֵּר יְהֹוָה אֶל־מֹשֶׁה לֵּאמֹר׃

26 Speak to the *Leviim* and say to them: When you receive from the Israelites their tithes, which I have assigned to you as your share, you shall set aside from them one-tenth of the tithe as a gift to *Hashem*.

כו וְאֶל־הַלְוִיִּם תְּדַבֵּר וְאָמַרְתָּ אֲלֵהֶם כִּי־תִקְחוּ מֵאֵת בְּנֵי־יִשְׂרָאֵל אֶת־הַמַּעֲשֵׂר אֲשֶׁר נָתַתִּי לָכֶם מֵאִתָּם בְּנַחֲלַתְכֶם וַהֲרֵמֹתֶם מִמֶּנּוּ תְּרוּמַת יְהֹוָה מַעֲשֵׂר מִן־הַמַּעֲשֵׂר׃

27 This shall be accounted to you as your gift. As with the new grain from the threshing floor or the flow from the vat,

כז וְנֶחְשַׁב לָכֶם תְּרוּמַתְכֶם כַּדָּגָן מִן־הַגֹּרֶן וְכַמְלֵאָה מִן־הַיָּקֶב׃

28 so shall you on your part set aside a gift for *Hashem* from all the tithes that you receive from the Israelites; and from them you shall bring the gift for *Hashem* to *Aharon* the *Kohen*.

כח כֵּן תָּרִימוּ גַם־אַתֶּם תְּרוּמַת יְהֹוָה מִכֹּל מַעְשְׂרֹתֵיכֶם אֲשֶׁר תִּקְחוּ מֵאֵת בְּנֵי יִשְׂרָאֵל וּנְתַתֶּם מִמֶּנּוּ אֶת־תְּרוּמַת יְהֹוָה לְאַהֲרֹן הַכֹּהֵן׃

29 You shall set aside all gifts due to *Hashem* from everything that is donated to you, from each thing its best portion, the part thereof that is to be consecrated.

כט מִכֹּל֙ מַתְּנֹ֣תֵיכֶ֔ם תָּרִ֕ימוּ אֵ֖ת כָּל־תְּרוּמַ֣ת יְהֹוָ֑ה מִכָּל־חֶלְבּ֔וֹ אֶת־מִקְדְּשׁ֖וֹ מִמֶּֽנּוּ׃

30 Say to them further: When you have removed the best part from it, you *Leviim* may consider it the same as the yield of threshing floor or vat.

ל וְאָמַרְתָּ֖ אֲלֵהֶ֑ם בַּהֲרִֽימְכֶ֤ם אֶת־חֶלְבּוֹ֙ מִמֶּ֔נּוּ וְנֶחְשַׁב֙ לַלְוִיִּ֔ם כִּתְבוּאַ֥ת גֹּ֖רֶן וְכִתְבוּאַ֥ת יָֽקֶב׃

31 You and your households may eat it anywhere, for it is your recompense for your services in the Tent of Meeting.

לא וַאֲכַלְתֶּ֤ם אֹתוֹ֙ בְּכָל־מָק֔וֹם אַתֶּ֖ם וּבֵיתְכֶ֑ם כִּֽי־שָׂכָ֥ר הוּא֙ לָכֶ֔ם חֵ֥לֶף עֲבֹֽדַתְכֶ֖ם בְּאֹ֥הֶל מוֹעֵֽד׃

32 You will incur no guilt through it, once you have removed the best part from it; but you must not profane the sacred donations of the Israelites, lest you die.

לב וְלֹֽא־תִשְׂא֤וּ עָלָיו֙ חֵ֔טְא בַּהֲרִֽימְכֶ֥ם אֶת־חֶלְבּ֖וֹ מִמֶּ֑נּוּ וְאֶת־קָדְשֵׁ֧י בְנֵֽי־יִשְׂרָאֵ֛ל לֹ֥א תְחַלְּל֖וּ וְלֹ֥א תָמֽוּתוּ׃

19 1 *Hashem* spoke to *Moshe* and *Aharon*, saying:

ט 🄰 וַיְדַבֵּ֣ר יְהֹוָ֔ה אֶל־מֹשֶׁ֥ה וְאֶֽל־אַהֲרֹ֖ן לֵאמֹֽר׃

2 This is the ritual law that *Hashem* has commanded: Instruct *B'nei Yisrael* to bring you a red cow without blemish, in which there is no defect and on which no yoke has been laid.

ב זֹ֚את חֻקַּ֣ת הַתּוֹרָ֔ה אֲשֶׁר־צִוָּ֥ה יְהֹוָ֖ה לֵאמֹ֑ר דַּבֵּ֣ר ׀ אֶל־בְּנֵ֣י יִשְׂרָאֵ֗ל וְיִקְח֣וּ אֵלֶ֩יךָ֩ פָרָ֨ה אֲדֻמָּ֜ה תְּמִימָ֗ה אֲשֶׁ֤ר אֵֽין־בָּהּ֙ מ֔וּם אֲשֶׁ֛ר לֹא־עָלָ֥ה עָלֶ֖יהָ עֹֽל׃

3 You shall give it to *Elazar* the *Kohen*. It shall be taken outside the camp and slaughtered in his presence.

ג וּנְתַתֶּ֣ם אֹתָ֔הּ אֶל־אֶלְעָזָ֖ר הַכֹּהֵ֑ן וְהוֹצִ֤יא אֹתָהּ֙ אֶל־מִח֣וּץ לַֽמַּחֲנֶ֔ה וְשָׁחַ֥ט אֹתָ֖הּ לְפָנָֽיו׃

4 *Elazar* the *Kohen* shall take some of its blood with his finger and sprinkle it seven times toward the front of the Tent of Meeting.

ד וְלָקַ֞ח אֶלְעָזָ֧ר הַכֹּהֵ֛ן מִדָּמָ֖הּ בְּאֶצְבָּע֑וֹ וְהִזָּ֞ה אֶל־נֹ֨כַח פְּנֵ֧י אֹֽהֶל־מוֹעֵ֛ד מִדָּמָ֖הּ שֶׁ֥בַע פְּעָמִֽים׃

5 The cow shall be burned in his sight – its hide, flesh, and blood shall be burned, its dung included –

ה וְשָׂרַ֥ף אֶת־הַפָּרָ֖ה לְעֵינָ֑יו אֶת־עֹרָ֤הּ וְאֶת־בְּשָׂרָהּ֙ וְאֶת־דָּמָ֔הּ עַל־פִּרְשָׁ֖הּ יִשְׂרֹֽף׃

6 and the *Kohen* shall take cedar wood, hyssop, and crimson stuff, and throw them into the fire consuming the cow.

ו וְלָקַ֣ח הַכֹּהֵ֗ן עֵ֥ץ אֶ֛רֶז וְאֵז֖וֹב וּשְׁנִ֣י תוֹלָ֑עַת וְהִשְׁלִ֕יךְ אֶל־תּ֖וֹךְ שְׂרֵפַ֥ת הַפָּרָֽה׃

7 The *Kohen* shall wash his garments and bathe his body in water; after that the *Kohen* may reenter the camp, but he shall be unclean until evening.

ז וְכִבֶּ֨ס בְּגָדָ֜יו הַכֹּהֵ֗ן וְרָחַ֤ץ בְּשָׂרוֹ֙ בַּמַּ֔יִם וְאַחַ֖ר יָבֹ֣א אֶל־הַֽמַּחֲנֶ֑ה וְטָמֵ֥א הַכֹּהֵ֖ן עַד־הָעָֽרֶב׃

8 He who performed the burning shall also wash his garments in water, bathe his body in water, and be unclean until evening.

ח וְהַשֹּׂרֵ֣ף אֹתָ֔הּ יְכַבֵּ֤ס בְּגָדָיו֙ בַּמַּ֔יִם וְרָחַ֥ץ בְּשָׂר֖וֹ בַּמָּ֑יִם וְטָמֵ֖א עַד־הָעָֽרֶב׃

9 A man who is clean shall gather up the ashes of the cow and deposit them outside the camp in a clean place, to be kept for water of lustration for the Israelite community. It is for cleansing.

ט וְאָסַ֣ף ׀ אִ֣ישׁ טָה֗וֹר אֵ֚ת אֵ֣פֶר הַפָּרָ֔ה וְהִנִּ֛יחַ מִח֥וּץ לַֽמַּחֲנֶ֖ה בְּמָק֣וֹם טָה֑וֹר וְ֠הָיְתָ֠ה לַעֲדַ֨ת בְּנֵֽי־יִשְׂרָאֵ֧ל לְמִשְׁמֶ֛רֶת לְמֵ֥י נִדָּ֖ה חַטָּ֥את הֽוּא׃

10 He who gathers up the ashes of the cow shall also wash his clothes and be unclean until evening. This shall be a permanent law for the Israelites and for the strangers who reside among you.

י וְכָבֶ֡ס הָאֹסֵף֩ אֶת־אֵ֨פֶר הַפָּרָ֜ה אֶת־בְּגָדָ֗יו וְטָמֵ֖א עַד־הָעָ֑רֶב וְהָֽיְתָ֞ה לִבְנֵ֣י יִשְׂרָאֵ֗ל וְלַגֵּ֛ר הַגָּ֥ר בְּתוֹכָ֖ם לְחֻקַּ֥ת עוֹלָֽם:

11   He who touches the corpse of any human being shall be unclean for seven days.

יא הַנֹּגֵ֛עַ בְּמֵ֥ת לְכָל־נֶ֥פֶשׁ אָדָ֖ם וְטָמֵ֖א שִׁבְעַ֥ת יָמִֽים:

ha-no-GAY-a b'-MAYT l'-khol NE-fesh a-DAM v'-ta-MAY shiv-AT ya-MEEM

12 He shall cleanse himself with it on the third day and on the seventh day, and then be clean; if he fails to cleanse himself on the third and seventh days, he shall not be clean.

יב ה֣וּא יִתְחַטָּא־ב֞וֹ בַּיּ֧וֹם הַשְּׁלִישִׁ֛י וּבַיּ֥וֹם הַשְּׁבִיעִ֖י יִטְהָ֑ר וְאִם־לֹ֨א יִתְחַטָּ֜א בַּיּ֧וֹם הַשְּׁלִישִׁ֛י וּבַיּ֥וֹם הַשְּׁבִיעִ֖י לֹ֥א יִטְהָֽר:

13 Whoever touches a corpse, the body of a person who has died, and does not cleanse himself, defiles *Hashem*'s *Mishkan*; that person shall be cut off from *Yisrael*. Since the water of lustration was not dashed on him, he remains unclean; his uncleanness is still upon him.

יג כָּל־הַנֹּגֵ֡עַ בְּמֵ֣ת בְּנֶפֶשׁ֩ הָאָדָ֨ם אֲשֶׁר־יָמ֜וּת וְלֹ֣א יִתְחַטָּ֗א אֶת־מִשְׁכַּ֤ן יְהֹוָה֙ טִמֵּ֔א וְנִכְרְתָ֛ה הַנֶּ֥פֶשׁ הַהִ֖וא מִיִּשְׂרָאֵ֑ל כִּי֩ מֵ֨י נִדָּ֜ה לֹא־זֹרַ֤ק עָלָיו֙ טָמֵ֣א יִהְיֶ֔ה ע֖וֹד טֻמְאָת֥וֹ בֽוֹ:

14 This is the ritual: When a person dies in a tent, whoever enters the tent and whoever is in the tent shall be unclean seven days;

יד זֹ֚את הַתּוֹרָ֔ה אָדָ֖ם כִּֽי־יָמ֣וּת בְּאֹ֑הֶל כָּל־הַבָּ֤א אֶל־הָאֹ֨הֶל֙ וְכָל־אֲשֶׁ֣ר בָּאֹ֔הֶל יִטְמָ֖א שִׁבְעַ֥ת יָמִֽים:

15 and every open vessel, with no lid fastened down, shall be unclean.

טו וְכֹל֙ כְּלִ֣י פָת֔וּחַ אֲשֶׁ֛ר אֵֽין־צָמִ֥יד פָּתִ֖יל עָלָ֑יו טָמֵ֥א הֽוּא:

16 And in the open, anyone who touches a person who was killed or who died naturally, or human bone, or a grave, shall be unclean seven days.

טז וְכֹ֨ל אֲשֶׁר־יִגַּ֜ע עַל־פְּנֵ֣י הַשָּׂדֶ֗ה בַּֽחֲלַל־חֶ֨רֶב֙ א֣וֹ בְמֵ֔ת אֽוֹ־בְעֶ֥צֶם אָדָ֖ם א֣וֹ בְקָ֑בֶר יִטְמָ֖א שִׁבְעַ֥ת יָמִֽים:

17 Some of the ashes from the fire of cleansing shall be taken for the unclean person, and fresh water shall be added to them in a vessel.

יז וְלָֽקְחוּ֙ לַטָּמֵ֔א מֵֽעֲפַ֖ר שְׂרֵפַ֣ת הַֽחַטָּ֑את וְנָתַ֥ן עָלָ֛יו מַ֥יִם חַיִּ֖ים אֶל־כֶּֽלִי:

18 A person who is clean shall take hyssop, dip it in the water, and sprinkle on the tent and on all the vessels and people who were there, or on him who touched the bones or the person who was killed or died naturally or the grave.

יח וְלָקַ֨ח אֵז֜וֹב וְטָבַ֣ל בַּמַּ֘יִם֮ אִ֣ישׁ טָהוֹר֒ וְהִזָּ֤ה עַל־הָאֹ֨הֶל֙ וְעַל־כָּל־הַכֵּלִ֔ים וְעַל־הַנְּפָשׁ֖וֹת אֲשֶׁ֣ר הָֽיוּ־שָׁ֑ם וְעַל־הַנֹּגֵ֗עַ בַּעֶ֨צֶם֙ א֣וֹ בֶֽחָלָ֔ל א֥וֹ בַמֵּ֖ת א֥וֹ בַקָּֽבֶר:

19:11 He who touches the corpse of any human being shall be unclean Chapter 19 discusses the laws of ritual impurity that result from coming into contact, directly or indirectly, with a dead body. Unlike other rituals that were performed inside the *Mishkan* or its courtyard, the purification process for these ritually impure individuals takes place outside the camp, in the place farthest from the *Mishkan*. When a person passes from this world, his body is left bereft of its soul, its Godliness. The absence of the soul is the antithesis of the spirituality of the *Mishkan*, where God's presence is most intensely concentrated. Entering the holy sanctuary after having encountered the absence of Godliness is incongruous. It is only after a person has become purified that he can regain entry into such a holy place.

Ruins of an ancient ritual bath from the time of the second *Beit Hamikdash* near the Temple Mount

Numbers

19 The clean person shall sprinkle it upon the unclean person on the third day and on the seventh day, thus cleansing him by the seventh day. He shall then wash his clothes and bathe in water, and at nightfall he shall be clean.

20 If anyone who has become unclean fails to cleanse himself, that person shall be cut off from the congregation, for he has defiled *Hashem*'s sanctuary. The water of lustration was not dashed on him: he is unclean.

21 That shall be for them a law for all time. Further, he who sprinkled the water of lustration shall wash his clothes; and whoever touches the water of lustration shall be unclean until evening.

22 Whatever that unclean person touches shall be unclean; and the person who touches him shall be unclean until evening.

20 1 The Israelites arrived in a body at the wilderness of Zin on the first new moon, and the people stayed at Kadesh. *Miriam* died there and was buried there.

2 The community was without water, and they joined against *Moshe* and *Aharon*.

3 The people quarreled with *Moshe*, saying, "If only we had perished when our brothers perished at the instance of *Hashem*!

4 Why have you brought *Hashem*'s congregation into this wilderness for us and our beasts to die there?

5 Why did you make us leave Egypt to bring us to this wretched place, a place with no grain or figs or vines or pomegranates? There is not even water to drink!"

6 *Moshe* and *Aharon* came away from the congregation to the entrance of the Tent of Meeting, and fell on their faces. The Presence of *Hashem* appeared to them,

7 and *Hashem* spoke to *Moshe*, saying,

8 "You and your brother *Aharon* take the rod and assemble the community, and before their very eyes order the rock to yield its water. Thus you shall produce water for them from the rock and provide drink for the congregation and their beasts."

9 *Moshe* took the rod from before *Hashem*, as He had commanded him.

יט וְהִזָּה הַטָּהֹר עַל־הַטָּמֵא בַּיּוֹם הַשְּׁלִישִׁי וּבַיּוֹם הַשְּׁבִיעִי וְחִטְּאוֹ בַּיּוֹם הַשְּׁבִיעִי וְכִבֶּס בְּגָדָיו וְרָחַץ בַּמַּיִם וְטָהֵר בָּעָרֶב:

כ וְאִישׁ אֲשֶׁר־יִטְמָא וְלֹא יִתְחַטָּא וְנִכְרְתָה הַנֶּפֶשׁ הַהִוא מִתּוֹךְ הַקָּהָל כִּי אֶת־מִקְדַּשׁ יְהֹוָה טִמֵּא מֵי נִדָּה לֹא־זֹרַק עָלָיו טָמֵא הוּא:

כא וְהָיְתָה לָהֶם לְחֻקַּת עוֹלָם וּמַזֵּה מֵי־ הַנִּדָּה יְכַבֵּס בְּגָדָיו וְהַנֹּגֵעַ בְּמֵי הַנִּדָּה יִטְמָא עַד־הָעָרֶב:

כב וְכֹל אֲשֶׁר־יִגַּע־בּוֹ הַטָּמֵא יִטְמָא וְהַנֶּפֶשׁ הַנֹּגַעַת תִּטְמָא עַד־הָעָרֶב:

כ א וַיָּבֹאוּ בְנֵי־יִשְׂרָאֵל כָּל־הָעֵדָה מִדְבַּר־צִן בַּחֹדֶשׁ הָרִאשׁוֹן וַיֵּשֶׁב הָעָם בְּקָדֵשׁ וַתָּמָת שָׁם מִרְיָם וַתִּקָּבֵר שָׁם:

ב וְלֹא־הָיָה מַיִם לָעֵדָה וַיִּקָּהֲלוּ עַל־מֹשֶׁה וְעַל־אַהֲרֹן:

ג וַיָּרֶב הָעָם עִם־מֹשֶׁה וַיֹּאמְרוּ לֵאמֹר וְלוּ גָוַעְנוּ בִּגְוַע אַחֵינוּ לִפְנֵי יְהֹוָה:

ד וְלָמָה הֲבֵאתֶם אֶת־קְהַל יְהֹוָה אֶל־ הַמִּדְבָּר הַזֶּה לָמוּת שָׁם אֲנַחְנוּ וּבְעִירֵנוּ:

ה וְלָמָה הֶעֱלִיתֻנוּ מִמִּצְרַיִם לְהָבִיא אֹתָנוּ אֶל־הַמָּקוֹם הָרָע הַזֶּה לֹא מְקוֹם זֶרַע וּתְאֵנָה וְגֶפֶן וְרִמּוֹן וּמַיִם אַיִן לִשְׁתּוֹת:

ו וַיָּבֹא מֹשֶׁה וְאַהֲרֹן מִפְּנֵי הַקָּהָל אֶל־ פֶּתַח אֹהֶל מוֹעֵד וַיִּפְּלוּ עַל־פְּנֵיהֶם וַיֵּרָא כְבוֹד־יְהֹוָה אֲלֵיהֶם:

ז וַיְדַבֵּר יְהֹוָה אֶל־מֹשֶׁה לֵּאמֹר:

ח קַח אֶת־הַמַּטֶּה וְהַקְהֵל אֶת־הָעֵדָה אַתָּה וְאַהֲרֹן אָחִיךָ וְדִבַּרְתֶּם אֶל־הַסֶּלַע לְעֵינֵיהֶם וְנָתַן מֵימָיו וְהוֹצֵאתָ לָהֶם מַיִם מִן־הַסֶּלַע וְהִשְׁקִיתָ אֶת־הָעֵדָה וְאֶת־בְּעִירָם:

ט וַיִּקַּח מֹשֶׁה אֶת־הַמַּטֶּה מִלִּפְנֵי יְהֹוָה כַּאֲשֶׁר צִוָּהוּ:

Numbers

10 *Moshe* and *Aharon* assembled the congregation in front of the rock; and he said to them, "Listen, you rebels, shall we get water for you out of this rock?"

יַּקְהִלוּ מֹשֶׁה וְאַהֲרֹן אֶת־הַקָּהָל אֶל־פְּנֵי הַסָּלַע וַיֹּאמֶר לָהֶם שִׁמְעוּ־נָא הַמֹּרִים הֲמִן־הַסֶּלַע הַזֶּה נוֹצִיא לָכֶם מָיִם:

11 And *Moshe* raised his hand and struck the rock twice with his rod. Out came copious water, and the community and their beasts drank.

יא וַיָּרֶם מֹשֶׁה אֶת־יָדוֹ וַיַּךְ אֶת־הַסֶּלַע בְּמַטֵּהוּ פַּעֲמָיִם וַיֵּצְאוּ מַיִם רַבִּים וַתֵּשְׁתְּ הָעֵדָה וּבְעִירָם:

12 But *Hashem* said to *Moshe* and *Aharon*, "Because you did not trust Me enough to affirm My sanctity in the sight of *B'nei Yisrael*, therefore you shall not lead this congregation into the land that I have given them."

יב וַיֹּאמֶר יְהֹוָה אֶל־מֹשֶׁה וְאֶל־אַהֲרֹן יַעַן לֹא־הֶאֱמַנְתֶּם בִּי לְהַקְדִּישֵׁנִי לְעֵינֵי בְּנֵי יִשְׂרָאֵל לָכֵן לֹא תָבִיאוּ אֶת־הַקָּהָל הַזֶּה אֶל־הָאָרֶץ אֲשֶׁר־נָתַתִּי לָהֶם:

va-YO-mer a-do-NAI el mo-SHEH v'-el a-ha-RON YA-an lo he-e-man-TEM BEE l'-HAK-dee-SHAY-nee l'-ay-NAY b'-NAY yis-ra-AYL la-KHAYN LO ta-VEE-u et ha-ka-HAL ha-ZEH el ha-A-retz a-sher na-TA-tee la-HEM

13 Those are the Waters of Meribah – meaning that the Israelites quarrelled with *Hashem* – through which He affirmed His sanctity.

יג הֵמָּה מֵי מְרִיבָה אֲשֶׁר־רָבוּ בְנֵי־יִשְׂרָאֵל אֶת־יְהֹוָה וַיִּקָּדֵשׁ בָּם:

14 From Kadesh, *Moshe* sent messengers to the king of Edom: "Thus says your brother *Yisrael*: You know all the hardships that have befallen us;

יד וַיִּשְׁלַח מֹשֶׁה מַלְאָכִים מִקָּדֵשׁ אֶל־מֶלֶךְ אֱדוֹם כֹּה אָמַר אָחִיךָ יִשְׂרָאֵל אַתָּה יָדַעְתָּ אֵת כָּל־הַתְּלָאָה אֲשֶׁר מְצָאָתְנוּ:

15 that our ancestors went down to Egypt, that we dwelt in Egypt a long time, and that the Egyptians dealt harshly with us and our ancestors.

טו וַיֵּרְדוּ אֲבֹתֵינוּ מִצְרַיְמָה וַנֵּשֶׁב בְּמִצְרַיִם יָמִים רַבִּים וַיָּרֵעוּ לָנוּ מִצְרַיִם וְלַאֲבֹתֵינוּ:

16 We cried to *Hashem* and He heard our plea, and He sent a messenger who freed us from Egypt. Now we are in Kadesh, the town on the border of your territory.

טז וַנִּצְעַק אֶל־יְהֹוָה וַיִּשְׁמַע קֹלֵנוּ וַיִּשְׁלַח מַלְאָךְ וַיֹּצִאֵנוּ מִמִּצְרָיִם וְהִנֵּה אֲנַחְנוּ בְקָדֵשׁ עִיר קְצֵה גְבוּלֶךָ:

17 Allow us, then, to cross your country. We will not pass through fields or vineyards, and we will not drink water from wells. We will follow the king's highway, turning off neither to the right nor to the left until we have crossed your territory."

יז נַעְבְּרָה־נָּא בְאַרְצֶךָ לֹא נַעֲבֹר בְּשָׂדֶה וּבְכֶרֶם וְלֹא נִשְׁתֶּה מֵי בְאֵר דֶּרֶךְ הַמֶּלֶךְ נֵלֵךְ לֹא נִטֶּה יָמִין וּשְׂמֹאול עַד אֲשֶׁר־נַעֲבֹר גְּבוּלֶךָ:

The Kziv river in the Galilee

20:12 Because you did not trust Me The account of *Moshe* hitting the rock to get water for his people is one of the most perplexing stories in the entire Bible. *Hashem* tells him to speak to the rock in order to bring forth water, but *Moshe* hits the rock instead and is punished by being prevented from entering the Land of Israel, "because you did not trust Me enough to affirm My sanctity in the sight of the *B'nei Yisrael*." What could be so terrible about hitting the rock instead of speaking to it? One explanation, given by *Rashi*, is that while *Moshe* understood that the water flowing from the rock was God's doing, he did not make this sufficiently clear to the rest of the Children of Israel. Instead of hitting the rock, which implied that it was his own power that brought forth the water, *Moshe* should have spoken to it. By failing to do this, he missed an opportunity to attribute greatness to *Hashem*. It is not enough for us to recognize *Hashem* in our lives or within history; we have a duty to make sure others recognize Him as well.

18 But Edom answered him, "You shall not pass through us, else we will go out against you with the sword."

יח וַיֹּ֤אמֶר אֵלָיו֙ אֱד֔וֹם לֹ֥א תַעֲבֹ֖ר בִּ֑י פֶּן־בַּחֶ֖רֶב אֵצֵ֥א לִקְרָאתֶֽךָ׃

19 "We will keep to the beaten track," the Israelites said to them, "and if we or our cattle drink your water, we will pay for it. We ask only for passage on foot – it is but a small matter."

יט וַיֹּאמְר֨וּ אֵלָ֜יו בְּנֵֽי־יִשְׂרָאֵ֗ל בַּֽמְסִלָּ֣ה נַֽעֲלֶ֔ה וְאִם־מֵימֶ֤יךָ נִשְׁתֶּה֙ אֲנִ֣י וּמִקְנַ֔י וְנָֽתַתִּ֖י מִכְרָ֑ם רַ֥ק אֵֽין־דָּבָ֖ר בְּרַגְלַ֥י אֶֽעֱבֹֽרָה׃

20 But they replied, "You shall not pass through!" And Edom went out against them in heavy force, strongly armed.

כ וַיֹּ֖אמֶר לֹ֣א תַעֲבֹ֑ר וַיֵּצֵ֤א אֱדוֹם֙ לִקְרָאת֔וֹ בְּעַ֥ם כָּבֵ֖ד וּבְיָ֥ד חֲזָקָֽה׃

21 So Edom would not let *Yisrael* cross their territory, and *Yisrael* turned away from them.

כא וַיְמָאֵ֣ן ׀ אֱד֗וֹם נְתֹן֙ אֶת־יִשְׂרָאֵ֔ל עֲבֹ֖ר בִּגְבֻל֑וֹ וַיֵּ֥ט יִשְׂרָאֵ֖ל מֵעָלָֽיו׃

22 Setting out from Kadesh, the Israelites arrived in a body at Mount Hor.

כב וַיִּסְע֖וּ מִקָּדֵ֑שׁ וַיָּבֹ֧אוּ בְנֵֽי־יִשְׂרָאֵ֛ל כָּל־הָעֵדָ֖ה הֹ֥ר הָהָֽר׃

23 At Mount Hor, on the boundary of the land of Edom, *Hashem* said to *Moshe* and *Aharon*,

כג וַיֹּ֧אמֶר יְהֹוָ֛ה אֶל־מֹשֶׁ֥ה וְאֶֽל־אַהֲרֹ֖ן בְּהֹ֣ר הָהָ֑ר עַל־גְּב֥וּל אֶֽרֶץ־אֱד֖וֹם לֵאמֹֽר׃

24 "Let *Aharon* be gathered to his kin: he is not to enter the land that I have assigned to *B'nei Yisrael*, because you disobeyed my command about the waters of Meribah.

כד יֵאָסֵ֤ף אַהֲרֹן֙ אֶל־עַמָּ֔יו כִּ֣י לֹ֤א יָבֹא֙ אֶל־הָאָ֔רֶץ אֲשֶׁ֥ר נָתַ֖תִּי לִבְנֵ֣י יִשְׂרָאֵ֑ל עַ֛ל אֲשֶׁר־מְרִיתֶ֥ם אֶת־פִּ֖י לְמֵ֥י מְרִיבָֽה׃

25 Take *Aharon* and his son *Elazar* and bring them up on Mount Hor.

כה קַ֚ח אֶֽת־אַהֲרֹ֔ן וְאֶת־אֶלְעָזָ֖ר בְּנ֑וֹ וְהַ֥עַל אֹתָ֖ם הֹ֥ר הָהָֽר׃

KAKH et a-ha-RON v'-et el-a-ZAR b'-NO v'-HA-al o-TAM hor ha-HAR

26 Strip *Aharon* of his vestments and put them on his son *Elazar*. There *Aharon* shall be gathered unto the dead."

כו וְהַפְשֵׁ֤ט אֶֽת־אַהֲרֹן֙ אֶת־בְּגָדָ֔יו וְהִלְבַּשְׁתָּ֖ם אֶת־אֶלְעָזָ֣ר בְּנ֑וֹ וְאַהֲרֹ֥ן יֵאָסֵ֖ף וּמֵ֥ת שָֽׁם׃

27 *Moshe* did as *Hashem* had commanded. They ascended Mount Hor in the sight of the whole community.

כז וַיַּ֣עַשׂ מֹשֶׁ֔ה כַּֽאֲשֶׁ֖ר צִוָּ֣ה יְהֹוָ֑ה וַֽיַּעֲל֛וּ אֶל־הֹ֥ר הָהָ֖ר לְעֵינֵ֥י כָּל־הָעֵדָֽה׃

28 *Moshe* stripped *Aharon* of his vestments and put them on his son *Elazar*, and *Aharon* died there on the summit of the mountain. When *Moshe* and *Elazar* came down from the mountain,

כח וַיַּפְשֵׁט֩ מֹשֶׁ֨ה אֶֽת־אַהֲרֹ֜ן אֶת־בְּגָדָ֗יו וַיַּלְבֵּ֤שׁ אֹתָם֙ אֶת־אֶלְעָזָ֣ר בְּנ֔וֹ וַיָּ֧מָת אַהֲרֹ֛ן שָׁ֖ם בְּרֹ֣אשׁ הָהָ֑ר וַיֵּ֧רֶד מֹשֶׁ֛ה וְאֶלְעָזָ֖ר מִן־הָהָֽר׃

29 the whole community knew that *Aharon* had breathed his last. All the house of *Yisrael* bewailed *Aharon* thirty days.

כט וַיִּרְאוּ֙ כָּל־הָ֣עֵדָ֔ה כִּ֥י גָוַ֖ע אַהֲרֹ֑ן וַיִּבְכּ֤וּ אֶֽת־אַהֲרֹן֙ שְׁלֹשִׁ֣ים י֔וֹם כֹּ֖ל בֵּ֥ית יִשְׂרָאֵֽל׃

21 1 When the Canaanite, king of Arad, who dwelt in the *Negev*, learned that *Yisrael* was coming by the way of Atharim, he engaged *Yisrael* in battle and took some of them captive.

כא א וַיִּשְׁמַ֞ע הַכְּנַעֲנִ֤י מֶֽלֶךְ־עֲרָד֙ יֹשֵׁ֣ב הַנֶּ֔גֶב כִּ֚י בָּ֣א יִשְׂרָאֵ֔ל דֶּ֖רֶךְ הָֽאֲתָרִ֑ים וַיִּלָּ֙חֶם֙ בְּיִשְׂרָאֵ֔ל וַיִּ֥שְׁבְּ ׀ מִמֶּ֖נּוּ שֶֽׁבִי׃

2 Then *Yisrael* made a vow to *Hashem* and said, "If You deliver this people into our hand, we will proscribe their towns."

3 *Hashem* heeded *Yisrael*'s plea and delivered up the Canaanites; and they and their cities were proscribed. So that place was named Hormah.

4 They set out from Mount Hor by way of the Sea of Reeds to skirt the land of Edom. But the people grew restive on the journey,

5 and the people spoke against *Hashem* and against *Moshe*, "Why did you make us leave Egypt to die in the wilderness? There is no bread and no water, and we have come to loathe this miserable food."

ב וַיִּדַּר יִשְׂרָאֵל נֶדֶר לַיהֹוָה וַיֹּאמַר אִם־נָתֹן תִּתֵּן אֶת־הָעָם הַזֶּה בְּיָדִי וְהַחֲרַמְתִּי אֶת־עָרֵיהֶם:

ג וַיִּשְׁמַע יְהֹוָה בְּקוֹל יִשְׂרָאֵל וַיִּתֵּן אֶת־הַכְּנַעֲנִי וַיַּחֲרֵם אֶתְהֶם וְאֶת־עָרֵיהֶם וַיִּקְרָא שֵׁם־הַמָּקוֹם חָרְמָה:

ד וַיִּסְעוּ מֵהֹר הָהָר דֶּרֶךְ יַם־סוּף לִסְבֹב אֶת־אֶרֶץ אֱדוֹם וַתִּקְצַר נֶפֶשׁ־הָעָם בַּדָּרֶךְ:

ה וַיְדַבֵּר הָעָם בֵּאלֹהִים וּבְמֹשֶׁה לָמָה הֶעֱלִיתֻנוּ מִמִּצְרַיִם לָמוּת בַּמִּדְבָּר כִּי אֵין לֶחֶם וְאֵין מַיִם וְנַפְשֵׁנוּ קָצָה בַּלֶּחֶם הַקְּלֹקֵל:

va-y'-da-BER ha-AM be-e-lo-HEEM u-v'-mo-SHE la-MA he-e'-lee-TU-nu mi-mitz-RA-yim la-MOOT ba-mid-BAR kee ayn LEH-khem v'-AYN MA-yim v'-naf-SHAY-nu ka-TZA ba-LE-khem ha-k'-lo-KEL

6 *Hashem* sent seraph serpents against the people. They bit the people and many of the Israelites died.

7 The people came to *Moshe* and said, "We sinned by speaking against *Hashem* and against you. Intercede with *Hashem* to take away the serpents from us!" And *Moshe* interceded for the people.

8 Then *Hashem* said to *Moshe*, "Make a seraph figure and mount it on a standard. And if anyone who is bitten looks at it, he shall recover."

9 *Moshe* made a copper serpent and mounted it on a standard; and when anyone was bitten by a serpent, he would look at the copper serpent and recover.

ו וַיְשַׁלַּח יְהֹוָה בָּעָם אֵת הַנְּחָשִׁים הַשְּׂרָפִים וַיְנַשְּׁכוּ אֶת־הָעָם וַיָּמָת עַם־רָב מִיִּשְׂרָאֵל:

ז וַיָּבֹא הָעָם אֶל־מֹשֶׁה וַיֹּאמְרוּ חָטָאנוּ כִּי־דִבַּרְנוּ בַיהֹוָה וָבָךְ הִתְפַּלֵּל אֶל־יְהֹוָה וְיָסֵר מֵעָלֵינוּ אֶת־הַנָּחָשׁ וַיִּתְפַּלֵּל מֹשֶׁה בְּעַד הָעָם:

ח וַיֹּאמֶר יְהֹוָה אֶל־מֹשֶׁה עֲשֵׂה לְךָ שָׂרָף וְשִׂים אֹתוֹ עַל־נֵס וְהָיָה כָּל־הַנָּשׁוּךְ וְרָאָה אֹתוֹ וָחָי:

ט וַיַּעַשׂ מֹשֶׁה נְחַשׁ נְחֹשֶׁת וַיְשִׂמֵהוּ עַל־הַנֵּס וְהָיָה אִם־נָשַׁךְ הַנָּחָשׁ אֶת־אִישׁ וְהִבִּיט אֶל־נְחַשׁ הַנְּחֹשֶׁת וָחָי:

va-YA-as mo-SHEH n'-KHASH n'-KHO-shet va-y'-si-MAY-hu al ha-NAYS v'-ha-YAH im na-SHAKH ha-na-KHASH et EESH v'-hi-BEET el n'-KHASH ha-n'-KHO-shet va-KHAI

10 The Israelites marched on and encamped at Oboth.

11 They set out from Oboth and encamped at Iye-abarim, in the wilderness bordering on Moab to the east.

י וַיִּסְעוּ בְּנֵי יִשְׂרָאֵל וַיַּחֲנוּ בְּאֹבֹת:

יא וַיִּסְעוּ מֵאֹבֹת וַיַּחֲנוּ בְּעִיֵּי הָעֲבָרִים בַּמִּדְבָּר אֲשֶׁר עַל־פְּנֵי מוֹאָב מִמִּזְרַח הַשָּׁמֶשׁ:

21:5 We have come to loathe this miserable food According to the Sages, the manna was a miraculous and wonderful food that tasted like anything a person would wish. If so, why did the Children of Israel complain so bitterly about it, and call it, "this miserable food"? According to the 13th century French scholar Rabbi Hezekiah ben Manoah, and known as *Chizkuni*, the Israelites were not complaining about the quality of the manna. Rather, they were expressing their impatience and eagerness to enter the Land of Israel where they would finally be able to eat the fruit of their own hands from the soil of the Holy Land.

Fruit of the land from Kibbutz Alumot

12 From there they set out and encamped at the wadi Zered.

יב מִשָּׁם נָסָעוּ וַיַּחֲנוּ בְּנַחַל זָרֶד:

13 From there they set out and encamped beyond the Arnon, that is, in the wilderness that extends from the territory of the Amorites. For the Arnon is the boundary of Moab, between Moab and the Amorites.

יג מִשָּׁם נָסָעוּ וַיַּחֲנוּ מֵעֵבֶר אַרְנוֹן אֲשֶׁר בַּמִּדְבָּר הַיֹּצֵא מִגְּבוּל הָאֱמֹרִי כִּי אַרְנוֹן גְּבוּל מוֹאָב בֵּין מוֹאָב וּבֵין הָאֱמֹרִי:

14 Therefore the Book of the Wars of *Hashem* speaks of "…Waheb in Suphah, and the wadis: the Arnon

יד עַל־כֵּן יֵאָמַר בְּסֵפֶר מִלְחֲמֹת יְהוָה אֶת־וָהֵב בְּסוּפָה וְאֶת־הַנְּחָלִים אַרְנוֹן:

15 with its tributary wadis, stretched along the settled country of Ar, hugging the territory of Moab…"

טו וְאֶשֶׁד הַנְּחָלִים אֲשֶׁר נָטָה לְשֶׁבֶת עָר וְנִשְׁעַן לִגְבוּל מוֹאָב:

16 And from there to Beer, which is the well where *Hashem* said to *Moshe*, "Assemble the people that I may give them water."

טז וּמִשָּׁם בְּאֵרָה הִוא הַבְּאֵר אֲשֶׁר אָמַר יְהוָה לְמֹשֶׁה אֱסֹף אֶת־הָעָם וְאֶתְּנָה לָהֶם מָיִם:

17 Then *Yisrael* sang this song: Spring up, O well – sing to it –

יז אָז יָשִׁיר יִשְׂרָאֵל אֶת־הַשִּׁירָה הַזֹּאת עֲלִי בְאֵר עֱנוּ־לָהּ:

18 The well which the chieftains dug, Which the nobles of the people started With maces, with their own staffs. And from Midbar to Mattanah,

יח בְּאֵר חֲפָרוּהָ שָׂרִים כָּרוּהָ נְדִיבֵי הָעָם בִּמְחֹקֵק בְּמִשְׁעֲנֹתָם וּמִמִּדְבָּר מַתָּנָה:

19 and from Mattanah to Nahaliel, and from Nahaliel to Bamoth,

יט וּמִמַּתָּנָה נַחֲלִיאֵל וּמִנַּחֲלִיאֵל בָּמוֹת:

20 and from Bamoth to the valley that is in the country of Moab, at the peak of Pisgah, overlooking the wasteland.

כ וּמִבָּמוֹת הַגַּיְא אֲשֶׁר בִּשְׂדֵה מוֹאָב רֹאשׁ הַפִּסְגָּה וְנִשְׁקָפָה עַל־פְּנֵי הַיְשִׁימֹן:

21 *Yisrael* now sent messengers to Sihon king of the Amorites, saying,

כא וַיִּשְׁלַח יִשְׂרָאֵל מַלְאָכִים אֶל־סִיחֹן מֶלֶךְ־הָאֱמֹרִי לֵאמֹר:

22 Let me pass through your country. We will not turn off into fields or vineyards, and we will not drink water from wells. We will follow the king's highway until we have crossed your territory."

כב אֶעְבְּרָה בְאַרְצֶךָ לֹא נִטֶּה בְּשָׂדֶה וּבְכֶרֶם לֹא נִשְׁתֶּה מֵי בְאֵר בְּדֶרֶךְ הַמֶּלֶךְ נֵלֵךְ עַד אֲשֶׁר־נַעֲבֹר גְּבֻלֶךָ:

23 But Sihon would not let *Yisrael* pass through his territory. Sihon gathered all his people and went out against *Yisrael* in the wilderness. He came to Jahaz and engaged *Yisrael* in battle.

כג וְלֹא־נָתַן סִיחֹן אֶת־יִשְׂרָאֵל עֲבֹר בִּגְבֻלוֹ וַיֶּאֱסֹף סִיחֹן אֶת־כָּל־עַמּוֹ וַיֵּצֵא לִקְרַאת יִשְׂרָאֵל הַמִּדְבָּרָה וַיָּבֹא יָהְצָה וַיִּלָּחֶם בְּיִשְׂרָאֵל:

24 But *Yisrael* put them to the sword, and took possession of their land, from the Arnon to the Jabbok, as far as [Az] of the Ammonites, for Az marked the boundary of the Ammonites.

כד וַיַּכֵּהוּ יִשְׂרָאֵל לְפִי־חָרֶב וַיִּירַשׁ אֶת־אַרְצוֹ מֵאַרְנֹן עַד־יַבֹּק עַד־בְּנֵי עַמּוֹן כִּי עַז גְּבוּל בְּנֵי עַמּוֹן:

25 *Yisrael* took all those towns. And *Yisrael* settled in all the towns of the Amorites, in Heshbon and all its dependencies.

כה וַיִּקַּח יִשְׂרָאֵל אֵת כָּל־הֶעָרִים הָאֵלֶּה וַיֵּשֶׁב יִשְׂרָאֵל בְּכָל־עָרֵי הָאֱמֹרִי בְּחֶשְׁבּוֹן וּבְכָל־בְּנֹתֶיהָ:

26 Now Heshbon was the city of Sihon king of the Amorites, who had fought against a former king of Moab and taken all his land from him as far as the Arnon.

כו כִּי חֶשְׁבּוֹן עִיר סִיחֹן מֶלֶךְ הָאֱמֹרִי הִוא וְהוּא נִלְחַם בְּמֶלֶךְ מוֹאָב הָרִאשׁוֹן וַיִּקַּח אֶת־כָּל־אַרְצוֹ מִיָּדוֹ עַד־אַרְנֹן:

27 Therefore the bards would recite: "Come to Heshbon; firmly built And well founded is Sihon's city.

כז עַל־כֵּן יֹאמְרוּ הַמֹּשְׁלִים בֹּאוּ חֶשְׁבּוֹן תִּבָּנֶה וְתִכּוֹנֵן עִיר סִיחוֹן:

28 For fire went forth from Heshbon, Flame from Sihon's city, Consuming Ar of Moab, The lords of Bamoth by the Arnon.

כח כִּי־אֵשׁ יָצְאָה מֵחֶשְׁבּוֹן לֶהָבָה מִקִּרְיַת סִיחֹן אָכְלָה עָר מוֹאָב בַּעֲלֵי בָּמוֹת אַרְנֹן:

29 Woe to you, O Moab! You are undone, O people of Chemosh! His sons are rendered fugitive And his daughters captive By an Amorite king, Sihon."

כט אוֹי־לְךָ מוֹאָב אָבַדְתָּ עַם־כְּמוֹשׁ נָתַן בָּנָיו פְּלֵיטִם וּבְנֹתָיו בַּשְּׁבִית לְמֶלֶךְ אֱמֹרִי סִיחוֹן:

30 Yet we have cast them down utterly, Heshbon along with Dibon; We have wrought desolation at Nophah, Which is hard by Medeba.

ל וַנִּירָם אָבַד חֶשְׁבּוֹן עַד־דִּיבוֹן וַנַּשִּׁים עַד־נֹפַח אֲשֶׁר עַד־מֵידְבָא:

31 So *Yisrael* occupied the land of the Amorites.

לא וַיֵּשֶׁב יִשְׂרָאֵל בְּאֶרֶץ הָאֱמֹרִי:

32 Then *Moshe* sent to spy out Jazer, and they captured its dependencies and dispossessed the Amorites who were there.

לב וַיִּשְׁלַח מֹשֶׁה לְרַגֵּל אֶת־יַעְזֵר וַיִּלְכְּדוּ בְּנֹתֶיהָ [וַיּוֹרֶשׁ] אֶת־הָאֱמֹרִי אֲשֶׁר־שָׁם:

33 They marched on and went up the road to Bashan, and King Og of Bashan, with all his people, came out to Edrei to engage them in battle.

לג וַיִּפְנוּ וַיַּעֲלוּ דֶּרֶךְ הַבָּשָׁן וַיֵּצֵא עוֹג מֶלֶךְ־הַבָּשָׁן לִקְרָאתָם הוּא וְכָל־עַמּוֹ לַמִּלְחָמָה אֶדְרֶעִי:

34 But *Hashem* said to *Moshe*, "Do not fear him, for I give him and all his people and his land into your hand. You shall do to him as you did to Sihon king of the Amorites who dwelt in Heshbon."

לד וַיֹּאמֶר יְהוָה אֶל־מֹשֶׁה אַל־תִּירָא אֹתוֹ כִּי בְיָדְךָ נָתַתִּי אֹתוֹ וְאֶת־כָּל־עַמּוֹ וְאֶת־אַרְצוֹ וְעָשִׂיתָ לּוֹ כַּאֲשֶׁר עָשִׂיתָ לְסִיחֹן מֶלֶךְ הָאֱמֹרִי אֲשֶׁר יוֹשֵׁב בְּחֶשְׁבּוֹן:

35 They defeated him and his sons and all his people, until no remnant was left him; and they took possession of his country.

לה וַיַּכּוּ אֹתוֹ וְאֶת־בָּנָיו וְאֶת־כָּל־עַמּוֹ עַד־בִּלְתִּי הִשְׁאִיר־לוֹ שָׂרִיד וַיִּירְשׁוּ אֶת־אַרְצוֹ:

*va-ya-KU o-TO v'-et ba-NAV v'-et kol a-MO ad bil-TEE
hish-eer LO sa-REED va-yee-r'-SHU et ar-TZO*

21:35 They defeated him In this section, the Israelites capture the lands of Sihon, king of the Amorites and Og, king of Bashan. *Moshe* initially asks these two kings for permission to pass peacefully through their lands in order to reach the Land of Israel. Instead of agreeing to the request, however, the Israelites were greeted with swords and spears. They thus had no choice but to go to war, from which they emerged victorious. While these lands were not included within the original borders of *Eretz Yisrael*, the capture of this territory marks the beginning of the successful conquest of the Promised Land.

The Golan Heights, part of biblical Bashan

Numbers

22 ¹ The Israelites then marched on and encamped in the steppes of Moab, across the *Yarden* from *Yericho*.

² Balak son of Zippor saw all that *Yisrael* had done to the Amorites.

³ Moab was alarmed because that people was so numerous. Moab dreaded the Israelites,

⁴ and Moab said to the elders of Midian, "Now this horde will lick clean all that is about us as an ox licks up the grass of the field." Balak son of Zippor, who was king of Moab at that time,

⁵ sent messengers to Balaam son of Beor in Pethor, which is by the Euphrates, in the land of his kinsfolk, to invite him, saying, "There is a people that came out of Egypt; it hides the earth from view, and it is settled next to me.

⁶ Come then, put a curse upon this people for me, since they are too numerous for me; perhaps I can thus defeat them and drive them out of the land. For I know that he whom you bless is blessed indeed, and he whom you curse is cursed."

⁷ The elders of Moab and the elders of Midian, versed in divination, set out. They came to Balaam and gave him Balak's message.

⁸ He said to them, "Spend the night here, and I shall reply to you as *Hashem* may instruct me." So the Moabite dignitaries stayed with Balaam.

⁹ *Hashem* came to Balaam and said, "What do these people want of you?"

¹⁰ Balaam said to *Hashem*, "Balak son of Zippor, king of Moab, sent me this message:

¹¹ Here is a people that came out from Egypt and hides the earth from view. Come now and curse them for me; perhaps I can engage them in battle and drive them off."

ב א וַיִּסְעוּ בְּנֵי יִשְׂרָאֵל וַיַּחֲנוּ בְּעַרְבוֹת מוֹאָב מֵעֵבֶר לְיַרְדֵּן יְרֵחוֹ׃

ב וַיַּרְא בָּלָק בֶּן־צִפּוֹר אֵת כָּל־אֲשֶׁר־עָשָׂה יִשְׂרָאֵל לָאֱמֹרִי׃

ג וַיָּגָר מוֹאָב מִפְּנֵי הָעָם מְאֹד כִּי רַב־הוּא וַיָּקָץ מוֹאָב מִפְּנֵי בְּנֵי יִשְׂרָאֵל׃

ד וַיֹּאמֶר מוֹאָב אֶל־זִקְנֵי מִדְיָן עַתָּה יְלַחֲכוּ הַקָּהָל אֶת־כָּל־סְבִיבֹתֵינוּ כִּלְחֹךְ הַשּׁוֹר אֵת יֶרֶק הַשָּׂדֶה וּבָלָק בֶּן־צִפּוֹר מֶלֶךְ לְמוֹאָב בָּעֵת הַהִוא׃

ה וַיִּשְׁלַח מַלְאָכִים אֶל־בִּלְעָם בֶּן־בְּעוֹר פְּתוֹרָה אֲשֶׁר עַל־הַנָּהָר אֶרֶץ בְּנֵי־עַמּוֹ לִקְרֹא־לוֹ לֵאמֹר הִנֵּה עַם יָצָא מִמִּצְרַיִם הִנֵּה כִסָּה אֶת־עֵין הָאָרֶץ וְהוּא יֹשֵׁב מִמֻּלִי׃

ו וְעַתָּה לְכָה־נָּא אָרָה־לִּי אֶת־הָעָם הַזֶּה כִּי־עָצוּם הוּא מִמֶּנִּי אוּלַי אוּכַל נַכֶּה־בּוֹ וַאֲגָרְשֶׁנּוּ מִן־הָאָרֶץ כִּי יָדַעְתִּי אֵת אֲשֶׁר־תְּבָרֵךְ מְבֹרָךְ וַאֲשֶׁר תָּאֹר יוּאָר׃

ז וַיֵּלְכוּ זִקְנֵי מוֹאָב וְזִקְנֵי מִדְיָן וּקְסָמִים בְּיָדָם וַיָּבֹאוּ אֶל־בִּלְעָם וַיְדַבְּרוּ אֵלָיו דִּבְרֵי בָלָק׃

ח וַיֹּאמֶר אֲלֵיהֶם לִינוּ פֹה הַלַּיְלָה וַהֲשִׁבֹתִי אֶתְכֶם דָּבָר כַּאֲשֶׁר יְדַבֵּר יְהֹוָה אֵלָי וַיֵּשְׁבוּ שָׂרֵי־מוֹאָב עִם־בִּלְעָם׃

ט וַיָּבֹא אֱלֹהִים אֶל־בִּלְעָם וַיֹּאמֶר מִי הָאֲנָשִׁים הָאֵלֶּה עִמָּךְ׃

י וַיֹּאמֶר בִּלְעָם אֶל־הָאֱלֹהִים בָּלָק בֶּן־צִפֹּר מֶלֶךְ מוֹאָב שָׁלַח אֵלָי׃

יא הִנֵּה הָעָם הַיֹּצֵא מִמִּצְרַיִם וַיְכַס אֶת־עֵין הָאָרֶץ עַתָּה לְכָה קָבָה־לִּי אֹתוֹ אוּלַי אוּכַל לְהִלָּחֶם בּוֹ וְגֵרַשְׁתִּיו׃

hi-NAY ha-AM ha-yo-TZAY mi-mitz-RA-yim vai-KHAS et AYN ha-A-retz a-TAH l'-KHAH ka-vah LEE o-TO u-LAI u-KHAL l'-hi-la-KHEM BO v'-gay-rash-TEEV

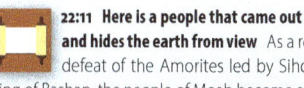

22:11 Here is a people that came out from Egypt and hides the earth from view As a result of the defeat of the Amorites led by Sihon and Og, king of Bashan, the people of Moab become afraid of the People of Israel. In an effort to stop the Israelites, their king, *Balak*, sends for the prophet Balaam to curse them. *Hashem*, however, has a different idea and puts a blessing into Balaam's mouth instead of his intended curses. This verse highlights Balaam's typically prejudicial attitude, in his description of the Israelites as a nation that covers the

12 But *Hashem* said to Balaam, "Do not go with them. You must not curse that people, for they are blessed."

יב וַיֹּאמֶר אֱלֹהִים אֶל־בִּלְעָם לֹא תֵלֵךְ עִמָּהֶם לֹא תָאֹר אֶת־הָעָם כִּי בָרוּךְ הוּא:

13 Balaam arose in the morning and said to Balak's dignitaries, "Go back to your own country, for *Hashem* will not let me go with you."

יג וַיָּקָם בִּלְעָם בַּבֹּקֶר וַיֹּאמֶר אֶל־שָׂרֵי בָלָק לְכוּ אֶל־אַרְצְכֶם כִּי מֵאֵן יְהֹוָה לְתִתִּי לַהֲלֹךְ עִמָּכֶם:

14 The Moabite dignitaries left, and they came to Balak and said, "Balaam refused to come with us."

יד וַיָּקוּמוּ שָׂרֵי מוֹאָב וַיָּבֹאוּ אֶל־בָּלָק וַיֹּאמְרוּ מֵאֵן בִּלְעָם הֲלֹךְ עִמָּנוּ:

15 Then Balak sent other dignitaries, more numerous and distinguished than the first.

טו וַיֹּסֶף עוֹד בָּלָק שְׁלֹחַ שָׂרִים רַבִּים וְנִכְבָּדִים מֵאֵלֶּה:

16 They came to Balaam and said to him, "Thus says Balak son of Zippor: Please do not refuse to come to me.

טז וַיָּבֹאוּ אֶל־בִּלְעָם וַיֹּאמְרוּ לוֹ כֹּה אָמַר בָּלָק בֶּן־צִפּוֹר אַל־נָא תִמָּנַע מֵהֲלֹךְ אֵלָי:

17 I will reward you richly and I will do anything you ask of me. Only come and damn this people for me."

יז כִּי־כַבֵּד אֲכַבֶּדְךָ מְאֹד וְכֹל אֲשֶׁר־תֹּאמַר אֵלַי אֶעֱשֶׂה וּלְכָה־נָּא קָבָה־לִּי אֵת הָעָם הַזֶּה:

18 Balaam replied to Balak's officials, "Though Balak were to give me his house full of silver and gold, I could not do anything, big or little, contrary to the command of *Hashem* my God.

יח וַיַּעַן בִּלְעָם וַיֹּאמֶר אֶל־עַבְדֵי בָלָק אִם־יִתֶּן־לִי בָלָק מְלֹא בֵיתוֹ כֶּסֶף וְזָהָב לֹא אוּכַל לַעֲבֹר אֶת־פִּי יְהֹוָה אֱלֹהָי לַעֲשׂוֹת קְטַנָּה אוֹ גְדוֹלָה:

19 So you, too, stay here overnight, and let me find out what else *Hashem* may say to me."

יט וְעַתָּה שְׁבוּ נָא בָזֶה גַּם־אַתֶּם הַלָּיְלָה וְאֵדְעָה מַה־יֹּסֵף יְהֹוָה דַּבֵּר עִמִּי:

20 That night *Hashem* came to Balaam and said to him, "If these men have come to invite you, you may go with them. But whatever I command you, that you shall do."

כ וַיָּבֹא אֱלֹהִים אֶל־בִּלְעָם לַיְלָה וַיֹּאמֶר לוֹ אִם־לִקְרֹא לְךָ בָּאוּ הָאֲנָשִׁים קוּם לֵךְ אִתָּם וְאַךְ אֶת־הַדָּבָר אֲשֶׁר־אֲדַבֵּר אֵלֶיךָ אֹתוֹ תַעֲשֶׂה:

21 When he arose in the morning, Balaam saddled his ass and departed with the Moabite dignitaries.

כא וַיָּקָם בִּלְעָם בַּבֹּקֶר וַיַּחֲבֹשׁ אֶת־אֲתֹנוֹ וַיֵּלֶךְ עִם־שָׂרֵי מוֹאָב:

22 But *Hashem* was incensed at his going; so an angel of *Hashem* placed himself in his way as an adversary. He was riding on his she-ass, with his two servants alongside,

כב וַיִּחַר־אַף אֱלֹהִים כִּי־הוֹלֵךְ הוּא וַיִּתְיַצֵּב מַלְאַךְ יְהֹוָה בַּדֶּרֶךְ לְשָׂטָן לוֹ וְהוּא רֹכֵב עַל־אֲתֹנוֹ וּשְׁנֵי נְעָרָיו עִמּוֹ:

entire earth. Even today, the Jewish people comprise less than 0.2% of the world population, yet they are often thought of as a nuisance that threatens the world. This story, however, also underscores the fact that anti-Semitism will not prevail. *Hashem* tells Balaam that the Jewish people "are blessed," and that those who try to curse them will not succeed, just as *Hashem* had promised *Avraham* long before, "I will bless those who bless you and curse him that curses you" (Genesis 12:3). The Jewish nation is indeed blessed, and has made enormous contributions to the world, as evidenced by the fact that despite their small number, between 1901 and 2015 over 20% of all Nobel laureates have either been Jewish, or of Jewish descent.

Promenade dedicated to Jewish Nobel Prize laureates in Rishon Letzion.

Numbers

²³ when the ass caught sight of the angel of *Hashem* standing in the way, with his drawn sword in his hand. The ass swerved from the road and went into the fields; and Balaam beat the ass to turn her back onto the road.

כג וַתֵּרֶא הָאָתוֹן אֶת־מַלְאַךְ יְהֹוָה נִצָּב בַּדֶּרֶךְ וְחַרְבּוֹ שְׁלוּפָה בְּיָדוֹ וַתֵּט הָאָתוֹן מִן־הַדֶּרֶךְ וַתֵּלֶךְ בַּשָּׂדֶה וַיַּךְ בִּלְעָם אֶת־הָאָתוֹן לְהַטֹּתָהּ הַדָּרֶךְ:

²⁴ The angel of *Hashem* then stationed himself in a lane between the vineyards, with a fence on either side.

כד וַיַּעֲמֹד מַלְאַךְ יְהֹוָה בְּמִשְׁעוֹל הַכְּרָמִים גָּדֵר מִזֶּה וְגָדֵר מִזֶּה:

²⁵ The ass, seeing the angel of *Hashem*, pressed herself against the wall and squeezed Balaam's foot against the wall; so he beat her again.

כה וַתֵּרֶא הָאָתוֹן אֶת־מַלְאַךְ יְהֹוָה וַתִּלָּחֵץ אֶל־הַקִּיר וַתִּלְחַץ אֶת־רֶגֶל בִּלְעָם אֶל־הַקִּיר וַיֹּסֶף לְהַכֹּתָהּ:

²⁶ Once more the angel of *Hashem* moved forward and stationed himself on a spot so narrow that there was no room to swerve right or left.

כו וַיּוֹסֶף מַלְאַךְ־יְהֹוָה עֲבוֹר וַיַּעֲמֹד בְּמָקוֹם צָר אֲשֶׁר אֵין־דֶּרֶךְ לִנְטוֹת יָמִין וּשְׂמֹאול:

²⁷ When the ass now saw the angel of *Hashem*, she lay down under Balaam; and Balaam was furious and beat the ass with his stick.

כז וַתֵּרֶא הָאָתוֹן אֶת־מַלְאַךְ יְהֹוָה וַתִּרְבַּץ תַּחַת בִּלְעָם וַיִּחַר־אַף בִּלְעָם וַיַּךְ אֶת־הָאָתוֹן בַּמַּקֵּל:

²⁸ Then *Hashem* opened the ass's mouth, and she said to Balaam, "What have I done to you that you have beaten me these three times?"

כח וַיִּפְתַּח יְהֹוָה אֶת־פִּי הָאָתוֹן וַתֹּאמֶר לְבִלְעָם מֶה־עָשִׂיתִי לְךָ כִּי הִכִּיתַנִי זֶה שָׁלֹשׁ רְגָלִים:

²⁹ Balaam said to the ass, "You have made a mockery of me! If I had a sword with me, I'd kill you."

כט וַיֹּאמֶר בִּלְעָם לָאָתוֹן כִּי הִתְעַלַּלְתְּ בִּי לוּ יֶשׁ־חֶרֶב בְּיָדִי כִּי עַתָּה הֲרַגְתִּיךְ:

³⁰ The ass said to Balaam, "Look, I am the ass that you have been riding all along until this day! Have I been in the habit of doing thus to you?" And he answered, "No."

ל וַתֹּאמֶר הָאָתוֹן אֶל־בִּלְעָם הֲלוֹא אָנֹכִי אֲתֹנְךָ אֲשֶׁר־רָכַבְתָּ עָלַי מֵעוֹדְךָ עַד־הַיּוֹם הַזֶּה הַהַסְכֵּן הִסְכַּנְתִּי לַעֲשׂוֹת לְךָ כֹּה וַיֹּאמֶר לֹא:

³¹ Then *Hashem* uncovered Balaam's eyes, and he saw the angel of *Hashem* standing in the way, his drawn sword in his hand; thereupon he bowed right down to the ground.

לא וַיְגַל יְהֹוָה אֶת־עֵינֵי בִלְעָם וַיַּרְא אֶת־מַלְאַךְ יְהֹוָה נִצָּב בַּדֶּרֶךְ וְחַרְבּוֹ שְׁלֻפָה בְּיָדוֹ וַיִּקֹּד וַיִּשְׁתַּחוּ לְאַפָּיו:

³² The angel of *Hashem* said to him, "Why have you beaten your ass these three times? It is I who came out as an adversary, for the errand is obnoxious to me.

לב וַיֹּאמֶר אֵלָיו מַלְאַךְ יְהֹוָה עַל־מָה הִכִּיתָ אֶת־אֲתֹנְךָ זֶה שָׁלוֹשׁ רְגָלִים הִנֵּה אָנֹכִי יָצָאתִי לְשָׂטָן כִּי־יָרַט הַדֶּרֶךְ לְנֶגְדִּי:

³³ And when the ass saw me, she shied away because of me those three times. If she had not shied away from me, you are the one I should have killed, while sparing her."

לג וַתִּרְאַנִי הָאָתוֹן וַתֵּט לְפָנַי זֶה שָׁלֹשׁ רְגָלִים אוּלַי נָטְתָה מִפָּנַי כִּי עַתָּה גַּם־אֹתְכָה הָרַגְתִּי וְאוֹתָהּ הֶחֱיֵיתִי:

³⁴ Balaam said to the angel of *Hashem*, "I erred because I did not know that you were standing in my way. If you still disapprove, I will turn back."

לד וַיֹּאמֶר בִּלְעָם אֶל־מַלְאַךְ יְהֹוָה חָטָאתִי כִּי לֹא יָדַעְתִּי כִּי אַתָּה נִצָּב לִקְרָאתִי בַּדָּרֶךְ וְעַתָּה אִם־רַע בְּעֵינֶיךָ אָשׁוּבָה לִּי:

35 But the angel of *Hashem* said to Balaam, "Go with the men. But you must say nothing except what I tell you." So Balaam went on with Balak's dignitaries.

לה וַיֹּאמֶר מַלְאַךְ יְהֹוָה אֶל־בִּלְעָם לֵךְ עִם־הָאֲנָשִׁים וְאֶפֶס אֶת־הַדָּבָר אֲשֶׁר־אֲדַבֵּר אֵלֶיךָ אֹתוֹ תְדַבֵּר וַיֵּלֶךְ בִּלְעָם עִם־שָׂרֵי בָלָק:

36 When Balak heard that Balaam was coming, he went out to meet him at Ir-moab, which is on the Arnon border, at its farthest point.

לו וַיִּשְׁמַע בָּלָק כִּי בָא בִלְעָם וַיֵּצֵא לִקְרָאתוֹ אֶל־עִיר מוֹאָב אֲשֶׁר עַל־גְּבוּל אַרְנֹן אֲשֶׁר בִּקְצֵה הַגְּבוּל:

37 Balak said to Balaam, "When I first sent to invite you, why didn't you come to me? Am I really unable to reward you?"

לז וַיֹּאמֶר בָּלָק אֶל־בִּלְעָם הֲלֹא שָׁלֹחַ שָׁלַחְתִּי אֵלֶיךָ לִקְרֹא־לָךְ לָמָּה לֹא־הָלַכְתָּ אֵלָי הַאֻמְנָם לֹא אוּכַל כַּבְּדֶךָ:

38 But Balaam said to Balak, "And now that I have come to you, have I the power to speak freely? I can utter only the word that *Hashem* puts into my mouth."

לח וַיֹּאמֶר בִּלְעָם אֶל־בָּלָק הִנֵּה־בָאתִי אֵלֶיךָ עַתָּה הֲיָכֹל אוּכַל דַּבֵּר מְאוּמָה הַדָּבָר אֲשֶׁר יָשִׂים אֱלֹהִים בְּפִי אֹתוֹ אֲדַבֵּר:

39 Balaam went with Balak and they came to Kiriath-huzoth.

לט וַיֵּלֶךְ בִּלְעָם עִם־בָּלָק וַיָּבֹאוּ קִרְיַת חֻצוֹת:

40 Balak sacrificed oxen and sheep, and had them served to Balaam and the dignitaries with him.

מ וַיִּזְבַּח בָּלָק בָּקָר וָצֹאן וַיְשַׁלַּח לְבִלְעָם וְלַשָּׂרִים אֲשֶׁר אִתּוֹ:

41 In the morning Balak took Balaam up to Bamoth-baal. From there he could see a portion of the people.

מא וַיְהִי בַבֹּקֶר וַיִּקַּח בָּלָק אֶת־בִּלְעָם וַיַּעֲלֵהוּ בָּמוֹת בָּעַל וַיַּרְא מִשָּׁם קְצֵה הָעָם:

23 1 Balaam said to Balak, "Build me seven altars here and have seven bulls and seven rams ready here for me."

כג א וַיֹּאמֶר בִּלְעָם אֶל־בָּלָק בְּנֵה־לִי בָזֶה שִׁבְעָה מִזְבְּחֹת וְהָכֵן לִי בָּזֶה שִׁבְעָה פָרִים וְשִׁבְעָה אֵילִם:

2 Balak did as Balaam directed; and Balak and Balaam offered up a bull and a ram on each altar.

ב וַיַּעַשׂ בָּלָק כַּאֲשֶׁר דִּבֶּר בִּלְעָם וַיַּעַל בָּלָק וּבִלְעָם פָּר וָאַיִל בַּמִּזְבֵּחַ:

3 Then Balaam said to Balak, "Stay here beside your offerings while I am gone. Perhaps *Hashem* will grant me a manifestation, and whatever He reveals to me I will tell you." And he went off alone.

ג וַיֹּאמֶר בִּלְעָם לְבָלָק הִתְיַצֵּב עַל־עֹלָתֶךָ וְאֵלְכָה אוּלַי יִקָּרֵה יְהֹוָה לִקְרָאתִי וּדְבַר מַה־יַּרְאֵנִי וְהִגַּדְתִּי לָךְ וַיֵּלֶךְ שֶׁפִי:

4 *Hashem* manifested Himself to Balaam, who said to Him, "I have set up the seven altars and offered up a bull and a ram on each altar."

ד וַיִּקָּר אֱלֹהִים אֶל־בִּלְעָם וַיֹּאמֶר אֵלָיו אֶת־שִׁבְעַת הַמִּזְבְּחֹת עָרַכְתִּי וָאַעַל פָּר וָאַיִל בַּמִּזְבֵּחַ:

5 And *Hashem* put a word in Balaam's mouth and said, "Return to Balak and speak thus."

ה וַיָּשֶׂם יְהֹוָה דָּבָר בְּפִי בִלְעָם וַיֹּאמֶר שׁוּב אֶל־בָּלָק וְכֹה תְדַבֵּר:

6 So he returned to him and found him standing beside his offerings, and all the Moabite dignitaries with him.

ו וַיָּשָׁב אֵלָיו וְהִנֵּה נִצָּב עַל־עֹלָתוֹ הוּא וְכָל־שָׂרֵי מוֹאָב:

7 He took up his theme, and said: From Aram has Balak brought me, Moab's king from the hills of the East: Come, curse me *Yaakov*, Come, tell *Yisrael*'s doom!

ז וַיִּשָּׂא מְשָׁלוֹ וַיֹּאמַר מִן־אֲרָם יַנְחֵנִי בָלָק מֶלֶךְ־מוֹאָב מֵהַרְרֵי־קֶדֶם לְכָה אָרָה־לִּי יַעֲקֹב וּלְכָה זֹעֲמָה יִשְׂרָאֵל:

Numbers

8 How can I damn whom *Hashem* has not damned,
How doom when *Hashem* has not doomed?

ח מָה אֶקֹּב לֹא קַבֹּה אֵל וּמָה אֶזְעֹם לֹא
זָעַם יְהֹוָה:

9 As I see them from the mountain tops, Gaze on
them from the heights, There is a people that
dwells apart, Not reckoned among the nations,

ט כִּי־מֵרֹאשׁ צֻרִים אֶרְאֶנּוּ וּמִגְּבָעוֹת
אֲשׁוּרֶנּוּ הֶן־עָם לְבָדָד יִשְׁכֹּן וּבַגּוֹיִם לֹא
יִתְחַשָּׁב:

*kee may-ROSH tzu-REEM er-E-nu u-mig-va-OT a-shu-RE-nu hen
AM l'-va-DAD yish-KON u-va-go-YEEM LO yit-kha-SHAV*

10 Who can count the dust of *Yaakov*, Number the
dust-cloud of *Yisrael*? May I die the death of the
upright, May my fate be like theirs!

י מִי מָנָה עֲפַר יַעֲקֹב וּמִסְפָּר אֶת־רֹבַע
יִשְׂרָאֵל תָּמֹת נַפְשִׁי מוֹת יְשָׁרִים וּתְהִי
אַחֲרִיתִי כָּמֹהוּ:

11 Then Balak said to Balaam, "What have you done to
me? Here I brought you to damn my enemies, and
instead you have blessed them!"

יא וַיֹּאמֶר בָּלָק אֶל־בִּלְעָם מֶה עָשִׂיתָ לִי
לָקֹב אֹיְבַי לְקַחְתִּיךָ וְהִנֵּה בֵּרַכְתָּ בָרֵךְ:

12 He replied, "I can only repeat faithfully what
Hashem puts in my mouth."

יב וַיַּעַן וַיֹּאמַר הֲלֹא אֵת אֲשֶׁר יָשִׂים יְהֹוָה
בְּפִי אֹתוֹ אֶשְׁמֹר לְדַבֵּר:

13 Then Balak said to him, "Come with me to another
place from which you can see them – you will
see only a portion of them; you will not see all of
them – and damn them for me from there."

יג וַיֹּאמֶר אֵלָיו בָּלָק לך־[לְכָה־] נָּא אִתִּי
אֶל־מָקוֹם אַחֵר אֲשֶׁר תִּרְאֶנּוּ מִשָּׁם
אֶפֶס קָצֵהוּ תִרְאֶה וְכֻלּוֹ לֹא תִרְאֶה
וְקָבְנוֹ־לִי מִשָּׁם:

14 With that, he took him to Sedehzophim, on the
summit of Pisgah. He built seven altars and offered
a bull and a ram on each altar.

יד וַיִּקָּחֵהוּ שְׂדֵה צֹפִים אֶל־רֹאשׁ הַפִּסְגָּה
וַיִּבֶן שִׁבְעָה מִזְבְּחֹת וַיַּעַל פָּר וָאַיִל
בַּמִּזְבֵּחַ:

15 And [Balaam] said to Balak, "Stay here beside your
offerings, while I seek a manifestation yonder."

טו וַיֹּאמֶר אֶל־בָּלָק הִתְיַצֵּב כֹּה עַל־עֹלָתֶךָ
וְאָנֹכִי אִקָּרֶה כֹּה:

16 *Hashem* manifested Himself to Balaam and put a
word in his mouth, saying, "Return to Balak and
speak thus."

טז וַיִּקָּר יְהֹוָה אֶל־בִּלְעָם וַיָּשֶׂם דָּבָר בְּפִיו
וַיֹּאמֶר שׁוּב אֶל־בָּלָק וְכֹה תְדַבֵּר:

17 He went to him and found him standing beside his
offerings, and the Moabite dignitaries with him.
Balak asked him, "What did *Hashem* say?"

יז וַיָּבֹא אֵלָיו וְהִנּוֹ נִצָּב עַל־עֹלָתוֹ וְשָׂרֵי
מוֹאָב אִתּוֹ וַיֹּאמֶר לוֹ בָּלָק מַה־דִּבֶּר
יְהֹוָה:

**23:9 There is a people that dwells apart, not
reckoned among the nations** This chapter is
one of three that describe the failed attempt
by Balaam to curse the People of Israel. His plan is foiled
by *Hashem*, and instead of a curse, Balaam utters a reluc-
tant compliment, "There is a people that dwells apart, not
reckoned among the nations." For better or for worse, the
Jews have always been set aside from among the nations
and singled out for special treatment. Today, Israel receives a disproportionate amount of coverage by the
media, most of it negative. However, we must recognize
the inherent lesson of this solitude: the People of Israel
have been singled out for a holy purpose. They were
chosen by *Hashem* to
remain faithful to Him
and to fulfill the biblical
mandate of teaching
His truths to the world.
While for most of his-
tory, the Jewish Nation
has indeed been an

The Chinese delegation in the
Jerusalem march, September 2013

isolated "people that dwells apart," that reality began to
change with the establishment of the State of Israel. For
the first time, millions of non-Jews have started to stand
together with the People of Israel, rejecting the curse of
Balaam.

18 And he took up his theme, and said: Up, Balak, attend, Give ear unto me, son of Zippor!

יח וַיִּשָּׂ֣א מְשָׁל֔וֹ וַיֹּאמַ֑ר ק֤וּם בָּלָק֙ וּֽשֲׁמָ֔ע הַאֲזִ֥ינָה עָדַ֖י בְּנ֥וֹ צִפֹּֽר׃

19 *Hashem* is not man to be capricious, Or mortal to change His mind. Would He speak and not act, Promise and not fulfill?

יט לֹ֣א אִ֥ישׁ אֵל֙ וִֽיכַזֵּ֔ב וּבֶן־אָדָ֖ם וְיִתְנֶחָ֑ם הַה֤וּא אָמַר֙ וְלֹ֣א יַעֲשֶׂ֔ה וְדִבֶּ֖ר וְלֹ֥א יְקִימֶֽנָּה׃

20 My message was to bless: When He blesses, I cannot reverse it.

כ הִנֵּ֥ה בָרֵ֖ךְ לָקָ֑חְתִּי וּבֵרֵ֖ךְ וְלֹ֥א אֲשִׁיבֶֽנָּה׃

21 No harm is in sight for *Yaakov*, No woe in view for *Yisrael*. *Hashem* their God is with them, And their King's acclaim in their midst.

כא לֹֽא־הִבִּ֥יט אָ֨וֶן֙ בְּיַֽעֲקֹ֔ב וְלֹא־רָאָ֥ה עָמָ֖ל בְּיִשְׂרָאֵ֑ל יְהֹוָ֤ה אֱלֹהָיו֙ עִמּ֔וֹ וּתְרוּעַ֥ת מֶ֖לֶךְ בּֽוֹ׃

22 *Hashem* who freed them from Egypt Is for them like the horns of the wild ox.

כב אֵ֖ל מֽוֹצִיאָ֣ם מִמִּצְרָ֑יִם כְּתֽוֹעֲפֹ֥ת רְאֵ֖ם לֽוֹ׃

23 Lo, there is no augury in *Yaakov*, No divining in *Yisrael*: *Yaakov* is told at once, Yea *Yisrael*, what *Hashem* has planned.

כג כִּ֤י לֹא־נַ֨חַשׁ֙ בְּיַֽעֲקֹ֔ב וְלֹא־קֶ֖סֶם בְּיִשְׂרָאֵ֑ל כָּעֵ֗ת יֵאָמֵ֤ר לְיַֽעֲקֹב֙ וּלְיִשְׂרָאֵ֔ל מַה־פָּ֖עַל אֵֽל׃

24 Lo, a people that rises like a lion, Leaps up like the king of beasts, Rests not till it has feasted on prey And drunk the blood of the slain.

כד הֶן־עָם֙ כְּלָבִ֣יא יָק֔וּם וְכַֽאֲרִ֖י יִתְנַשָּׂ֑א לֹ֤א יִשְׁכַּב֙ עַד־יֹ֣אכַל טֶ֔רֶף וְדַם־חֲלָלִ֖ים יִשְׁתֶּֽה׃

25 Thereupon Balak said to Balaam, "Don't curse them and don't bless them!"

כה וַיֹּ֤אמֶר בָּלָק֙ אֶל־בִּלְעָ֔ם גַּם־קֹ֖ב לֹ֣א תִקֳּבֶ֑נּוּ גַּם־בָּרֵ֖ךְ לֹ֥א תְבָֽרֲכֶֽנּוּ׃

26 In reply, Balaam said to Balak, "But I told you: Whatever *Hashem* says, that I must do."

כו וַיַּ֣עַן בִּלְעָ֔ם וַיֹּ֖אמֶר אֶל־בָּלָ֑ק הֲלֹ֗א דִּבַּ֤רְתִּי אֵלֶ֨יךָ֙ לֵאמֹ֔ר כֹּ֛ל אֲשֶׁר־יְדַבֵּ֥ר יְהֹוָ֖ה אֹת֥וֹ אֶֽעֱשֶֽׂה׃

27 Then Balak said to Balaam, "Come now, I will take you to another place. Perhaps *Hashem* will deem it right that you damn them for me there."

כז וַיֹּ֤אמֶר בָּלָק֙ אֶל־בִּלְעָ֔ם לְכָה־נָּא֙ אֶקָּ֣חֲךָ֔ אֶל־מָק֖וֹם אַחֵ֑ר אוּלַ֤י יִישַׁר֙ בְּעֵינֵ֣י הָֽאֱלֹהִ֔ים וְקַבֹּ֥תוֹ לִ֖י מִשָּֽׁם׃

28 Balak took Balaam to the peak of Peor, which overlooks the wasteland.

כח וַיִּקַּ֥ח בָּלָ֖ק אֶת־בִּלְעָ֑ם רֹ֖אשׁ הַפְּע֑וֹר הַנִּשְׁקָ֖ף עַל־פְּנֵ֥י הַיְשִׁימֹֽן׃

29 Balaam said to Balak, "Build me here seven altars, and have seven bulls and seven rams ready for me here."

כט וַיֹּ֤אמֶר בִּלְעָם֙ אֶל־בָּלָ֔ק בְּנֵה־לִ֥י בָזֶ֖ה שִׁבְעָ֣ה מִזְבְּחֹ֑ת וְהָכֵ֥ן לִ֛י בָּזֶ֖ה שִׁבְעָ֥ה פָרִ֖ים וְשִׁבְעָ֥ה אֵילִֽים׃

30 Balak did as Balaam said: he offered up a bull and a ram on each altar.

ל וַיַּ֣עַשׂ בָּלָ֔ק כַּֽאֲשֶׁ֖ר אָמַ֣ר בִּלְעָ֑ם וַיַּ֛עַל פָּ֥ר וָאַ֖יִל בַּמִּזְבֵּֽחַ׃

24 1 Now Balaam, seeing that it pleased *Hashem* to bless *Yisrael*, did not, as on previous occasions, go in search of omens, but turned his face toward the wilderness.

כד א וַיַּ֣רְא בִּלְעָ֗ם כִּ֣י ט֞וֹב בְּעֵינֵ֤י יְהֹוָה֙ לְבָרֵ֣ךְ אֶת־יִשְׂרָאֵ֔ל וְלֹֽא־הָלַ֥ךְ כְּפַֽעַם־בְּפַ֖עַם לִקְרַ֣את נְחָשִׁ֑ים וַיָּ֥שֶׁת אֶל־הַמִּדְבָּ֖ר פָּנָֽיו׃

2 As Balaam looked up and saw *Yisrael* encamped tribe by tribe, the spirit of *Hashem* came upon him.

ב וַיִּשָּׂ֨א בִלְעָ֜ם אֶת־עֵינָ֗יו וַיַּרְא֙ אֶת־יִשְׂרָאֵ֔ל שֹׁכֵ֖ן לִשְׁבָטָ֑יו וַתְּהִ֥י עָלָ֖יו ר֥וּחַ אֱלֹהִֽים׃

Numbers

3 Taking up his theme, he said: Word of Balaam son of Beor, Word of the man whose eye is true,

ג וַיִּשָּׂא מְשָׁלוֹ וַיֹּאמַר נְאֻם בִּלְעָם בְּנוֹ בְעֹר וּנְאֻם הַגֶּבֶר שְׁתֻם הָעָיִן:

4 Word of him who hears *Hashem*'s speech, Who beholds visions from the Almighty, Prostrate, but with eyes unveiled:

ד נְאֻם שֹׁמֵעַ אִמְרֵי־אֵל אֲשֶׁר מַחֲזֵה שַׁדַּי יֶחֱזֶה נֹפֵל וּגְלוּי עֵינָיִם:

5 How fair are your tents, O *Yaakov*, Your dwellings, O *Yisrael*!

ה מַה־טֹּבוּ אֹהָלֶיךָ יַעֲקֹב מִשְׁכְּנֹתֶיךָ יִשְׂרָאֵל:

ma TO-vu o-ha-LE-kha ya-a-KOV mish-k'-no-TE-kha yis-ra-AYL

6 Like palm-groves that stretch out, Like gardens beside a river, Like aloes planted by *Hashem*, Like cedars beside the water;

ו כִּנְחָלִים נִטָּיוּ כְּגַנֹּת עֲלֵי נָהָר כַּאֲהָלִים נָטַע יְהוָה כַּאֲרָזִים עֲלֵי־מָיִם:

7 Their boughs drip with moisture, Their roots have abundant water. Their king shall rise above Agag, Their kingdom shall be exalted.

ז יִזַּל־מַיִם מִדָּלְיָו וְזַרְעוֹ בְּמַיִם רַבִּים וְיָרֹם מֵאֲגַג מַלְכּוֹ וְתִנַּשֵּׂא מַלְכֻתוֹ:

8 *Hashem* who freed them from Egypt Is for them like the horns of the wild ox. They shall devour enemy nations, Crush their bones, And smash their arrows.

ח אֵל מוֹצִיאוֹ מִמִּצְרַיִם כְּתוֹעֲפֹת רְאֵם לוֹ יֹאכַל גּוֹיִם צָרָיו וְעַצְמֹתֵיהֶם יְגָרֵם וְחִצָּיו יִמְחָץ:

9 They crouch, they lie down like a lion, Like the king of beasts; who dare rouse them? Blessed are they who bless you, Accursed they who curse you!

ט כָּרַע שָׁכַב כַּאֲרִי וּכְלָבִיא מִי יְקִימֶנּוּ מְבָרֲכֶיךָ בָרוּךְ וְאֹרְרֶיךָ אָרוּר:

10 Enraged at Balaam, Balak struck his hands together. "I called you," Balak said to Balaam, "to damn my enemies, and instead you have blessed them these three times!

י וַיִּחַר־אַף בָּלָק אֶל־בִּלְעָם וַיִּסְפֹּק אֶת־כַּפָּיו וַיֹּאמֶר בָּלָק אֶל־בִּלְעָם לָקֹב אֹיְבַי קְרָאתִיךָ וְהִנֵּה בֵּרַכְתָּ בָרֵךְ זֶה שָׁלֹשׁ פְּעָמִים:

11 Back with you at once to your own place! I was going to reward you richly, but *Hashem* has denied you the reward."

יא וְעַתָּה בְּרַח־לְךָ אֶל־מְקוֹמֶךָ אָמַרְתִּי כַּבֵּד אֲכַבֶּדְךָ וְהִנֵּה מְנָעֲךָ יְהוָה מִכָּבוֹד:

12 Balaam replied to Balak, "But I even told the messengers you sent to me,

יב וַיֹּאמֶר בִּלְעָם אֶל־בָּלָק הֲלֹא גַּם אֶל־מַלְאָכֶיךָ אֲשֶׁר־שָׁלַחְתָּ אֵלַי דִּבַּרְתִּי לֵאמֹר:

13 'Though Balak were to give me his house full of silver and gold, I could not of my own accord do anything good or bad contrary to *Hashem*'s command. What *Hashem* says, that I must say.'

יג אִם־יִתֶּן־לִי בָלָק מְלֹא בֵיתוֹ כֶּסֶף וְזָהָב לֹא אוּכַל לַעֲבֹר אֶת־פִּי יְהוָה לַעֲשׂוֹת טוֹבָה אוֹ רָעָה מִלִּבִּי אֲשֶׁר־יְדַבֵּר יְהוָה אֹתוֹ אֲדַבֵּר:

 24:5 How fair are your tents, O *Yaakov*, your dwellings, O *Yisrael* *Ramban* points out that when referring to the homes of the Children of Israel, the verse first mentions tents of *Yaakov* and then dwellings of Israel. He explains that "tents" are temporary living quarters, referring to Israel's sojourn in the desert, while

The modern city of Be'er Sheva

"dwellings" implies a permanent living space, hinting to the established life of the Jews in the Holy Land. Just as they are taken care of and protected in the desert, the Children of Israel will ultimately be blessed with success, prosperity and security in *Eretz Yisrael*.

14 And now, as I go back to my people, let me inform you of what this people will do to your people in days to come."

יד וְעַתָּ֗ה הִנְנִ֤י הוֹלֵךְ֙ לְעַמִּ֔י לְכָה֙ אִיעָ֣צְךָ֔ אֲשֶׁ֨ר יַעֲשֶׂ֜ה הָעָ֥ם הַזֶּ֛ה לְעַמְּךָ֖ בְּאַחֲרִ֥ית הַיָּמִֽים:

15 He took up his theme, and said: Word of Balaam son of Beor, Word of the man whose eye is true,

טו וַיִּשָּׂ֥א מְשָׁל֖וֹ וַיֹּאמַ֑ר נְאֻ֤ם בִּלְעָם֙ בְּנ֣וֹ בְעֹ֔ר וּנְאֻ֥ם הַגֶּ֖בֶר שְׁתֻ֥ם הָעָֽיִן:

16 Word of him who hears *Hashem*'s speech, Who obtains knowledge from the Most High, And beholds visions from the Almighty, Prostrate, but with eyes unveiled:

טז נְאֻ֗ם שֹׁמֵ֙עַ֙ אִמְרֵי־אֵ֔ל וְיֹדֵ֖עַ דַּ֣עַת עֶלְי֑וֹן מַחֲזֵ֤ה שַׁדַּי֙ יֶֽחֱזֶ֔ה נֹפֵ֖ל וּגְל֥וּי עֵינָֽיִם:

17 What I see for them is not yet, What I behold will not be soon: A star rises from *Yaakov*, A scepter comes forth from *Yisrael*; It smashes the brow of Moab, The foundation of all children of *Shet*.

יז אֶרְאֶ֙נּוּ֙ וְלֹ֣א עַתָּ֔ה אֲשׁוּרֶ֖נּוּ וְלֹ֣א קָר֑וֹב דָּרַ֨ךְ כּוֹכָ֜ב מִֽיַּעֲקֹ֗ב וְקָ֥ם שֵׁ֙בֶט֙ מִיִּשְׂרָאֵ֔ל וּמָחַץ֙ פַּאֲתֵ֣י מוֹאָ֔ב וְקַרְקַ֖ר כָּל־בְּנֵי־שֵֽׁת:

18 Edom becomes a possession, Yea, Seir a possession of its enemies; But *Yisrael* is triumphant.

יח וְהָיָ֨ה אֱד֜וֹם יְרֵשָׁ֗ה וְהָיָ֧ה יְרֵשָׁ֛ה שֵׂעִ֖יר אֹיְבָ֑יו וְיִשְׂרָאֵ֖ל עֹ֥שֶׂה חָֽיִל:

19 A victor issues from *Yaakov* To wipe out what is left of Ir.

יט וְיֵ֖רְדְּ מִֽיַּעֲקֹ֑ב וְהֶאֱבִ֥יד שָׂרִ֖יד מֵעִֽיר:

20 He saw Amalek and, taking up his theme, he said: A leading nation is Amalek; But its fate is to perish forever.

כ וַיַּרְא֙ אֶת־עֲמָלֵ֔ק וַיִּשָּׂ֥א מְשָׁל֖וֹ וַיֹּאמַ֑ר רֵאשִׁ֤ית גּוֹיִם֙ עֲמָלֵ֔ק וְאַחֲרִית֖וֹ עֲדֵ֥י אֹבֵֽד:

21 He saw the Kenites and, taking up his theme, he said: Though your abode be secure, And your nest be set among cliffs,

כא וַיַּרְא֙ אֶת־הַקֵּינִ֔י וַיִּשָּׂ֥א מְשָׁל֖וֹ וַיֹּאמַ֑ר אֵיתָן֙ מֽוֹשָׁבֶ֔ךָ וְשִׂ֥ים בַּסֶּ֖לַע קִנֶּֽךָ:

22 Yet shall Kain be consumed, When Assyria takes you captive.

כב כִּ֤י אִם־יִֽהְיֶה֙ לְבָ֣עֵ֣ר קָ֔יִן עַד־מָ֖ה אַשּׁ֥וּר תִּשְׁבֶּֽךָּ:

23 He took up his theme and said: Alas, who can survive except *Hashem* has willed it!

כג וַיִּשָּׂ֥א מְשָׁל֖וֹ וַיֹּאמַ֑ר א֕וֹי מִ֥י יִחְיֶ֖ה מִשֻּׂמ֥וֹ אֵֽל:

24 Ships come from the quarter of Kittim; They subject Assyria, subject Eber. They, too, shall perish forever.

כד וְצִים֙ מִיַּ֣ד כִּתִּ֔ים וְעִנּ֥וּ אַשּׁ֖וּר וְעִנּוּ־עֵ֑בֶר וְגַם־ה֖וּא עֲדֵ֥י אֹבֵֽד:

25 Then Balaam set out on his journey back home; and Balak also went his way.

כה וַיָּ֣קָם בִּלְעָ֔ם וַיֵּ֖לֶךְ וַיָּ֣שָׁב לִמְקֹמ֑וֹ וְגַם־בָּלָ֖ק הָלַ֥ךְ לְדַרְכּֽוֹ:

25 1 While *Yisrael* was staying at Shittim, the people profaned themselves by whoring with the Moabite women,

כה א וַיֵּ֥שֶׁב יִשְׂרָאֵ֖ל בַּשִּׁטִּ֑ים וַיָּ֣חֶל הָעָ֔ם לִזְנ֖וֹת אֶל־בְּנ֥וֹת מוֹאָֽב:

2 who invited the people to the sacrifices for their god. The people partook of them and worshiped that god.

ב וַתִּקְרֶ֣אןָ לָעָ֔ם לְזִבְחֵ֖י אֱלֹהֵיהֶ֑ן וַיֹּ֣אכַל הָעָ֔ם וַיִּֽשְׁתַּחֲו֖וּ לֵֽאלֹהֵיהֶֽן:

3 Thus *Yisrael* attached itself to Baal-peor, and *Hashem* was incensed with *Yisrael*.

ג וַיִּצָּ֥מֶד יִשְׂרָאֵ֖ל לְבַ֣עַל פְּע֑וֹר וַיִּֽחַר־אַ֥ף יְהוָֹ֖ה בְּיִשְׂרָאֵֽל:

Numbers

4 *Hashem* said to *Moshe*, "Take all the ringleaders and have them publicly impaled before *Hashem*, so that *Hashem*'s wrath may turn away from *Yisrael*."

ד וַיֹּאמֶר יְהֹוָה אֶל־מֹשֶׁה קַח אֶת־כָּל־רָאשֵׁי הָעָם וְהוֹקַע אוֹתָם לַיהֹוָה נֶגֶד הַשָּׁמֶשׁ וְיָשֹׁב חֲרוֹן אַף־יְהֹוָה מִיִּשְׂרָאֵל:

5 So *Moshe* said to *Yisrael*'s officials, "Each of you slay those of his men who attached themselves to Baal-peor."

ה וַיֹּאמֶר מֹשֶׁה אֶל־שֹׁפְטֵי יִשְׂרָאֵל הִרְגוּ אִישׁ אֲנָשָׁיו הַנִּצְמָדִים לְבַעַל פְּעוֹר:

6 Just then one of the Israelites came and brought a Midianite woman over to his companions, in the sight of *Moshe* and of the whole Israelite community who were weeping at the entrance of the Tent of Meeting.

ו וְהִנֵּה אִישׁ מִבְּנֵי יִשְׂרָאֵל בָּא וַיַּקְרֵב אֶל־אֶחָיו אֶת־הַמִּדְיָנִית לְעֵינֵי מֹשֶׁה וּלְעֵינֵי כָּל־עֲדַת בְּנֵי־יִשְׂרָאֵל וְהֵמָּה בֹכִים פֶּתַח אֹהֶל מוֹעֵד:

7 When *Pinchas*, son of *Elazar* son of *Aharon* the *Kohen*, saw this, he left the assembly and, taking a spear in his hand,

ז וַיַּרְא פִּינְחָס בֶּן־אֶלְעָזָר בֶּן־אַהֲרֹן הַכֹּהֵן וַיָּקָם מִתּוֹךְ הָעֵדָה וַיִּקַּח רֹמַח בְּיָדוֹ:

8 he followed the Israelite into the Hamber and stabbed both of them, the Israelite and the woman, through the belly. Then the plague against the Israelites was checked.

ח וַיָּבֹא אַחַר אִישׁ־יִשְׂרָאֵל אֶל־הַקֻּבָּה וַיִּדְקֹר אֶת־שְׁנֵיהֶם אֵת אִישׁ יִשְׂרָאֵל וְאֶת־הָאִשָּׁה אֶל־קֳבָתָהּ וַתֵּעָצַר הַמַּגֵּפָה מֵעַל בְּנֵי יִשְׂרָאֵל:

9 Those who died of the plague numbered twenty-four thousand.

ט וַיִּהְיוּ הַמֵּתִים בַּמַּגֵּפָה אַרְבָּעָה וְעֶשְׂרִים אָלֶף:

10 *Hashem* spoke to *Moshe*, saying,

י וַיְדַבֵּר יְהֹוָה אֶל־מֹשֶׁה לֵּאמֹר:

11 "*Pinchas*, son of *Elazar* son of *Aharon* the *Kohen*, has turned back My wrath from the Israelites by displaying among them his passion for Me, so that I did not wipe out *B'nei Yisrael* in My passion.

יא פִּינְחָס בֶּן־אֶלְעָזָר בֶּן־אַהֲרֹן הַכֹּהֵן הֵשִׁיב אֶת־חֲמָתִי מֵעַל בְּנֵי־יִשְׂרָאֵל בְּקַנְאוֹ אֶת־קִנְאָתִי בְּתוֹכָם וְלֹא־כִלִּיתִי אֶת־בְּנֵי־יִשְׂרָאֵל בְּקִנְאָתִי:

12 Say, therefore, 'I grant him My pact of friendship.

יב לָכֵן אֱמֹר הִנְנִי נֹתֵן לוֹ אֶת־בְּרִיתִי שָׁלוֹם:

la-KHAYN e-MOR hin-NEE no-TAYN LO et b'-ree-TEE sha-LOM

13 It shall be for him and his descendants after him a pact of priesthood for all time, because he took impassioned action for his God, thus making expiation for the Israelites.'"

יג וְהָיְתָה לּוֹ וּלְזַרְעוֹ אַחֲרָיו בְּרִית כְּהֻנַּת עוֹלָם תַּחַת אֲשֶׁר קִנֵּא לֵאלֹהָיו וַיְכַפֵּר עַל־בְּנֵי יִשְׂרָאֵל:

ברית שלום

 25:12 I grant him My pact of friendship The zealot, *Pinchas*, sees immoral behavior among the camp of Israel, and immediately responds with an iron fist and a sharp spear. Ironically, *Pinchas* is rewarded for his violent action with *Hashem*'s "pact of friendship," known in Hebrew as *brit shalom* (שלום ברית), literally 'covenant of peace.' With this striking detail, the *Torah* illustrates a vital lesson. Genuine peace is not merely the absence of conflict. *Pinchas* did not negotiate with the perpetrators and attempt to achieve a compromise solution. By standing up for his principles, *Pinchas* demonstrated that only when based on eternal principles of truth and justice can true peace be achieved. A person who internalizes this idea and acts accordingly is a true "friend" of God.

A prayer for peace at the Western Wall

14 The name of the Israelite who was killed, the one who was killed with the Midianite woman, was *Zimri* son of Salu, chieftain of a Simeonite ancestral house.

יד וְשֵׁם אִישׁ יִשְׂרָאֵל הַמֻּכֶּה אֲשֶׁר הֻכָּה אֶת־הַמִּדְיָנִית זִמְרִי בֶּן־סָלוּא נְשִׂיא בֵית־אָב לַשִּׁמְעֹנִי:

15 The name of the Midianite woman who was killed was Cozbi daughter of Zur; he was the tribal head of an ancestral house in Midian.

טו וְשֵׁם הָאִשָּׁה הַמֻּכָּה הַמִּדְיָנִית כָּזְבִּי בַת־צוּר רֹאשׁ אֻמּוֹת בֵּית־אָב בְּמִדְיָן הוּא:

16 *Hashem* spoke to *Moshe*, saying,

טז וַיְדַבֵּר יְהֹוָה אֶל־מֹשֶׁה לֵּאמֹר:

17 "Assail the Midianites and defeat them

יז צָרוֹר אֶת־הַמִּדְיָנִים וְהִכִּיתֶם אוֹתָם:

18 for they assailed you by the trickery they practiced against you – because of the affair of Peor and because of the affair of their kinswoman Cozbi, daughter of the Midianite chieftain, who was killed at the time of the plague on account of Peor."

יח כִּי צֹרְרִים הֵם לָכֶם בְּנִכְלֵיהֶם אֲשֶׁר־נִכְּלוּ לָכֶם עַל־דְּבַר־פְּעוֹר וְעַל־דְּבַר כָּזְבִּי בַת־נְשִׂיא מִדְיָן אֲחֹתָם הַמֻּכָּה בְיוֹם־הַמַּגֵּפָה עַל־דְּבַר־פְּעוֹר:

26 1 When the plague was over, *Hashem* said to *Moshe* and to *Elazar* son of *Aharon* the *Kohen*,

כו א וַיְהִי אַחֲרֵי הַמַּגֵּפָה וַיֹּאמֶר יְהֹוָה אֶל־מֹשֶׁה וְאֶל אֶלְעָזָר בֶּן־אַהֲרֹן הַכֹּהֵן לֵאמֹר:

2 "Take a census of the whole Israelite community from the age of twenty years up, by their ancestral houses, all Israelites able to bear arms."

ב שְׂאוּ אֶת־רֹאשׁ כָּל־עֲדַת בְּנֵי־יִשְׂרָאֵל מִבֶּן עֶשְׂרִים שָׁנָה וָמַעְלָה לְבֵית אֲבֹתָם כָּל־יֹצֵא צָבָא בְּיִשְׂרָאֵל:

*s'-U et ROSH kol a-DAT b'-nay yis-ra-AYL mi-BEN es-REEM sha-NAH
va-MA-lah l'-VAYT a-vo-TAM kol yo-TZAY tza-VA b'-yis-ra-AYL*

3 So *Moshe* and *Elazar* the *Kohen*, on the steppes of Moab, at the *Yarden* near *Yericho*, gave instructions about them, namely,

ג וַיְדַבֵּר מֹשֶׁה וְאֶלְעָזָר הַכֹּהֵן אֹתָם בְּעַרְבֹת מוֹאָב עַל־יַרְדֵּן יְרֵחוֹ לֵאמֹר:

4 those from twenty years up, as *Hashem* had commanded *Moshe*. The descendants of the Israelites who came out of the land of Egypt were:

ד מִבֶּן עֶשְׂרִים שָׁנָה וָמָעְלָה כַּאֲשֶׁר צִוָּה יְהֹוָה אֶת־מֹשֶׁה וּבְנֵי יִשְׂרָאֵל הַיֹּצְאִים מֵאֶרֶץ מִצְרָיִם:

5 *Reuven*, *Yisrael*'s first-born. Descendants of *Reuven*: [Of] Enoch, the clan of the Enochites; of Pallu, the clan of the Palluites;

ה רְאוּבֵן בְּכוֹר יִשְׂרָאֵל בְּנֵי רְאוּבֵן חֲנוֹךְ מִשְׁפַּחַת הַחֲנֹכִי לְפַלּוּא מִשְׁפַּחַת הַפַּלֻּאִי:

6 of *Chetzron*, the clan of the Chetzronites; of Carmi, the clan of the Carmites.

ו לְחֶצְרֹן מִשְׁפַּחַת הַחֶצְרוֹנִי לְכַרְמִי מִשְׁפַּחַת הַכַּרְמִי:

26:2 Take a census of the whole Israelite community This chapter discusses the second census found in the book of *Bamidbar*. The forty years of wandering in the desert are now over, and the people are finally going to conquer, inherit and divide the land. A count is now necessary, to determine how big their army will be and among how many people the land must be divided. By counting each individual, *Hashem* conveys the message that each person's role in conquering and inhabiting the Promised Land is vital. Each person receives his portion, and with it a responsibility to contribute his part to *Hashem*, the country and the nation.

IDF recruits at their swearing in ceremony

7 Those are the clans of the Reubenites. The persons enrolled came to 43,730.

ז אֵלֶּה מִשְׁפְּחֹת הָרֽאוּבֵנִי וַיִּהְיוּ פְקֻדֵיהֶם שְׁלֹשָׁה וְאַרְבָּעִים אֶלֶף וּשְׁבַע מֵאוֹת וּשְׁלֹשִֽׁים:

8 Born to Pallu: *Eliav.*

ח וּבְנֵי פַלּוּא אֱלִיאָֽב:

9 The sons of *Eliav* were Nemuel, and *Datan* and *Aviram.* These are the same *Datan* and *Aviram,* chosen in the assembly, who agitated against *Moshe* and *Aharon* as part of *Korach*'s band when they agitated against *Hashem.*

ט וּבְנֵי אֱלִיאָב נְמוּאֵל וְדָתָן וַֽאֲבִירָם הֽוּא־דָתָן וַֽאֲבִירָם קרואי [קְרִיאֵי] הָֽעֵדָה אֲשֶׁר הִצּוּ עַל־מֹשֶׁה וְעַל־אַֽהֲרֹן בַּֽעֲדַת־קֹרַח בְּהַצֹּתָם עַל־יְהוָֹֽה:

10 Whereupon the earth opened its mouth and swallowed them up with *Korach* – when that band died, when the fire consumed the two hundred and fifty men – and they became an example.

י וַתִּפְתַּח הָאָרֶץ אֶת־פִּיהָ וַתִּבְלַע אֹתָם וְאֶת־קֹרַח בְּמוֹת הָֽעֵדָה בַּֽאֲכֹל הָאֵשׁ אֵת חֲמִשִּׁים וּמָאתַיִם אִישׁ וַיִּֽהְיוּ לְנֵֽס:

11 The sons of *Korach*, however, did not die.

יא וּבְנֵי־קֹרַח לֹא־מֵֽתוּ:

12 Descendants of *Shimon* by their clans: Of Nemuel, the clan of the Nemuelites; of Jamin, the clan of the Jaminites; of Jachin, the clan of the Jachinites;

יב בְּנֵי שִׁמְעוֹן לְמִשְׁפְּחֹתָם לִנְמוּאֵל מִשְׁפַּחַת הַנְּמֽוּאֵלִי לְיָמִין מִשְׁפַּחַת הַיָּֽמִינִי לְיָכִין מִשְׁפַּחַת הַיָּֽכִינִי:

13 of Zerach, the clan of the Zerahites; of *Shaul*, the clan of the Shaulites.

יג לְזֶרַח מִשְׁפַּחַת הַזַּרְחִי לְשָׁאוּל מִשְׁפַּחַת הַשָּׁאוּלִֽי:

14 Those are the clans of the Simeonites; [persons enrolled:] 22,200.

יד אֵלֶּה מִשְׁפְּחֹת הַשִּׁמְעֹנִי שְׁנַיִם וְעֶשְׂרִים אֶלֶף וּמָאתָֽיִם:

15 Descendants of *Gad* by their clans: Of Zephon, the clan of the Zephonites; of Haggi, the clan of the Haggites; of Shuni, the clan of the Shunites;

טו בְּנֵי גָד לְמִשְׁפְּחֹתָם לִצְפוֹן מִשְׁפַּחַת הַצְּפוֹנִי לְחַגִּי מִשְׁפַּחַת הַֽחַגִּי לְשׁוּנִי מִשְׁפַּחַת הַשּׁוּנִֽי:

16 of Ozni, the clan of the Oznites; of Eri, the clan of the Erites;

טז לְאָזְנִי מִשְׁפַּחַת הָֽאָזְנִי לְעֵרִי מִשְׁפַּחַת הָֽעֵרִֽי:

17 of Arod, the clan of the Arodites; of Areli, the clan of the Arelites.

יז לַֽאֲרוֹד מִשְׁפַּחַת הָֽאֲרוֹדִי לְאַרְאֵלִי מִשְׁפַּחַת הָֽאַרְאֵלִֽי:

18 Those are the clans of *Gad*'s descendants; persons enrolled: 40,500.

יח אֵלֶּה מִשְׁפְּחֹת בְּנֵי־גָד לִפְקֻדֵיהֶם אַרְבָּעִים אֶלֶף וַֽחֲמֵשׁ מֵאֽוֹת:

19 Born to *Yehuda*: Er and *Onan.* Er and *Onan* died in the land of Canaan.

יט בְּנֵי יְהוּדָה עֵר וְאוֹנָן וַיָּמָת עֵר וְאוֹנָן בְּאֶרֶץ כְּנָֽעַן:

20 Descendants of *Yehuda* by their clans: Of *Sheilah*, the clan of the Shelanites; of *Peretz*, the clan of the Peretzites; of *Zerach*, the clan of the Zerahites.

כ וַיִּֽהְיוּ בְנֵֽי־יְהוּדָה לְמִשְׁפְּחֹתָם לְשֵׁלָה מִשְׁפַּחַת הַשֵּֽׁלָנִי לְפֶרֶץ מִשְׁפַּחַת הַפַּרְצִי לְזֶרַח מִשְׁפַּחַת הַזַּרְחִֽי:

21 Descendants of *Peretz*: of *Chetzron*, the clan of the Chetzronites; of Hamul, the clan of the Hamulites.

כא וַיִּֽהְיוּ בְנֵי־פֶרֶץ לְחֶצְרֹן מִשְׁפַּחַת הַֽחֶצְרֹנִי לְחָמוּל מִשְׁפַּחַת הֶֽחָמוּלִֽי:

22 Those are the clans of *Yehuda*; persons enrolled: 76,500.

כב אֵלֶּה מִשְׁפְּחֹת יְהוּדָה לִפְקֻדֵיהֶם שִׁשָּׁה וְשִׁבְעִים אֶלֶף וַֽחֲמֵשׁ מֵאֽוֹת:

23 Descendants of *Yissachar* by their clans: [Of] *Tola*, the clan of the Tolaites; of Puvah, the clan of the Punites;

כג בְּנֵי יִשָּׂשכָר לְמִשְׁפְּחֹתָם תּוֹלָע מִשְׁפַּחַת הַתּוֹלָעִי לְפֻוָּה מִשְׁפַּחַת הַפּוּנִי:

24 of Yashuv, the clan of the Yashuvites; of Shimron, the clan of the Shimronites.

כד לְיָשׁוּב מִשְׁפַּחַת הַיָּשׁוּבִי לְשִׁמְרֹן מִשְׁפַּחַת הַשִּׁמְרֹנִי:

25 Those are the clans of *Yissachar*; persons enrolled: 64,300.

כה אֵלֶּה מִשְׁפְּחֹת יִשָּׂשכָר לִפְקֻדֵיהֶם אַרְבָּעָה וְשִׁשִּׁים אֶלֶף וּשְׁלֹשׁ מֵאוֹת:

26 Descendants of *Zevulun* by their clans: Of Sered, the clan of the Seredites; of Eilon, the clan of the Elonites; of Jahleel, the clan of the Jahleelites.

כו בְּנֵי זְבוּלֻן לְמִשְׁפְּחֹתָם לְסֶרֶד מִשְׁפַּחַת הַסַּרְדִּי לְאֵלוֹן מִשְׁפַּחַת הָאֵלֹנִי לְיַחְלְאֵל מִשְׁפַּחַת הַיַּחְלְאֵלִי:

27 Those are the clans of the Zebulunites; persons enrolled: 60,500.

כז אֵלֶּה מִשְׁפְּחֹת הַזְּבוּלֹנִי לִפְקֻדֵיהֶם שִׁשִּׁים אֶלֶף וַחֲמֵשׁ מֵאוֹת:

28 The sons of *Yosef* were *Menashe* and *Efraim* – by their clans.

כח בְּנֵי יוֹסֵף לְמִשְׁפְּחֹתָם מְנַשֶּׁה וְאֶפְרָיִם:

29 Descendants of *Menashe*: Of Machir, the clan of the Machirites. – Machir begot *Gilad*. – Of *Gilad*, the clan of the Giladites.

כט בְּנֵי מְנַשֶּׁה לְמָכִיר מִשְׁפַּחַת הַמָּכִירִי וּמָכִיר הוֹלִיד אֶת־גִּלְעָד לְגִלְעָד מִשְׁפַּחַת הַגִּלְעָדִי:

30 These were the descendants of *Gilad*: [Of] Iezer, the clan of the Iezerites; of Helek, the clan of the Helekites;

ל אֵלֶּה בְּנֵי גִלְעָד אִיעֶזֶר מִשְׁפַּחַת הָאִיעֶזְרִי לְחֵלֶק מִשְׁפַּחַת הַחֶלְקִי:

31 [of] Asriel, the clan of the Asrielites; [of] *Shechem*, the clan of the Sh'chemites;

לא וְאַשְׂרִיאֵל מִשְׁפַּחַת הָאַשְׂרִאֵלִי וְשֶׁכֶם מִשְׁפַּחַת הַשִּׁכְמִי:

32 [of] Shemida, the clan of the Shemidaites; [of] Hepher, the clan of the Hepherites. –

לב וּשְׁמִידָע מִשְׁפַּחַת הַשְּׁמִידָעִי וְחֵפֶר מִשְׁפַּחַת הַחֶפְרִי:

33 Now *Tzelofchad* son of Hepher had no sons, only daughters. The names of *Tzelofchad*'s daughters were *Machla, Noa, Chagla, Milka,* and *Tirtza*.

לג וּצְלָפְחָד בֶּן־חֵפֶר לֹא־הָיוּ לוֹ בָּנִים כִּי אִם־בָּנוֹת וְשֵׁם בְּנוֹת צְלָפְחָד מַחְלָה וְנֹעָה חָגְלָה מִלְכָּה וְתִרְצָה:

34 Those are the clans of *Menashe*; persons enrolled: 52,700.

לד אֵלֶּה מִשְׁפְּחֹת מְנַשֶּׁה וּפְקֻדֵיהֶם שְׁנַיִם וַחֲמִשִּׁים אֶלֶף וּשְׁבַע מֵאוֹת:

35 These are the descendants of *Efraim* by their clans: Of Shuthelah, the clan of the Shuthelahites; of Becher, the clan of the Becherites; of Tahan, the clan of the Tahanites.

לה אֵלֶּה בְנֵי־אֶפְרַיִם לְמִשְׁפְּחֹתָם לְשׁוּתֶלַח מִשְׁפַּחַת הַשֻּׁתַלְחִי לְבֶכֶר מִשְׁפַּחַת הַבַּכְרִי לְתַחַן מִשְׁפַּחַת הַתַּחֲנִי:

36 These are the descendants of Shuthelah: Of Eran, the clan of the Eranites.

לו וְאֵלֶּה בְּנֵי שׁוּתָלַח לְעֵרָן מִשְׁפַּחַת הָעֵרָנִי:

37 Those are the clans of *Efraim*'s descendants; persons enrolled: 32,500. Those are the descendants of *Yosef* by their clans.

לז אֵלֶּה מִשְׁפְּחֹת בְּנֵי־אֶפְרַיִם לִפְקֻדֵיהֶם שְׁנַיִם וּשְׁלֹשִׁים אֶלֶף וַחֲמֵשׁ מֵאוֹת אֵלֶּה בְנֵי־יוֹסֵף לְמִשְׁפְּחֹתָם:

38 The descendants of *Binyamin* by their clans: Of Bela, the clan of the Belaites; of Ashbel, the clan of the Ashbelites; of Ahiram, the clan of the Ahiramites;

לח בְּנֵי בִנְיָמִן לְמִשְׁפְּחֹתָם לְבֶלַע מִשְׁפַּחַת הַבַּלְעִי לְאַשְׁבֵּל מִשְׁפַּחַת הָאַשְׁבֵּלִי לַאֲחִירָם מִשְׁפַּחַת הָאֲחִירָמִי:

Numbers

³⁹ of Shephupham, the clan of the Shuphamites; of Hupham, the clan of the Huphamites.

לט לִשְׁפוּפָ֗ם מִשְׁפַּ֙חַת֙ הַשּׁוּפָמִ֔י לְחוּפָ֕ם מִשְׁפַּ֖חַת הַחוּפָמִֽי׃

⁴⁰ The sons of Bela were Ard and Naaman: [Of Ard,] the clan of the Ardites; of Naaman, the clan of the Naamanites.

מ וַיִּהְי֥וּ בְנֵי־בֶ֖לַע אַ֣רְדְּ וְנַעֲמָ֑ן מִשְׁפַּ֙חַת֙ הָֽאַרְדִּ֔י לְנַ֣עֲמָ֔ן מִשְׁפַּ֖חַת הַֽנַּעֲמִֽי׃

⁴¹ Those are the descendants of *Binyamin* by their clans; persons enrolled: 45,600.

מא אֵ֥לֶּה בְנֵֽי־בִנְיָמִ֖ן לְמִשְׁפְּחֹתָ֑ם וּפְקֻ֣דֵיהֶ֔ם חֲמִשָּׁ֧ה וְאַרְבָּעִ֛ים אֶ֖לֶף וְשֵׁ֥שׁ מֵאֽוֹת׃

⁴² These are the descendants of *Dan* by their clans: Of Shuham, the clan of the Shuhamites. Those are the clans of *Dan*, by their clans.

מב אֵ֤לֶּה בְנֵי־דָן֙ לְמִשְׁפְּחֹתָ֔ם לְשׁוּחָ֕ם מִשְׁפַּ֖חַת הַשּׁוּחָמִ֑י אֵ֛לֶּה מִשְׁפְּחֹ֥ת דָּ֖ן לְמִשְׁפְּחֹתָֽם׃

⁴³ All the clans of the Shuhamites; persons enrolled: 64,400.

מג כׇּל־מִשְׁפְּחֹ֥ת הַשּׁוּחָמִ֖י לִפְקֻדֵיהֶ֑ם אַרְבָּעָ֧ה וְשִׁשִּׁ֛ים אֶ֖לֶף וְאַרְבַּ֥ע מֵאֽוֹת׃

⁴⁴ Descendants of *Asher* by their clans: Of Imnah, the clan of the Imnites; of Ishvi, the clan of the Ishvites; of Beriah, the clan of the Beriites.

מד בְּנֵ֣י אָשֵׁר֮ לְמִשְׁפְּחֹתָם֒ לְיִמְנָ֗ה מִשְׁפַּ֙חַת֙ הַיִּמְנָ֔ה לְיִשְׁוִ֕י מִשְׁפַּ֖חַת הַיִּשְׁוִ֑י לִבְרִיעָ֕ה מִשְׁפַּ֖חַת הַבְּרִיעִֽי׃

⁴⁵ Of the descendants of Beriah: Of *Chever*, the clan of the Heberites; of Malchiel, the clan of the Malchielites.

מה לִבְנֵ֣י בְרִיעָ֔ה לְחֶ֕בֶר מִשְׁפַּ֖חַת הַֽחֶבְרִ֑י לְמַ֨לְכִּיאֵ֔ל מִשְׁפַּ֖חַת הַמַּלְכִּיאֵלִֽי׃

⁴⁶ The name of *Asher*'s daughter was Serah.

מו וְשֵׁ֥ם בַּת־אָשֵׁ֖ר שָֽׂרַח׃

⁴⁷ These are the clans of *Asher*'s descendants; persons enrolled: 53,400.

מז אֵ֛לֶּה מִשְׁפְּחֹ֥ת בְּנֵֽי־אָשֵׁ֖ר לִפְקֻדֵיהֶ֑ם שְׁלֹשָׁ֧ה וַחֲמִשִּׁ֛ים אֶ֖לֶף וְאַרְבַּ֥ע מֵאֽוֹת׃

⁴⁸ Descendants of *Naftali* by their clans: Of Jahzeel, the clan of the Jahzeelites; of Guni, the clan of the Gunites;

מח בְּנֵ֤י נַפְתָּלִי֙ לְמִשְׁפְּחֹתָ֔ם לְיַ֨חְצְאֵ֔ל מִשְׁפַּ֖חַת הַיַּחְצְאֵלִ֑י לְגוּנִ֕י מִשְׁפַּ֖חַת הַגּוּנִֽי׃

⁴⁹ of Jezer, the clan of the Jezerites; of Shillem, the clan of the Shillemites.

מט לְיֵ֕צֶר מִשְׁפַּ֖חַת הַיִּצְרִ֑י לְשִׁלֵּ֕ם מִשְׁפַּ֖חַת הַשִּׁלֵּמִֽי׃

⁵⁰ Those are the clans of the Naphtalites, clan by clan; persons enrolled: 45,400.

נ אֵ֛לֶּה מִשְׁפְּחֹ֥ת נַפְתָּלִ֖י לְמִשְׁפְּחֹתָ֑ם וּפְקֻ֣דֵיהֶ֔ם חֲמִשָּׁ֧ה וְאַרְבָּעִ֛ים אֶ֖לֶף וְאַרְבַּ֥ע מֵאֽוֹת׃

⁵¹ This is the enrollment of the Israelites: 601,730.

נא אֵ֗לֶּה פְּקוּדֵי֙ בְּנֵ֣י יִשְׂרָאֵ֔ל שֵׁשׁ־מֵא֥וֹת אֶ֖לֶף וָאָ֑לֶף שְׁבַ֥ע מֵא֖וֹת וּשְׁלֹשִֽׁים׃

⁵² *Hashem* spoke to *Moshe*, saying,

נב וַיְדַבֵּ֥ר יְהֹוָ֖ה אֶל־מֹשֶׁ֥ה לֵּאמֹֽר׃

⁵³ "Among these shall the land be apportioned as shares, according to the listed names:

נג לָאֵ֗לֶּה תֵּחָלֵ֥ק הָאָ֛רֶץ בְּנַחֲלָ֖ה בְּמִסְפַּ֥ר שֵׁמֽוֹת׃

⁵⁴ with larger groups increase the share, with smaller groups reduce the share. Each is to be assigned its share according to its enrollment.

נד לָרַ֗ב תַּרְבֶּה֙ נַחֲלָת֔וֹ וְלַמְעַ֖ט תַּמְעִ֣יט נַחֲלָת֑וֹ אִ֚ישׁ לְפִ֣י פְקֻדָ֔יו יֻתַּ֖ן נַחֲלָתֽוֹ׃

⁵⁵ The land, moreover, is to be apportioned by lot; and the allotment shall be made according to the listings of their ancestral tribes.

נה אַךְ־בְּגוֹרָ֕ל יֵחָלֵ֖ק אֶת־הָאָ֑רֶץ לִשְׁמ֥וֹת מַטּוֹת־אֲבֹתָ֖ם יִנְחָֽלוּ׃

56 Each portion shall be assigned by lot, whether for larger or smaller groups."

נו עַל־פִּי הַגּוֹרָל תֵּחָלֵק נַחֲלָתוֹ בֵּין רַב לִמְעָט:

57 This is the enrollment of the *Leviim* by their clans: Of *Gershon*, the clan of the Gershonites; of *Kehat*, the clan of the Kohathites; of *Merari*, the clan of the Merarites.

נז וְאֵלֶּה פְקוּדֵי הַלֵּוִי לְמִשְׁפְּחֹתָם לְגֵרְשׁוֹן מִשְׁפַּחַת הַגֵּרְשֻׁנִּי לִקְהָת מִשְׁפַּחַת הַקְּהָתִי לִמְרָרִי מִשְׁפַּחַת הַמְּרָרִי:

58 These are the clans of *Levi*: The clan of the Libnites, the clan of the Chevronites, the clan of the Mahlites, the clan of the Mushites, the clan of the Korahites. – *Kehat* begot *Amram*.

נח אֵלֶּה מִשְׁפְּחֹת לֵוִי מִשְׁפַּחַת הַלִּבְנִי מִשְׁפַּחַת הַחֶבְרֹנִי מִשְׁפַּחַת הַמַּחְלִי מִשְׁפַּחַת הַמּוּשִׁי מִשְׁפַּחַת הַקָּרְחִי וּקְהָת הוֹלִד אֶת־עַמְרָם:

59 The name of *Amram's* wife was *Yocheved* daughter of *Levi*, who was born to *Levi* in Egypt; she bore to *Amram Aharon* and *Moshe* and their sister *Miriam*.

נט וְשֵׁם אֵשֶׁת עַמְרָם יוֹכֶבֶד בַּת־לֵוִי אֲשֶׁר יָלְדָה אֹתָהּ לְלֵוִי בְּמִצְרָיִם וַתֵּלֶד לְעַמְרָם אֶת־אַהֲרֹן וְאֶת־מֹשֶׁה וְאֵת מִרְיָם אֲחֹתָם:

60 To *Aharon* were born *Nadav* and *Avihu, Elazar* and *Itamar*.

ס וַיִּוָּלֵד לְאַהֲרֹן אֶת־נָדָב וְאֶת־אֲבִיהוּא אֶת־אֶלְעָזָר וְאֶת־אִיתָמָר:

61 *Nadav* and *Avihu* died when they offered alien fire before *Hashem*.

סא וַיָּמָת נָדָב וַאֲבִיהוּא בְּהַקְרִיבָם אֵשׁ־זָרָה לִפְנֵי יְהֹוָה:

62 Their enrollment of 23,000 comprised all males from a month up. They were not part of the regular enrollment of the Israelites, since no share was assigned to them among the Israelites.

סב וַיִּהְיוּ פְקֻדֵיהֶם שְׁלֹשָׁה וְעֶשְׂרִים אֶלֶף כָּל־זָכָר מִבֶּן־חֹדֶשׁ וָמָעְלָה כִּי לֹא הָתְפָּקְדוּ בְּתוֹךְ בְּנֵי יִשְׂרָאֵל כִּי לֹא־נִתַּן לָהֶם נַחֲלָה בְּתוֹךְ בְּנֵי יִשְׂרָאֵל:

63 These are the persons enrolled by *Moshe* and *Elazar* the *Kohen* who registered the Israelites on the steppes of Moab, at the *Yarden* near *Yericho*.

סג אֵלֶּה פְּקוּדֵי מֹשֶׁה וְאֶלְעָזָר הַכֹּהֵן אֲשֶׁר פָּקְדוּ אֶת־בְּנֵי יִשְׂרָאֵל בְּעַרְבֹת מוֹאָב עַל יַרְדֵּן יְרֵחוֹ:

64 Among these there was not one of those enrolled by *Moshe* and *Aharon* the *Kohen* when they recorded the Israelites in the wilderness of Sinai.

סד וּבְאֵלֶּה לֹא־הָיָה אִישׁ מִפְּקוּדֵי מֹשֶׁה וְאַהֲרֹן הַכֹּהֵן אֲשֶׁר פָּקְדוּ אֶת־בְּנֵי יִשְׂרָאֵל בְּמִדְבַּר סִינָי:

65 For *Hashem* had said of them, "They shall die in the wilderness." Not one of them survived, except *Kalev* son of Jephunneh and *Yehoshua* son of Nun.

סה כִּי־אָמַר יְהֹוָה לָהֶם מוֹת יָמֻתוּ בַּמִּדְבָּר וְלֹא־נוֹתַר מֵהֶם אִישׁ כִּי אִם־כָּלֵב בֶּן־יְפֻנֶּה וִיהוֹשֻׁעַ בִּן־נוּן:

27 1 The daughters of *Tzelofchad*, of Manassite family – son of Hepher son of *Gilad* son of Machir son of *Menashe* son of *Yosef* – came forward. The names of the daughters were *Machla, Noa, Chagla, Milka,* and *Tirtza*.

כז א וַתִּקְרַבְנָה בְּנוֹת צְלָפְחָד בֶּן־חֵפֶר בֶּן־גִּלְעָד בֶּן־מָכִיר בֶּן־מְנַשֶּׁה לְמִשְׁפְּחֹת מְנַשֶּׁה בֶן־יוֹסֵף וְאֵלֶּה שְׁמוֹת בְּנֹתָיו מַחְלָה נֹעָה וְחָגְלָה וּמִלְכָּה וְתִרְצָה:

2 They stood before *Moshe, Elazar* the *Kohen,* the chieftains, and the whole assembly, at the entrance of the Tent of Meeting, and they said,

ב וַתַּעֲמֹדְנָה לִפְנֵי מֹשֶׁה וְלִפְנֵי אֶלְעָזָר הַכֹּהֵן וְלִפְנֵי הַנְּשִׂיאִם וְכָל־הָעֵדָה פֶּתַח אֹהֶל־מוֹעֵד לֵאמֹר:

3 "Our father died in the wilderness. He was not one of the faction, *Korach's* faction, which banded together against *Hashem,* but died for his own sin; and he has left no sons.

ג אָבִינוּ מֵת בַּמִּדְבָּר וְהוּא לֹא־הָיָה בְּתוֹךְ הָעֵדָה הַנּוֹעָדִים עַל־יְהֹוָה בַּעֲדַת־קֹרַח כִּי־בְחֶטְאוֹ מֵת וּבָנִים לֹא־הָיוּ לוֹ:

Numbers

⁴ Let not our father's name be lost to his clan just because he had no son! Give us a holding among our father's kinsmen!"

ד לָמָּה יִגָּרַע שֵׁם־אָבִינוּ מִתּוֹךְ מִשְׁפַּחְתּוֹ כִּי אֵין לוֹ בֵּן תְּנָה־לָּנוּ אֲחֻזָּה בְּתוֹךְ אֲחֵי אָבִינוּ:

LA-mah yi-ga-RA shaym a-VEE-nu mi-TOKH mish-pakh-TO KEE AYN LO BAYN t'-NAH LA-nu a-khu-ZAH b'-TOKH a-KHAY a-VEE-nu

⁵ *Moshe* brought their case before *Hashem*.

ה וַיַּקְרֵב מֹשֶׁה אֶת־מִשְׁפָּטָן לִפְנֵי יְהֹוָה:

⁶ And *Hashem* said to *Moshe*,

ו וַיֹּאמֶר יְהֹוָה אֶל־מֹשֶׁה לֵּאמֹר:

⁷ "The plea of *Tzelofchad*'s daughters is just: you should give them a hereditary holding among their father's kinsmen; transfer their father's share to them.

ז כֵּן בְּנוֹת צְלָפְחָד דֹּבְרֹת נָתֹן תִּתֵּן לָהֶם אֲחֻזַּת נַחֲלָה בְּתוֹךְ אֲחֵי אֲבִיהֶם וְהַעֲבַרְתָּ אֶת־נַחֲלַת אֲבִיהֶן לָהֶן:

⁸ "Further, speak to *B'nei Yisrael* as follows: 'If a man dies without leaving a son, you shall transfer his property to his daughter.

ח וְאֶל־בְּנֵי יִשְׂרָאֵל תְּדַבֵּר לֵאמֹר אִישׁ כִּי־יָמוּת וּבֵן אֵין לוֹ וְהַעֲבַרְתֶּם אֶת־נַחֲלָתוֹ לְבִתּוֹ:

⁹ If he has no daughter, you shall assign his property to his brothers.

ט וְאִם־אֵין לוֹ בַּת וּנְתַתֶּם אֶת־נַחֲלָתוֹ לְאֶחָיו:

¹⁰ If he has no brothers, you shall assign his property to his father's brothers.

י וְאִם־אֵין לוֹ אַחִים וּנְתַתֶּם אֶת־נַחֲלָתוֹ לַאֲחֵי אָבִיו:

¹¹ If his father had no brothers, you shall assign his property to his nearest relative in his own clan, and he shall inherit it.' This shall be the law of procedure for the Israelites, in accordance with *Hashem*'s command to *Moshe*."

יא וְאִם־אֵין אַחִים לְאָבִיו וּנְתַתֶּם אֶת־נַחֲלָתוֹ לִשְׁאֵרוֹ הַקָּרֹב אֵלָיו מִמִּשְׁפַּחְתּוֹ וְיָרַשׁ אֹתָהּ וְהָיְתָה לִבְנֵי יִשְׂרָאֵל לְחֻקַּת מִשְׁפָּט כַּאֲשֶׁר צִוָּה יְהֹוָה אֶת־מֹשֶׁה:

¹² *Hashem* said to *Moshe*, "Ascend these heights of Abarim and view the land that I have given to *B'nei Yisrael*.

יב וַיֹּאמֶר יְהֹוָה אֶל־מֹשֶׁה עֲלֵה אֶל־הַר הָעֲבָרִים הַזֶּה וּרְאֵה אֶת־הָאָרֶץ אֲשֶׁר נָתַתִּי לִבְנֵי יִשְׂרָאֵל:

va-YO-mer a-do-NAI el mo-SHEH a-LAY el HAR ha-a-va-REEM ha-ZEH ur-AY et ha-A-RETZ a-SHER na-TA-tee liv-NAY yis-ra-AYL

27:4 Give us a holding among our father's kinsmen After it is determined among whom *Eretz Yisrael* will be divided, the daughters of a deceased man named *Tzelofchad* approach *Moshe* with a complaint. The rule of inheritance is that a father's land is inherited by his sons, but the late *Tzelofchad* had no sons who could inherit his portion. Moved by a deep love for the Land of Israel, *Tzelofchad's* daughters complain that if nothing is done, their family will forever lose its portion of land. *Rashi* points out that it is no coincidence that the verse traces their lineage back to their forefather *Yosef*, who served as a model of love for the Promised Land when he made his brothers

promise that they would take his remains with them out of Egypt, for burial in *Eretz Yisrael*. The women are relieved when *Hashem* clarifies to *Moshe* that in the absence of sons, a man's land is to be inherited by his daughters. The passion for Israel exhibited by the daughters of *Tzelofchad* serves as a model for the special role that women have always played in settling *Eretz Yisrael*.

27:12 And view the land Though *Moshe* was not allowed to enter the Land of Israel, he is given an opportunity to see the land from atop the mountain of *Avarim*. In verse 12, *Hashem* tells him to go up to the mountain and "view the land", and in verse 13 He repeats "when you have seen it." The double language reflects the notion that *Moshe* saw beyond the land's physical beauty. In addition, he was able to perceive its spiritual grandeur as well.

A view of the land from Mount Avarim (Mount Nebo)

13 When you have seen it, you too shall be gathered to your kin, just as your brother *Aharon* was.

יג וְרָאִיתָה אֹתָהּ וְנֶאֱסַפְתָּ אֶל־עַמֶּיךָ גַּם־אָתָּה כַּאֲשֶׁר נֶאֱסַף אַהֲרֹן אָחִיךָ:

14 For, in the wilderness of Zin, when the community was contentious, you disobeyed My command to uphold My sanctity in their sight by means of the water." Those are the Waters of Meribath-kadesh, in the wilderness of Zin.

יד כַּאֲשֶׁר מְרִיתֶם פִּי בְּמִדְבַּר־צִן בִּמְרִיבַת הָעֵדָה לְהַקְדִּישֵׁנִי בַמַּיִם לְעֵינֵיהֶם הֵם מֵי־מְרִיבַת קָדֵשׁ מִדְבַּר־צִן:

15 *Moshe* spoke to *Hashem*, saying,

טו וַיְדַבֵּר מֹשֶׁה אֶל־יְהוָֹה לֵאמֹר:

16 "Let *Hashem*, Source of the breath of all flesh, appoint someone over the community

טז יִפְקֹד יְהוָֹה אֱלֹהֵי הָרוּחֹת לְכָל־בָּשָׂר אִישׁ עַל־הָעֵדָה:

17 who shall go out before them and come in before them, and who shall take them out and bring them in, so that *Hashem*'s community may not be like sheep that have no shepherd."

יז אֲשֶׁר־יֵצֵא לִפְנֵיהֶם וַאֲשֶׁר יָבֹא לִפְנֵיהֶם וַאֲשֶׁר יוֹצִיאֵם וַאֲשֶׁר יְבִיאֵם וְלֹא תִהְיֶה עֲדַת יְהוָֹה כַּצֹּאן אֲשֶׁר אֵין־לָהֶם רֹעֶה:

18 And *Hashem* answered *Moshe*, "Single out *Yehoshua* son of *Nun*, an inspired man, and lay your hand upon him.

יח וַיֹּאמֶר יְהוָֹה אֶל־מֹשֶׁה קַח־לְךָ אֶת־יְהוֹשֻׁעַ בִּן־נוּן אִישׁ אֲשֶׁר־רוּחַ בּוֹ וְסָמַכְתָּ אֶת־יָדְךָ עָלָיו:

19 Have him stand before *Elazar* the *Kohen* and before the whole community, and commission him in their sight.

יט וְהַעֲמַדְתָּ אֹתוֹ לִפְנֵי אֶלְעָזָר הַכֹּהֵן וְלִפְנֵי כָּל־הָעֵדָה וְצִוִּיתָה אֹתוֹ לְעֵינֵיהֶם:

20 Invest him with some of your authority, so that the whole Israelite community may obey.

כ וְנָתַתָּה מֵהוֹדְךָ עָלָיו לְמַעַן יִשְׁמְעוּ כָּל־עֲדַת בְּנֵי יִשְׂרָאֵל:

21 But he shall present himself to *Elazar* the *Kohen*, who shall on his behalf seek the decision of the Urim before *Hashem*. By such instruction they shall go out and by such instruction they shall come in, he and all the Israelites, the whole community."

כא וְלִפְנֵי אֶלְעָזָר הַכֹּהֵן יַעֲמֹד וְשָׁאַל לוֹ בְּמִשְׁפַּט הָאוּרִים לִפְנֵי יְהוָֹה עַל־פִּיו יֵצְאוּ וְעַל־פִּיו יָבֹאוּ הוּא וְכָל־בְּנֵי־יִשְׂרָאֵל אִתּוֹ וְכָל־הָעֵדָה:

22 *Moshe* did as *Hashem* commanded him. He took *Yehoshua* and had him stand before *Elazar* the *Kohen* and before the whole community.

כב וַיַּעַשׂ מֹשֶׁה כַּאֲשֶׁר צִוָּה יְהוָֹה אֹתוֹ וַיִּקַּח אֶת־יְהוֹשֻׁעַ וַיַּעֲמִדֵהוּ לִפְנֵי אֶלְעָזָר הַכֹּהֵן וְלִפְנֵי כָּל־הָעֵדָה:

23 He laid his hands upon him and commissioned him – as *Hashem* had spoken through *Moshe*.

כג וַיִּסְמֹךְ אֶת־יָדָיו עָלָיו וַיְצַוֵּהוּ כַּאֲשֶׁר דִּבֶּר יְהוָֹה בְּיַד־מֹשֶׁה:

28 1 *Hashem* spoke to *Moshe*, saying:

כח א וַיְדַבֵּר יְהוָֹה אֶל־מֹשֶׁה לֵּאמֹר:

2 Command *B'nei Yisrael* and say to them: Be punctilious in presenting to Me at stated times the offerings of food due Me, as offerings by fire of pleasing odor to Me.

ב צַו אֶת־בְּנֵי יִשְׂרָאֵל וְאָמַרְתָּ אֲלֵהֶם אֶת־קָרְבָּנִי לַחְמִי לְאִשַּׁי רֵיחַ נִיחֹחִי תִּשְׁמְרוּ לְהַקְרִיב לִי בְּמוֹעֲדוֹ:

3 Say to them: These are the offerings by fire that you are to present to *Hashem*: As a regular burnt offering every day, two yearling lambs without blemish.

ג וְאָמַרְתָּ לָהֶם זֶה הָאִשֶּׁה אֲשֶׁר תַּקְרִיבוּ לַיהוָֹה כְּבָשִׂים בְּנֵי־שָׁנָה תְמִימִם שְׁנַיִם לַיּוֹם עֹלָה תָמִיד:

Numbers

⁴ You shall offer one lamb in the morning, and the other lamb you shall offer at twilight.

ד אֶת־הַכֶּבֶשׂ אֶחָד תַּעֲשֶׂה בַבֹּקֶר וְאֵת הַכֶּבֶשׂ הַשֵּׁנִי תַּעֲשֶׂה בֵּין הָעַרְבָּיִם:

⁵ And as a meal offering, there shall be a tenth of an *efah* of choice flour with a quarter of a *hin* of beaten oil mixed in

ה וַעֲשִׂירִית הָאֵיפָה סֹלֶת לְמִנְחָה בְּלוּלָה בְּשֶׁמֶן כָּתִית רְבִיעִת הַהִין:

⁶ the regular burnt offering instituted at *Har Sinai* – an offering by fire of pleasing odor to *Hashem*.

ו עֹלַת תָּמִיד הָעֲשֻׂיָה בְּהַר סִינַי לְרֵיחַ נִיחֹחַ אִשֶּׁה לַיהוָה:

⁷ The libation with it shall be a quarter of a *hin* for each lamb, to be poured in the sacred precinct as an offering of fermented drink to *Hashem*.

ז וְנִסְכּוֹ רְבִיעִת הַהִין לַכֶּבֶשׂ הָאֶחָד בַּקֹּדֶשׁ הַסֵּךְ נֶסֶךְ שֵׁכָר לַיהוָה:

⁸ The other lamb you shall offer at twilight, preparing the same meal offering and libation as in the morning – an offering by fire of pleasing odor to *Hashem*.

ח וְאֵת הַכֶּבֶשׂ הַשֵּׁנִי תַּעֲשֶׂה בֵּין הָעַרְבָּיִם כְּמִנְחַת הַבֹּקֶר וּכְנִסְכּוֹ תַּעֲשֶׂה אִשֵּׁה רֵיחַ נִיחֹחַ לַיהוָה:

⁹ On the *Shabbat* day: two yearling lambs without blemish, together with two-tenths of a measure of choice flour with oil mixed in as a meal offering, and with the proper libation –

ט וּבְיוֹם הַשַּׁבָּת שְׁנֵי־כְבָשִׂים בְּנֵי־שָׁנָה תְּמִימִם וּשְׁנֵי עֶשְׂרֹנִים סֹלֶת מִנְחָה בְּלוּלָה בַשֶּׁמֶן וְנִסְכּוֹ:

uv-YOM ha-sha-BAT sh'-nay kh'-va-SEEM b'-nay sha-NAH t'-mee-MIM
u-sh'-NAY es-ro-NEEM SO-let min-KHAH b'-lu-LAH va-SHE-men v'-nis-KO

¹⁰ a burnt offering for every *Shabbat*, in addition to the regular burnt offering and its libation.

י עֹלַת שַׁבַּת בְּשַׁבַּתּוֹ עַל־עֹלַת הַתָּמִיד וְנִסְכָּהּ:

¹¹ On your new moons you shall present a burnt offering to *Hashem*: two bulls of the herd, one ram, and seven yearling lambs, without blemish.

יא וּבְרָאשֵׁי חָדְשֵׁיכֶם תַּקְרִיבוּ עֹלָה לַיהוָה פָּרִים בְּנֵי־בָקָר שְׁנַיִם וְאַיִל אֶחָד כְּבָשִׂים בְּנֵי־שָׁנָה שִׁבְעָה תְּמִימִם:

uv-ro-SHAY khod-shay-KHEM tak-REE-vu o-LAH la-do-NAI
pa-REEM b'-nay va-KAR sh'-NA-yim v'-A-yil e-KHAD
k'-va-SEEM b'-NAY sha-NAH shiv-AH t'-mee-MIM

28:9 On the *Shabbat* day *Shabbat*, the seventh day of the week, is a reminder that God is the creator of the entire world. Just as He created the world in six days and rested on the seventh, we use our creative powers to work for six days, but rest on the seventh. *Shabbat* also serves as a remembrance of the exodus from Egypt (see Deuteronomy 5:14). Through the miracles associated with the exodus, *Hashem* demonstrated that He is still very much involved in the world, though He generally works behind the scenes. By

Shabbat candles, wine and Challah

keeping the *Shabbat*, we affirm our belief in *Hashem* as the Creator who is continuously responsible for everything that happens in the world. The Land of Israel also has a *Shabbat* of its own, once every seven years. By abandoning the fields during the Sabbatical year and putting our sustenance in the hands of the Lord, we affirm our belief that He is intimately involved in everything that happens in our lives. We owe all of our success to Him, and we believe that He will provide for us, even if we are not working the land.

28:11 On your new moons Judaism follows a calendar with both lunar and solar components. The months are determined by the cycle

12 As meal offering for each bull: three-tenths of a measure of choice flour with oil mixed in. As meal offering for each ram: two-tenths of a measure of choice flour with oil mixed in.

13 As meal offering for each lamb: a tenth of a measure of fine flour with oil mixed in. Such shall be the burnt offering of pleasing odor, an offering by fire to *Hashem*.

14 Their libations shall be: half a *hin* of wine for a bull, a third of a *hin* for a ram, and a quarter of a *hin* for a lamb. That shall be the monthly burnt offering for each new moon of the year.

15 And there shall be one goat as a sin offering to *Hashem*, to be offered in addition to the regular burnt offering and its libation.

16 In the first month, on the fourteenth day of the month, there shall be a *Pesach* sacrifice to *Hashem*,

17 and on the fifteenth day of that month a festival. Unleavened bread shall be eaten for seven days.

18 The first day shall be a sacred occasion: you shall not work at your occupations.

19 You shall present an offering by fire, a burnt offering, to *Hashem*: two bulls of the herd, one ram, and seven yearling lambs – see that they are without blemish.

20 The meal offering with them shall be of choice flour with oil mixed in: prepare three-tenths of a measure for a bull, two-tenths for a ram;

21 and for each of the seven lambs prepare one-tenth of a measure.

22 And there shall be one goat for a sin offering, to make expiation in your behalf.

23 You shall present these in addition to the morning portion of the regular burnt offering.

יב וּשְׁלֹשָׁה עֶשְׂרֹנִים סֹלֶת מִנְחָה בְּלוּלָה בַשֶּׁמֶן לַפָּר הָאֶחָד וּשְׁנֵי עֶשְׂרֹנִים סֹלֶת מִנְחָה בְּלוּלָה בַשֶּׁמֶן לָאַיִל הָאֶחָד:

יג וְעִשָּׂרֹן עִשָּׂרוֹן סֹלֶת מִנְחָה בְּלוּלָה בַשֶּׁמֶן לַכֶּבֶשׂ הָאֶחָד עֹלָה רֵיחַ נִיחֹחַ אִשֶּׁה לַיהוָֹה:

יד וְנִסְכֵּיהֶם חֲצִי הַהִין יִהְיֶה לַפָּר וּשְׁלִישִׁת הַהִין לָאַיִל וּרְבִיעִת הַהִין לַכֶּבֶשׂ יָיִן זֹאת עֹלַת חֹדֶשׁ בְּחָדְשׁוֹ לְחָדְשֵׁי הַשָּׁנָה:

טו וּשְׂעִיר עִזִּים אֶחָד לְחַטָּאת לַיהוָֹה עַל־עֹלַת הַתָּמִיד יֵעָשֶׂה וְנִסְכּוֹ:

טז וּבַחֹדֶשׁ הָרִאשׁוֹן בְּאַרְבָּעָה עָשָׂר יוֹם לַחֹדֶשׁ פֶּסַח לַיהוָֹה:

יז וּבַחֲמִשָּׁה עָשָׂר יוֹם לַחֹדֶשׁ הַזֶּה חָג שִׁבְעַת יָמִים מַצּוֹת יֵאָכֵל:

יח בַּיּוֹם הָרִאשׁוֹן מִקְרָא־קֹדֶשׁ כָּל־מְלֶאכֶת עֲבֹדָה לֹא תַעֲשׂוּ:

יט וְהִקְרַבְתֶּם אִשֶּׁה עֹלָה לַיהוָֹה פָּרִים בְּנֵי־בָקָר שְׁנַיִם וְאַיִל אֶחָד וְשִׁבְעָה כְבָשִׂים בְּנֵי שָׁנָה תְּמִימִם יִהְיוּ לָכֶם:

כ וּמִנְחָתָם סֹלֶת בְּלוּלָה בַשָּׁמֶן שְׁלֹשָׁה עֶשְׂרֹנִים לַפָּר וּשְׁנֵי עֶשְׂרֹנִים לָאַיִל תַּעֲשׂוּ:

כא עִשָּׂרוֹן עִשָּׂרוֹן תַּעֲשֶׂה לַכֶּבֶשׂ הָאֶחָד לְשִׁבְעַת הַכְּבָשִׂים:

כב וּשְׂעִיר חַטָּאת אֶחָד לְכַפֵּר עֲלֵיכֶם:

כג מִלְּבַד עֹלַת הַבֹּקֶר אֲשֶׁר לְעֹלַת הַתָּמִיד תַּעֲשׂוּ אֶת־אֵלֶּה:

of the moon, with the new month beginning when the first sliver of moon reappears in the sky at the beginning of a new lunar cycle. At the same time, though, the Jewish calendar has a solar component. Each of the festivals are supposed to fall out during a specific season in Israel, reflected in the agricultural aspects of the holiday. *Pesach* must fall out during the springtime as the grain begins to ripen, *Shavuot* celebrates the wheat harvest and the beginning of the fruit harvest in early summer, and *Sukkot* is celebrated in the beginning of the autumn, at the end of the harvest season. There is, however, an eleven-day discrepancy between the number of days in twelve lunar months and a solar year. To enable the months to follow the cycle of the moon while also ensuring that the holidays are celebrated in the appropriate seasons, a thirteenth month is added to the year seven times in every nineteen-year cycle.

The moon in the Negev desert

24 You shall offer the like daily for seven days as food, an offering by fire of pleasing odor to *Hashem*; they shall be offered, with their libations, in addition to the regular burnt offering.

כד כָּאֵ֗לֶּה תַּעֲשׂ֤וּ לַיּוֹם֙ שִׁבְעַ֣ת יָמִ֔ים לֶ֚חֶם אִשֵּׁ֣ה רֵֽיחַ־נִיחֹ֖חַ לַיהֹוָ֑ה עַל־עוֹלַ֧ת הַתָּמִ֛יד יֵעָשֶׂ֖ה וְנִסְכּֽוֹ:

25 And the seventh day shall be a sacred occasion for you: you shall not work at your occupations.

כה וּבַיּוֹם֙ הַשְּׁבִיעִ֔י מִקְרָא־קֹ֖דֶשׁ יִהְיֶ֣ה לָכֶ֑ם כָּל־מְלֶ֥אכֶת עֲבֹדָ֖ה לֹ֥א תַעֲשֽׂוּ:

26 On the day of the first fruits, your festival of *Shavuot*, when you bring an offering of new grain to *Hashem*, you shall observe a sacred occasion: you shall not work at your occupations.

כו וּבְי֣וֹם הַבִּכּוּרִ֗ים בְּהַקְרִ֨יבְכֶ֤ם מִנְחָ֣ה חֲדָשָׁה֙ לַֽיהֹוָ֔ה בְּשָׁבֻעֹֽתֵיכֶ֑ם מִקְרָא־קֹ֙דֶשׁ֙ יִהְיֶ֣ה לָכֶ֔ם כָּל־מְלֶ֥אכֶת עֲבֹדָ֖ה לֹ֥א תַעֲשֽׂוּ:

27 You shall present a burnt offering of pleasing odor to *Hashem*: two bulls of the herd, one ram, seven yearling lambs.

כז וְהִקְרַבְתֶּ֨ם עוֹלָ֜ה לְרֵ֤יחַ נִיחֹ֨חַ֙ לַֽיהֹוָ֔ה פָּרִ֧ים בְּנֵֽי־בָקָ֛ר שְׁנַ֖יִם אַ֣יִל אֶחָ֑ד שִׁבְעָ֥ה כְבָשִׂ֖ים בְּנֵ֥י שָׁנָֽה:

28 The meal offering with them shall be of choice flour with oil mixed in, three-tenths of a measure for a bull, two-tenths for a ram,

כח וּמִ֨נְחָתָ֔ם סֹ֖לֶת בְּלוּלָ֣ה בַשָּׁ֑מֶן שְׁלֹשָׁ֣ה עֶשְׂרֹנִ֗ים לַפָּ֤ר הָֽאֶחָד֙ שְׁנֵ֣י עֶשְׂרֹנִ֔ים לָאַ֖יִל הָֽאֶחָֽד:

29 and one-tenth for each of the seven lambs.

כט עִשָּׂר֤וֹן עִשָּׂרוֹן֙ לַכֶּ֣בֶשׂ הָֽאֶחָ֔ד לְשִׁבְעַ֖ת הַכְּבָשִֽׂים:

30 And there shall be one goat for expiation in your behalf.

ל שְׂעִ֥יר עִזִּ֖ים אֶחָ֑ד לְכַפֵּ֖ר עֲלֵיכֶֽם:

31 You shall present them – see that they are without blemish – with their libations, in addition to the regular burnt offering and its meal offering.

לא מִלְּבַ֞ד עֹלַ֧ת הַתָּמִ֛יד וּמִנְחָת֖וֹ תַּעֲשׂ֑וּ תְּמִימִ֥ם יִֽהְיוּ־לָכֶ֖ם וְנִסְכֵּיהֶֽם:

29 1 In the seventh month, on the first day of the month, you shall observe a sacred occasion: you shall not work at your occupations. You shall observe it as a day when the *shofar* is sounded.

ט א וּבַחֹ֨דֶשׁ הַשְּׁבִיעִ֜י בְּאֶחָ֣ד לַחֹ֗דֶשׁ מִקְרָא־קֹ֙דֶשׁ֙ יִהְיֶ֣ה לָכֶ֔ם כָּל־מְלֶ֥אכֶת עֲבֹדָ֖ה לֹ֣א תַעֲשׂ֑וּ י֥וֹם תְּרוּעָ֖ה יִהְיֶ֥ה לָכֶֽם:

2 You shall present a burnt offering of pleasing odor to *Hashem*: one bull of the herd, one ram, and seven yearling lambs, without blemish.

ב וַעֲשִׂיתֶ֨ם עֹלָ֜ה לְרֵ֤יחַ נִיחֹ֨חַ֙ לַֽיהֹוָ֔ה פַּ֧ר בֶּן־בָּקָ֛ר אֶחָ֖ד אַ֣יִל אֶחָ֑ד כְּבָשִׂ֧ים בְּנֵֽי־שָׁנָ֛ה שִׁבְעָ֖ה תְּמִימִֽם:

3 The meal offering with them – choice flour with oil mixed in – shall be: three-tenths of a measure for a bull, two-tenths for a ram,

ג וּמִ֨נְחָתָ֔ם סֹ֖לֶת בְּלוּלָ֣ה בַשָּׁ֑מֶן שְׁלֹשָׁ֣ה עֶשְׂרֹנִ֗ים לַפָּ֛ר שְׁנֵ֥י עֶשְׂרֹנִ֖ים לָאָֽיִל:

4 and one-tenth for each of the seven lambs.

ד וְעִשָּׂר֣וֹן אֶחָ֔ד לַכֶּ֖בֶשׂ הָֽאֶחָ֑ד לְשִׁבְעַ֖ת הַכְּבָשִֽׂים:

5 And there shall be one goat for a sin offering, to make expiation in your behalf

ה וּשְׂעִיר־עִזִּ֥ים אֶחָ֖ד חַטָּ֑את לְכַפֵּ֖ר עֲלֵיכֶֽם:

6 in addition to the burnt offering of the new moon with its meal offering and the regular burnt offering with its meal offering, each with its libation as prescribed, offerings by fire of pleasing odor to *Hashem*.

ו מִלְּבַד֩ עֹלַ֨ת הַחֹ֜דֶשׁ וּמִנְחָתָ֗הּ וְעֹלַ֤ת הַתָּמִיד֙ וּמִנְחָתָ֔הּ וְנִסְכֵּיהֶ֖ם כְּמִשְׁפָּטָ֑ם לְרֵ֣יחַ נִיחֹ֔חַ אִשֶּׁ֖ה לַֽיהֹוָֽה:

⁷ On the tenth day of the same seventh month you shall observe a sacred occasion when you shall practice self-denial. You shall do no work.

⁸ You shall present to *Hashem* a burnt offering of pleasing odor: one bull of the herd, one ram, seven yearling lambs; see that they are without blemish.

⁹ The meal offering with them – of choice flour with oil mixed in – shall be: three-tenths of a measure for a bull, two-tenths for the one ram,

¹⁰ one-tenth for each of the seven lambs.

¹¹ And there shall be one goat for a sin offering, in addition to the sin offering of expiation and the regular burnt offering with its meal offering, each with its libation.

¹² On the fifteenth day of the seventh month, you shall observe a sacred occasion: you shall not work at your occupations. – Seven days you shall observe a festival of *Hashem*.

¹³ You shall present a burnt offering, an offering by fire of pleasing odor to *Hashem*: Thirteen bulls of the herd, two rams, fourteen yearling lambs; they shall be without blemish.

¹⁴ The meal offerings with them – of choice flour with oil mixed in – shall be: three-tenths of a measure for each of the thirteen bulls, two-tenths for each of the two rams,

¹⁵ and one-tenth for each of the fourteen lambs.

¹⁶ And there shall be one goat for a sin offering – in addition to the regular burnt offering, its meal offering and libation.

¹⁷ Second day: Twelve bulls of the herd, two rams, fourteen yearling lambs, without blemish;

¹⁸ the meal offerings and libations for the bulls, rams, and lambs, in the quantities prescribed;

¹⁹ and one goat for a sin offering – in addition to the regular burnt offering, its meal offering and libations.

ז וּבֶעָשׂוֹר לַחֹדֶשׁ הַשְּׁבִיעִי הַזֶּה מִקְרָא־קֹדֶשׁ יִהְיֶה לָכֶם וְעִנִּיתֶם אֶת־נַפְשֹׁתֵיכֶם כָּל־מְלָאכָה לֹא תַעֲשֽׂוּ:

ח וְהִקְרַבְתֶּם עֹלָה לַיהוָֹה רֵיחַ נִיחֹחַ פַּר בֶּן־בָּקָר אֶחָד אַיִל אֶחָד כְּבָשִׂים בְּנֵי־שָׁנָה שִׁבְעָה תְּמִימִם יִהְיוּ לָכֶֽם:

ט וּמִנְחָתָם סֹלֶת בְּלוּלָה בַשָּׁמֶן שְׁלֹשָׁה עֶשְׂרֹנִים לַפָּר שְׁנֵי עֶשְׂרֹנִים לָאַיִל הָאֶחָֽד:

י עִשָּׂרוֹן עִשָּׂרוֹן לַכֶּבֶשׂ הָאֶחָד לְשִׁבְעַת הַכְּבָשִֽׂים:

יא שְׂעִיר־עִזִּים אֶחָד חַטָּאת מִלְּבַד חַטַּאת הַכִּפֻּרִים וְעֹלַת הַתָּמִיד וּמִנְחָתָהּ וְנִסְכֵּיהֶֽם:

יב וּבַחֲמִשָּׁה עָשָׂר יוֹם לַחֹדֶשׁ הַשְּׁבִיעִי מִקְרָא־קֹדֶשׁ יִהְיֶה לָכֶם כָּל־מְלֶאכֶת עֲבֹדָה לֹא תַעֲשׂוּ וְחַגֹּתֶם חַג לַיהוָֹה שִׁבְעַת יָמִֽים:

יג וְהִקְרַבְתֶּם עֹלָה אִשֵּׁה רֵיחַ נִיחֹחַ לַיהוָֹה פָּרִים בְּנֵי־בָקָר שְׁלֹשָׁה עָשָׂר אֵילִם שְׁנָיִם כְּבָשִׂים בְּנֵי־שָׁנָה אַרְבָּעָה עָשָׂר תְּמִימִם יִהְיֽוּ:

יד וּמִנְחָתָם סֹלֶת בְּלוּלָה בַשֶּׁמֶן שְׁלֹשָׁה עֶשְׂרֹנִים לַפָּר הָאֶחָד לִשְׁלֹשָׁה עָשָׂר פָּרִים שְׁנֵי עֶשְׂרֹנִים לָאַיִל הָאֶחָד לִשְׁנֵי הָאֵילִֽם:

טו וְעִשָּׂרוֹן עִשָּׂרוֹן לַכֶּבֶשׂ הָאֶחָד לְאַרְבָּעָה עָשָׂר כְּבָשִֽׂים:

טז וּשְׂעִיר־עִזִּים אֶחָד חַטָּאת מִלְּבַד עֹלַת הַתָּמִיד מִנְחָתָהּ וְנִסְכָּֽהּ:

יז וּבַיּוֹם הַשֵּׁנִי פָּרִים בְּנֵי־בָקָר שְׁנֵים עָשָׂר אֵילִם שְׁנָיִם כְּבָשִׂים בְּנֵי־שָׁנָה אַרְבָּעָה עָשָׂר תְּמִימִֽם:

יח וּמִנְחָתָם וְנִסְכֵּיהֶם לַפָּרִים לָאֵילִם וְלַכְּבָשִׂים בְּמִסְפָּרָם כַּמִּשְׁפָּֽט:

יט וּשְׂעִיר־עִזִּים אֶחָד חַטָּאת מִלְּבַד עֹלַת הַתָּמִיד וּמִנְחָתָהּ וְנִסְכֵּיהֶֽם:

²⁰ Third day: Eleven bulls, two rams, fourteen yearling lambs, without blemish;

כ וּבַיּוֹם הַשְּׁלִישִׁי פָּרִים עַשְׁתֵּי־עָשָׂר אֵילִם שְׁנָיִם כְּבָשִׂים בְּנֵי־שָׁנָה אַרְבָּעָה עָשָׂר תְּמִימִם:

²¹ the meal offerings and libations for the bulls, rams, and lambs, in the quantities prescribed;

כא וּמִנְחָתָם וְנִסְכֵּיהֶם לַפָּרִים לָאֵילִם וְלַכְּבָשִׂים בְּמִסְפָּרָם כַּמִּשְׁפָּט:

²² and one goat for a sin offering – in addition to the regular burnt offering, its meal offering and libation.

כב וּשְׂעִיר חַטָּאת אֶחָד מִלְּבַד עֹלַת הַתָּמִיד וּמִנְחָתָהּ וְנִסְכָּהּ:

²³ Fourth day: Ten bulls, two rams, fourteen yearling lambs, without blemish;

כג וּבַיּוֹם הָרְבִיעִי פָּרִים עֲשָׂרָה אֵילִם שְׁנָיִם כְּבָשִׂים בְּנֵי־שָׁנָה אַרְבָּעָה עָשָׂר תְּמִימִם:

²⁴ the meal offerings and libations for the bulls, rams, and lambs, in the quantities prescribed;

כד מִנְחָתָם וְנִסְכֵּיהֶם לַפָּרִים לָאֵילִם וְלַכְּבָשִׂים בְּמִסְפָּרָם כַּמִּשְׁפָּט:

²⁵ and one goat for a sin offering – in addition to the regular burnt offering, its meal offering and libation.

כה וּשְׂעִיר־עִזִּים אֶחָד חַטָּאת מִלְּבַד עֹלַת הַתָּמִיד מִנְחָתָהּ וְנִסְכָּהּ:

²⁶ Fifth day: Nine bulls, two rams, fourteen yearling lambs, without blemish;

כו וּבַיּוֹם הַחֲמִישִׁי פָּרִים תִּשְׁעָה אֵילִם שְׁנָיִם כְּבָשִׂים בְּנֵי־שָׁנָה אַרְבָּעָה עָשָׂר תְּמִימִם:

²⁷ the meal offerings and libations for the bulls, rams, and lambs, in the quantities prescribed;

כז וּמִנְחָתָם וְנִסְכֵּיהֶם לַפָּרִים לָאֵילִם וְלַכְּבָשִׂים בְּמִסְפָּרָם כַּמִּשְׁפָּט:

²⁸ and one goat for a sin offering – in addition to the regular burnt offering, its meal offering and libation.

כח וּשְׂעִיר חַטָּאת אֶחָד מִלְּבַד עֹלַת הַתָּמִיד וּמִנְחָתָהּ וְנִסְכָּהּ:

²⁹ Sixth day: Eight bulls, two rams, fourteen yearling lambs, without blemish;

כט וּבַיּוֹם הַשִּׁשִּׁי פָּרִים שְׁמֹנָה אֵילִם שְׁנָיִם כְּבָשִׂים בְּנֵי־שָׁנָה אַרְבָּעָה עָשָׂר תְּמִימִם:

³⁰ the meal offerings and libations for the bulls, rams, and lambs, in the quantities prescribed;

ל וּמִנְחָתָם וְנִסְכֵּיהֶם לַפָּרִים לָאֵילִם וְלַכְּבָשִׂים בְּמִסְפָּרָם כַּמִּשְׁפָּט:

³¹ and one goat for a sin offering – in addition to the regular burnt offering, its meal offering and libations.

לא וּשְׂעִיר חַטָּאת אֶחָד מִלְּבַד עֹלַת הַתָּמִיד מִנְחָתָהּ וּנְסָכֶיהָ:

³² Seventh day: Seven bulls, two rams, fourteen yearling lambs, without blemish;

לב וּבַיּוֹם הַשְּׁבִיעִי פָּרִים שִׁבְעָה אֵילִם שְׁנָיִם כְּבָשִׂים בְּנֵי־שָׁנָה אַרְבָּעָה עָשָׂר תְּמִימִם:

³³ the meal offerings and libations for the bulls, rams, and lambs, in the quantities prescribed;

לג וּמִנְחָתָם וְנִסְכֵּהֶם לַפָּרִים לָאֵילִם וְלַכְּבָשִׂים בְּמִסְפָּרָם כְּמִשְׁפָּטָם:

³⁴ and one goat for a sin offering – in addition to the regular burnt offering, its meal offering and libation.

לד וּשְׂעִיר חַטָּאת אֶחָד מִלְּבַד עֹלַת הַתָּמִיד מִנְחָתָהּ וְנִסְכָּהּ:

35 On the eighth day you shall hold a solemn gathering; you shall not work at your occupations.

לה בַּיּוֹם הַשְּׁמִינִי עֲצֶרֶת תִּהְיֶה לָכֶם כָּל־מְלֶאכֶת עֲבֹדָה לֹא תַעֲשׂוּ:

ba-YOM ha-sh'-mee-NEE a-TZE-ret tih-YEH la-KHEM kol m'-LE-khet a-vo-DAH LO ta-a-SU

36 You shall present a burnt offering, an offering by fire of pleasing odor to *Hashem*; one bull, one ram, seven yearling lambs, without blemish;

לו וְהִקְרַבְתֶּם עֹלָה אִשֵּׁה רֵיחַ נִיחֹחַ לַיהוָה פַּר אֶחָד אַיִל אֶחָד כְּבָשִׂים בְּנֵי־שָׁנָה שִׁבְעָה תְּמִימִם:

37 the meal offerings and libations for the bull, the ram, and the lambs, in the quantities prescribed;

לז מִנְחָתָם וְנִסְכֵּיהֶם לַפָּר לָאַיִל וְלַכְּבָשִׂים בְּמִסְפָּרָם כַּמִּשְׁפָּט:

38 and one goat for a sin offering – in addition to the regular burnt offering, its meal offering and libation.

לח וּשְׂעִיר חַטָּאת אֶחָד מִלְּבַד עֹלַת הַתָּמִיד וּמִנְחָתָהּ וְנִסְכָּהּ:

39 All these you shall offer to *Hashem* at the stated times, in addition to your votive and freewill offerings, be they burnt offerings, meal offerings, libations, or offerings of well-being.

לט אֵלֶּה תַּעֲשׂוּ לַיהוָה בְּמוֹעֲדֵיכֶם לְבַד מִנִּדְרֵיכֶם וְנִדְבֹתֵיכֶם לְעֹלֹתֵיכֶם וּלְמִנְחֹתֵיכֶם וּלְנִסְכֵּיכֶם וּלְשַׁלְמֵיכֶם:

ל 1 So *Moshe* spoke to the Israelites just as *Hashem* had commanded *Moshe*.

א וַיֹּאמֶר מֹשֶׁה אֶל־בְּנֵי יִשְׂרָאֵל כְּכֹל אֲשֶׁר־צִוָּה יְהוָה אֶת־מֹשֶׁה:

2 *Moshe* spoke to the heads of the Israelite tribes, saying: This is what *Hashem* has commanded:

וַיְדַבֵּר מֹשֶׁה אֶל־רָאשֵׁי הַמַּטּוֹת לִבְנֵי יִשְׂרָאֵל לֵאמֹר זֶה הַדָּבָר אֲשֶׁר צִוָּה יְהוָה:

3 If a man makes a vow to *Hashem* or takes an oath imposing an obligation on himself, he shall not break his pledge; he must carry out all that has crossed his lips.

ג אִישׁ כִּי־יִדֹּר נֶדֶר לַיהוָה אוֹ־הִשָּׁבַע שְׁבֻעָה לֶאְסֹר אִסָּר עַל־נַפְשׁוֹ לֹא יַחֵל דְּבָרוֹ כְּכָל־הַיֹּצֵא מִפִּיו יַעֲשֶׂה:

EESH kee yi-DOR NE-der la-do-NAI o hi-SHA-va sh'-vu-AH le-SOR i-SAR al naf-SHO LO ya-KHAYL d'-va-RO k'-khol ha-yo-TZAY mi-PEEV ya-a-SEH

29:35 On the eighth day you shall hold a solemn gathering This verse mandates an additional "solemn gathering" to be held on the day immediately following the seven days of *Sukkot*. According to the Sages (*Sukkah* 55b), the festival of *Sukkot* has a universal message, demonstrated by the fact that over the course of these seven days, seventy special sacrifices were brought in the *Beit Hamikdash*, corresponding to the seventy primordial nations of the world. At the completion of the *Sukkot* holiday, *Hashem* adds an extra day, as if to say to His people "I don't want you to leave yet. Let us celebrate one more day together so I can enjoy your ex-

Dancing with the *Torah* on *Simchat Torah*, celebrated on *Shemini Atzeret*

clusive, intimate company." After celebrating *Rosh Hashana*, *Yom Kippur* and finally *Sukkot*, *Hashem* doesn't want the special time to end. He asks His chosen nation to celebrate with Him alone for one more day. This final day is known as *Shemini Atzeret*, the 'eighth day of assembly.'

30:3 He shall not break his pledge This chapter elaborates on the laws regarding vows and oaths. *Hashem* takes these matters very seriously, and commands that any commitment to do something must be fulfilled. In fact, violating one's vows is a sin. This commandment teaches how important it is to be true to one's word: *Hashem* expects us to keep our word, just as He keeps His. Today, we are witness to *Hashem*'s fulfillment of His promise, made through His prophets, to return His people to the Promised Land. We hope to see the fulfillment of the rest of the divine promise, that the People of Israel will live peacefully in the Promised Land, very soon.

Numbers

4 If a woman makes a vow to *Hashem* or assumes an obligation while still in her father's household by reason of her youth,

5 and her father learns of her vow or her self-imposed obligation and offers no objection, all her vows shall stand and every self-imposed obligation shall stand.

6 But if her father restrains her on the day he finds out, none of her vows or self-imposed obligations shall stand; and *Hashem* will forgive her, since her father restrained her.

7 If she should marry while her vow or the commitment to which she bound herself is still in force,

8 and her husband learns of it and offers no objection on the day he finds out, her vows shall stand and her self-imposed obligations shall stand.

9 But if her husband restrains her on the day that he learns of it, he thereby annuls her vow which was in force or the commitment to which she bound herself; and *Hashem* will forgive her.

10 The vow of a widow or of a divorced woman, however, whatever she has imposed on herself, shall be binding upon her.

11 So, too, if, while in her husband's household, she makes a vow or imposes an obligation on herself by oath,

12 and her husband learns of it, yet offers no objection – thus failing to restrain her – all her vows shall stand and all her self-imposed obligations shall stand.

13 But if her husband does annul them on the day he finds out, then nothing that has crossed her lips shall stand, whether vows or self-imposed obligations. Her husband has annulled them, and *Hashem* will forgive her.

14 Every vow and every sworn obligation of self-denial may be upheld by her husband or annulled by her husband.

15 If her husband offers no objection from that day to the next, he has upheld all the vows or obligations she has assumed: he has upheld them by offering no objection on the day he found out.

ד וְאִשָּׁה כִּי־תִדֹּר נֶדֶר לַיהֹוָה וְאָסְרָה אִסָּר בְּבֵית אָבִיהָ בִּנְעֻרֶיהָ:

ה וְשָׁמַע אָבִיהָ אֶת־נִדְרָהּ וֶאֱסָרָהּ אֲשֶׁר אָסְרָה עַל־נַפְשָׁהּ וְהֶחֱרִישׁ לָהּ אָבִיהָ וְקָמוּ כָּל־נְדָרֶיהָ וְכָל־אִסָּר אֲשֶׁר־אָסְרָה עַל־נַפְשָׁהּ יָקוּם:

ו וְאִם־הֵנִיא אָבִיהָ אֹתָהּ בְּיוֹם שָׁמְעוֹ כָּל־נְדָרֶיהָ וֶאֱסָרֶיהָ אֲשֶׁר־אָסְרָה עַל־נַפְשָׁהּ לֹא יָקוּם וַיהֹוָה יִסְלַח־לָהּ כִּי־הֵנִיא אָבִיהָ אֹתָהּ:

ז וְאִם־הָיוֹ תִהְיֶה לְאִישׁ וּנְדָרֶיהָ עָלֶיהָ אוֹ מִבְטָא שְׂפָתֶיהָ אֲשֶׁר אָסְרָה עַל־נַפְשָׁהּ:

ח וְשָׁמַע אִישָׁהּ בְּיוֹם שָׁמְעוֹ וְהֶחֱרִישׁ לָהּ וְקָמוּ נְדָרֶיהָ וֶאֱסָרֶהָ אֲשֶׁר־אָסְרָה עַל־נַפְשָׁהּ יָקֻמוּ:

ט וְאִם בְּיוֹם שְׁמֹעַ אִישָׁהּ יָנִיא אוֹתָהּ וְהֵפֵר אֶת־נִדְרָהּ אֲשֶׁר עָלֶיהָ וְאֵת מִבְטָא שְׂפָתֶיהָ אֲשֶׁר אָסְרָה עַל־נַפְשָׁהּ וַיהֹוָה יִסְלַח־לָהּ:

י וְנֵדֶר אַלְמָנָה וּגְרוּשָׁה כֹּל אֲשֶׁר־אָסְרָה עַל־נַפְשָׁהּ יָקוּם עָלֶיהָ:

יא וְאִם־בֵּית אִישָׁהּ נָדָרָה אוֹ־אָסְרָה אִסָּר עַל־נַפְשָׁהּ בִּשְׁבֻעָה:

יב וְשָׁמַע אִישָׁהּ וְהֶחֱרִשׁ לָהּ לֹא הֵנִיא אֹתָהּ וְקָמוּ כָּל־נְדָרֶיהָ וְכָל־אִסָּר אֲשֶׁר־אָסְרָה עַל־נַפְשָׁהּ יָקוּם:

יג וְאִם־הָפֵר יָפֵר אֹתָם אִישָׁהּ בְּיוֹם שָׁמְעוֹ כָּל־מוֹצָא שְׂפָתֶיהָ לִנְדָרֶיהָ וּלְאִסַּר נַפְשָׁהּ לֹא יָקוּם אִישָׁהּ הֲפֵרָם וַיהֹוָה יִסְלַח־לָהּ:

יד כָּל־נֵדֶר וְכָל־שְׁבֻעַת אִסָּר לְעַנֹּת נָפֶשׁ אִישָׁהּ יְקִימֶנּוּ וְאִישָׁהּ יְפֵרֶנּוּ:

טו וְאִם־הַחֲרֵשׁ יַחֲרִישׁ לָהּ אִישָׁהּ מִיּוֹם אֶל־יוֹם וְהֵקִים אֶת־כָּל־נְדָרֶיהָ אוֹ אֶת־כָּל־אֱסָרֶיהָ אֲשֶׁר עָלֶיהָ הֵקִים אֹתָם כִּי־הֶחֱרִשׁ לָהּ בְּיוֹם שָׁמְעוֹ:

16 But if he annuls them after [the day] he finds out, he shall bear her guilt.

טז וְאִם־הָפֵר יָפֵר אֹתָם אַחֲרֵי שָׁמְעוֹ וְנָשָׂא אֶת־עֲוֺנָהּ:

17 Those are the laws that *Hashem* enjoined upon *Moshe* between a man and his wife, and as between a father and his daughter while in her father's household by reason of her youth.

יז אֵלֶּה הַחֻקִּים אֲשֶׁר צִוָּה יְהֹוָה אֶת־מֹשֶׁה בֵּין אִישׁ לְאִשְׁתּוֹ בֵּין־אָב לְבִתּוֹ בִּנְעֻרֶיהָ בֵּית אָבִיהָ:

לא 1 *Hashem* spoke to *Moshe*, saying,

א וַיְדַבֵּר יְהֹוָה אֶל־מֹשֶׁה לֵּאמֹר: **לא**

2 "Avenge *B'nei Yisrael* on the Midianites; then you shall be gathered to your kin."

ב נְקֹם נִקְמַת בְּנֵי יִשְׂרָאֵל מֵאֵת הַמִּדְיָנִים אַחַר תֵּאָסֵף אֶל־עַמֶּיךָ:

3 *Moshe* spoke to the people, saying, "Let men be picked out from among you for a campaign, and let them fall upon Midian to wreak *Hashem*'s vengeance on Midian.

ג וַיְדַבֵּר מֹשֶׁה אֶל־הָעָם לֵאמֹר הֵחָלְצוּ מֵאִתְּכֶם אֲנָשִׁים לַצָּבָא וְיִהְיוּ עַל־מִדְיָן לָתֵת נִקְמַת־יְהֹוָה בְּמִדְיָן:

4 You shall dispatch on the campaign a thousand from every one of the tribes of *Yisrael*."

ד אֶלֶף לַמַּטֶּה אֶלֶף לַמַּטֶּה לְכֹל מַטּוֹת יִשְׂרָאֵל תִּשְׁלְחוּ לַצָּבָא:

5 So a thousand from each tribe were furnished from the divisions of *Yisrael*, twelve thousand picked for the campaign.

ה וַיִּמָּסְרוּ מֵאַלְפֵי יִשְׂרָאֵל אֶלֶף לַמַּטֶּה שְׁנֵים־עָשָׂר אֶלֶף חֲלוּצֵי צָבָא:

6 *Moshe* dispatched them on the campaign, a thousand from each tribe, with *Pinchas* son of *Elazar* serving as a *Kohen* on the campaign, equipped with the sacred utensils and the trumpets for sounding the blasts.

ו וַיִּשְׁלַח אֹתָם מֹשֶׁה אֶלֶף לַמַּטֶּה לַצָּבָא אֹתָם וְאֶת־פִּינְחָס בֶּן־אֶלְעָזָר הַכֹּהֵן לַצָּבָא וּכְלֵי הַקֹּדֶשׁ וַחֲצֹצְרוֹת הַתְּרוּעָה בְּיָדוֹ:

7 They took the field against Midian, as *Hashem* had commanded *Moshe*, and slew every male.

ז וַיִּצְבְּאוּ עַל־מִדְיָן כַּאֲשֶׁר צִוָּה יְהֹוָה אֶת־מֹשֶׁה וַיַּהַרְגוּ כָּל־זָכָר:

8 Along with their other victims, they slew the kings of Midian: Evi, Rekem, Zur, Hur, and Reba, the five kings of Midian. They also put Balaam son of Beor to the sword.

ח וְאֶת־מַלְכֵי מִדְיָן הָרְגוּ עַל־חַלְלֵיהֶם אֶת־אֱוִי וְאֶת־רֶקֶם וְאֶת־צוּר וְאֶת־חוּר וְאֶת־רֶבַע חֲמֵשֶׁת מַלְכֵי מִדְיָן וְאֵת בִּלְעָם בֶּן־בְּעוֹר הָרְגוּ בֶּחָרֶב:

9 The Israelites took the women and children of the Midianites captive, and seized as booty all their beasts, all their herds, and all their wealth.

ט וַיִּשְׁבּוּ בְנֵי־יִשְׂרָאֵל אֶת־נְשֵׁי מִדְיָן וְאֶת־טַפָּם וְאֵת כָּל־בְּהֶמְתָּם וְאֶת־כָּל־מִקְנֵהֶם וְאֶת־כָּל־חֵילָם בָּזָזוּ:

10 And they destroyed by fire all the towns in which they were settled, and their encampments.

י וְאֵת כָּל־עָרֵיהֶם בְּמוֹשְׁבֹתָם וְאֵת כָּל־טִירֹתָם שָׂרְפוּ בָּאֵשׁ:

11 They gathered all the spoil and all the booty, man and beast,

יא וַיִּקְחוּ אֶת־כָּל־הַשָּׁלָל וְאֵת כָּל־הַמַּלְקוֹחַ בָּאָדָם וּבַבְּהֵמָה:

12 and they brought the captives, the booty, and the spoil to *Moshe*, *Elazar* the *Kohen*, and the whole Israelite community, at the camp in the steppes of Moab, at the *Yarden* near *Yericho*.

יב וַיָּבִאוּ אֶל־מֹשֶׁה וְאֶל־אֶלְעָזָר הַכֹּהֵן וְאֶל־עֲדַת בְּנֵי־יִשְׂרָאֵל אֶת־הַשְּׁבִי וְאֶת־הַמַּלְקוֹחַ וְאֶת־הַשָּׁלָל אֶל־הַמַּחֲנֶה אֶל־עַרְבֹת מוֹאָב אֲשֶׁר עַל־יַרְדֵּן יְרֵחוֹ:

13 *Moshe, Elazar* the *Kohen,* and all the chieftains of the community came out to meet them outside the camp.

יג וַיֵּצְא֡וּ מֹשֶׁ֣ה וְאֶלְעָזָ֣ר הַכֹּהֵ֗ן וְכָל־נְשִׂיאֵ֤י הָֽעֵדָ֛ה לִקְרָאתָ֖ם אֶל־מִח֥וּץ לַֽמַּחֲנֶֽה:

14 *Moshe* became angry with the commanders of the army, the officers of thousands and the officers of hundreds, who had come back from the military campaign.

יד וַיִּקְצֹ֣ף מֹשֶׁ֔ה עַ֖ל פְּקוּדֵ֣י הֶחָ֑יִל שָׂרֵ֤י הָֽאֲלָפִים֙ וְשָׂרֵ֣י הַמֵּא֔וֹת הַבָּאִ֖ים מִצְּבָ֥א הַמִּלְחָמָֽה:

15 *Moshe* said to them, "You have spared every female!

טו וַיֹּ֥אמֶר אֲלֵיהֶ֖ם מֹשֶׁ֑ה הַֽחִיִּיתֶ֖ם כָּל־נְקֵבָֽה:

16 Yet they are the very ones who, at the bidding of Balaam, induced the Israelites to trespass against *Hashem* in the matter of Peor, so that *Hashem*'s community was struck by the plague.

טז הֵ֣ן הֵ֜נָּה הָי֨וּ לִבְנֵ֤י יִשְׂרָאֵל֙ בִּדְבַ֣ר בִּלְעָ֔ם לִמְסָר־מַ֥עַל בַּֽיהוָֹ֖ה עַל־דְּבַר־פְּע֑וֹר וַתְּהִ֥י הַמַּגֵּפָ֖ה בַּֽעֲדַ֥ת יְהוָֹֽה:

17 Now, therefore, slay every male among the children, and slay also every woman who has known a man carnally;

יז וְעַתָּ֕ה הִרְג֥וּ כָל־זָכָ֖ר בַּטָּ֑ף וְכָל־אִשָּׁ֗ה יֹדַ֥עַת אִ֛ישׁ לְמִשְׁכַּ֥ב זָכָ֖ר הֲרֹֽגוּ:

18 but spare every young woman who has not had carnal relations with a man.

יח וְכֹל֙ הַטַּ֣ף בַּנָּשִׁ֔ים אֲשֶׁ֥ר לֹא־יָֽדְע֖וּ מִשְׁכַּ֣ב זָכָ֑ר הַֽחֲי֖וּ לָכֶֽם:

19 "You shall then stay outside the camp seven days; every one among you or among your captives who has slain a person or touched a corpse shall cleanse himself on the third and seventh days.

יט וְאַתֶּ֗ם חֲנ֛וּ מִח֥וּץ לַֽמַּחֲנֶ֖ה שִׁבְעַ֣ת יָמִ֑ים כֹּל֩ הֹרֵ֨ג נֶ֜פֶשׁ וְכֹ֣ל | נֹגֵ֣עַ בֶּחָלָ֗ל תִּֽתְחַטְּא֞וּ בַּיּ֤וֹם הַשְּׁלִישִׁי֙ וּבַיּ֣וֹם הַשְּׁבִיעִ֔י אַתֶּ֖ם וּשְׁבִֽיכֶֽם:

20 You shall also cleanse every cloth, every article of skin, everything made of goats' hair, and every object of wood."

כ וְכָל־בֶּ֧גֶד וְכָל־כְּלִי־ע֛וֹר וְכָל־מַֽעֲשֵׂ֥ה עִזִּ֖ים וְכָל־כְּלִי־עֵ֑ץ תִּתְחַטָּֽאוּ:

21 *Elazar* the *Kohen* said to the troops who had taken part in the fighting, "This is the ritual law that *Hashem* has enjoined upon *Moshe*:

כא וַיֹּ֨אמֶר אֶלְעָזָ֣ר הַכֹּהֵן֮ אֶל־אַנְשֵׁ֣י הַצָּבָא֒ הַבָּאִ֖ים לַמִּלְחָמָ֑ה זֹ֚את חֻקַּ֣ת הַתּוֹרָ֔ה אֲשֶׁר־צִוָּ֥ה יְהוָֹ֖ה אֶת־מֹשֶֽׁה:

22 Gold and silver, copper, iron, tin, and lead

כב אַ֥ךְ אֶת־הַזָּהָ֖ב וְאֶת־הַכָּ֑סֶף אֶֽת־הַנְּחֹ֨שֶׁת֙ אֶת־הַבַּרְזֶ֔ל אֶֽת־הַבְּדִ֖יל וְאֶת־הָֽעֹפָֽרֶת:

23 any article that can withstand fire – these you shall pass through fire and they shall be clean, except that they must be cleansed with water of lustration; and anything that cannot withstand fire you must pass through water.

כג כָּל־דָּבָ֞ר אֲשֶׁר־יָבֹ֣א בָאֵ֗שׁ תַּֽעֲבִ֤ירוּ בָאֵשׁ֙ וְטָהֵ֔ר אַ֕ךְ בְּמֵ֥י נִדָּ֖ה יִתְחַטָּ֑א וְכֹ֛ל אֲשֶׁ֧ר לֹֽא־יָבֹ֛א בָּאֵ֖שׁ תַּֽעֲבִ֥ירוּ בַמָּֽיִם:

24 On the seventh day you shall wash your clothes and be clean, and after that you may enter the camp."

כד וְכִבַּסְתֶּ֧ם בִּגְדֵיכֶ֛ם בַּיּ֥וֹם הַשְּׁבִיעִ֖י וּטְהַרְתֶּ֑ם וְאַחַ֖ר תָּבֹ֥אוּ אֶל־הַמַּֽחֲנֶֽה:

25 *Hashem* said to *Moshe*:

כה וַיֹּ֥אמֶר יְהוָֹ֖ה אֶל־מֹשֶׁ֥ה לֵּאמֹֽר:

26 "You and *Elazar* the *Kohen* and the family heads of the community take an inventory of the booty that was captured, man and beast,

כו שָׂ֗א אֵ֣ת רֹ֤אשׁ מַלְק֨וֹחַ֙ הַשְּׁבִ֔י בָּֽאָדָ֖ם וּבַבְּהֵמָ֑ה אַתָּה֙ וְאֶלְעָזָ֣ר הַכֹּהֵ֔ן וְרָאשֵׁ֖י אֲב֥וֹת הָֽעֵדָֽה:

27 and divide the booty equally between the combatants who engaged in the campaign and the rest of the community.

כז וְחָצִ֙יתָ֙ אֶת־הַמַּלְק֔וֹחַ בֵּ֚ין תֹּפְשֵׂ֣י הַמִּלְחָמָ֔ה הַיֹּצְאִ֖ים לַצָּבָ֑א וּבֵ֖ין כָּל־הָעֵדָֽה:

v'-kha-TZEE-ta et ha-mal-KO-akh BAYN to-f'-SAY ha-mil-kha-MAH ha-yo-tz'-EEM la-tza-VA u-VAYN kol ha-ay-DAH

28 You shall exact a levy for *Hashem*: in the case of the warriors who engaged in the campaign, one item in five hundred, of persons, oxen, asses, and sheep,

כח וַהֲרֵמֹתָ֨ מֶ֜כֶס לַֽיהֹוָ֗ה מֵאֵ֞ת אַנְשֵׁ֤י הַמִּלְחָמָה֙ הַיֹּצְאִ֣ים לַצָּבָ֔א אֶחָ֥ד נֶ֖פֶשׁ מֵחֲמֵ֣שׁ הַמֵּא֑וֹת מִן־הָֽאָדָם֙ וּמִן־הַבָּקָ֔ר וּמִן־הַחֲמֹרִ֖ים וּמִן־הַצֹּֽאן:

29 shall be taken from their half-share and given to *Elazar* the *Kohen* as a contribution to *Hashem*;

כט מִמַּֽחֲצִיתָ֖ם תִּקָּ֑חוּ וְנָֽתַתָּ֛ה לְאֶלְעָזָ֥ר הַכֹּהֵ֖ן תְּרוּמַ֥ת יְהֹוָֽה:

30 and from the half-share of the other Israelites you shall withhold one in every fifty human beings as well as cattle, asses, and sheep – all the animals – and give them to the *Leviim*, who attend to the duties of *Hashem*'s *Mishkan*."

ל וּמִמַּֽחֲצִ֨ת בְּנֵֽי־יִשְׂרָאֵ֜ל תִּקַּ֣ח ׀ אֶחָ֣ד ׀ אָחֻ֣ז מִן־הַֽחֲמִשִּׁ֗ים מִן־הָֽאָדָ֤ם מִן־הַבָּקָר֙ מִן־הַֽחֲמֹרִ֣ים וּמִן־הַצֹּ֔אן מִכָּל־הַבְּהֵמָ֑ה וְנָֽתַתָּ֤ה אֹתָם֙ לַֽלְוִיִּ֔ם שֹֽׁמְרֵ֕י מִשְׁמֶ֖רֶת מִשְׁכַּ֥ן יְהֹוָֽה:

31 *Moshe* and *Elazar* the *Kohen* did as *Hashem* commanded *Moshe*.

לא וַיַּ֣עַשׂ מֹשֶׁ֔ה וְאֶלְעָזָ֖ר הַכֹּהֵ֑ן כַּֽאֲשֶׁ֛ר צִוָּ֥ה יְהֹוָ֖ה אֶת־מֹשֶֽׁה:

32 The amount of booty, other than the spoil that the troops had plundered, came to 675,000 sheep,

לב וַיְהִי֙ הַמַּלְק֔וֹחַ יֶ֣תֶר הַבָּ֔ז אֲשֶׁ֥ר בָּֽזְז֖וּ עַ֣ם הַצָּבָ֑א צֹ֗אן שֵׁשׁ־מֵא֥וֹת אֶ֛לֶף וְשִׁבְעִ֥ים אֶ֖לֶף וַֽחֲמֵֽשֶׁת־אֲלָפִֽים:

33 72,000 head of cattle,

לג וּבָקָ֕ר שְׁנַ֥יִם וְשִׁבְעִ֖ים אָֽלֶף:

34 61,000 asses,

לד וַֽחֲמֹרִ֕ים אֶחָ֥ד וְשִׁשִּׁ֖ים אָֽלֶף:

35 and a total of 32,000 human beings, namely, the women who had not had carnal relations.

לה וְנֶ֣פֶשׁ אָדָ֔ם מִן־הַ֨נָּשִׁ֔ים אֲשֶׁ֥ר לֹֽא־יָֽדְע֖וּ מִשְׁכַּ֣ב זָכָ֑ר כָּל־נֶ֕פֶשׁ שְׁנַ֥יִם וּשְׁלֹשִׁ֖ים אָֽלֶף:

36 Thus, the half-share of those who had engaged in the campaign [was as follows]: The number of sheep was 337,500,

לו וַתְּהִי֙ הַמֶּֽחֱצָ֔ה חֵ֕לֶק הַיֹּֽצְאִ֖ים בַּצָּבָ֑א מִסְפַּ֣ר הַצֹּ֗אן שְׁלֹשׁ־מֵא֥וֹת אֶ֙לֶף֙ וּשְׁלֹשִׁ֣ים אֶ֔לֶף וְשִׁבְעַ֥ת אֲלָפִ֖ים וַֽחֲמֵ֥שׁ מֵאֽוֹת:

37 and *Hashem*'s levy from the sheep was 675;

לז וַיְהִ֛י הַמֶּ֥כֶס לַֽיהֹוָ֖ה מִן־הַצֹּ֑אן שֵׁ֥שׁ מֵא֖וֹת חָמֵ֥שׁ וְשִׁבְעִֽים:

An Israeli soldier and an ultra-Orthodox Jew praying together at the Western Wall

31:27 And the rest of the community Chapter 31 describes the war waged by the Israelites against the Midianites as retribution for the immorality and idolatry that the Midianites caused, which lead to the death of twenty-four thousand Israelites. *Moshe* commands that an equal number of men from each tribe be chosen to fight, and at the conclusion of the battle, the spoils of war are divided among the entire congregation. The fact that each tribe is equally represented in battle, and that everyone, even those who did not fight, is given a share in the spoils, highlights the unity of the congregation of Israel. Since they are functioning as one cohesive unit, united in the service of *Hashem*, they are finally ready to enter the Land of Israel and complete the journey their parents had started forty years earlier.

38 the cattle came to 36,000, from which *Hashem*'s levy was 72;

לח וְהַבָּקָר שִׁשָּׁה וּשְׁלֹשִׁים אָלֶף וּמִכְסָם לַיהֹוָה שְׁנַיִם וְשִׁבְעִים:

39 the asses came to 30,500, from which *Hashem*'s levy was 61.

לט וַחֲמֹרִים שְׁלֹשִׁים אֶלֶף וַחֲמֵשׁ מֵאוֹת וּמִכְסָם לַיהֹוָה אֶחָד וְשִׁשִּׁים:

40 And the number of human beings was 16,000, from which *Hashem*'s levy was 32.

מ וְנֶפֶשׁ אָדָם שִׁשָּׁה עָשָׂר אָלֶף וּמִכְסָם לַיהֹוָה שְׁנַיִם וּשְׁלֹשִׁים נָפֶשׁ:

41 *Moshe* gave the contributions levied for *Hashem* to *Elazar* the *Kohen*, as *Hashem* had commanded *Moshe*.

מא וַיִּתֵּן מֹשֶׁה אֶת־מֶכֶס תְּרוּמַת יְהֹוָה לְאֶלְעָזָר הַכֹּהֵן כַּאֲשֶׁר צִוָּה יְהֹוָה אֶת־מֹשֶׁה:

42 As for the half-share of the other Israelites, which *Moshe* withdrew from the men who had taken the field,

מב וּמִמַּחֲצִית בְּנֵי יִשְׂרָאֵל אֲשֶׁר חָצָה מֹשֶׁה מִן־הָאֲנָשִׁים הַצֹּבְאִים:

43 that half-share of the community consisted of 337,500 sheep,

מג וַתְּהִי מֶחֱצַת הָעֵדָה מִן־הַצֹּאן שְׁלֹשׁ־מֵאוֹת אֶלֶף וּשְׁלֹשִׁים אֶלֶף שִׁבְעַת אֲלָפִים וַחֲמֵשׁ מֵאוֹת:

44 36,000 head of cattle,

מד וּבָקָר שִׁשָּׁה וּשְׁלֹשִׁים אָלֶף:

45 30,500 asses,

מה וַחֲמֹרִים שְׁלֹשִׁים אֶלֶף וַחֲמֵשׁ מֵאוֹת:

46 and 16,000 human beings.

מו וְנֶפֶשׁ אָדָם שִׁשָּׁה עָשָׂר אָלֶף:

47 From this half-share of the Israelites, *Moshe* withheld one in every fifty humans and animals; and he gave them to the *Leviim*, who attended to the duties of *Hashem*'s *Mishkan*, as *Hashem* had commanded *Moshe*.

מז וַיִּקַּח מֹשֶׁה מִמַּחֲצִת בְּנֵי־יִשְׂרָאֵל אֶת־הָאָחֻז אֶחָד מִן־הַחֲמִשִּׁים מִן־הָאָדָם וּמִן־הַבְּהֵמָה וַיִּתֵּן אֹתָם לַלְוִיִּם שֹׁמְרֵי מִשְׁמֶרֶת מִשְׁכַּן יְהֹוָה כַּאֲשֶׁר צִוָּה יְהֹוָה אֶת־מֹשֶׁה:

48 The commanders of the troop divisions, the officers of thousands and the officers of hundreds, approached *Moshe*.

מח וַיִּקְרְבוּ אֶל־מֹשֶׁה הַפְּקֻדִים אֲשֶׁר לְאַלְפֵי הַצָּבָא שָׂרֵי הָאֲלָפִים וְשָׂרֵי הַמֵּאוֹת:

49 They said to *Moshe*, "Your servants have made a check of the warriors in our charge, and not one of us is missing.

מט וַיֹּאמְרוּ אֶל־מֹשֶׁה עֲבָדֶיךָ נָשְׂאוּ אֶת־רֹאשׁ אַנְשֵׁי הַמִּלְחָמָה אֲשֶׁר בְּיָדֵנוּ וְלֹא־נִפְקַד מִמֶּנּוּ אִישׁ:

50 So we have brought as an offering to *Hashem* such articles of gold as each of us came upon: armlets, bracelets, signet rings, earrings, and pendants, that expiation may be made for our persons before *Hashem*."

נ וַנַּקְרֵב אֶת־קָרְבַּן יְהֹוָה אִישׁ אֲשֶׁר מָצָא כְלִי־זָהָב אֶצְעָדָה וְצָמִיד טַבַּעַת עָגִיל וְכוּמָז לְכַפֵּר עַל־נַפְשֹׁתֵינוּ לִפְנֵי יְהֹוָה:

51 *Moshe* and *Elazar* the *Kohen* accepted the gold from them, all kinds of wrought articles.

נא וַיִּקַּח מֹשֶׁה וְאֶלְעָזָר הַכֹּהֵן אֶת־הַזָּהָב מֵאִתָּם כֹּל כְּלִי מַעֲשֶׂה:

52 All the gold that was offered by the officers of thousands and the officers of hundreds as a contribution to *Hashem* came to 16,750 *shekalim*.

נב וַיְהִי כָּל־זְהַב הַתְּרוּמָה אֲשֶׁר הֵרִימוּ לַיהֹוָה שִׁשָּׁה עָשָׂר אֶלֶף שְׁבַע־מֵאוֹת וַחֲמִשִּׁים שָׁקֶל מֵאֵת שָׂרֵי הָאֲלָפִים וּמֵאֵת שָׂרֵי הַמֵּאוֹת:

⁵³ But in the ranks, everyone kept his booty for himself.

נג אַנְשֵׁי הַצָּבָא בָּזְזוּ אִישׁ לוֹ:

⁵⁴ So *Moshe* and *Elazar* the *Kohen* accepted the gold from the officers of thousands and the officers of hundreds and brought it to the Tent of Meeting, as a reminder in behalf of the Israelites before *Hashem*.

נד וַיִּקַּח מֹשֶׁה וְאֶלְעָזָר הַכֹּהֵן אֶת־הַזָּהָב מֵאֵת שָׂרֵי הָאֲלָפִים וְהַמֵּאוֹת וַיָּבִאוּ אֹתוֹ אֶל־אֹהֶל מוֹעֵד זִכָּרוֹן לִבְנֵי־יִשְׂרָאֵל לִפְנֵי יְהוָה:

2 ¹ The Reubenites and the Gadites owned cattle in very great numbers. Noting that the lands of Jazer and *Gilad* were a region suitable for cattle,

לב א וּמִקְנֶה רַב הָיָה לִבְנֵי רְאוּבֵן וְלִבְנֵי־גָד עָצוּם מְאֹד וַיִּרְאוּ אֶת־אֶרֶץ יַעְזֵר וְאֶת־אֶרֶץ גִּלְעָד וְהִנֵּה הַמָּקוֹם מְקוֹם מִקְנֶה:

² the Gadites and the Reubenites came to *Moshe*, *Elazar* the *Kohen*, and the chieftains of the community, and said,

ב וַיָּבֹאוּ בְנֵי־גָד וּבְנֵי רְאוּבֵן וַיֹּאמְרוּ אֶל־מֹשֶׁה וְאֶל־אֶלְעָזָר הַכֹּהֵן וְאֶל־נְשִׂיאֵי הָעֵדָה לֵאמֹר:

³ "Ataroth, Dibon, Jazer, Nimrah, Heshbon, Elealeh, Sebam, Nebo, and Beon

ג עֲטָרוֹת וְדִיבֹן וְיַעְזֵר וְנִמְרָה וְחֶשְׁבּוֹן וְאֶלְעָלֵה וּשְׂבָם וּנְבוֹ וּבְעֹן:

⁴ the land that *Hashem* has conquered for the community of *Yisrael* is cattle country, and your servants have cattle.

ד הָאָרֶץ אֲשֶׁר הִכָּה יְהוָה לִפְנֵי עֲדַת יִשְׂרָאֵל אֶרֶץ מִקְנֶה הִוא וְלַעֲבָדֶיךָ מִקְנֶה:

⁵ It would be a favor to us," they continued, "if this land were given to your servants as a holding; do not move us across the *Yarden*."

ה וַיֹּאמְרוּ אִם־מָצָאנוּ חֵן בְּעֵינֶיךָ יֻתַּן אֶת־הָאָרֶץ הַזֹּאת לַעֲבָדֶיךָ לַאֲחֻזָּה אַל־תַּעֲבִרֵנוּ אֶת־הַיַּרְדֵּן:

⁶ *Moshe* replied to the Gadites and the Reubenites, "Are your brothers to go to war while you stay here?

ו וַיֹּאמֶר מֹשֶׁה לִבְנֵי־גָד וְלִבְנֵי רְאוּבֵן הַאַחֵיכֶם יָבֹאוּ לַמִּלְחָמָה וְאַתֶּם תֵּשְׁבוּ פֹה:

⁷ Why will you turn the minds of the Israelites from crossing into the land that *Hashem* has given them?

ז וְלָמָּה תנואון [תְנִיאוּן] אֶת־לֵב בְּנֵי יִשְׂרָאֵל מֵעֲבֹר אֶל־הָאָרֶץ אֲשֶׁר־נָתַן לָהֶם יְהוָה:

⁸ That is what your fathers did when I sent them from Kadesh-barnea to survey the land.

ח כֹּה עָשׂוּ אֲבֹתֵיכֶם בְּשָׁלְחִי אֹתָם מִקָּדֵשׁ בַּרְנֵעַ לִרְאוֹת אֶת־הָאָרֶץ:

*KO a-SU a-vo-tay-KHEM b'-shol-KHEE o-TAM
mi-ka-DAYSH bar-NAY-a lir-OT et ha-A-retz*

32:8 That is what your fathers did When the tribes of *Reuven* and *Gad* request to settle in the lands conquered from Sihon and Og on the east bank of the Jordan River, instead of settling in the Land of Israel proper, *Moshe*'s reaction is very strong and negative. In his eyes, they are rejecting the land given to them by God, and he fears that they will influence others to also refrain from crossing into the land of Israel. He wonders: Have they learned nothing from the sin of the spies? *Moshe* acquiesces only when he becomes convinced that the request stems neither from a rejection of God's land, nor from a desire to be relieved of the long and hard upcoming struggle to conquer the Promised Land. That mistake had already been made once and the people suffered the consequences; they have learned not to make the same mistake again. Let us make sure that neither our actions nor our speech in anyway rejects or belittles *Eretz Yisrael*.

The Golan Heights, part of biblical Bashan inherited by *Reuven* and *Gad*

9 After going up to the wadi Eshcol and surveying the land, they turned the minds of the Israelites from invading the land that *Hashem* had given them.

ט וַיַּעֲלוּ עַד־נַחַל אֶשְׁכּוֹל וַיִּרְאוּ אֶת־הָאָרֶץ וַיָּנִיאוּ אֶת־לֵב בְּנֵי יִשְׂרָאֵל לְבִלְתִּי־בֹא אֶל־הָאָרֶץ אֲשֶׁר־נָתַן לָהֶם יְהֹוָה:

10 Thereupon *Hashem* was incensed and He swore,

י וַיִּחַר־אַף יְהֹוָה בַּיּוֹם הַהוּא וַיִּשָּׁבַע לֵאמֹר:

11 'None of the men from twenty years up who came out of Egypt shall see the land that I promised on oath to *Avraham, Yitzchak,* and *Yaakov,* for they did not remain loyal to Me –

יא אִם־יִרְאוּ הָאֲנָשִׁים הָעֹלִים מִמִּצְרַיִם מִבֶּן עֶשְׂרִים שָׁנָה וָמַעְלָה אֵת הָאֲדָמָה אֲשֶׁר נִשְׁבַּעְתִּי לְאַבְרָהָם לְיִצְחָק וּלְיַעֲקֹב כִּי לֹא־מִלְאוּ אַחֲרָי:

12 none except *Kalev* son of Jephunneh the Kenizzite and *Yehoshua* son of Nun, for they remained loyal to *Hashem.*'

יב בִּלְתִּי כָּלֵב בֶּן־יְפֻנֶּה הַקְּנִזִּי וִיהוֹשֻׁעַ בִּן־נוּן כִּי מִלְאוּ אַחֲרֵי יְהֹוָה:

13 *Hashem* was incensed at *Yisrael,* and for forty years He made them wander in the wilderness, until the whole generation that had provoked *Hashem*'s displeasure was gone.

יג וַיִּחַר־אַף יְהֹוָה בְּיִשְׂרָאֵל וַיְנִעֵם בַּמִּדְבָּר אַרְבָּעִים שָׁנָה עַד־תֹּם כָּל־הַדּוֹר הָעֹשֶׂה הָרַע בְּעֵינֵי יְהֹוָה:

14 And now you, a breed of sinful men, have replaced your fathers, to add still further to *Hashem*'s wrath against *Yisrael.*

יד וְהִנֵּה קַמְתֶּם תַּחַת אֲבֹתֵיכֶם תַּרְבּוּת אֲנָשִׁים חַטָּאִים לִסְפּוֹת עוֹד עַל חֲרוֹן אַף־יְהֹוָה אֶל־יִשְׂרָאֵל:

15 If you turn away from Him and He abandons them once more in the wilderness, you will bring calamity upon all this people."

טו כִּי תְשׁוּבֻן מֵאַחֲרָיו וְיָסַף עוֹד לְהַנִּיחוֹ בַּמִּדְבָּר וְשִׁחַתֶּם לְכָל־הָעָם הַזֶּה:

16 Then they stepped up to him and said, "We will build here sheepfolds for our flocks and towns for our children.

טז וַיִּגְּשׁוּ אֵלָיו וַיֹּאמְרוּ גִּדְרֹת צֹאן נִבְנֶה לְמִקְנֵנוּ פֹּה וְעָרִים לְטַפֵּנוּ:

17 And we will hasten as shock-troops in the van of the Israelites until we have established them in their home, while our children stay in the fortified towns because of the inhabitants of the land.

יז וַאֲנַחְנוּ נֵחָלֵץ חֻשִׁים לִפְנֵי בְּנֵי יִשְׂרָאֵל עַד אֲשֶׁר אִם־הֲבִיאֹנֻם אֶל־מְקוֹמָם וְיָשַׁב טַפֵּנוּ בְּעָרֵי הַמִּבְצָר מִפְּנֵי יֹשְׁבֵי הָאָרֶץ:

18 We will not return to our homes until every one of the Israelites is in possession of his portion.

יח לֹא נָשׁוּב אֶל־בָּתֵּינוּ עַד הִתְנַחֵל בְּנֵי יִשְׂרָאֵל אִישׁ נַחֲלָתוֹ:

19 But we will not have a share with them in the territory beyond the *Yarden,* for we have received our share on the east side of the *Yarden.*"

יט כִּי לֹא נִנְחַל אִתָּם מֵעֵבֶר לַיַּרְדֵּן וָהָלְאָה כִּי בָאָה נַחֲלָתֵנוּ אֵלֵינוּ מֵעֵבֶר הַיַּרְדֵּן מִזְרָחָה:

20 *Moshe* said to them, "If you do this, if you go to battle as shock-troops, at the instance of *Hashem,*

כ וַיֹּאמֶר אֲלֵיהֶם מֹשֶׁה אִם־תַּעֲשׂוּן אֶת־הַדָּבָר הַזֶּה אִם־תֵּחָלְצוּ לִפְנֵי יְהֹוָה לַמִּלְחָמָה:

21 and every shock-fighter among you crosses the *Yarden*, at the instance of *Hashem*, until He has dispossessed His enemies before Him,

כא וְעָבַר לָכֶם כָּל־חָלוּץ אֶת־הַיַּרְדֵּן לִפְנֵי יְהֹוָה עַד הוֹרִישׁוֹ אֶת־אֹיְבָיו מִפָּנָיו:

*v'-a-VAR la-KHEM kol kha-LUTZ et ha-yar-DAYN lif-NAY
a-do-NAI AD ho-ree-SHO et o-y'-VAV mi-pa-NAV*

22 and the land has been subdued, at the instance of *Hashem*, and then you return – you shall be clear before *Hashem* and before *Yisrael*; and this land shall be your holding under *Hashem*.

כב וְנִכְבְּשָׁה הָאָרֶץ לִפְנֵי יְהֹוָה וְאַחַר תָּשֻׁבוּ וִהְיִיתֶם נְקִיִּם מֵיְהֹוָה וּמִיִּשְׂרָאֵל וְהָיְתָה הָאָרֶץ הַזֹּאת לָכֶם לַאֲחֻזָּה לִפְנֵי יְהֹוָה:

23 But if you do not do so, you will have sinned against *Hashem*; and know that your sin will overtake you.

כג וְאִם־לֹא תַעֲשׂוּן כֵּן הִנֵּה חֲטָאתֶם לַיְהֹוָה וּדְעוּ חַטַּאתְכֶם אֲשֶׁר תִּמְצָא אֶתְכֶם:

24 Build towns for your children and sheepfolds for your flocks, but do what you have promised."

כד בְּנוּ־לָכֶם עָרִים לְטַפְּכֶם וּגְדֵרֹת לְצֹנַאֲכֶם וְהַיֹּצֵא מִפִּיכֶם תַּעֲשׂוּ:

25 The Gadites and the Reubenites answered *Moshe*, "Your servants will do as my lord commands.

כה וַיֹּאמֶר בְּנֵי־גָד וּבְנֵי רְאוּבֵן אֶל־מֹשֶׁה לֵאמֹר עֲבָדֶיךָ יַעֲשׂוּ כַּאֲשֶׁר אֲדֹנִי מְצַוֶּה:

26 Our children, our wives, our flocks, and all our other livestock will stay behind in the towns of *Gilad*;

כו טַפֵּנוּ נָשֵׁינוּ מִקְנֵנוּ וְכָל־בְּהֶמְתֵּנוּ יִהְיוּ־שָׁם בְּעָרֵי הַגִּלְעָד:

27 while your servants, all those recruited for war, cross over, at the instance of *Hashem*, to engage in battle – as my lord orders."

כז וַעֲבָדֶיךָ יַעַבְרוּ כָּל־חֲלוּץ צָבָא לִפְנֵי יְהֹוָה לַמִּלְחָמָה כַּאֲשֶׁר אֲדֹנִי דֹּבֵר:

28 Then *Moshe* gave instructions concerning them to *Elazar* the *Kohen*, *Yehoshua* son of *Nun*, and the family heads of the Israelite tribes.

כח וַיְצַו לָהֶם מֹשֶׁה אֵת אֶלְעָזָר הַכֹּהֵן וְאֵת יְהוֹשֻׁעַ בִּן־נוּן וְאֶת־רָאשֵׁי אֲבוֹת הַמַּטּוֹת לִבְנֵי יִשְׂרָאֵל:

29 *Moshe* said to them, "If every shock-fighter among the Gadites and the Reubenites crosses the *Yarden* with you to do battle, at the instance of *Hashem*, and the land is subdued before you, you shall give them the land of *Gilad* as a holding.

כט וַיֹּאמֶר מֹשֶׁה אֲלֵהֶם אִם־יַעַבְרוּ בְנֵי־גָד וּבְנֵי־רְאוּבֵן אִתְּכֶם אֶת־הַיַּרְדֵּן כָּל־חָלוּץ לַמִּלְחָמָה לִפְנֵי יְהֹוָה וְנִכְבְּשָׁה הָאָרֶץ לִפְנֵיכֶם וּנְתַתֶּם לָהֶם אֶת־אֶרֶץ הַגִּלְעָד לַאֲחֻזָּה:

32:21 And every shock-fighter among you crosses the *Yarden* *Moshe* was willing to accept the request of *Reuven* and *Gad* to settle on the east of the *Yarden* River only after they promised to help fight to inherit the Land of Israel. We learn a powerful lesson of responsibility from this story. While they already possess the land that was going to be their home, these tribes are not allowed to settle down until every other tribe in Israel also has land of their own in which to settle. Life in *Eretz Yisrael* demands and engenders the concept that every-one is responsible for his fellow. This spirit of collective cooperation can be seen in the *Kibbutz* movement formed by the original Zionist pioneers. These unique farms, known as *Kibbutzim*, took collective responsibility so far that members didn't even own their own clothing or personal property. Everything was shared equally among the members.

Members of Kibbutz Amir heading to work, 1940

Numbers

30 But if they do not cross over with you as shock-troops, they shall receive holdings among you in the land of Canaan."

ל וְאִם־לֹא יַעַבְרֻוּ חֲלוּצִים אִתְּכֶם וְנֹאחֲזֻוּ בְתֹכְכֶם בְּאֶרֶץ כְּנָעַן:

31 The Gadites and the Reubenites said in reply, "Whatever *Hashem* has spoken concerning your servants, that we will do.

לא וַיַּעֲנֻוּ בְנֵי־גָד וּבְנֵי רְאוּבֵן לֵאמֹר אֵת אֲשֶׁר דִּבֶּר יְהוָֹה אֶל־עֲבָדֶיךָ כֵּן נַעֲשֶׂה:

32 We ourselves will cross over as shock-troops, at the instance of *Hashem*, into the land of Canaan; and we shall keep our hereditary holding across the *Yarden*."

לב נַחְנוּ נַעֲבֹר חֲלוּצִים לִפְנֵי יְהוָֹה אֶרֶץ כְּנָעַן וְאִתָּנוּ אֲחֻזַּת נַחֲלָתֵנוּ מֵעֵבֶר לַיַּרְדֵּן:

33 So *Moshe* assigned to them – to the Gadites, the Reubenites, and the half-tribe of *Menashe* son of *Yosef* – the kingdom of Sihon king of the Amorites and the kingdom of King Og of Bashan, the land with its various cities and the territories of their surrounding towns.

לג וַיִּתֵּן לָהֶם מֹשֶׁה לִבְנֵי־גָד וְלִבְנֵי רְאוּבֵן וְלַחֲצִי שֵׁבֶט מְנַשֶּׁה בֶן־יוֹסֵף אֶת־מַמְלֶכֶת סִיחֹן מֶלֶךְ הָאֱמֹרִי וְאֶת־מַמְלֶכֶת עוֹג מֶלֶךְ הַבָּשָׁן הָאָרֶץ לְעָרֶיהָ בִּגְבֻלֹת עָרֵי הָאָרֶץ סָבִיב:

34 The Gadites rebuilt Dibon, Ataroth, Aroer,

לד וַיִּבְנֻוּ בְנֵי־גָד אֶת־דִּיבֹן וְאֶת־עֲטָרֹת וְאֵת עֲרֹעֵר:

35 Atroth-shophan, Jazer, Jogbehah,

לה וְאֶת־עַטְרֹת שׁוֹפָן וְאֶת־יַעְזֵר וְיָגְבֳּהָה:

36 Beth-nimrah, and Beth-haran as fortified towns or as enclosures for flocks.

לו וְאֶת־בֵּית נִמְרָה וְאֶת־בֵּית הָרָן עָרֵי מִבְצָר וְגִדְרֹת צֹאן:

37 The Reubenites rebuilt Heshbon, Elealeh, Kiriathaim,

לז וּבְנֵי רְאוּבֵן בָּנֻוּ אֶת־חֶשְׁבּוֹן וְאֶת־אֶלְעָלֵא וְאֵת קִרְיָתָיִם:

38 Nebo, Baal-meon – some names being changed – and Sibmah; they gave [their own] names to towns that they rebuilt.

לח וְאֶת־נְבוֹ וְאֶת־בַּעַל מְעוֹן מוּסַבֹּת שֵׁם וְאֶת־שִׂבְמָה וַיִּקְרְאוּ בְשֵׁמֹת אֶת־שְׁמֹות הֶעָרִים אֲשֶׁר בָּנֻו:

39 The descendants of Machir son of *Menashe* went to *Gilad* and captured it, dispossessing the Amorites who were there;

לט וַיֵּלְכוּ בְּנֵי מָכִיר בֶּן־מְנַשֶּׁה גִּלְעָדָה וַיִּלְכְּדֻהָ וַיּוֹרֶשׁ אֶת־הָאֱמֹרִי אֲשֶׁר־בָּהּ:

40 so *Moshe* gave *Gilad* to Machir son of *Menashe*, and he settled there.

מ וַיִּתֵּן מֹשֶׁה אֶת־הַגִּלְעָד לְמָכִיר בֶּן־מְנַשֶּׁה וַיֵּשֶׁב בָּהּ:

41 *Yair* son of *Menashe* went and captured their villages, which he renamed Havvoth-jair.

מא וְיָאִיר בֶּן־מְנַשֶּׁה הָלַךְ וַיִּלְכֹּד אֶת־חַוֹּתֵיהֶם וַיִּקְרָא אֶתְהֶן חַוֹּת יָאִיר:

42 And Nobah went and captured Kenath and its dependencies, renaming it Nobah after himself.

מב וְנֹבַח הָלַךְ וַיִּלְכֹּד אֶת־קְנָת וְאֶת־בְּנֹתֶיהָ וַיִּקְרָא לָה נֹבַח בִּשְׁמוֹ:

Numbers

33 1 These were the marches of the Israelites who
started out from the land of Egypt, troop by troop,
in the charge of *Moshe* and *Aharon*.

א אֵלֶּה מַסְעֵי בְנֵי־יִשְׂרָאֵל אֲשֶׁר יָצְאוּ
מֵאֶרֶץ מִצְרַיִם לְצִבְאֹתָם בְּיַד־מֹשֶׁה
וְאַהֲרֹן:

*AY-leh mas-AY v'-nay yis-ra-AYL a-SHER ya-tz'-U may-E-retz
mitz-RA-yim l'-tziv-o-TAM b'-yad mo-SHEH v'-a-ha-RON*

2 *Moshe* recorded the starting points of their various
marches as directed by *Hashem*. Their marches, by
starting points, were as follows:

ב וַיִּכְתֹּב מֹשֶׁה אֶת־מוֹצָאֵיהֶם לְמַסְעֵיהֶם
עַל־פִּי יְהוָה וְאֵלֶּה מַסְעֵיהֶם
לְמוֹצָאֵיהֶם:

3 They set out from Rameses in the first month, on
the fifteenth day of the first month. It was on the
morrow of the *Pesach* offering that the Israelites
started out defiantly, in plain view of all the
Egyptians.

ג וַיִּסְעוּ מֵרַעְמְסֵס בַּחֹדֶשׁ הָרִאשׁוֹן
בַּחֲמִשָּׁה עָשָׂר יוֹם לַחֹדֶשׁ הָרִאשׁוֹן
מִמָּחֳרַת הַפֶּסַח יָצְאוּ בְנֵי־יִשְׂרָאֵל בְּיָד
רָמָה לְעֵינֵי כָּל־מִצְרָיִם:

4 The Egyptians meanwhile were burying those
among them whom *Hashem* had struck down, every
first-born – whereby *Hashem* executed judgment on
their gods.

ד וּמִצְרַיִם מְקַבְּרִים אֵת אֲשֶׁר הִכָּה יְהוָה
בָּהֶם כָּל־בְּכוֹר וּבֵאלֹהֵיהֶם עָשָׂה יְהוָה
שְׁפָטִים:

5 The Israelites set out from Rameses and encamped
at Succoth.

ה וַיִּסְעוּ בְנֵי־יִשְׂרָאֵל מֵרַעְמְסֵס וַיַּחֲנוּ
בְּסֻכֹּת:

6 They set out from Succoth and encamped at Etham,
which is on the edge of the wilderness.

ו וַיִּסְעוּ מִסֻּכֹּת וַיַּחֲנוּ בְאֵתָם אֲשֶׁר בִּקְצֵה
הַמִּדְבָּר:

7 They set out from Etham and turned about toward
Pi-hahiroth, which faces Baal-zephon, and they
encamped before Migdol.

ז וַיִּסְעוּ מֵאֵתָם וַיָּשָׁב עַל־פִּי הַחִירֹת
אֲשֶׁר עַל־פְּנֵי בַּעַל צְפוֹן וַיַּחֲנוּ לִפְנֵי
מִגְדֹּל:

8 They set out from Pene-hahiroth and passed
through the sea into the wilderness; and they made
a three-days' journey in the wilderness of Etham
and encamped at Marah.

ח וַיִּסְעוּ מִפְּנֵי הַחִירֹת וַיַּעַבְרוּ בְתוֹךְ־הַיָּם
הַמִּדְבָּרָה וַיֵּלְכוּ דֶּרֶךְ שְׁלֹשֶׁת יָמִים
בְּמִדְבַּר אֵתָם וַיַּחֲנוּ בְּמָרָה:

9 They set out from Marah and came to Elim. There
were twelve springs in Elim and seventy palm trees,
so they encamped there.

ט וַיִּסְעוּ מִמָּרָה וַיָּבֹאוּ אֵילִמָה וּבְאֵילִם
שְׁתֵּים עֶשְׂרֵה עֵינֹת מַיִם וְשִׁבְעִים
תְּמָרִים וַיַּחֲנוּ־שָׁם:

10 They set out from Elim and encamped by the Sea
of Reeds.

י וַיִּסְעוּ מֵאֵילִם וַיַּחֲנוּ עַל־יַם־סוּף:

33:1 These were the marches of the Israelites
This chapter summarizes the journey that the
People of Israel took to the Promised Land,
starting with the flight from Egypt until they stood on the
bank of the *Yarden* River, ready to enter the land. Overall,
there were forty-two encampments in the desert: fourteen before the sin of the spies which took place in the
second year, and eight in the fortieth year, leaving only
twenty stops during the thirty-eight years in between.
Rashi points out that this highlights *Hashem*'s compassion
for His people. Although
they were punished with
forty years of wandering in
the desert, He did not force
them to continuously move
around, as this would have
been too physically grueling.
Instead, they were allowed
much opportunity to rest between their wanderings.

A man stands on a mountain ridge in the Negev desert

Numbers

¹¹ They set out from the Sea of Reeds and encamped in the wilderness of Sin.

יא וַיִּסְעוּ מִיַּם־סוּף וַיַּחֲנוּ בְּמִדְבַּר־סִין:

¹² They set out from the wilderness of Sin and encamped at Dophkah.

יב וַיִּסְעוּ מִמִּדְבַּר־סִין וַיַּחֲנוּ בְּדָפְקָה:

¹³ They set out from Dophkah and encamped at Alush.

יג וַיִּסְעוּ מִדָּפְקָה וַיַּחֲנוּ בְּאָלוּשׁ:

¹⁴ They set out from Alush and encamped at Rephidim; it was there that the people had no water to drink.

יד וַיִּסְעוּ מֵאָלוּשׁ וַיַּחֲנוּ בִּרְפִידִם וְלֹא־הָיָה שָׁם מַיִם לָעָם לִשְׁתּוֹת:

¹⁵ They set out from Rephidim and encamped in the wilderness of Sinai.

טו וַיִּסְעוּ מֵרְפִידִם וַיַּחֲנוּ בְּמִדְבַּר סִינָי:

¹⁶ They set out from the wilderness of Sinai and encamped at Kibroth-hattaavah.

טז וַיִּסְעוּ מִמִּדְבַּר סִינָי וַיַּחֲנוּ בְּקִבְרֹת הַתַּאֲוָה:

¹⁷ They set out from Kibroth-hattaavah and encamped at Hazeroth.

יז וַיִּסְעוּ מִקִּבְרֹת הַתַּאֲוָה וַיַּחֲנוּ בַּחֲצֵרֹת:

¹⁸ They set out from Hazeroth and encamped at Rithmah.

יח וַיִּסְעוּ מֵחֲצֵרֹת וַיַּחֲנוּ בְּרִתְמָה:

¹⁹ They set out from Rithmah and encamped at Rimmon-perez.

יט וַיִּסְעוּ מֵרִתְמָה וַיַּחֲנוּ בְּרִמֹּן פָּרֶץ:

²⁰ They set out from Rimmon-perez and encamped at Libnah.

כ וַיִּסְעוּ מֵרִמֹּן פָּרֶץ וַיַּחֲנוּ בְּלִבְנָה:

²¹ They set out from Libnah and encamped at Rissah.

כא וַיִּסְעוּ מִלִּבְנָה וַיַּחֲנוּ בְּרִסָּה:

²² They set out from Rissah and encamped at Kehelath.

כב וַיִּסְעוּ מֵרִסָּה וַיַּחֲנוּ בִּקְהֵלָתָה:

²³ They set out from Kehelath and encamped at Mount Shepher.

כג וַיִּסְעוּ מִקְּהֵלָתָה וַיַּחֲנוּ בְּהַר־שָׁפֶר:

²⁴ They set out from Mount Shepher and encamped at Haradah.

כד וַיִּסְעוּ מֵהַר־שָׁפֶר וַיַּחֲנוּ בַּחֲרָדָה:

²⁵ They set out from Haradah and encamped at Makheloth.

כה וַיִּסְעוּ מֵחֲרָדָה וַיַּחֲנוּ בְּמַקְהֵלֹת:

²⁶ They set out from Makheloth and encamped at Tahath.

כו וַיִּסְעוּ מִמַּקְהֵלֹת וַיַּחֲנוּ בְּתָחַת:

²⁷ They set out from Tahath and encamped at Terah.

כז וַיִּסְעוּ מִתָּחַת וַיַּחֲנוּ בְּתָרַח:

²⁸ They set out from Terah and encamped at Mithkah.

כח וַיִּסְעוּ מִתָּרַח וַיַּחֲנוּ בְּמִתְקָה:

²⁹ They set out from Mithkah and encamped at Hashmonah.

כט וַיִּסְעוּ מִמִּתְקָה וַיַּחֲנוּ בְּחַשְׁמֹנָה:

³⁰ They set out from Hashmonah and encamped at Moseroth.

ל וַיִּסְעוּ מֵחַשְׁמֹנָה וַיַּחֲנוּ בְּמֹסֵרוֹת:

³¹ They set out from Moseroth and encamped at Bene-jaakan.

לא וַיִּסְעוּ מִמֹּסֵרוֹת וַיַּחֲנוּ בִּבְנֵי יַעֲקָן:

Masei

32 They set out from Bene-jaakan and encamped at Hor-haggidgad.

לב וַיִּסְעוּ מִבְּנֵי יַעֲקָן וַיַּחֲנוּ בְּחֹר הַגִּדְגָּד:

33 They set out from Hor-haggidgad and encamped at Jotbath.

לג וַיִּסְעוּ מֵחֹר הַגִּדְגָּד וַיַּחֲנוּ בְּיָטְבָתָה:

34 They set out from Jotbath and encamped at Abronah.

לד וַיִּסְעוּ מִיָּטְבָתָה וַיַּחֲנוּ בְּעַבְרֹנָה:

35 They set out from Abronah and encamped at Ezion-geber.

לה וַיִּסְעוּ מֵעַבְרֹנָה וַיַּחֲנוּ בְּעֶצְיוֹן גָּבֶר:

36 They set out from Ezion-geber and encamped in the wilderness of Zin, that is, Kadesh.

לו וַיִּסְעוּ מֵעֶצְיוֹן גָּבֶר וַיַּחֲנוּ בְמִדְבַּר־צִן הִוא קָדֵשׁ:

37 They set out from Kadesh and encamped at Mount Hor, on the edge of the land of Edom.

לז וַיִּסְעוּ מִקָּדֵשׁ וַיַּחֲנוּ בְּהֹר הָהָר בִּקְצֵה אֶרֶץ אֱדוֹם:

38 *Aharon* the *Kohen* ascended Mount Hor at the command of *Hashem* and died there, in the fortieth year after the Israelites had left the land of Egypt, on the first day of the fifth month.

לח וַיַּעַל אַהֲרֹן הַכֹּהֵן אֶל־הֹר הָהָר עַל־פִּי יְהֹוָה וַיָּמָת שָׁם בִּשְׁנַת הָאַרְבָּעִים לְצֵאת בְּנֵי־יִשְׂרָאֵל מֵאֶרֶץ מִצְרַיִם בַּחֹדֶשׁ הַחֲמִישִׁי בְּאֶחָד לַחֹדֶשׁ:

39 *Aharon* was a hundred and twenty-three years old when he died on Mount Hor.

לט וְאַהֲרֹן בֶּן־שָׁלֹשׁ וְעֶשְׂרִים וּמְאַת שָׁנָה בְּמֹתוֹ בְּהֹר הָהָר:

40 And the Canaanite, king of Arad, who dwelt in the *Negev*, in the land of Canaan, learned of the coming of the Israelites.

מ וַיִּשְׁמַע הַכְּנַעֲנִי מֶלֶךְ עֲרָד וְהוּא־יֹשֵׁב בַּנֶּגֶב בְּאֶרֶץ כְּנָעַן בְּבֹא בְּנֵי יִשְׂרָאֵל:

41 They set out from Mount Hor and encamped at Zalmonah.

מא וַיִּסְעוּ מֵהֹר הָהָר וַיַּחֲנוּ בְּצַלְמֹנָה:

42 They set out from Zalmonah and encamped at Punon.

מב וַיִּסְעוּ מִצַּלְמֹנָה וַיַּחֲנוּ בְּפוּנֹן:

43 They set out from Punon and encamped at Oboth.

מג וַיִּסְעוּ מִפּוּנֹן וַיַּחֲנוּ בְּאֹבֹת:

44 They set out from Oboth and encamped at Iye-abarim, in the territory of Moab.

מד וַיִּסְעוּ מֵאֹבֹת וַיַּחֲנוּ בְּעִיֵּי הָעֲבָרִים בִּגְבוּל מוֹאָב:

45 They set out from Iyim and encamped at Dibon-gad.

מה וַיִּסְעוּ מֵעִיִּים וַיַּחֲנוּ בְּדִיבֹן גָּד:

46 They set out from Dibon-gad and encamped at Almon-diblathaim.

מו וַיִּסְעוּ מִדִּיבֹן גָּד וַיַּחֲנוּ בְּעַלְמֹן דִּבְלָתָיְמָה:

47 They set out from Almon-diblathaim and encamped in the hills of Abarim, before Nebo.

מז וַיִּסְעוּ מֵעַלְמֹן דִּבְלָתָיְמָה וַיַּחֲנוּ בְּהָרֵי הָעֲבָרִים לִפְנֵי נְבוֹ:

48 They set out from the hills of Abarim and encamped in the steppes of Moab, at the *Yarden* near *Yericho*;

מח וַיִּסְעוּ מֵהָרֵי הָעֲבָרִים וַיַּחֲנוּ בְּעַרְבֹת מוֹאָב עַל יַרְדֵּן יְרֵחוֹ:

49 they encamped by the *Yarden* from Beth-jeshimoth as far as Abel-shittim, in the steppes of Moab.

מט וַיַּחֲנוּ עַל־הַיַּרְדֵּן מִבֵּית הַיְשִׁמֹת עַד אָבֵל הַשִּׁטִּים בְּעַרְבֹת מוֹאָב:

Numbers

⁵⁰ In the steppes of Moab, at the *Yarden* near *Yericho*,
Hashem spoke to *Moshe*, saying:

נ וַיְדַבֵּר יְהֹוָה אֶל־מֹשֶׁה בְּעַרְבֹת מוֹאָב
עַל־יַרְדֵּן יְרֵחוֹ לֵאמֹר:

⁵¹ Speak to *B'nei Yisrael* and say to them: When you
cross the *Yarden* into the land of Canaan,

נא דַּבֵּר אֶל־בְּנֵי יִשְׂרָאֵל וְאָמַרְתָּ אֲלֵהֶם כִּי
אַתֶּם עֹבְרִים אֶת־הַיַּרְדֵּן אֶל־אֶרֶץ כְּנָעַן:

⁵² you shall dispossess all the inhabitants of the land;
you shall destroy all their figured objects; you
shall destroy all their molten images, and you shall
demolish all their cult places.

נב וְהוֹרַשְׁתֶּם אֶת־כָּל־יֹשְׁבֵי הָאָרֶץ
מִפְּנֵיכֶם וְאִבַּדְתֶּם אֵת כָּל־מַשְׂכִּיֹּתָם
וְאֵת כָּל־צַלְמֵי מַסֵּכֹתָם תְּאַבֵּדוּ וְאֵת
כָּל־בָּמֹתָם תַּשְׁמִידוּ:

⁵³ And you shall take possession of the land and settle
in it, for I have assigned the land to you to possess.

נג וְהוֹרַשְׁתֶּם אֶת־הָאָרֶץ וִישַׁבְתֶּם־בָּהּ כִּי
לָכֶם נָתַתִּי אֶת־הָאָרֶץ לָרֶשֶׁת אֹתָהּ:

*v'-ho-rash-TEM et ha-A-retz vee-shav-tem BAH KEE
la-KHEM na-TA-tee et ha-A-retz la-RE-shet o-TAH*

⁵⁴ You shall apportion the land among yourselves
by lot, clan by clan: with larger groups increase
the share, with smaller groups reduce the share.
Wherever the lot falls for anyone, that shall be his.
You shall have your portions according to your
ancestral tribes.

נד וְהִתְנַחַלְתֶּם אֶת־הָאָרֶץ בְּגוֹרָל
לְמִשְׁפְּחֹתֵיכֶם לָרַב תַּרְבּוּ אֶת־נַחֲלָתוֹ
וְלַמְעַט תַּמְעִיט אֶת־נַחֲלָתוֹ אֶל אֲשֶׁר־
יֵצֵא לוֹ שָׁמָּה הַגּוֹרָל לוֹ יִהְיֶה לְמַטּוֹת
אֲבֹתֵיכֶם תִּתְנֶחָלוּ:

*v'-hit-na-khal-TEM et ha-A-retz b'-go-RAL l'-mish-p'-kho-tay-KHEM la-RAV
tar-BU et na-kha-la-TO v'-lam-AT tam-EET et na-kha-la-TO EL a-sher yay-TZAY
LO SHA-mah ha-go-RAL LO yih-YEH l'-ma-TOT a-vo-TAY-khem tit-ne-KHA-lu*

⁵⁵ But if you do not dispossess the inhabitants of the
land, those whom you allow to remain shall be
stings in your eyes and thorns in your sides, and
they shall harass you in the land in which you live;

נה וְאִם־לֹא תוֹרִישׁוּ אֶת־יֹשְׁבֵי הָאָרֶץ
מִפְּנֵיכֶם וְהָיָה אֲשֶׁר תּוֹתִירוּ מֵהֶם
לְשִׂכִּים בְּעֵינֵיכֶם וְלִצְנִינִם בְּצִדֵּיכֶם
וְצָרְרוּ אֶתְכֶם עַל־הָאָרֶץ אֲשֶׁר אַתֶּם
יֹשְׁבִים בָּהּ:

⁵⁶ so that I will do to you what I planned to do to
them.

נו וְהָיָה כַּאֲשֶׁר דִּמִּיתִי לַעֲשׂוֹת לָהֶם
אֶעֱשֶׂה לָכֶם:

34 ¹ Hashem spoke to *Moshe*, saying:

לד א וַיְדַבֵּר יְהֹוָה אֶל־מֹשֶׁה לֵּאמֹר:

33:53 I have assigned the land to you to possess
This verse is the source for the biblical command to settle and inhabit the Land of Israel. It
emphasizes the importance of living in the land and,
according to many, hints to a prohibition of leaving Israel
without a compelling reason. As *Sefer Bamidbar* draws to
a close, the people are on the verge of entering the Promised Land and fulfilling these words. They would remain
in the land for hundreds of years, but sin and transgression eventually led to their exile. For centuries, the Jewish
people yearned to return and resettle their land. While
over the centuries, some individuals were able to fulfill
these dreams, the founding
of the State of Israel in
1948 made it possible for
any Jew who wishes to re-
turn to come and settle in
their homeland. Today, there
are approximately six million
Jews and eight million total
residents in *Eretz Yisrael*.
How fortunate we are to live
in a time when the Land of
Israel is so accessible to all.

Holocaust survivors yearning for Israel

Numbers

2 Instruct *B'nei Yisrael* and say to them: When you enter the land of Canaan, this is the land that shall fall to you as your portion, the land of Canaan with its various boundaries:

ב צַו אֶת־בְּנֵי יִשְׂרָאֵל וְאָמַרְתָּ אֲלֵהֶם כִּי־אַתֶּם בָּאִים אֶל־הָאָרֶץ כְּנָעַן זֹאת הָאָרֶץ אֲשֶׁר תִּפֹּל לָכֶם בְּנַחֲלָה אֶרֶץ כְּנַעַן לִגְבֻלֹתֶיהָ:

TZAV et b'-NAY yis-ra-AYL v'-a-mar-TA a-lay-HEM kee a-TEM ba-EEM el ha-A-retz k'-NA-an ZOT ha-A-retz a-SHER ti-POL la-KHEM b'-na-kha-LAH E-retz k'-NA-an lig-vu-lo-TE-ha

3 Your southern sector shall extend from the wilderness of Zin alongside Edom. Your southern boundary shall start on the east from the tip of the Dead Sea.

ג וְהָיָה לָכֶם פְּאַת־נֶגֶב מִמִּדְבַּר־צִן עַל־יְדֵי אֱדוֹם וְהָיָה לָכֶם גְּבוּל נֶגֶב מִקְצֵה יָם־הַמֶּלַח קֵדְמָה:

4 Your boundary shall then turn to pass south of the ascent of Akrabbim and continue to Zin, and its limits shall be south of Kadesh-barnea, reaching Hazar-addar and continuing to Azmon.

ד וְנָסַב לָכֶם הַגְּבוּל מִנֶּגֶב לְמַעֲלֵה עַקְרַבִּים וְעָבַר צִנָה והיה [וְהָיוּ] תוֹצְאֹתָיו מִנֶּגֶב לְקָדֵשׁ בַּרְנֵעַ וְיָצָא חֲצַר־אַדָּר וְעָבַר עַצְמֹנָה:

5 From Azmon the boundary shall turn toward the Wadi of Egypt and terminate at the Sea.

ה וְנָסַב הַגְּבוּל מֵעַצְמוֹן נַחְלָה מִצְרָיִם וְהָיוּ תוֹצְאֹתָיו הַיָּמָּה:

6 For the western boundary you shall have the coast of the Great Sea; that shall serve as your western boundary.

ו וּגְבוּל יָם וְהָיָה לָכֶם הַיָּם הַגָּדוֹל וּגְבוּל זֶה־יִהְיֶה לָכֶם גְּבוּל יָם:

7 This shall be your northern boundary: Draw a line from the Great Sea to Mount Hor;

ז וְזֶה־יִהְיֶה לָכֶם גְּבוּל צָפוֹן מִן־הַיָּם הַגָּדֹל תְּתָאוּ לָכֶם הֹר הָהָר:

8 from Mount Hor draw a line to Lebo-hamath, and let the boundary reach Zedad.

ח מֵהֹר הָהָר תְּתָאוּ לְבֹא חֲמָת וְהָיוּ תוֹצְאֹת הַגְּבֻל צְדָדָה:

9 The boundary shall then run to Ziphron and terminate at Hazar-enan. That shall be your northern boundary.

ט וְיָצָא הַגְּבֻל זִפְרֹנָה וְהָיוּ תוֹצְאֹתָיו חֲצַר עֵינָן זֶה־יִהְיֶה לָכֶם גְּבוּל צָפוֹן:

10 For your eastern boundary you shall draw a line from Hazar-enan to Shepham.

י וְהִתְאַוִּיתֶם לָכֶם לִגְבוּל קֵדְמָה מֵחֲצַר עֵינָן שְׁפָמָה:

11 From Shepham the boundary shall descend to Riblah on the east side of Ain; from there the boundary shall continue downward and abut on the eastern slopes of the Sea of Chinnereth.

יא וְיָרַד הַגְּבֻל מִשְּׁפָם הָרִבְלָה מִקֶּדֶם לָעָיִן וְיָרַד הַגְּבֻל וּמָחָה עַל־כֶּתֶף יָם־כִּנֶּרֶת קֵדְמָה:

A tractor ploughing a field in the Negev desert

34:2 The land of *Canaan* with its various boundaries Chapter 34 describes the biblical boundaries of the Land of Israel. These boundaries are important, since a number of *mitzvot* (מצוות), 'commandments,' apply only within these borders. Many of the biblical laws that apply specifically inside *Eretz Yisrael* are agricultural ones that are intrinsically connected to the land. Many of them mandate providing for those who cannot provide for themselves, either because they are poor or because they do not have their own portion of land. How special is the Land of Israel: Caring for others is inherent in living there.

Numbers

12 The boundary shall then descend along the *Yarden* and terminate at the Dead Sea. That shall be your land as defined by its boundaries on all sides.

יב וְיָרַד הַגְּבוּל הַיַּרְדֵּנָה וְהָיוּ תוֹצְאֹתָיו יָם הַמֶּלַח זֹאת תִּהְיֶה לָכֶם הָאָרֶץ לִגְבֻלֹתֶיהָ סָבִיב:

13 *Moshe* instructed the Israelites, saying: This is the land you are to receive by lot as your hereditary portion, which *Hashem* has commanded to be given to the nine and a half tribes.

יג וַיְצַו מֹשֶׁה אֶת־בְּנֵי יִשְׂרָאֵל לֵאמֹר זֹאת הָאָרֶץ אֲשֶׁר תִּתְנַחֲלוּ אֹתָהּ בְּגוֹרָל אֲשֶׁר צִוָּה יְהוָה לָתֵת לְתִשְׁעַת הַמַּטּוֹת וַחֲצִי הַמַּטֶּה:

14 For the Reubenite tribe by its ancestral houses, the Gadite tribe by its ancestral houses, and the half-tribe of *Menashe* have already received their portions:

יד כִּי לָקְחוּ מַטֵּה בְנֵי הָראוּבֵנִי לְבֵית אֲבֹתָם וּמַטֵּה בְנֵי־הַגָּדִי לְבֵית אֲבֹתָם וַחֲצִי מַטֵּה מְנַשֶּׁה לָקְחוּ נַחֲלָתָם:

15 those two and a half tribes have received their portions across the *Yarden*, opposite *Yericho*, on the east, the orient side.

טו שְׁנֵי הַמַּטּוֹת וַחֲצִי הַמַּטֶּה לָקְחוּ נַחֲלָתָם מֵעֵבֶר לְיַרְדֵּן יְרֵחוֹ קֵדְמָה מִזְרָחָה:

16 *Hashem* spoke to *Moshe*, saying:

טז וַיְדַבֵּר יְהוָה אֶל־מֹשֶׁה לֵּאמֹר:

17 These are the names of the men through whom the land shall be apportioned for you: *Elazar* the *Kohen* and *Yehoshua* son of *Nun*.

יז אֵלֶּה שְׁמוֹת הָאֲנָשִׁים אֲשֶׁר־יִנְחֲלוּ לָכֶם אֶת־הָאָרֶץ אֶלְעָזָר הַכֹּהֵן וִיהוֹשֻׁעַ בִּן־נוּן:

18 And you shall also take a chieftain from each tribe through whom the land shall be apportioned.

יח וְנָשִׂיא אֶחָד נָשִׂיא אֶחָד מִמַּטֶּה תִּקְחוּ לִנְחֹל אֶת־הָאָרֶץ:

19 These are the names of the men: from the tribe of *Yehuda*: *Kalev* son of Jephunneh.

יט וְאֵלֶּה שְׁמוֹת הָאֲנָשִׁים לְמַטֵּה יְהוּדָה כָּלֵב בֶּן־יְפֻנֶּה:

20 From the Simeonite tribe: *Shmuel* son of Ammihud.

כ וּלְמַטֵּה בְּנֵי שִׁמְעוֹן שְׁמוּאֵל בֶּן־עַמִּיהוּד:

21 From the tribe of *Binyamin*: *Elidad* son of Chislon.

כא לְמַטֵּה בִנְיָמִן אֱלִידָד בֶּן־כִּסְלוֹן:

22 From the Danite tribe: a chieftain, *Buki* son of Jogli.

כב וּלְמַטֵּה בְנֵי־דָן נָשִׂיא בֻּקִּי בֶּן־יָגְלִי:

23 For the descendants of *Yosef*: from the Manassite tribe: a chieftain, *Chaniel* son of Ephod;

כג לִבְנֵי יוֹסֵף לְמַטֵּה בְנֵי־מְנַשֶּׁה נָשִׂיא חַנִּיאֵל בֶּן־אֵפֹד:

24 and from the Ephraimite tribe: a chieftain, *Kemuel* son of Shiphtan.

כד וּלְמַטֵּה בְנֵי־אֶפְרַיִם נָשִׂיא קְמוּאֵל בֶּן־שִׁפְטָן:

25 From the Zebulunite tribe: a chieftain, *Elitzafan* son of Parnach.

כה וּלְמַטֵּה בְנֵי־זְבוּלֻן נָשִׂיא אֱלִיצָפָן בֶּן־פַּרְנָךְ:

26 From the Issacharite tribe: a chieftain, *Paltiel* son of Azzan.

כו וּלְמַטֵּה בְנֵי־יִשָּׂשכָר נָשִׂיא פַּלְטִיאֵל בֶּן־עַזָּן:

27 From the Asherite tribe: a chieftain, *Achihud* son of Shelomi.

כז וּלְמַטֵּה בְנֵי־אָשֵׁר נָשִׂיא אֲחִיהוּד בֶּן־שְׁלֹמִי:

28 From the Naphtalite tribe: a chieftain, *Pedahel* son of Ammihud.

כח וּלְמַטֵּה בְנֵי־נַפְתָּלִי נָשִׂיא פְּדַהְאֵל בֶּן־עַמִּיהוּד:

29 It was these whom *Hashem* designated to allot portions to the Israelites in the land of Canaan.

כט אֵלֶּה אֲשֶׁר צִוָּה יְהוָֹה לְנַחֵל אֶת־בְּנֵי־יִשְׂרָאֵל בְּאֶרֶץ כְּנָעַן:

לה 1 *Hashem* spoke to *Moshe* in the steppes of Moab at the *Yarden* near *Yericho*, saying:

א וַיְדַבֵּר יְהוָֹה אֶל־מֹשֶׁה בְּעַרְבֹת מוֹאָב עַל־יַרְדֵּן יְרֵחוֹ לֵאמֹר:

2 Instruct *B'nei Yisrael* to assign, out of the holdings apportioned to them, towns for the *Leviim* to dwell in; you shall also assign to the *Leviim* pasture land around their towns.

ב צַו אֶת־בְּנֵי יִשְׂרָאֵל וְנָתְנוּ לַלְוִיִּם מִנַּחֲלַת אֲחֻזָּתָם עָרִים לָשָׁבֶת וּמִגְרָשׁ לֶעָרִים סְבִיבֹתֵיהֶם תִּתְּנוּ לַלְוִיִּם:

TZAV et b'-NAY yis-ra-AYL v'-na-t'-NU lal-vee-YIM
mi-na-kha-LAT a-khu-za-TAM a-REEM la-SHA-vet u-mig-RASH
le-a-REEM s'-vee-vo-tay-HEM ti-t'-NU lal-vee-YIM

3 The towns shall be theirs to dwell in, and the pasture shall be for the cattle they own and all their other beasts.

ג וְהָיוּ הֶעָרִים לָהֶם לָשָׁבֶת וּמִגְרְשֵׁיהֶם יִהְיוּ לִבְהֶמְתָּם וְלִרְכֻשָׁם וּלְכֹל חַיָּתָם:

4 The town pasture that you are to assign to the *Leviim* shall extend a thousand *amot* outside the town wall all around.

ד וּמִגְרְשֵׁי הֶעָרִים אֲשֶׁר תִּתְּנוּ לַלְוִיִּם מִקִּיר הָעִיר וָחוּצָה אֶלֶף אַמָּה סָבִיב:

5 You shall measure off two thousand *amot* outside the town on the east side, two thousand on the south side, two thousand on the west side, and two thousand on the north side, with the town in the center. That shall be the pasture for their towns.

ה וּמַדֹּתֶם מִחוּץ לָעִיר אֶת־פְּאַת־קֵדְמָה אַלְפַּיִם בָּאַמָּה וְאֶת־פְּאַת־נֶגֶב אַלְפַּיִם בָּאַמָּה וְאֶת־פְּאַת־יָם אַלְפַּיִם בָּאַמָּה וְאֵת פְּאַת צָפוֹן אַלְפַּיִם בָּאַמָּה וְהָעִיר בַּתָּוֶךְ זֶה יִהְיֶה לָהֶם מִגְרְשֵׁי הֶעָרִים:

6 The towns that you assign to the *Leviim* shall comprise the six cities of refuge that you are to designate for a manslayer to flee to, to which you shall add forty-two towns.

ו וְאֵת הֶעָרִים אֲשֶׁר תִּתְּנוּ לַלְוִיִּם אֵת שֵׁשׁ־עָרֵי הַמִּקְלָט אֲשֶׁר תִּתְּנוּ לָנֻס שָׁמָּה הָרֹצֵחַ וַעֲלֵיהֶם תִּתְּנוּ אַרְבָּעִים וּשְׁתַּיִם עִיר:

7 Thus the total of the towns that you assign to the *Leviim* shall be forty-eight towns, with their pasture.

ז כָּל־הֶעָרִים אֲשֶׁר תִּתְּנוּ לַלְוִיִּם אַרְבָּעִים וּשְׁמֹנֶה עִיר אֶתְהֶן וְאֶת־מִגְרְשֵׁיהֶן:

8 In assigning towns from the holdings of the Israelites, take more from the larger groups and less from the smaller, so that each assigns towns to the *Leviim* in proportion to the share it receives.

ח וְהֶעָרִים אֲשֶׁר תִּתְּנוּ מֵאֲחֻזַּת בְּנֵי־יִשְׂרָאֵל מֵאֵת הָרַב תַּרְבּוּ וּמֵאֵת הַמְעַט תַּמְעִיטוּ אִישׁ כְּפִי נַחֲלָתוֹ אֲשֶׁר יִנְחָלוּ יִתֵּן מֵעָרָיו לַלְוִיִּם:

9 *Hashem* spoke further to *Moshe*:

ט וַיְדַבֵּר יְהוָֹה אֶל־מֹשֶׁה לֵּאמֹר:

10 Speak to *B'nei Yisrael* and say to them: When you cross the *Yarden* into the land of Canaan,

י דַּבֵּר אֶל־בְּנֵי יִשְׂרָאֵל וְאָמַרְתָּ אֲלֵהֶם כִּי אַתֶּם עֹבְרִים אֶת־הַיַּרְדֵּן אַרְצָה כְּנָעַן:

35:2 Towns for the *Leviim* to dwell in The Children of Israel are commanded to set aside forty-eight cities throughout the length and breadth of the Land of Israel as residences for the *Leviim* (Levites). The people are required to live holy lives in the Promised Land, and it is the *Leviim* who are given the task of instructing them about how to live this way. By scattering the *Leviim* among the nation in- stead of giving them their own portion of land, *Hashem* ensures that everyone will have the op- portunity to be exposed to the spiritual leaders of the people and to learn from them and by their example.

Excavations in *Beit Shemesh*, one of the Levitical cities in the portion of *Yehuda*

11 you shall provide yourselves with places to serve you as cities of refuge to which a manslayer who has killed a person unintentionally may flee.

יא וְהִקְרִיתֶם לָכֶם עָרִים עָרֵי מִקְלָט תִּהְיֶינָה לָכֶם וְנָס שָׁמָּה רֹצֵחַ מַכֵּה־נֶפֶשׁ בִּשְׁגָגָה:

12 The cities shall serve you as a refuge from the avenger, so that the manslayer may not die unless he has stood trial before the assembly.

יב וְהָיוּ לָכֶם הֶעָרִים לְמִקְלָט מִגֹּאֵל וְלֹא יָמוּת הָרֹצֵחַ עַד־עָמְדוֹ לִפְנֵי הָעֵדָה לַמִּשְׁפָּט:

13 The towns that you thus assign shall be six cities of refuge in all.

יג וְהֶעָרִים אֲשֶׁר תִּתֵּנוּ שֵׁשׁ־עָרֵי מִקְלָט תִּהְיֶינָה לָכֶם:

14 Three cities shall be designated beyond the *Yarden*, and the other three shall be designated in the land of Canaan: they shall serve as cities of refuge.

יד אֵת שְׁלֹשׁ הֶעָרִים תִּתְּנוּ מֵעֵבֶר לַיַּרְדֵּן וְאֵת שְׁלֹשׁ הֶעָרִים תִּתְּנוּ בְּאֶרֶץ כְּנָעַן עָרֵי מִקְלָט תִּהְיֶינָה:

15 These six cities shall serve the Israelites and the resident aliens among them for refuge, so that anyone who kills a person unintentionally may flee there.

טו לִבְנֵי יִשְׂרָאֵל וְלַגֵּר וְלַתּוֹשָׁב בְּתוֹכָם תִּהְיֶינָה שֵׁשׁ־הֶעָרִים הָאֵלֶּה לְמִקְלָט לָנוּס שָׁמָּה כָּל־מַכֵּה־נֶפֶשׁ בִּשְׁגָגָה:

16 Anyone, however, who strikes another with an iron object so that death results is a murderer; the murderer must be put to death.

טז וְאִם־בִּכְלִי בַרְזֶל הִכָּהוּ וַיָּמֹת רֹצֵחַ הוּא מוֹת יוּמַת הָרֹצֵחַ:

17 If he struck him with a stone tool that could cause death, and death resulted, he is a murderer; the murderer must be put to death.

יז וְאִם בְּאֶבֶן יָד אֲשֶׁר־יָמוּת בָּהּ הִכָּהוּ וַיָּמֹת רֹצֵחַ הוּא מוֹת יוּמַת הָרֹצֵחַ:

18 Similarly, if the object with which he struck him was a wooden tool that could cause death, and death resulted, he is a murderer; the murderer must be put to death.

יח אוֹ בִּכְלִי עֵץ־יָד אֲשֶׁר־יָמוּת בּוֹ הִכָּהוּ וַיָּמֹת רֹצֵחַ הוּא מוֹת יוּמַת הָרֹצֵחַ:

19 The blood-avenger himself shall put the murderer to death; it is he who shall put him to death upon encounter.

יט גֹּאֵל הַדָּם הוּא יָמִית אֶת־הָרֹצֵחַ בְּפִגְעוֹ־בוֹ הוּא יְמִיתֶנּוּ:

20 So, too, if he pushed him in hate or hurled something at him on purpose and death resulted,

כ וְאִם־בְּשִׂנְאָה יֶהְדָּפֶנּוּ אוֹ־הִשְׁלִיךְ עָלָיו בִּצְדִיָּה וַיָּמֹת:

21 or if he struck him with his hand in enmity and death resulted, the assailant shall be put to death; he is a murderer. The blood-avenger shall put the murderer to death upon encounter.

כא אוֹ בְאֵיבָה הִכָּהוּ בְיָדוֹ וַיָּמֹת מוֹת־יוּמַת הַמַּכֶּה רֹצֵחַ הוּא גֹּאֵל הַדָּם יָמִית אֶת־הָרֹצֵחַ בְּפִגְעוֹ־בוֹ:

22 But if he pushed him without malice aforethought or hurled any object at him unintentionally,

כב וְאִם־בְּפֶתַע בְּלֹא־אֵיבָה הֲדָפוֹ אוֹ־הִשְׁלִיךְ עָלָיו כָּל־כְּלִי בְּלֹא צְדִיָּה:

23 or inadvertently dropped upon him any deadly object of stone, and death resulted – though he was not an enemy of his and did not seek his harm

כג אוֹ בְכָל־אֶבֶן אֲשֶׁר־יָמוּת בָּהּ בְּלֹא רְאוֹת וַיַּפֵּל עָלָיו וַיָּמֹת וְהוּא לֹא־אוֹיֵב לוֹ וְלֹא מְבַקֵּשׁ רָעָתוֹ:

24 in such cases the assembly shall decide between the slayer and the blood-avenger.

כד וְשָׁפְטוּ הָעֵדָה בֵּין הַמַּכֶּה וּבֵין גֹּאֵל הַדָּם עַל הַמִּשְׁפָּטִים הָאֵלֶּה:

²⁵ The assembly shall protect the manslayer from the blood-avenger, and the assembly shall restore him to the city of refuge to which he fled, and there he shall remain until the death of the *Kohen Gadol* who was anointed with the sacred oil.

²⁶ But if the manslayer ever goes outside the limits of the city of refuge to which he has fled,

²⁷ and the blood-avenger comes upon him outside the limits of his city of refuge, and the blood-avenger kills the manslayer, there is no bloodguilt on his account.

²⁸ For he must remain inside his city of refuge until the death of the *Kohen Gadol*; after the death of the *Kohen Gadol*, the manslayer may return to his land holding.

²⁹ Such shall be your law of procedure throughout the ages in all your settlements.

³⁰ If anyone kills a person, the manslayer may be executed only on the evidence of witnesses; the testimony of a single witness against a person shall not suffice for a sentence of death.

³¹ You may not accept a ransom for the life of a murderer who is guilty of a capital crime; he must be put to death.

³² Nor may you accept ransom in lieu of flight to a city of refuge, enabling one to return to live on his land before the death of the *Kohen*.

³³ You shall not pollute the land in which you live; for blood pollutes the land, and the land can have no expiation for blood that is shed on it, except by the blood of him who shed it.

³⁴ You shall not defile the land in which you live, in which I Myself abide, for I *Hashem* abide among *B'nei Yisrael*.

36 ¹ The family heads in the clan of the descendants of *Gilad* son of *Machir* son of *Menashe*, one of the Yosefite clans, came forward and appealed to *Moshe* and the chieftains, family heads of the Israelites.

² They said, "*Hashem* commanded my lord to assign the land to the Israelites as shares by lot, and my lord was further commanded by *Hashem* to assign the share of our kinsman *Tzelofchad* to his daughters.

כה וְהִצִּ֨ילוּ הָעֵדָ֜ה אֶת־הָרֹצֵ֗חַ מִיַּד֮ גֹּאֵ֣ל הַדָּם֒ וְהֵשִׁ֤יבוּ אֹתוֹ֙ הָ֣עֵדָ֔ה אֶל־עִ֣יר מִקְלָט֖וֹ אֲשֶׁר־נָ֣ס שָׁ֑מָּה וְיָ֣שַׁב בָּ֗הּ עַד־מוֹת֙ הַכֹּהֵ֣ן הַגָּדֹ֔ל אֲשֶׁר־מָשַׁ֥ח אֹת֖וֹ בְּשֶׁ֥מֶן הַקֹּֽדֶשׁ:

כו וְאִם־יָצֹ֥א יֵצֵ֖א הָרֹצֵ֑חַ אֶת־גְּבוּל֙ עִ֣יר מִקְלָט֔וֹ אֲשֶׁ֥ר יָנ֖וּס שָֽׁמָּה:

כז וּמָצָ֤א אֹתוֹ֙ גֹּאֵ֣ל הַדָּ֔ם מִח֕וּץ לִגְב֖וּל עִ֣יר מִקְלָט֑וֹ וְרָצַ֞ח גֹּאֵ֤ל הַדָּם֙ אֶת־הָ֣רֹצֵ֔חַ אֵ֥ין ל֖וֹ דָּֽם:

כח כִּ֣י בְעִ֤יר מִקְלָטוֹ֙ יֵשֵׁ֔ב עַד־מ֖וֹת הַכֹּהֵ֣ן הַגָּדֹ֑ל וְאַֽחֲרֵי֙ מוֹת֙ הַכֹּהֵ֣ן הַגָּדֹ֔ל יָשׁוּב֙ הָ֣רֹצֵ֔חַ אֶל־אֶ֖רֶץ אֲחֻזָּתֽוֹ:

כט וְהָי֨וּ אֵ֧לֶּה לָכֶ֛ם לְחֻקַּ֥ת מִשְׁפָּ֖ט לְדֹרֹֽתֵיכֶ֑ם בְּכֹ֖ל מֽוֹשְׁבֹֽתֵיכֶֽם:

ל כָּל־מַ֨כֵּה־נֶ֔פֶשׁ לְפִ֣י עֵדִ֔ים יִרְצַ֖ח אֶת־הָֽרֹצֵ֑חַ וְעֵ֣ד אֶחָ֔ד לֹא־יַֽעֲנֶ֥ה בְנֶ֖פֶשׁ לָמֽוּת:

לא וְלֹֽא־תִקְח֥וּ כֹ֨פֶר֙ לְנֶ֣פֶשׁ רֹצֵ֔חַ אֲשֶׁר־ה֥וּא רָשָׁ֖ע לָמ֑וּת כִּי־מ֖וֹת יוּמָֽת:

לב וְלֹֽא־תִקְח֣וּ כֹ֔פֶר לָנ֖וּס אֶל־עִ֣יר מִקְלָט֑וֹ לָשׁוּב֙ לָשֶׁ֣בֶת בָּאָ֔רֶץ עַד־מ֖וֹת הַכֹּהֵֽן:

לג וְלֹֽא־תַֽחֲנִ֣יפוּ אֶת־הָאָ֗רֶץ אֲשֶׁ֤ר אַתֶּם֙ בָּ֔הּ כִּ֣י הַדָּ֔ם ה֥וּא יַֽחֲנִ֖יף אֶת־הָאָ֑רֶץ וְלָאָ֣רֶץ לֹֽא־יְכֻפַּ֗ר לַדָּם֙ אֲשֶׁ֣ר שֻׁפַּךְ־בָּ֔הּ כִּי־אִ֖ם בְּדַ֥ם שֹֽׁפְכֽוֹ:

לד וְלֹ֧א תְטַמֵּ֣א אֶת־הָאָ֗רֶץ אֲשֶׁ֤ר אַתֶּם֙ יֹֽשְׁבִ֣ים בָּ֔הּ אֲשֶׁ֥ר אֲנִ֖י שֹׁכֵ֣ן בְּתוֹכָ֑הּ כִּ֚י אֲנִ֣י יְהֹוָ֔ה שֹׁכֵ֕ן בְּת֖וֹךְ בְּנֵ֥י יִשְׂרָאֵֽל:

לו א וַיִּקְרְב֞וּ רָאשֵׁ֣י הָֽאָב֗וֹת לְמִשְׁפַּ֣חַת בְּנֵֽי־גִלְעָ֡ד בֶּן־מָכִ֣יר בֶּן־מְנַשֶּׁה֮ מִמִּשְׁפְּחֹ֣ת בְּנֵ֣י יוֹסֵף֒ וַיְדַבְּר֞וּ לִפְנֵ֤י מֹשֶׁה֙ וְלִפְנֵ֣י הַנְּשִׂאִ֔ים רָאשֵׁ֥י אָב֖וֹת לִבְנֵ֥י יִשְׂרָאֵֽל:

ב וַיֹּֽאמְר֗וּ אֶת־אֲדֹנִי֙ צִוָּ֣ה יְהֹוָ֔ה לָתֵ֨ת אֶת־הָאָ֧רֶץ בְּנַֽחֲלָ֛ה בְּגוֹרָ֖ל לִבְנֵ֣י יִשְׂרָאֵ֑ל וַֽאדֹנִי֙ צֻוָּ֣ה בַֽיהֹוָ֔ה לָתֵ֗ת אֶת־נַֽחֲלַ֛ת צְלָפְחָ֥ד אָחִ֖ינוּ לִבְנֹתָֽיו:

Numbers

³ Now, if they marry persons from another Israelite tribe, their share will be cut off from our ancestral portion and be added to the portion of the tribe into which they marry; thus our allotted portion will be diminished.

ג וְהָיוּ לְאֶחָד מִבְּנֵי שִׁבְטֵי בְנֵי־יִשְׂרָאֵל לְנָשִׁים וְנִגְרְעָה נַחֲלָתָן מִנַּחֲלַת אֲבֹתֵינוּ וְנוֹסַף עַל נַחֲלַת הַמַּטֶּה אֲשֶׁר תִּהְיֶינָה לָהֶם וּמִגֹּרַל נַחֲלָתֵנוּ יִגָּרֵעַ:

> *v'-ha-YU l'-e-KHAD mi-b'-NAY shiv-TAY v'-nay yis-ra-AYL*
> *l'-na-SHEEM v'-nig-r'-AH na-kha-la-TAN mi-na-kha-LAT*
> *a-vo-TAY-nu v'-no-SAF AL na-kha-LAT ha-ma-TEH a-SHER*
> *tih-YE-nah la-HEM u-mi-go-RAL na-kha-la-TAY-nu yi-ga-RAY-a*

⁴ And even when the Israelites observe the jubilee, their share will be added to that of the tribe into which they marry, and their share will be cut off from the ancestral portion of our tribe."

ד וְאִם־יִהְיֶה הַיֹּבֵל לִבְנֵי יִשְׂרָאֵל וְנוֹסְפָה נַחֲלָתָן עַל נַחֲלַת הַמַּטֶּה אֲשֶׁר תִּהְיֶינָה לָהֶם וּמִנַּחֲלַת מַטֵּה אֲבֹתֵינוּ יִגָּרַע נַחֲלָתָן:

⁵ So *Moshe*, at *Hashem*'s bidding, instructed the Israelites, saying: "The plea of the Josephite tribe is just.

ה וַיְצַו מֹשֶׁה אֶת־בְּנֵי יִשְׂרָאֵל עַל־פִּי יְהוָה לֵאמֹר כֵּן מַטֵּה בְנֵי־יוֹסֵף דֹּבְרִים:

⁶ This is what *Hashem* has commanded concerning the daughters of *Tzelofchad*: They may marry anyone they wish, provided they marry into a clan of their father's tribe.

ו זֶה הַדָּבָר אֲשֶׁר־צִוָּה יְהוָה לִבְנוֹת צְלָפְחָד לֵאמֹר לַטּוֹב בְּעֵינֵיהֶם תִּהְיֶינָה לְנָשִׁים אַךְ לְמִשְׁפַּחַת מַטֵּה אֲבִיהֶם תִּהְיֶינָה לְנָשִׁים:

⁷ No inheritance of the Israelites may pass over from one tribe to another, but the Israelites must remain bound each to the ancestral portion of his tribe.

ז וְלֹא־תִסֹּב נַחֲלָה לִבְנֵי יִשְׂרָאֵל מִמַּטֶּה אֶל־מַטֶּה כִּי אִישׁ בְּנַחֲלַת מַטֵּה אֲבֹתָיו יִדְבְּקוּ בְּנֵי יִשְׂרָאֵל:

⁸ Every daughter among the Israelite tribes who inherits a share must marry someone from a clan of her father's tribe, in order that every Israelite may keep his ancestral share.

ח וְכָל־בַּת יֹרֶשֶׁת נַחֲלָה מִמַּטּוֹת בְּנֵי יִשְׂרָאֵל לְאֶחָד מִמִּשְׁפַּחַת מַטֵּה אָבִיהָ תִּהְיֶה לְאִשָּׁה לְמַעַן יִירְשׁוּ בְּנֵי יִשְׂרָאֵל אִישׁ נַחֲלַת אֲבֹתָיו:

⁹ Thus no inheritance shall pass over from one tribe to another, but the Israelite tribes shall remain bound each to its portion."

ט וְלֹא־תִסֹּב נַחֲלָה מִמַּטֶּה לְמַטֶּה אַחֵר כִּי־אִישׁ בְּנַחֲלָתוֹ יִדְבְּקוּ מַטּוֹת בְּנֵי יִשְׂרָאֵל:

🔶 **36:3 Their share will be cut off from our ancestral portion** Motivated by a deep sense of passion for the Land of Israel, *Tzelofchad's* daughters pleaded with *Moshe* for the right to inherit their father's land in the absence of sons, and their request was granted (see Chapter 27). Now, the elders of the tribe of *Menashe*, who share the same love of the land, approach

A rainbow over Tal Menashe, a settlement in the portion of Menashe

Moshe concerned that this ruling could adversely affect their tribe. The Land of Israel will soon be divided among the tribes through lots, for eternal inheritance. If *Tzelofchad's* daughters would marry men from

other tribes, their father's land that they inherit, which will ultimately be inherited by their husbands and sons, will be permanently transferred to other tribes. The prospect of their tribe losing title to a piece of *Eretz Yisrael* is distressing to the tribal leaders, and they approach *Moshe* with their dilemma. To resolve the issue, the daughters of *Tzelofchad* are instructed to marry men from their own tribe, thus guaranteeing that the tribe of *Menashe* will maintain every inch of the precious land in its possession. The Book of *Bamidbar* tells the story of many times that the Children of Israel provoked *Hashem* in the desert. The most unsettling of these was the sin of the spies, the rejection of the Promised Land that led to forty years of wandering in the desert and the death of an entire generation. However, in contrast, the book concludes with an inspiring example of deep love for *Eretz Yisrael*.

10 The daughters of *Tzelofchad* did as *Hashem* had commanded *Moshe*:

11 *Machla, Tirtza, Chagla, Milka*, and *Noa, Tzelofchad's* daughters, were married to sons of their uncles,

12 marrying into clans of descendants of *Menashe* son of *Yosef*; and so their share remained in the tribe of their father's clan.

13 These are the commandments and regulations that *Hashem* enjoined upon the Israelites, through *Moshe*, on the steppes of Moab, at the *Yarden* near *Yericho*.

י כַּאֲשֶׁר צִוָּה יְהֹוָה אֶת־מֹשֶׁה כֵּן עָשׂוּ בְּנוֹת צְלׇפְחָד:

יא וַתִּהְיֶינָה מַחְלָה תִרְצָה וְחׇגְלָה וּמִלְכָּה וְנֹעָה בְּנוֹת צְלׇפְחָד לִבְנֵי דֹדֵיהֶן לְנָשִׁים:

יב מִמִּשְׁפְּחֹת בְּנֵי־מְנַשֶּׁה בֶן־יוֹסֵף הָיוּ לְנָשִׁים וַתְּהִי נַחֲלָתָן עַל־מַטֵּה מִשְׁפַּחַת אֲבִיהֶן:

יג אֵלֶּה הַמִּצְוֺת וְהַמִּשְׁפָּטִים אֲשֶׁר צִוָּה יְהֹוָה בְּיַד־מֹשֶׁה אֶל־בְּנֵי יִשְׂרָאֵל בְּעַרְבֹת מוֹאָב עַל יַרְדֵּן יְרֵחוֹ:

List of Transliterated
Words in *The Israel Bible*

The following is a list of nouns which have been transliterated into Hebrew in the English translation and commentary of *The Israel Bible*:

Hebrew Name	English Name	Pronunciation	Hebrew
Achan	Achan	a-KHAN	עָכָן
Achav	Ahab	akh-AV	אַחְאָב
Achaz	Ahaz	a-KHAZ	אָחָז
Achazyahu	Ahaziah	a-khaz-YA-hu	אֲחַזְיָהוּ
Achiezer	Ahiezer	a-khee-E-zer	אֲחִיעֶזֶר
Achihud	Ahihud	a-khee-HUD	אֲחִיהוּד
Achikam	Ahikam	a-khee-KAM	אֲחִיקָם
Achilud	Ahilud	a-khee-LUD	אֲחִילוּד
Achimelech	Ahimelech	a-khee-ME-lekh	אֲחִימֶלֶךְ
Achira	Ahira	a-khee-RA	אֲחִירַע
Achisamach	Ahisamach	a-khee-sa-MAKH	אֲחִיסָמָךְ
Achitofel	Ahithophel	a-khee-TO-fel	אֲחִיתֹפֶל
Achituv	Ahitub	a-khee-TUV	אֲחִיטוּב
Achiya	Ahijah	a-khi-YAH	אֲחִיָּה
Adam	Adam	a-DAM	אָדָם
Adar	Adar	a-DAR	אֲדָר
Adoniyahu	Adonijah	a-do-ni-YA-hu	אֲדֹנִיָּהוּ
Adulam	Adullam	a-du-LAM	עֲדֻלָּם
Agur	Agur	a-GUR	אָגוּר
Aharon	Aaron	a-ha-RON	אַהֲרֹן
Amasa	Amasa	a-ma-SA	עֲמָשָׂא
Amatzya	Amaziah	a-matz-YAH	אֲמַצְיָה
Amen	Amen	a-MAYN	אָמֵן
Amiel	Ammiel	a-mee-AYL	עַמִּיאֵל
Aminadav	Amminadab	a-mee-na-DAV	עַמִּינָדָב
Amitai	Amittai	a-mi-TAI	אֲמִתַּי
Amnon	Amnon	am-NON	אַמְנֹן

107

Hebrew Name	English Name	Pronunciation	Hebrew
Amon	Amon	a-MON	אָמוֹן
Amos	Amos	a-MOS	עָמוֹס
Amotz	Amoz	a-MOTZ	אָמוֹץ
Amram	Amram	am-RAM	עַמְרָם
Anatot	Anathoth	a-na-TOT	עֲנָתוֹת
Aron	Ark	a-RON	אָרוֹן
Aron HaBrit	Ark of the Covenant	a-RON ha-b'-REET	אָרוֹן הַבְּרִית
Arpachshad	Arpachshad	ar-pakh-SHAD	אַרְפַּכְשַׁד
Asa	Asa	a-SA	אָסָא
Asael	Asahel	a-sah-AYL	עֲשָׂהאֵל
Asaf	Asaph	a-SAF	אָסָף
Ashdod	Ashdod	ash-DOD	אַשְׁדּוֹד
Asher	Asher	a-SHAYR	אָשֵׁר
Ashkelon	Ashkelon	ash-k'-LON	אַשְׁקְלוֹן
Atalya	Athaliah	a-tal-YAH	עֲתַלְיָה
Avdon	Abdon	av-DON	עַבְדּוֹן
Avichayil	Abihail	a-vee-KHA-yil	אֲבִיחַיִל
Avidan	Abidan	a-vee-DAN	אֲבִידָן
Avigail	Abigail	a-vee-GA-yil	אֲבִיגַיִל
Avihu	Abihu	a-vee-HU	אֲבִיהוּא
Avimelech	Abimelech	a-vee-ME-lekh	אֲבִימָלֶךְ
Avinadav	Abinadab	a-vee-na-DAV	אֲבִינָדָב
Aviram	Abiram	a-vee-RAM	אֲבִירָם
Avishai	Abishai	a-vee-SHAI	אֲבִישַׁי
Aviya	Abijah	a-vi-YAH	אֲבִיָּה
Aviyam	Abijam	a-vi-YAM	אֲבִיָּם
Avner	Abner	av-NAYR	אַבְנֵר
Avraham	Abraham	av-ra-HAM	אַבְרָהָם
Avram	Abram	av-RAM	אַבְרָם
Avshalom	Absalom	av-sha-LOM	אַבְשָׁלוֹם
Azarya	Azariah	a-zar-YAH	עֲזַרְיָה
Azeika	Azekah	a-zay-KAH	עֲזֵקָה
Azza	Gaza	a-ZAH	עַזָּה

108

Hebrew Name	English Name	Pronunciation	Hebrew
B'nei Yisrael	The Children of Israel	b'-NAY yis-ra-AYL	בְּנֵי יִשְׂרָאֵל
Barak	Barak	ba-rakh-AYL	בָּרָק
Baruch	Baruch	ba-RUKH	בָּרוּךְ
Barzilai	Barzillai	bar-zi-LAI	בַּרְזִלַּי
Basha	Baasa	ba-SHA	בַּעְשָׁא
Batsheva	Bath-sheba	bat-SHE-va	בַּת־שֶׁבַע
Be'er Sheva	Beer-sheba	b'-AYR SHE-va	בְּאֵר שֶׁבַע
Be'eri	Beeri	b'-ay-REE	בְּאֵרִי
Beit Aven	Beth-aven	bayt A-ven	בֵּית אָוֶן
Beit El	Beth-el	bayt el	בֵּית אֵל
Beit Hamikdash	Temple	bayt ha-mik-DASH	בֵּית הַמִּקְדָּשׁ
Beit Lechem	Beth-lehem	bayt LE-khem	בֵּית לָחֶם
Beit Shean	Beth-shean	bayt sh'-AN	בֵּית שְׁאָן
Beit Shemesh	Beth-shemesh	bayt SHE-mesh	בֵּית שֶׁמֶשׁ
Berechya	Berechiah	be-rekh-YAH	בֶּרֶכְיָה
Betzalel	Bezalel	b'-tzal-AYL	בְּצַלְאֵל
Bilha	Bilhah	bil-HAH	בִּלְהָה
Binyamin	Benjamin	bin-ya-MIN	בִּנְיָמִין
Boaz	Boaz	BO-az	בֹּעַז
Buki	Bukki	bu-KEE	בֻּקִּי
Buzi	Buzi	bu-ZEE	בּוּזִי
Carmel	Carmel	kar-MEL	כַּרְמֶל
Chachalya	Hacaliah	kha-khal-YAH	חֲכַלְיָה
Chagai	Haggai	kha-GAI	חַגַּי
Chana	Hannah	kha-NAH	חַנָּה
Chanamel	Hanamel	kha-nam-AYL	חֲנַמְאֵל
Chanani	Hanani	kha-NA-nee	חֲנָנִי
Chananya	Hananiah	kha-nan-YAH	חֲנַנְיָה
Chaniel	Hanniel	kha-nee-AYL	חַנִּיאֵל
Chanoch	Enoch	kha-NOKH	חֲנוֹךְ
Chava	Eve	kha-VAH	חַוָּה
Chavakuk	Habakkuk	kha-va-KUK	חֲבַקּוּק
Chermon	Hermon	kher-MON	חֶרְמוֹן

109

Hebrew Name	English Name	Pronunciation	Hebrew
Chetzron	Hezron	khetz-RON	חֶצְרוֹן
Chever	Heber	KHE-ver	חֶבֶר
Chevron	Hebron	khev-RON	חֶבְרוֹן
Chilkiyahu	Hilkiah	khil-ki-YA-hu	חִלְקִיָּהוּ
Chizkiyahu	Hezekiah	khiz-ki-YA-hu	חִזְקִיָּהוּ
Chofni	Hophni	khof-NEE	חָפְנִי
Chogla	Hoglah	khog-LAH	חָגְלָה
Chulda	Hulda	khul-DAH	חֻלְדָּה
Chur	Hur	Khur	חוּר
Dan	Dan	Dan	דָּן
Daniel	Daniel	da-ni-YAYL	דָּנִיֵּאל
Datan	Dathan	da-TAN	דָּתָן
David	David	da-VID	דָּוִד
Devora	Deborah	d'-vo-RAH	דְּבוֹרָה
Dina	Dinah	DEE-nah	דִּינָה
Doeg Ha'adomi	Doeg the Edomite	do-AYG ha-a-do-MEE	דּוֹאֵג הָאֲדֹמִי
Efraim	Ephraim	ef-RA-yim	אֶפְרַיִם
Efrat	Ephrat	ef-RAT	אֶפְרָתָה
Efrat	Ephrathah	ef-RA-tah	אֶפְרָתָה
Ehud	Ehud	ay-HUD	אֵהוּד
Eila	Elah	AY-lah	אֵלָה
Eilon	Elon	ay-LON	אֵילוֹן
Ein Gedi	En-gedi	ayn GE-dee	עֵין גֶּדִי
Elazar	Eleazar	el-a-ZAR	אֶלְעָזָר
Elchanan	Elhanan	el-kha-NAN	אֶלְחָנָן
Eli	Eli	ay-LEE	עֵלִי
Eliav	Eliab	e-lee-AV	אֱלִיאָב
Elidad	Elidad	e-lee-DAD	אֱלִידָד
Eliezer	Eliezer	e-lee-E-zer	אֱלִיעֶזֶר
Elimelech	Elimelech	e-lee-ME-lekh	אֱלִימֶלֶךְ
Elisha	Elisha	e-lee-SHA	אֱלִישָׁע
Elishama	Elishama	e-lee-sha-MA	אֱלִישָׁמָע
Elisheva	Elisheba	e-lee-SHE-va	אֱלִישֶׁבַע

Hebrew Name	English Name	Pronunciation	Hebrew
Elitzafan	Eli-zaphan	e-lee-tza-FAN	אֱלִיצָפָן
Elitzur	Elizur	e-lee-TZUR	אֱלִיצוּר
Eliyahu	Elijah	ay-li-YA-hu	אֵלִיָּהוּ
Elkana	Elkanah	el-ka-NAH	אֶלְקָנָה
Elyasaf	Eliasaph	el-ya-SAF	אֶלְיָסָף
Elyashiv	Eliashib	el-ya-SHEEV	אֶלְיָשִׁיב
Enosh	Enosh	e-NOSH	אֱנוֹשׁ
Er	Er	ayr	עֵר
Eshtaol	Eshtaol	esh-ta-OL	אֶשְׁתָּאֹל
Esther	Esther	es-TAYR	אֶסְתֵּר
Eved Melech	Ebed-melech	E-ved ME-lekh	עֶבֶד־מֶלֶךְ
Even Ha-Ezer	Eben-Ezer	E-ven ha-E-zer	אֶבֶן הָעֵזֶר
Ever	Eber	AY-ver	עֵבֶר
Evyatar	Abiathar	ev-ya-TAR	אֶבְיָתָר
Ezra	Ezra	ez-RA	עֶזְרָא
Gad	Gad	gad	גָּד
Gadi	Gaddi	ga-DEE	גַּדִּי
Gadiel	Gaddiel	ga-dee-AYL	גַּדִּיאֵל
Gamliel	Gamaliel	gam-lee-AYL	גַּמְלִיאֵל
Gedalia	Gedaliah	g'-dal-YA (hu)	גְּדַלְיָהוּ
Gedera	Gederah	g'-day-RAH	גְּדֵרָה
Gershom	Gershom	gay-r'-SHOM	גֵּרְשׁוֹם
Gershon	Gershon	gay-r'-SHON	גֵּרְשׁוֹן
Geshem	Geshem	GE-shem	גֶּשֶׁם
Geuel	Geuel	g'-u-AYL	גְּאוּאֵל
Gidon	Gideon	gid-ON	גִּדְעוֹן
Gilad	Gilead	gil-AD	גִּלְעָד
Gilgal	Gilgal	gil-GAL	גִּלְגָּל
Giva	Gibeah	giv-AH	גִּבְעָה
Givon	Gibeon	giv-ON	גִּבְעוֹן
Hadassa	Hadassah	ha-da-SAH	הֲדַסָּה
Har Eival	Mount Ebal	ay-VAL	הַר עֵיבָל
Har Gerizim	Mount Gerizim	g'-ri-ZEEM	הַר גְּרִזִים

Hebrew Name	English Name	Pronunciation	Hebrew
Har HaBayit	Temple Mount	har ha-BA-yit	הַר הַבַּיִת
Har HaZeitim	the Mount of Olives	har ha-zay-TEEM	הַר הַזֵּיתִים
Hashem	Lord/God		
Hayman	Heman	hay-MAN	הֵימָן
Hoshea	Hosea	ho-SHAY-a	הוֹשֵׁעַ
Ido	Iddo	i-DO	עִדּוֹ
Imanu-El	Immanuel	i-MA-nu ayl	עִמָּנוּ אֵל
Ish-boshet	Ish-bosheth	eesh BO-shet	אִישׁ־בֹּשֶׁת
Itamar	Ithamar	ee-ta-MAR	אִיתָמָר
Itiel	Ithiel	ee-tee-AYL	אִיתִיאֵל
Ivtzan	Ibzan	iv-TZAN	אִבְצָן
Iyov	Job	i-YOV	אִיּוֹב
Kadmiel	Kadmiel	kad-mee-AYL	קַדְמִיאֵל
Kalev	Caleb	ka-LAYV	כָּלֵב
Keesh	Kish	keesh	קִישׁ
Kehat	Kohath	k'-HAT	קְהָת
Keinan	Kenan	kay-NAN	קֵינָן
Kemuel	Kemuel	k'-mu-AYL	קְמוּאֵל
Keruvim	Cherubim	k'-ru-VEEM	כְּרוּבִים
Kilyon	Chilion	kil-YON	כִּלְיוֹן
Kiryat Arba	Kiriath-arba	keer-YAT AR-bah	קִרְיַת אַרְבַּע
Kiryat Sefer	Kiriath-sepher	keer-YAT SAY-fer	קִרְיַת־סֵפֶר
Kiryat Ye'arim	Kiriath-jearim	keer-YAT y'-a-REEM	קִרְיַת יְעָרִים
Kislev	Chislev	kis-LAYV	כִּסְלוֹ
Kohanim	Priests	ko-ha-NEEM	כֹּהֲנִים
Kohelet	Koheleth	ko-HE-let	קֹהֶלֶת
Kohen	Priest	ko-HAYN	כֹּהֵן
Kohen Gadol	High Priest	ko-HAYN ga-DOL	כֹּהֵן גָּדוֹל
Korach	Korah	KO-rakh	קֹרַח
Kushi	Cushi	ku-SHEE	כּוּשִׁי
Lachish	Lachish	la-KHEESH	לָכִישׁ
Leah	Leah	lay-AH	לֵאָה
Lemech	Lamech	LE-mekh	לֶמֶךְ

Hebrew Name	English Name	Pronunciation	Hebrew
Lemuel	Lemuel	l'-mu-AYL	לְמוּאֵל
Levi	Levi	lay-VEE	לֵוִי
Leviim	Levites	l'-vee-IM	לְוִיִם
Machla	Mahlah	makh-LAH	מַחְלָה
Machlon	Mahlon	makh-LON	מַחְלוֹן
Machseya	Mahseiah	makh-say-YAH	מַחְסֵיָה
Malachi	Malachi	mal-a-KHEE	מַלְאָכִי
Manoach	Manoah	ma-NO-akh	מָנוֹחַ
Mashiach	Messiah	ma-SHEE-akh	מָשִׁיחַ
Mefiboshet	Mephibosheth	m'-fee-VO-shet	מְפִיבֹשֶׁת
Mehalalel	Mahalalel	ma-ha-lal-AYL	מַהֲלַלְאֵל
Menachem	Menahem	m'-na-KHAYM	מְנַחֵם
Menashe	Menasseh	m'-na-SHEH	מְנַשֶּׁה
Menorah	Candlestick	m'-no-RAH	מְנֹרָה
Merari	Merari	m'-ra-REE	מְרָרִי
Metushelach	Methusaleh	m'-tu-SHE-lakh	מְתוּשָׁלַח
Micha	Micah	mee-KHAH	מִיכָה
Michael	Michael	mee-kha-AYL	מִיכָאֵל
Michaihu	Micaiah	mee-KHAI-hu	מִיכָיְהוּ
Michal	Michal	mee-KHAL	מִיכַל
Milka	Milcah	mil-KAH	מִלְכָּה
Miriam	Miriam	mir-YAM	מִרְיָם
Mishael	Mishael	mee-sha-AYL	מִישָׁאֵל
Mishkan	Tabernacle	mish-KAN	מִשְׁכָּן
Mitzpa	Mizpah	mitz-PAH	מִצְפָּה
Mizbayach	Altar	miz-BAY-akh	מִזְבֵּחַ
Mordechai	Mordecai	mor-d'-KHAI	מָרְדֳּכַי
Moriah	Moriah	mo-ri-YAH	מוֹרִיָּה
Moshe	Moses	mo-SHEH	מֹשֶׁה
Nachbi	Nahbi	nakh-BEE	נַחְבִּי
Nachor	Nahor	na-KHOR	נָחוֹר
Nachshon	Nahshon	nakh-SHON	נַחְשׁוֹן
Nachum	Nahum	na-KHUM	נַחוּם

Hebrew Name	English Name	Pronunciation	Hebrew
Nadav	Nadab	na-DAV	נָדָב
Naftali	Naphtali	naf-ta-LEE	נַפְתָּלִי
Naomi	Naomi	na-o-MEE	נָעֳמִי
Natan	Nathan	na-TAN	נָתָן
Naval	Nabal	na-VAL	נָבָל
Navi	Prophet	na-VEE	נָבִיא
Navot	Naboth	na-VAL	נָבָל
Nechemya	Nehemiah	n'-khem-YAH	נְחֶמְיָה
Negev	Negeb	NE-gev	נֶגֶב
Nerya	Neriah	nay-ri-YAH	נֵרִיָּה
Netanel	Nethanel	n'-tan-AYL	נְתַנְאֵל
Neviah	Prophetess	n'-vee-AH	נְבִיאָה
Neviim	Prophets	n'-vee-EEM	נְבִיאִים
Nisan	Nisan	nee-SAN	נִיסָן
Noa	Noah	no-AH	נֹעָה
Noach	Noah	NO-akh	נֹחַ
Nov	Nob	nov	נֹב
Nun	Nun	nun	נוּן
Oded	Oded	o-DAYD	עוֹדֵד
Ohola	Oholah	a-ho-LAH	אָהֳלָה
Oholiav	Oholiab	o-ha-lee-AV	אָהֳלִיאָב
Oholiva	Oholibah	a-ho-lee-VAH	אָהֳלִיבָה
Omri	Omri	om-REE	עָמְרִי
Onan	Onan	o-NAN	אוֹנָן
Otniel	Othniel	ot-nee-AYL	עָתְנִיאֵל
Ovadya	Obadiah	o-vad-YAH	עֹבַדְיָה
Oved	Obed	o-VAYD	עוֹבֵד
Oved Edom	Obed Edom	o-VAYD e-DOM	עוֹבֵד אֱדֹם
Pagiel	Pagiel	pag-ee-AYL	פַּגְעִיאֵל
Palti	Palti	pal-TEE	פַּלְטִי
Paltiel	Paltiel	pal-tee-AYL	פַּלְטִיאֵל
Pekach	Pekah	PE-kakh	פֶּקַח
Pedael	Pedahel	p'-da-AYL	פְּדָהאֵל

114

Hebrew Name	English Name	Pronunciation	Hebrew
Pekachya	Pekahiah	p'-kakh-YAH	פְּקַחְיָה
Peleg	Peleg	PE-leg	פֶּלֶג
Penina	Peninnah	p'-ni-NAH	פְּנִנָּה
Peretz	Perez	PE-retz	פֶּרֶץ
Petuel	Pethuel	p'-tu-AYL	פְּתוּאֵל
Pinchas	Phinehas	peen-KHAS	פִּינְחָס
Rachel	Rachel	ra-KHAYL	רָחֵל
Ram	Ram	ram	רָם
Rama	Ramah	ra-MAH	רָמָה
Re'u	Reu	r'-U	רְעוּ
Rechovam	Rehoboam	r'-khav-AM	רְחַבְעָם
Reuven	Reuben	r'-u-VAYN	רְאוּבֵן
Rivka	Rebecca	riv-KAH	רִבְקָה
Rut	Ruth	rut	רוּת
Salma	Salmon/Salmah	sal-MAH	שַׂלְמָה
Salmon	Salmon	sal-MON	שַׂלְמוֹן
Sara	Sarah	sa-RAH	שָׂרָה
Sarai	Sarai	sa-RAI	שָׂרַי
Selah	Selah	SE-lah	סֶלָה
Seraya	Seraiah	s'-ra-YAH	שְׂרָיָה
Serug	Serug	s'-RUG	שְׂרוּג
Setur	Sethur	s'-TUR	סְתוּר
Shaarayim	Shaaraim	sha-a-RA-yim	שַׁעֲרָיִם
Shabbat	Sabbath	sha-BAT	שַׁבָּת
Shabbatot	Sabbaths	sha-ba-TOT	שַׁבָּתוֹת
Shafan	Shaphan	sha-FAN	שָׁפָן
Shafat	Shaphat	sha-FAT	שָׁפָט
Shalem	Salem	sha-LAYM	שָׁלֵם
Shalum	Shallum	sha-LUM	שַׁלּוּם
Shamgar	Shamgar	sham-GAR	שַׁמְגַּר
Shamua	Shammua	sha-MU-a	שַׁמּוּעַ
Shaul	Saul	sha-UL	שָׁאוּל
Shealtiel	Shealtiel	sh'-al-tee-AYL	שְׁאַלְתִּיאֵל

Hebrew Name	English Name	Pronunciation	Hebrew
Shear Yashuv	Shear-Jashub	sh'-AR ya-SHUV	שְׁאָר יָשׁוּב
Shechanya	Shecaniah	sh'-khan-YAH	שְׁכַנְיָה
Shechem	Shechem	sh'-KHEM	שְׁכֶם
Sheila	Shelah	shay-LAH	שֵׁלָה
Shelach	Shelah	SHE-lakh	שָׁלַח
Shelumiel	Shelumiel	sh'-lu-mee-AYL	שְׁלֻמִיאֵל
Shem	Shem	Shaym	שֵׁם
Shemaya	Shemaiah	sh'-ma-YAH	שְׁמַעְיָה
Sheshbatzar	Sheshbazzar	shaysh-ba-TZAR	שֵׁשְׁבַּצַּר
Shet	Seth	Shayt	שֵׁת
Shevat	Shebat	sh'-VAT	שְׁבָט
Shilo	Shiloh	shi-LOH	שלה
Shim'i	Shimei	shim-EE	שִׁמְעִי
Shimon	Simeon	shim-ON	שִׁמְעוֹן
Shimshon	Samson	shim-SHON	שִׁמְשׁוֹן
Shlomo	Solomon	sh'-lo-MOH	שְׁלֹמֹה
Shmuel	Samuel	sh'-mu-AYL	שְׁמוּאֵל
Shofar	Horn	sho-FAR	שׁוֹפָר
Shofarot	Horns	sho-fa-ROT	שׁוֹפָרוֹת
Shomron	Samaria	sho-m'-RON	שֹׁמְרוֹן
Sivan	Sivan	see-VAN	סִיוָן
Tamar	Tamar	ta-MAR	תָּמָר
Tanakh	Hebrew Bible	ta-NAKH	תָּנַ"ךְ
Tapuach	Tappuah	ta-PU-akh	תַּפּוּחַ
Tavor	Tabor	ta-VOR	תָּבוֹר
Tekoa	Tekoa	t'-KO-a	תְּקוֹעַה
Terach	Terah	TE-rakh	תֶּרַח
Teveria	Tiberias	t'-ver-YAH	טְבֶרְיָה
Tevet	Tebeth	tay-VAYT	טֵבֵת
Tirtza	Tirzah	tir-TZAH	תִּרְצָה
Tola	Tola	to-LA	תּוֹלָע
Tzadok	Zadok	tza-DOK	צָדוֹק
Tzefanya	Zephaniah	tz'-fan-YAH	צְפַנְיָה

Hebrew Name	English Name	Pronunciation	Hebrew
Tzelofchad	Zelophehad	tz'-lo-f-KHAD	צְלָפְחָד
Tzeruya	Zeruiah	tz'-ru-YAH	צְרוּיָה
Tzfat	Safed	tz'-FAT	צְפַת
Tzidkiyahu	Zedekiah	tzid-ki-YA-hu	צִדְקִיָהוּ
Tziklag	Ziklag	tzi-k'-LAG	צִקְלַג
Tzion	Zion	tzi-YON	צִיּוֹן
Tzipora	Zipporah	tzi-po-RAH	צִפֹּרָה
Tzora	Zorah	tzor-AH	צָרְעָה
Tzuriel	Zuriel	tzu-ree-AYL	צוּרִיאֵל
Ukal	Ucal	u-KAL	אֻכָל
Uri	Uri	u-REE	אוּרִי
Uriya	Uriah	u-ri-YAH	אוּרִיָה
Utz	Uz	Utz	עוּץ
Uzziyahu	Uzziah	u-zi-YA-hu	עֻזִיָהוּ
Yaakov	Jacob	ya-a-KOV	יַעֲקֹב
Yachaziel	Jahaziel	ya-kha-zee-AYL	יַחֲזִיאֵל
Yael	Jael	ya-AYL	יָעֵל
Yaffo	Joppa/Jaffa	ya-FO	יָפוֹ
Yair	Jair	ya-EER	יָאִיר
Yakeh	Jakeh	ya-KEH	יָקֶה
Yarden	Jordan	yar-DAYN	יַרְדֵן
Yarmut	Jarmuth	yar-MUT	יַרְמוּת
Yechezkel	Ezekiel	y'-khez-KAYL	יְחֶזְקֵאל
Yechiel	Jehiel	y'-khee-AYL	יְחִיאֵל
Yechonya	Jeconiah	y'-khon-YAH	יְכָנְיָה
Yedutun	Jeduthun	y'-du-TUN	יְדוּתוּן
Yehoachaz	Jehoahaz	y'-ho-a-KHAZ	יְהוֹאָחָז
Yehoash	Jehoash	y'-ho-ASH	יְהוֹאָשׁ
Yehochanan	Jehohanan	y'-ho-kha-NAN	יְהוֹחָנָן
Yehonatan	Jonathan	y'-ho-na-TAN	יְהוֹנָתָן
Yehoram	Jehoram	y'-ho-RAM	יְהוֹרָם
Yehoshafat	Jehoshaphat	y'-ho-sha-FAT	יְהוֹשָׁפָט
Yehoshavat	Jehoshabeath	y'-ho-shav-AT	יְהוֹשַׁבְעַת

117

Hebrew Name	English Name	Pronunciation	Hebrew
Yehosheva	Jehosheba	y-ho-SHE-va	יְהוֹשֶׁבַע
Yehoshua	Joshua	y'-ho-SHU-a	יְהוֹשֻׁעַ
Yehotzadak	Jehozadak	y'-ho-tza-DAK	יְהוֹצָדָק
Yehoyachin	Jehoiachin	y'-ho-ya-KHEEN	יְהוֹיָכִין
Yehoyada	Jehoiada	y'-ho-ya-DA	יְהוֹיָדָע
Yehoyakim	Jehoiakim	y'-ho-ya-KEEM	יְהוֹיָקִים
Yehu	Jehu	yay-HU	יֵהוּא
Yehuda	Judah	y'-hu-DAH	יְהוּדָה
Yehudi	Jew	y'-hu-DEE	יְהוּדִי
Yehudim	Jews	y'-hu-DEEM	יְהוּדִים
Yered	Jared	YE-red	יֶרֶד
Yericho	Jericho	y'-ree-KHO	יְרִיחוֹ
Yerovam	Jeroboam	ya-rov-AM	יָרָבְעָם
Yerubaal	Jerubbaal	y'-ru-BA-al	יְרֻבַּעַל
Yerushalayim	Jerusalem	y'-ru-sha-LA-yim	יְרוּשָׁלַיִם
Yeshayahu	Isaiah	y'-sha-YA-hu	יְשַׁעְיָהוּ
Yeshua	Jeshua	yay-SHU-a	יֵשׁוּעַ
Yiftach	Jephthah	yif-TAKH	יִפְתָּח
Yigal	Igal	yig-AL	יִגְאָל
Yirmiyahu	Jeremiah	yir-m'-YA-hu	יִרְמִיָהוּ
Yishai	Jesse	yi-SHAI	יִשַׁי
Yisrael	Israel	yis-ra-AYL	יִשְׂרָאֵל
Yissachar	Issachar	yi-sa-KHAR	יִשָּׂשכָר
Yitzchak	Issac	yitz-KHAK	יִצְחָק
Yizrael	Jezreel	yiz-r'-EL	יִזְרְעָאל
Yoash	Joash	yo-ASH	יוֹאָשׁ
Yoav	Joab	yo-AV	יוֹאָב
Yochanan	Johanan	yo-kha-NAN	יוֹחָנָן
Yocheved	Jochebed	yo-KHE-ved	יוֹכֶבֶד
Yoel	Joel	yo-AYL	יוֹאֵל
Yona	Jonah	yo-NAH	יוֹנָה
Yonadav	Jonadab	yo-na-DAV	יוֹנָדָב
Yonatan	Jonathan	yo-na-TAN	יוֹנָתָן

Hebrew Name	English Name	Pronunciation	Hebrew
Yoram	Joram	yo-RAM	יוֹרָם
Yosef	Joseph	yo-SAYF	יוֹסֵף
Yoshiyahu	Josiah	yo-shi-YA-hu	יֹאשִׁיָּהוּ
Yotam	Jotham	yo-TAM	יוֹתָם
Yotzadak	Jozadak	yo-tza-DAK	יוֹצָדָק
Yozavad	Jozabad	yo-za-VAD	יוֹזָבָד
Zanoach	Zanoah	za-NO-akh	זָנוֹחַ
Zecharya	Zechariah	z'-khar-YAH	זְכַרְיָה
Zerach	Zerah	ZE-rakh	זֶרַח
Zerubavel	Zerubbabel	z'-ru-ba-VEL	זְרֻבָּבֶל
Zevulun	Zebulun	z'-vu-LUN	זְבוּלֻן
Zilpa	Zilpah	zil-PAH	זִלְפָּה
Zimri	Zimri	zim-REE	זִמְרִי

Jewish Holidays

Chanukah	Hanukkah	kha-nu-KAH	חֲנֻכָּה
Pesach	Passover	PE-sakh	פֶּסַח
Purim	Purim	pu-REEM	פּוּרִים
Rosh Hashana	Jewish New Year	rosh ha-sha-NAH	רֹאשׁ הַשָּׁנָה
Shavuot	Feast of Weeks	sha-vu-OT	שָׁבוּעוֹת
Shemini Atzeret	Eight Day of Assembly	sh'-mee-NEE a-TZE-ret	שְׁמִינִי עֲצֶרֶת
Sukkot	Feast of Tabernacles	su-KOT	סֻכּוֹת
Yom Kippur	Day of Atonement	yom kee-PUR	יוֹם כִּפּוּר

Biblical Measurements

Amah	Cubit	a-MAH	אַמָּה
Amot	Cubits	a-MOT	אַמּוֹת
Bat	Bath	bat	בַּת
Batim	Baths	ba-TEEM	בַּתִּים
Beka	half-shekel	BE-ka	בֶּקַע
Chomarim	Homers	kho-ma-REEM	חֳמָרִים
Chomer	Homer	KHO-mer	חֹמֶר
Efah	Ephah	ay-FAH	אֵיפָה
Geira	Gerah	gay-RAH	גֵּרָה

119

Hebrew Name	English Name	Pronunciation	Hebrew
Gomed	Gomed	GO- med	גֹּמֶד
Hin	Hin	heen	הִין
Kav	kab	kav	קַב
Kesita	kesitah	k'-see-TAH	קְשִׂיטָה
Kikar	talent	ki-KAR	כִּכָּר
Kikarim	talents	ki-ka-RIM	כִּכָּרִים
Kor	kor	kor	כֹּר
Letek	lethech	LE-tek	לֶתֶךְ
Log	Log	log	לֹג
Maneh	Mina	ma-NEH	מָנֶה
Manim	Minas	ma-NEEM	מָנִים
Omer	Omer	O-mer	עֹמֶר
Pim	Pim	peem	פִּים
Se'ah	Seah	say-AH	סְאָה
Se'eem	Seahs	s'-EEM	סְאִים
Shekalim	Shekels	sh'-ka-LEEM	שְׁקָלִים
Shekel	Shekel	SHE-kel	שֶׁקֶל
Tefach	Handbreadth	TE-fakh	טֶפַח
Zeret	Span	ZE-ret	זֶרֶת

Photo Credits

1:1 John Theodor/Shutterstock.com, 1:52 Zachi Evenor, goisrael.com, 2:3 Shlomo, Wikimedia Commons, 3:1 Courtesy of Israel365, 4:18 len4ik/Shutterstock.com, 5:6 Inna Reznik/Shutterstock.com 6:14 Yair Aronshtam/Shutterstock.com, 6:26 Mark Neyman, Government Press Office (Israel), 7:10 Mikhail Semenov/Shutterstock.com, 8:2 Avi Ohayon, Government Press Office (Israel), 9:5 Public Domain, 10:35 Courtesy of Israel365, 11:17 Ariely, Wikimedia Commons, 12:8 kavram/Shutterstock.com, 13:27 PhotoStock-Israel/Shutterstock.com, 14:1 Amos Ben Gershom, Government Press Office (Israel), 14:7 Oren Ravid/Shutterstock.com, 15:21 Nate photos/Shutterstock.com, 15:38 Blueeyes/Shutterstock.com, 16:3 MIA Studio/Shutterstock.com, 17:23 Michal Levinsky, Wikimedia Commons, 18:8 Shabtay/Shutterstock.com, 19:11 Dmitriy Feldman svarshik/Shutterstock.com, 20:12 Noam Armonn/Shutterstock.com, 21:5 Amos Ben Gershom, Government Press Office (Israel), 21:35 Protasov AN/Shutterstock.com, 22:11 By צילום: ד"ר אבישי טייכר, CC BY 2.5, https://commons.wikimedia.org/w/index.php?curid=11838202, 23:9 By Idont – Own work, CC BY-SA 3.0, https://commons.wikimedia.org/w/index.php?curid=33278674, 24:5 S1001/Shutterstock.com, 25:12 Alexandre Rotenberg/Shutterstock.com, 26:2 Moshe Milner, Government Press Office (Israel), 27:12 Denny George/Shutterstock.com, 28:9 Tomer Tu/Shutterstock.com, 29:35 By Gady Munz Pikiwiki Israel, CC BY 2.5, https://commons.wikimedia.org/w/index.php?curid=64758661, 31:27 mikhail/Shutterstock.com, 32:8 RnDmS/Shutterstock.com, 32:21 Government Press Office (Israel), 33:1 Evgeny Subbotsky/Shutterstock.com, 33:53 Zoltan Kluger, Government Press Office (Israel), 34:2 PhotoStock-Israel/Shutterstock.com, 35:2 Seth Aronstam/Shutterstock.com, 36:3 By Mendelson.avi – Own work, CC BY-SA 3.0, https://commons.wikimedia.org/w/index.php?curid=5798581

Map of Modern-Day Israel and its Neighbors

The following is a map of modern-day Israel and the surrounding countries

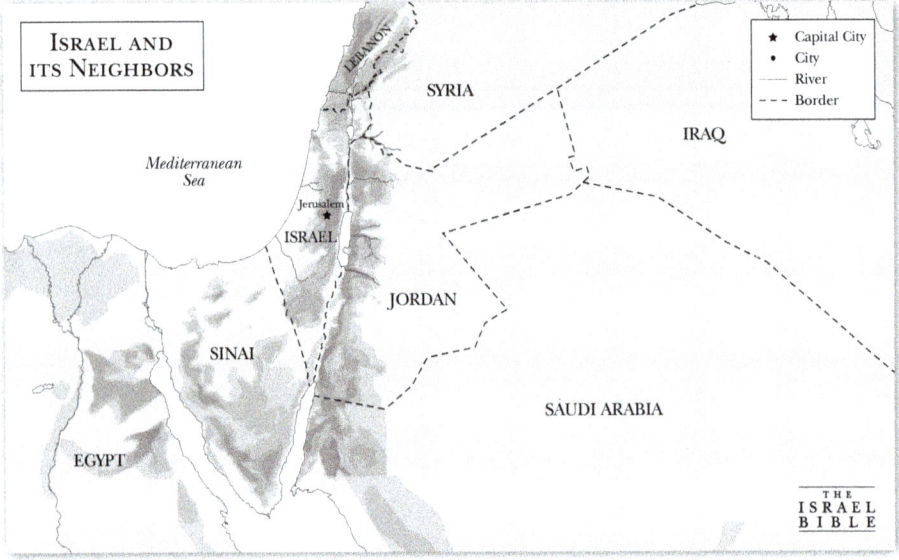

NOTES

NOTES

NOTES

NOTES

NOTES

For more inspiring commentary,
interactive maps, educational videos,
vivid photographs and more,
please visit our website

www.TheIsraelBible.com

THE
ISRAEL
BIBLE